HEROES OF THE
SUNLIT SKY

Books by Arch Whitehouse

HEROES OF THE SUNLIT SKY

Arch Whitehouse

Garden City, New York

DOUBLEDAY & COMPANY, INC.

1967

Library of Congress Catalog Card Number 67-19088
Copyright © 1967 by Arch Whitehouse
All Rights Reserved. Printed in the United States of America
First Edition

Dedicated to

AIR VICE-MARSHAL RAYMOND COLLISHAW

D.S.O. & Bar, D.S.C., D.F.C.

and *Croix de Guerre*

CONTENTS

(No attempt has been made to include all high-scoring aces of all countries. Instead, the author has presented the backgrounds, personalities and some outstanding feature of a representative group of World War I airmen from both sides of the line.)

ILLUSTRATIONS

INTRODUCTION

A very learned gentleman, Ralph Waldo Emerson, once wrote: "War educates the senses, calls into action the will, perfects the physical constitution, brings men into such swift and close collision in critical moments that man measures man." How such a temperate scholar, poet and preacher could be so knowledgeable about war is one of the mysteries of literature, for at no time in his life did he ever so much as fire a gun or take part in any physically strenuous pastime.

Yet how true is every word of that famous quotation.

In this day and age we are deeply concerned with the propriety of war, the extravagance of war, the apparent uselessness of war, and hope that war may soon be outlawed forever.

We who write about war, its actions and its personalities, are expected to delve deeply into our bag of words and continually denounce the horrors of war, and rack our minds for new phrases, new evidence, new reasons for banishing this international conflict. I know of no historian who would not willingly do so.

This antiwar fervor often assumes fantastic highlights. The man who burns his draft card, or openly proclaims his determination to be a conscientious objector receives wide-spread publicity. The young man who willingly enlists or volunteers to serve becomes just another name on a draftee list pinned up outside some unnamed reception center. The highly touted athletic star will enjoy the warmth of acclaim when by a strange consensus of medical opinion he is relieved of his service responsibilities on the premise that a minor injury received on the football field may detract eventually from his usefulness as a serving soldier. At the same time his classmate, a bespectacled, studious idealist, is accepted eagerly because of his basic intelligence that fits him for a regimental role where possible physical limitations will in no way interfere with his military potential.

Strangely enough, this paradox is not exploited by pacifists when they denounce the national service program. But the man who writes engrossing reports of military action that detail bravery, idealism, or a soldier's patriotism is deeply suspect. The pacifists are certain he must have some sinister motive. Someone—usually the munitions makers—must be paying him a stipend, as tainted as the thirty pieces of silver, to describe the deeds, sacrifices, or intent of the men who willingly fought the good fight. It is not considered important that these heroes eventually brought victory and comfort to those who cringed by their firesides; or that their stories should be written or their names heralded so that other men may one day strive to emulate their courage and dedication. Any historian who persists in retelling military heroics is branded a warmonger.

On the other hand; to take the opposite attitude is commercially attractive. To downgrade war, debunk the heroes, discount the generals, and weed out the diplomats who failed either to foresee the conflict or head it off, is a profitable proposition. For the same reason that crowds gathered at the guillotine or before the scaffold at Newgate Prison, the antiwar segment of the populace will rush to buy any volume that anticipates or garnishes its viewpoint. At this writing there are a baker's dozen of books denouncing the war in Vietnam, all of which have apparently sold well, but few of the purchasers are interested in the young American officer who won the first Medal of Honor to be awarded in that hapless campaign. (His name is Captain Roger H. C. Donlon.)

If we study history we see that the ratio of public determination to fight for a cause is directly related to the interest shown and respect expressed for its military heroes. This was illustrated in the American Revolution when a handful of rebels, Nathan Hale, Israel Putnam, Anthony Wayne, Ethan Allen, Francis Marion, and others became household heroes and encouraged others to take up the fight. History records it was well that there was such personal inspiration to bolster the cause.

Unquestionably, war is a senseless and bloody extravaganza, but it took a war to establish the United States of America, and it has taken several more to maintain its dignity, its honor, its traditions. Our real problem is not the justification for battle, but the control of men's passions, greed, power, and blood lust. Trying to ignore war is as hopeless a task as the legendary feat attempted by King Canute.

As long as men hunger for power, so long shall we have conflict. As long as we send men to fight our wars, we shall have heroes, and there will always be scribes and minstrels to tell of their deeds and valor. This book continues that centuries-old project, trusting that in its pages there may be the inspiration, the courage, and valor that is always necessary when a nation faces its great moment of truth.

It will be noted that I have selected a representative list of men who fought in that memorable campaign; *not necessarily all* who ran up lengthy scores. Such a volume would be repetitious and dull. I have picked out individuals who brought a special essence to the war, men who came from unusual backgrounds, men who performed with a certain *élan* or military style, and particularly to show what type of man willingly *volunteered* to fight for his country. It will be seen that most of them were outstanding in their accomplishments and many were (or were not) rewarded with the highest decorations or honors their country could bestow. But so many looked upon their service as a personal responsibility, and their right to serve became something dearer than life.

Arch Whitehouse
Montvale, N.J.

PART ONE

American

AMERICAN

World War I produced many new types of military heroes. It was an entirely new war, totally unlike those illustrated in the picture books of the late nineteenth century, and it was fought with a brand-new arsenal of weapons. We had never before met heroes who displayed high courage against massed machine guns, men who exhibited great heroism in the face of trench mortars or hand grenades. We were astonished to read of men who fought from armored vehicles known as tanks. Flame-throwers, poison gas, and aerial bombs had not been used before in martial combat.

The broad realm of the sea also created new heroes, particularly in submarine warfare. There were men who displayed their bravery on the gritty sands of deserts, amid the crags and defiles of Alpine mountains, and behind sodden revetments in Flanders fields, but it was in the sunlit skies that we were afforded the most fascinating list of valorous men. In that high vault of heaven men manned, or destroyed, giant Zeppelins, bombed armament plants, scouted the enemy deep inside his own lines, and fought one another to the death.

Strange to relate, World War I has never drawn the rapt attention of the American public, and with the years its importance, its place in history, and the valor of Americans who went overseas to fight has gradually become little more than a misty, glad-to-be-forgotten memory. Trifling reminders appear in song booklets used at service-club luncheons, in the reruns of ancient Hollywood films, and the annual capers of American Legionnaires, and rusty steel helmets that wound up as flower pots in suburban gardens.

It was not a popular war, and the country never embarked on the conflict in complete unity. Ethnic groups took determined sides, and for many months native Americans showed little or no interest in the cause or progress of the war. In fact, while approaching the threshold of complete involvement, Woodrow Wilson was elected to his second term as President in 1916 on the popular slogan, "He kept us out of war."

Few American servicemen returned from France with any animosity for the German people, but it was routine to berate the French for their barnyard sanitation, and the British for not paying their war debts. In fact, eighteen months after the Armistice the enemy had been welcomed back into the American fold. German comics again held top billing in vaudeville; Liberty cabbage was once more sauerkraut; and "Swiss" bartenders assumed their original Bavarian status.

"The Great War? We won it, so now let's forget it."

The "boys" were brought home as fast as they could be loaded aboard transports, and put back to work to maintain the high standard of living Americans had always demanded. Some returned to the colleges they had deserted when the call first rang out, and considered their service overseas in the same light as a Grand Tour of Europe. Some returned to their old jobs, some to new and better posts. A few malcontents took up pacifism or their old Tommy guns and continued to fight in the campaign aroused by Prohibition. Ex-sailors were recruited into the rumrunning business, piloting Eagle boats from supply ships to shore.

Little was written about the United States' important role in World War I. The generals had their say, as they always will, but their output seldom justified more than one edition, for few people were interested in reading about "that European war." For a time the stage offered *What Price Glory?*, a resounding drama by Maxwell Anderson and Laurence Stallings, and a British comedy, Bruce Bairnsfather's *The Better 'Ole* which added testimony to the American opinion that this was how the Limeys had fought the war.

Cynicism was widely encouraged. A Bible-thumping mountaineer, Alvin C. York, had been credited with capturing half a German regiment, several dozen machine guns, and a broad sector of the enemy front, singlehanded, but he made poor copy for he refused to show off his Medal of Honor on the vaudeville circuit, and in fact regretted he had had a part in that campaign.

Another Medal of Honor winner was Major Charles W. Whittlesey who had commanded the Lost Battalion, and is said to have committed suicide after the war by jumping from a steamship that was taking him on a vacation to Cuba, thus contributing further to the general opinion that the "war" had not been worth any red-blooded American's effort.

There were no naval heroes of the stature of John Paul Jones, Oliver Hazard Perry, or even Admiral George Dewey, for there had been no outstanding naval action after the Battle of Jutland in 1916.

The war in the air? Late in 1918 Major Billy Bishop, a Canadian who was credited with downing seventy-two aircraft on the Western Front, wrote a book *Winged Warfare* that, like those of the generals, never went through more than one edition. But then, Bishop was only a Canadian. A year or so later Captain Eddie Rickenbacker, America's Ace-of-Aces, produced his autobiography *Fighting the Flying Circus*. At the end of the war Captain Rickenbacker was credited with twenty-five victories. Since then he has proved that he was entitled to one more. His story enjoyed some fair success, but nothing that encouraged booksellers to enlarge their premises. No motion picture company considered putting Captain Eddie's career on the screen, and had his name not been attached to the radiator emblem of a motorcar he might have faded into oblivion with the spiral puttees and campaign hats of 1918.

Other books delineating the aerial successes of several British aces, such as Edward C. Mannock, Albert Ball, and James B. Mc-Cudden, were published in Great Britain, but none of these excited the interest of the book-buying public. Today, they all are out of print and bring a prince's ransom for a dog-eared copy.

Then suddenly, about 1927, World War I exploded like a latent bombshell when, to relieve the boredom of inheriting a multimillion-dollar cotton mill, Elliott White Springs, a typical Princeton playboy of that era, started writing stories set against the wartime airfields, cities, and fronts of the Great War. These sexy epistles first appeared in a number of glossy magazines, and Springs was so inspired by this unexpected spotlight, he deserted the cotton mill and soon wrote *War Birds—A Diary of an Unknown Aviator* that was offered as the personal journal of an American aviator who had been killed in the war. This was widely read, first in magazine form and later in a best-selling book.

At about the same time Floyd Gibbons, a flamboyant journalist who had been a war correspondent, wrote *The Red Knight of Germany* that was presented as the authentic story of Baron Manfred von Richthofen who had claimed to have shot down eighty British aircraft during his career on the Western Front.

Unquestionably, it was these two books that rescued World War I from the caverns of oblivion. Springs, who had presented the war in the air as a gay, bibulous, and lacy adventure, titillated the public's taste buds for more, but it was Gibbons' well-documented story of Germany's premier airman that lured hundreds of hack writers to this lush field of adventure. In these two books can be found the accepted doctrine of supply and demand.

Overnight, the newsstands were crowded with stacks of pulp magazines that offered more and more of this new element of warfare and heroics. At the peak of production there were thirty-eight aviation pulp magazines, all gleaming with the standard Fokker-versus-Spad combat covers. For anything from a dime to a quarter one could enjoy more air action than was experienced throughout the whole of that campaign. The movies took up the grim history, and within a few months a number of unbelievable air epics were released, each one based on some hair-raising dawn patrol. From all accounts there was no air action Over There after luncheon. Each six-reeler clamored to outdo anything produced previously in this frantic field of "yammering guns," "crates," German barons—complete with sneers and monocles—and slit-eyed American pilots, but each and every one was provided with devastating French girls who always were on hand to bind up a wound, bestow the Legion of Honor, or adjust a carburetor while the air hero staggered away to show his despair over the loss of a comrade. He gulped his cognac, gurgled one chorus of *Stand to Your Glasses Steady,* and then tossed the Emile Gallé glassware into the fireplace.

This was the standard pattern of air-war stories, filmed or written, between 1927 and 1939, when World War II put an end to these bogus presentations. The German pilots always were Prussian noblemen with lengthy strings of victories over "helpless two-seaters." They always flew Fokker D-VIIs no matter in what year of the war the action was set. Their aircraft were always artistically decorated in fantastic colors, and bore heraldic designs that identified the pilot, his background, *Jasta,* and the degree of his swinishness. Also, by some miraculous system of ground maintenance, these Germans always flew the same plane on every patrol.

The American pilots—there were no French, Belgian or British airmen in any of these production-line adventures—always sat high in the cockpit with a white silk handkerchief fluttering from the tops of their helmets. It was never made clear what the helmet handkerchief was supposed to indicate, but no American pilot worth his cognac would be seen in the air without that fluttering streamer. How many suffered broken necks as a result of this pointless affectation was never recorded.

Few movie or pulp-magazine pilots ever wore their goggles. After all, while dicing with death at 5000 meters, how would Baron von Schweinhund recognize our Yank hero if he were jousting incognito? American airmen always flew Spads that were suitably adorned with some identifying squadron crest or personal arabesque. In this manner, their feud that had originated in some Brooklyn delicatessen store a few years before could be continued—month after month, or reel after reel.

Another requirement in the pulp-movie, air-war story of this period was that practically all pilots in the U. S. Air Service were presented as true sons of the Auld Sod. From all accounts no volunteer was accepted unless he had a 'Mc' or an 'O' in front of his name and a bloodline that went back to Rory O'More. This Hibernian inheritance provided the two-fisted belligerency most necessary in all these stories. How Eddie Rickenbacker and Jimmie Meissner ever made it is one of World War I's continuing mysteries.

It was much the same whenever a British airman ever got a foot in the doorway of an air-war adventure. Though he had been most valiant and eventually worsted by a snarling German baron, he was always provided with a Mick ancestry and spirit. Weren't the Irish always fighting England's wars? Any American who could not produce some strain of Donnybrook descent was relegated to the Lafayette Escadrille where all those crazy New England college lads had migrated in 1916.

These distortions, inaccuracies, and ridiculous features marked American history of war in the air for years, and no dedicated historian can ever correct them; they have been established too long, and have left too deep an impression to ever be discarded. A World War I air hero must be an "ace," he must fly a single-seater "crate," and down a titled Prussian every time he takes off into the blue—*on a dawn patrol.* He must put his battered Spad down "on the Tarmac," and be greeted by a luscious Parisian damsel who will daintily dab at his wounded shoulder, and then "go tickle zee carburetor" while he searches for some expensive crystal to toss into the fireplace. There were no heroes in the two-seater, bomber, or artillery-observation squadrons. There were no Nieuports, Sopwith Camels, Caudrons, Salmsons, Albatros, or Rumpler aircraft in the pulp-movie combats—only Fokkers and Spads.

But of course there *were* other aircraft, and few of them could be considered "crates" by any standard of material or workmanship. There were hundreds of Americans who willingly fought with the French or British long before President Woodrow Wilson declared war, and many of them performed heroic achievements without ever appearing in the "ace" lists, or being rewarded with premier decorations. There were hundreds of Americans who had never seen a Spad, or who flew planes that bore their personal insignia. Dozens of these air heroes performed valorous acts from the wicker baskets of kite balloons, many fought valiantly as gunner-observers in the two-seater fighter squadrons. Some carried out determined bombing raids that eventually laid the foundation for strategic aviation. To be sure, not all their widely publicized stories were basically true. Many were conceived in the behind-the-lines bistros, or in Jack's American Bar in Paris, and cabled home by American correspondents who were determined to prove that Yank airmen were the elite of the flying services. There were some phonies, but by the same token there were hundreds who served manfully and well. Their stories are still worth relating.

J. JAMES BACH

In February 1959 a man named J. James Buck died in the Latter-Day Saints Hospital in Salt Lake City, Utah. He was seventy-four years of age, and had been teaching French at the University of Utah for more than fifteen years. It was disclosed in his obituary that Mr. Buck had used the name of Bach during World War I when he had served as a pilot in the French Air Service. He was of Danish descent and at the outset of World War II had changed his name to the less Germanic Buck. The French government had awarded him the Legion of Honor, the Médaille Militaire, and the Croix de Guerre.

Mr. Buck has long been credited with being the first American airman to destroy an enemy aircraft on the old Western Front. He may well have been, but by the same token the story of his feat may be apocryphal as it does not appear in all histories. However, Edwin C. Parsons who also flew with the French has attested to its authenticity, and it is well worth including in this list of American air heroes.

*

Jimmy Bach is completely unknown in American aviation history, but if the truth be told, it was he who inspired the formation of the Lafayette Escadrille. He never was actually a member of that volunteer organization, for it did not come into being until April 10, 1916, by which time Jimmy Bach had been a prisoner of war for more than six months.

As was the case with several other men who volunteered to fight with the French before the United States entered the war, James Bach had been born in Paris of American parents, and had spent a number of years in other European cities where he had worked as a mechanical engineer. When the war broke out in August 1914 Bach enlisted in the French Foreign Legion.

Many of the American volunteers who had even a smattering of French were quickly promoted, among them Bill Thaw, Charles Sweeney, and Jimmy Bach. Their service in the line was no more spectacular than that endured by any infantryman in those early days, but after about four months of trench warfare a few of these volunteers were shrewd enough to see that there was little future in that branch of the service. So, like many others, they felt the French Aviation Service promised at least a surcease from the mud and blood of the trenches. One by one, they scribbled out applications for transfers to the military air squadrons.

But it should not be assumed that because they were American volunteers they were quickly and enthusiastically accepted into the air service. Physically they were no better than any other youthful group. They showed no outstanding ability for flying, and only one or two could boast of having seen or been close to an airplane. On the other hand, France had hundreds of first-class candidates, particularly in the ranks of the well-trained, but frustrated cavalry regiments. These Frenchmen were experienced soldiers, inherently loyal to their homeland, and all spoke French. It should be remembered, too, that the Aviation Service had become the elite force in the opposing armies, for only airmen were visibly active enough to provide headlines for the war correspondents. The infantry was wallowing in the mud and mire of the trenches, and there were no sparkling naval engagements after Admiral Jellicoe's victory at Jutland. Only the air afforded contests worthy of day-by-day interest.

It was political implications that first opened the path for the Americans, as French officials quickly realized that if it could be shown that a number of neutrals—particularly Americans—were willing to serve with the French it would convince the neutral world of France's honorable stand in the campaign. It was also hoped that any success these American volunteers might have would be played up in the United States and perhaps have some influence in encouraging America to support the Allies.

The story of how the first handful of Americans managed to join the French Aviation Service reads much the same, whether we consider similar conditions in the British or German situations. Infantrymen who had experienced the opening phases of the war, men who had lived through the early development of trench warfare invariably attempted to transfer to what they considered to be a less hazardous, and certainly more endurable regime. Also, many of them felt that the time required for aviation training would prolong their potential lifespan. Not all volunteers for the air service were idealistic candidates for conquest in the skies.

William Thaw, son of a Pittsburgh industrial tycoon, was the leading light in this planned exodus from the trenches. He had had flying instruction before the war while a student at Yale. He, Jimmy Bach, and Bert Hall, a self-proclaimed soldier of fortune, are said to have walked thirty-two kilometers to put their petition before Colonel Felix Brocard who commanded an aviation squadron. This was in December 1914. A short time later all three men were rewarded with orders to turn in their trench equipment and report to French Aviation Headquarters where they were interviewed. All three men passed a list of rudimentary tests, were given a medical examination, and sent to a primary ground school.

Jimmy Bach did not encounter any real flying equipment until March 10, 1915, when he was sent to Pau, a primary flight school where the students ran up and down a turfed area aboard "Penguin" aircraft, old Blériot monoplanes with sharply clipped wings. These trainers could not get off the ground, but did give the pupil a rudimentary concept of the controls, how to run the engine, and in that way get the feel of flying. By early July Jimmy had soloed on an old Caudron and was given his pilot's certificate. By late August he had been made a corporal pilot and was transferred to Escadrille M.S.38, flying Morane Saulniers. He was at last back at the front.

The Morane Saulnier was a two-seater monoplane, powered by a Le Rhône rotary engine. The wing was mounted high above the fuselage, ostensibly for visibility purposes, and it became known as the Parasol. The Morane was originally intended for reconnaissance, bearing a pilot and a trained military observer, but as the air war intensified a few models were armed with two machine guns. One, fixed to fire forward, was mounted high enough to clear the arc of the propeller, the other, intended for the use of the observer, was set on a primary type of flexible mount and could be fired over a fairly wide arc to engage enemy aircraft attacking from the rear or broadside.

Air duels, as such, were rare until the early summer of 1915. The idea of plane-to-plane combat was not taken seriously, but here and there such encounters were recorded.

It was Jimmy Bach's good fortune to be involved in one of these rare engagements. In those days piloting was not considered the premier duty, for France had learned that practically anyone could be taught to fly, but that men who could scout and return with valuable military information were few. In fact, most all French—and German—observers were commissioned officers. The pilot was just an aerial chauffeur.

In this instance—the date is not on record—Jimmy had a Lieutenant Giroux as his observer, and while on a reconnaissance in the vicinity of Mézières they encountered a German Aviatik B-II returning from a similar mission. The observer in the German plane fired a long-range burst at the Parasol. Jimmy resented enemy bullets perforating the clean taut linen of his Morane; in fact one slug tore through the folds of his coverall.

"Get your gun ready," he bellowed at Lieutenant Giroux. He put the monoplane into a tight bank, and the 80-horsepower Le Rhône screeched under full throttle as he went after the Aviatik. The German pilot nosed down to get away, but in this instance the Parasol was faster and Jimmy was soon in a position to fire a few short bursts from the front fixed gun. The chase was continued until Giroux feared his pilot would follow the enemy machine all the way back to Berlin. He entreated, begged, and ordered Jimmy to return to his own lines, but the little American continued the chase, firing burst after burst into the fleeing Aviatik.

Then, as so often happened in many of these wartime stories, once he had reached the point where he could pour in the *coup de grâce* Jimmy's gun jammed—or perhaps he had used all the rounds in the single drum. He gripped the stick between his knees, and flew on while he attempted to remedy the stoppage—or replace the empty drum.

During this interruption in the chase he noticed that the German observer appeared to have been hit as he was sprawled over his gun mounting. Also, the Aviatik was flying on a very erratic course. And with that, Jimmy's observer tapped him on the shoulder and yelled, "I'll finish him for you!"

Jimmy nodded and gave the Le Rhône full throttle again and tried to bring the Morane below the faltering Aviatik. It took all the fragile Parasol's wing had, but the risk seemed worth the reward. Giroux poured two telling bursts into the enemy plane, and they saw the propeller break up, and then run wild.

"Don't let him glide to safety!" Jimmy yelled.

Giroux took another careful shot, and the Aviatik staggered under the fusillade. Another burst made the wings of the biplane fold as though battered by an invisible hammer. The doomed plane rolled and the body tore itself clear of the tangle and roared off like a gigantic dart. The runaway engine wrote its mournful story down the sky lane, dragging a long, greasy plume behind it.

This initial success demanded its price. Now Jimmy was praying that his precarious monoplane wing would hold when he pulled out of his wild dive. He had cut the throttle and carefully brought the Morane out of her great strain, and tried to turn for home. When he rammed the throttle up again the engine choked and coughed, and he realized he must have fouled the plugs while gliding with the ignition off. The chase had taken them well inside the enemy lines, and as matters stood, with the prevailing wind against them, they knew they would have to be very lucky to get back safely.

"You chased him too far," Lieutenant Giroux shouted.

"I had to. He would have gotten away."

"I'll admit you got him, but now it looks as though they'll get us."

"Don't give up so easily," Jimmy countered, and turned back to his controls.

The jagged pattern of trenches and sapheads that marked the front line seemed miles away as the wind blew telltale ground smoke toward the enemy back areas. Risking everything, even a deadly spin that comes with losing flying speed, Jimmy stretched his glide, mile after mile. The French lines were now ahead, plainly marked by the dull browns and whites of the various excavations where thousands of infantrymen huddled and watched the tiny airplane as it fluttered on in its effort to reach safety.

But luck was with them and they made it with just a few yards to spare. There was no flat or cleared area anywhere, and as they touched down, they floundered through tangles of barbed wire and flopped into a water-filled shell hole that ripped off the undercarriage. What was left slithered along on its belly and finally came to a halt. Lieutenant Giroux, who had been standing up telling Jimmy how to handle the landing, was tossed out and suffered a broken arm. Jimmy being well-belted in did not have a scratch.

On their return to their squadron, and after full details had been written and interpreted by the squadron commander, credit for the victory over the Aviatik was given to Corporal Bach who had resolutely given chase, delivered the first telling blow and "courageously" stayed in action until his observer could finish the destruction of their enemy.

This was an auspicious beginning, and it was unfortunate that Jimmy could not continue and add to the reputation of the Americans. But such was not to be.

A short time later, while engaged in a mission to drop a French agent inside the enemy lines, Jimmy Bach was captured. Although he made several brave attempts to escape, he finished his service as a prisoner of war, enduring more than three years behind enemy-compound wire.

WILLIAM T. BADHAM

Just to disprove that one had to be a single-seater pilot to become an ace, William T. Badham of Birmingham, Alabama, racked up five victories while flying DH-4 two-seater observation planes. Born in 1895, he attended Lawrenceville Preparatory School, and went on from there to Yale. About a month after the United States declared war on Germany, Badham volunteered for what was known then as the Aviation Section. After passing through the training program in the United States, he was commissioned on November 27, 1917, and shipped to France.

In order to get some experience, he volunteered to fly two-seaters with a French observation squadron, with which he served from February 7 to May 24, 1918. He was next transferred to the 91st Aero Squadron, a Corps Observation outfit, flying DH-4s.

While carrying out routine photographic and visual observation missions, Lieutenant Badham gained his first victory on September 15. On October 23 he scored over two more enemy aircraft and was awarded the D.S.C. Two more enemy planes fell under his attacks before October ended, but apparently because Lieutenant Badham was "only a two-seater pilot," few details of his successes have been recorded officially. He remained with the 91st Aero Squadron until January 17, 1919. Until recently he was president of the Naphthalene Products Company in Birmingham.

CLYDE BALSLEY

Clyde Balsley was born in San Antonio, Texas, but had the appearance, manners, and speech of a British university man. Aristocratic in bearing and dress, he was a remarkable contribution to France's part in the war, and had he had a reasonable share of luck he might have become one of the outstanding air heroes of the war. As it was, he was fortunate to live to see the Armistice.

As did so many other Lafayette Escadrille fliers, Clyde first went to France as an ambulance driver with the American Field Service. By mid-September 1915, he enlisted in the French Aviation Service and gained his pilot's brevet by January 2, 1916, passing his final tests on a Blériot.

He was then assigned to Escadrille V.97, which at the time was assuming the duties of Air Guard of Paris. Flying two-seater Voisins, these gallant men covered the outskirts of Paris on both day and night patrols, hoping to intercept German Zeppelins that might raid the City of Light. Balsley spent only six weeks on this work, and no German dirigibles appeared to offer him his chance for glory. After a short time in the Réserve Général Aéronautique he was posted to the Escadrille Américaine, arriving there May 29, 1916.

On June 18 Balsley, along with Norman Prince, Kiffin Rockwell, and Captain Georges Thénault, their French commander, went off on what was Clyde's first active-service patrol. Their task was to provide air protection for a couple of French artillery-spotting machines. The Nieuport scouts, flown by the American formation, were cruising at about 10,000 feet and were well over the enemy line when a formation of Aviatik two-seaters moved in to attack.

Balsley dived on one enemy plane and was in good position, but his Lewis fired only one cartridge and then jammed. There was little opportunity under these conditions to remedy the stoppage as the only gun on those early Nieuports was bolted to its wing bracket and could only be reached by loosening one's belt and trying to stand up to get at the recalcitrant weapon.

Clyde pulled out of the melee to clear the stoppage, and then found himself under the gun of an Aviatik observer. A second enemy plane joined the fun, and, according to one report, Clyde was struck by an "explosive" bullet which severely wounded him in the hip.

(There were no "explosive" bullets in use on either side of the line. The word "explosive" bullet has been used time and time again, when the report should state "tracer" or "incendiary" bullet. It is a fact that the Germans had no explosive bullet in 1916, and, when they learned that the British had devised such a round sometime later—a bullet intended for use against Zeppelins—they protested vigorously, arguing that such ammunition was illegal. But early in the war it was almost routine to call any bullet that sparkled, fizzed, or displayed some smoke, an "explosive" bullet. There is considerable difference between tracers, incendiaries, and explosive bullets. But we shall come upon these "explosive" bullets time and time again.)

At any rate Clyde Balsley was badly injured, and unable to use his right leg. It was explained later that his sciatic nerve had been damaged. Fortunately, he had about 6000 feet in which to reach his own side of the line. He landed in a wheat field just inside the French support lines, but turned over and was thrown out. He was not certain where he was until German artillery began shelling his wrecked machine. He crawled about for some time searching for a convenient shell hole, but eventually some French soldiers rescued him.

He was seriously hurt and had lost a lot of blood. He was first taken to a general hospital at Vadelaincourt where his life was despaired of for a time. He was then removed to the American hospital at Neuilly where he underwent several operations over the next twelve months for the removal of bullet fragments. This type of wound is often caused by soft-nosed, or dum dum bullets that break up immediately on impact. Even a regulation slug may break up after striking hard wood, sheet metal, or tightly woven fabric.

Not until late in 1917 was Clyde able to leave the hospital and return to the United States. By that time he had been elevated to the rank of sergeant, and the French government had awarded him the Médaille Militaire and the Croix de Guerre with one Palm.

Although crippled permanently, Balsley offered his services to the

United States, was commissioned a captain, and served through the rest of the war in the Pursuit Division, U. S. Air Service, in Washington, D.C.

FRANK BAYLIES

Frank Baylies of New Bedford, Massachusetts, is credited with twelve enemy aircraft. One of the more modest of our representatives in the French Aviation Service, he was candid, kind, friendly in appearance and manner, and probably the last to be marked as a "killer." In any company he was never boastful or belligerent, seldom talked of his accomplishments, and when pinned down always declared that he was very lucky in his contests.

Son of a New England doctor, Frank early in life learned to drive his father's automobile, a skill that enabled him to serve as an ambulance driver with the American Field Service in France and Salonika between February 1916 and May 1917. He was a conscientious worker, showed no fear under shellfire, and was always available in any emergency. He was awarded the Croix de Guerre during this period.

He transferred to the French Aviation Service on May 21, 1917, and for a time flew as a corporal pilot with Escadrille S.73. Then, on December 18, 1917, he was posted to the famous Spad 3, an escadrille of the Storks Group, and in a short time was one of their outstanding fighters. He ran up his "ace" score of five enemy planes within a very short time and was promoted to sergeant and given the leadership of a flight.

While with Spad 3, Baylies flew with such noted airmen as Dorme, Heurteaux, Deullin, and Guynemer from whom he learned a great deal. His escadrille was engaged on the important war fronts including the Somme, Noyon, and Montdidier where it daily encountered first-class enemy Staffeln. Baylies became a deadly shot, a first-class tactician, and a valuable leader. Once he took on an enemy airman, he stayed with him to the end. On one memorable occasion while patrolling miles behind the German lines, he engaged an Albatros and followed it all the way down to the farmhouse level. With a final burst he made sure his enemy had crashed, and then turned for home. On the way back his Spad was riddled time and time again by enemy ground fire, and before he had reached the security of the French lines, his Hisso engine began to lose power, and finally stopped altogether. He had to land inside the German lines.

During his final glide Baylies took stock and calculated where he would touch down, and before the Spad had stopped rolling, he had leaped from the cockpit, dodged two German infantrymen who tried to head him off, and then did a low hurdles' sprint across trenches, barbed-wire entanglements, and sandbag fortifications until he was in an advanced machine-gun post. How he weathered the storm of enemy fire that tried to cut him down, is one of the legendary stories of the French Aviation Service.

Instead of instilling caution, this experience only gave the New Bedford man more daring, and while he lasted he seemed invincible. He attacked, no matter how many enemy planes were in the area. He never fired until it was a matter of point-blank attack, and after three months service with Spad 3 he was officially credited with twelve enemy planes.

Frank Baylies disappeared on June 17, 1918, while fighting along the west side of the Marne salient. He had taken off with Ted Parsons, another New Englander, and had challenged four German single-seaters. Parsons reported later that Baylies had gone down in flames. Other American pilots stated that the German ships were Fokker triplanes, and that Baylies had rushed in before other French planes in the area could join him. There is no question but that Frank was shot down in flames.

It is interesting to note that Sergeant Frank Baylies had been accepted by the U. S. Aviation Service and commissioned a second lieutenant on May 20, 1918, but the papers did not come through immediately, so Frank stayed on, determined to repay the French for the training they had given him. He was awarded the Médaille Militaire and the Croix de Guerre with six Palms and one Star.

CHARLES JOHN BIDDLE

Charles J. Biddle was born in the small town of Andalusia, in Bucks County, Pennsylvania, and probably is the least known of the American aces of World War I. Although he scored but one victory during his service with two French squadrons, he added seven more after he joined the U. S. Air Service early in 1918. Never an especially glamorous type, he nevertheless performed so well he received the French Legion of Honor, the Croix de Guerre, and the Belgian Order of Leopold. He served eight months with two French Spad squadrons, transferred to the U. S. Air Service and ended his military career as Commanding Officer of the U. S. Fourth Pursuit Group. After the war he headed a noted law firm in Philadelphia and became counsel for the Drexel Institute of Technology.

There was nothing of the playboy about Charlie Biddle. He took his training seriously, and not only became an excellent pilot, but while he was at Le Plessis-Belleville awaiting assignment to an active service squadron, he used every opportunity to fly as many types of aircraft as were available instead of spending his free time along the boulevards of nearby Paris. He also gained complete technical knowledge of any aircraft engines on the test benches.

In this respect he was unlike most young airmen who were seldom interested in the power plants, and often used the old chestnut, "If my engine stops up there, I can't get out and fix it, can I?"

As a result Charles Biddle became not only a book-learning theorist, but a practical man of action.

He went to the front with Escadrille S.73 (Spads) on July 28, 1917, and served with this squadron until January 10, 1918, when he was assigned to the Lafayette Escadrille (S.124). In all that period of time he was credited with only one air victory but he had used his time in learning the art of air fighting from ground to ceiling.

He made a careful study of all phases of fighting and tactics that brought victory. Interestingly enough, his only score in that time was made over a two-seater Albatros that he downed near Langemarck in Belgium, although some authorities have argued that he must have destroyed many others that could not be confirmed—a statement that can be applied to any wartime aviator who fought deep inside the enemy lines.

Biddle kept a careful record of all his patrols and listed his various experiences during his five months with the French. He also interrogated many noted pilots to learn their views and the favorite maneuvers they employed under different combat conditions. The end result was an instruction book, complete with photographs and diagrams, produced to teach aerial combat. This valuable treatise was adopted later for the instruction of U. S. Air Service pilots who immediately appreciated its general merit and readability. If Charlie

Biddle had never flown one offensive patrol, this contribution would have more than justified his lengthy service.

Along with many other members of the Lafayette Escadrille Charlie was received into the U. S. Aviation Service on February 18, 1918. As were so many pilots, he was shunted into a period of wasteful idleness. He had actually been commissioned a captain on November 7, 1917, but because of the sluggish movement of the American war effort, the squadron that was formed with the men transferred from the Lafayette Escadrille did not get into real action until March 1918. In fact, this organization, to be known as the 103rd Pursuit Squadron, claims to have registered the first official victory for the U. S. Air Service when Paul Baer destroyed an Albatros near Rheims on March 11, 1918.

This victory is not to be confused with another American "first" that was scored by Douglas Campbell who downed a German aircraft on April 14, 1918, and is cited as being the "first American-trained pilot" to score. Campbell was a member of the original 94th Aero Squadron.

It is of interest to note that although the "French-trained" pilots were accepted for service in American squadrons they were cavalierly listed in a different category from those who had joined the service at home and were trained on American fields by American instructors, but their victories were always channeled into the American combat lists. Even those men who did not transfer to the U. S. Aviation Service saw their scores, made while serving with the French or British, eventually added to the all-American victory figures.

Charlie Biddle racked up his second victory on April 12 when he downed a Halberstadt two-seater near Corbeny (Chemin des Dames). Some historians have taken the stand that downing a two-seater requires twice the skill, daring and resolution, but Biddle would have none of this, always making it clear that fighting two-seaters simply needed different tactics and maneuvers to counteract the arc of fire available to the rear gunner. Of Biddle's eight victories, three were scored against two-seaters.

Charlie was concerned about kite balloons and had noted the ease with which some aircraft pilots could destroy these gasbags. He was particularly incensed with the manner in which German airmen could fire Allied balloons, and was to learn that the incendiary rounds used by the French were not efficient against German balloons. He hoped to encourage the development of a more potent bullet, but the war ended before he could bring his plans to fruition.

His most memorable day came on May 15, 1918, when during an offensive patrol he was shot down, wounded, and piled up in no man's land. This also occurred in the Langemarck area, and from all accounts Charlie's nemesis was a new German Junkers low-level attack plane that was said to be stoutly armored. Actually, the Junkers, a sesquiplane, was covered with 5-millimeter steel plating that made it singularly invulnerable. The pilot had no guns, but the observer was equipped with a flexible Parabellum and another gun mounted to fire down through a panel in the cockpit floor. In some variations of the Junkers a tail tunnel was provided through which the observer could fire at enemy aircraft approaching from below and behind.

"It was the slowest bus I ever encountered," Charlie said later, and well he might for the Junkers though powered with a 230-horsepower Benz could attain a maximum speed of only 97 miles per hour. However, it served well as a ground-attack plane.

Biddle was fascinated with this enemy machine, though its gunner had bested him in what he considered a fair battle. Probably he had been trying to get behind and below the two-seater, not knowing the observer could fire on him either through a tunnel or an open floor panel. But he was certain the machine was armored in some manner.

The telling burst spattered along the top of Charlie's Hisso engine, but one slug continued on through and pierced his left knee. The engine quit cold under the battering, and Charlie had to nose down and glide for home. He landed in a maze of shell holes, rusty barbed wire, and abandoned trenches. The instant his Spad touched down it became entangled in the maze of debris, but despite this emergency Charlie sensed where he was and in which direction safety lay. He crawled, waded, and scurried a distance of nearly seventy yards under heavy machine-gun fire and finally flopped into a British observation post where the Tommies took good care of him and at the first opportunity moved him out and forwarded him on to an advanced medical post.

That experience kept Charlie Biddle grounded for about a month, after which he was made CO of the 13th Pursuit Squadron. Leading a flight on August 1, Biddle brought down his third and fourth enemy machines during a patrol over Preny north of Pont-à-Mousson. In this case his victims flew Albatros single-seaters.

On August 16 Charlie trapped a Rumpler two-seater over

Bouxieres-aux-Dames and forced the enemy pilot to land his air-craft well inside the French lines. The plane was intact and Charlie spent several hours making a complete study of the machine—for future reference. Two Fokker fighters fell before his guns in the Argonne sector. After running his score up to eight, he was given command of the Fourth Pursuit Group and promoted to major. On his return to the United States, following the Armistice, he wrote a book of his experiences, *Way of the Eagle,* that, unfortunately, is now out of print.

DOUGLAS CAMPBELL

As noted before, Douglas Campbell of the 94th Aero Squadron is credited with being the first "American-trained" pilot to score a victory over an enemy airman. In this instance he nosed out Alan Winslow by a few minutes, for these two fliers were on a stand-by alert when two German airmen who had become lost during an earlier period of fog, were trapped and shot down while floundering over Allied territory. The records are not clear concerning the types of machines involved. In his book *Fighting the Flying Circus* Eddie Rickenbacker makes no mention of the types shot down, but some reports state that Campbell downed a Pfalz D-III, while Winslow opened his score on an Albatros D-V.

"You pays your money, and you takes your choice."

Douglas Campbell was born in San Francisco. His father was head of the Lick Observatory on Mount Wilson. Douglas put in his early years at the local public schools and eventually entered Harvard. On the outbreak of war in 1917 Doug left college and joined the U. S. Aviation Section and received most of his training in the United States. On his arrival in France, however, he did absorb some air-fighting and gunnery training at the Number 3 Training Depot at Issoudun. He was then assigned to the 94th Aero Squadron that was to become known as the Hat-in-the-Ring Squadron.

Campbell, Rickenbacker, and Raoul Lufbery made the first patrol flown by the squadron on March 19, 1918, but it was almost a month later before Campbell and Winslow scored their historic "double." Much was made of this. Both planes were put on display at Toul, much champagne was drunk, and then Colonel Billy Mitchell turned up to pen a laudatory report that was rapidly cabled to Washington. The American public relations machine then went into high gear, and it was generally assumed that even rookie American airmen were equally as good as any German, no matter how experienced or what "Circus" plane he flew.

By May 31, Campbell had continued his success, racking up five victories and qualifying as an "ace," but as so often happens, his luck ran out early in June during a two-ship foray with Jimmy Meissner. These two men were close companions, and whenever possible would hare off on crazy intrusions of Hun country looking for trouble.

The two pilots had taken off on the morning of June 6 on some special show they had cooked up, but after a couple of tours up and down the Pont-à-Mousson area, they became separated. Campbell continued the patrol and then, to his delight, spotted a Rumpler two-seater coursing out of Germany obviously heading for Nancy. He decided it was on a photographic mission, so eased up into the sun to pick off what looked like a sitting duck.

He moved carefully, but at the first opportunity nosed down and gave the Rumpler a stiff burst of Vickers fire. To his astonishment the two-seater continued on, ignoring his attack. While Doug tried to stage more dives, the German observer made the most of his chances and Campbell's Nieuport soon looked the worse for wear. At this point Jimmy Meissner appeared again and took a hand, but the Rumpler team handled itself well, and both Campbell and Meissner soon realized that if they were going to down this photoreconnaissance bus one or the other would have to put in a telling burst.

Working smoothly together, Jimmy and Doug attacked from opposite sides. Campbell moved into his approach first and received the brunt of the observer's fire. He had dived sharply to get below the Rumpler, and in fact put a burst up through the cockpit floor. By this time the German observer had spotted Meissner moving in and had swung his free gun around, and just as he was about to draw a bead on Jimmy, Doug came up out of nowhere and presented the enemy with a perfect target.

Doug was just leveling off from his zoom and was planning to circle for position to get a shot at the front elevation of the Rumpler when a heavy crash exploded just behind his seat. A burning pain swept across his shoulders, and he knew he had been hit. There was nothing to do but head for home and hope his machine would get him there. Jimmy stayed long enough to drive the two-seater down to a rocky landing just inside the enemy lines.

Again, we encounter an "explosive" bullet story. Ever since that fight it has been reported that Campbell had been downed by such a round, but he seems to have been hit by an incendiary or tracer that broke up on impact because of its hollow casing, and several fragments lodged in his back. He returned to his own field and after hospital treatment in France, was sent to the United States to recuperate. He did not return to his squadron until a few days after the Armistice.

After the war Douglas Campbell became affiliated with W. R. Grace and Company, and eventually was associated with Pan American Airways. In 1939 he held a post of vice-president, and in 1948 was made vice-president and general manager of that airline. He is now retired and lives in Connecticut.

THOMAS G. CASSADY

Another almost unknown American air hero of World War I is Thomas G. Cassady, a native of Spencer, Indiana. A curly-haired, pleasant man with a most youthful appearance, he joined the French Aviation Service in July 1917, went through the Avord-Tours-Pau and Le Plessis-Belleville routine and completed his training December 24, 1917. Two days later he was posted to Escadrille Spad 157, and stayed there until February 16, 1918, attaining the rank of sergeant.

By February 22, the United States had taken Cassady under consideration and he was commissioned in the U. S. Aviation Service as a first lieutenant. But there was no opportunity to fly and fight, so Tommy requested a return to the French, and on May 14 was attached to Escadrille Spad 163 with which he served until September 8, 1918, when he was posted to the U. S. 28th Aero Squadron. While with this American unit he took part in many aerial engagements, most of the time as a flight commander.

He ended his war with nine official victories, the Distinguished Service Cross, the French Legion of Honor, and the Croix de Guerre.

REED McKINLEY CHAMBERS

The popular Reed Chambers, victor in seven enemy combats, was born at Onaga, Kansas, in 1894. During his public school period his family moved to Memphis, Tennessee. He joined the Tennessee National Guard in 1916 and served on the Mexican border. After America's declaration of war on Germany, he immediately enlisted in the Aviation Section of the Signal Corps and completed his training in the United States. By March 1, 1918, he had been posted to the small group that was to comprise the 94th Aero Squadron then being formed at Toul.

Chambers proved to be a splendid air fighter, most popular with his comrades, and a capable leader. In fact, he gave so much time to his squadron duties he unquestionably sacrificed many opportunities to run up his score. He served well, first as a flight commander and later as commander of the First Pursuit Group.

After the war Reed Chambers teamed with Eddie Rickenbacker to form the Reed M. Chambers Co., an aerial photograph service, but this was not a well-paying proposition. In 1926 he organized the Florida Airways, and two years later established the U. S. Aircraft Insurance Group. When last heard of he was serving as Chairman of the Board of the U. S. Aviation Insurance Underwriters, Inc., of New York.

VICTOR CHAPMAN

One of the most beloved members of the Lafayette Escadrille was Victor Chapman, a native New Yorker who had been studying architecture in Paris during the spring of 1914. When the war broke out Victor was touring England with his family, but determined to fight for France, he left London and hurried back to Paris where he enlisted in the Foreign Legion.

Victor was assigned to the 3rd Marching Regiment of the Foreign Legion and received his early training at the Reuilly Caserne, Paris. He was given machine-gun instruction and for a time was the close companion of George Preston Ames, an American volunteer from Paraguay whose father was practicing dentistry there. Chapman and Ames had many exciting experiences as infantrymen during the three months they were in the trenches. Shortly thereafter Chapman heard of the plan to organize an American flying group and put in for a transfer to the French Aviation, although trench fighting held a certain fascination for him. He was to see plenty more before his transfer came through on August 1, 1915.

Because of his skill with the machine gun Victor was assigned first to V.B. 108 (Voisin bombers) and put in more than a month with this long-distance bomber escadrille as a machine gunner during which time he proved his worth. He was then released and sent to Avord for pilot training.

Chapman was the perfect candidate for war flying. He had the artistic touch that is necessary for scout piloting. He ignored the horror and blood of combat; his eye took in only the poetry of the scene. The shell-torn landscape, the battered villages, and the ruin of beautiful forests were tucked away for future reference. He loved to fly and willingly volunteered for extra patrols, and it is still a mystery he lived as long as he did.

The New York man gained his pilot's ticket by January 9, 1916, after passing out on a Maurice Farman biplane. He joined the Escadrille Américaine on April 20, 1916, and was killed on June 23, some eight weeks later. On June 17 Victor was wounded while on a lone patrol when he came upon a formation of two Aviatik C-III two-seaters that were being escorted by three Fokker fighters. The Aviatiks were carrying out a reconnaissance over French territory.

At first Chapman had to curb his desire to plunge headlong into the enemy formation. When he saw that it included three single-seater fighters he eased off and circled nearby hoping to pick off a laggard. The German planes held their formation and made no attempt to tackle the lone Nieuport. But when the Aviatiks split up to make their individual photographic runs over their assigned strips, Victor decided to move in.

He swooped like a hawk, his lone Lewis gun chattered and stitched a seam up the back of one of the photography planes. Believing he had scored, Victor then banked hard with the intent of moving into a position below the three-ship formation of Fokkers to keep away from their guns and hope to get in a final burst at the photography ship. He emptied his first drum into the fish-tailed two-seater. The Aviatik banked, staggered, and the pilot fell for-

ward on the stick with a number of slugs in his back. The enemy
gunner had been killed before he could bob up from his camera that
was mounted in the floor. The Aviatik then burst into flames and
plunged to the earth.

The Fokker pilots bore down on this impudent Nieuport airman,
all three pouring sharp bursts in his direction. Victor looked the
situation over and decided that these three were members of Oswald
Boelcke's first circus formation that had been brought into the area
for the Battle of the Somme. Certainly they flew well and moved
cleverly to trap him. They came in on three sharp angles, firing short,
telling bursts. In fact it seemed that they were using this loner for
target practice.

Victor had to use every maneuver in the book. He darted and
dived in all directions, knowing that he had used his original drum
of ammunition on the two-seater. It was impossible under these
conditions to replace the empty pan. Bullets hissed from every direction. Tracers drew their silver lines across the cloudless sky and
crashed into his frail machine until at last the stick acted slug-
gishly and Victor knew some control cable had been cut. On glancing
around he saw that one bullet had severed the metal aileron bracket
that protruded from the upper wing. The same bullet had slashed
through Victor's helmet and hacked a four-inch gash across his scalp.

He had no aileron control and the plane went into a flat spin. His
vision was obscured by blood streaming from his wound, but he had
sense enough to reach up and draw the broken bracket together,
holding it fast with his gloved hand. In some small way this provided
neutral aileron effect, allowing him to fly level while darting back
and forth with his rudder to evade the continuing storm of enemy
fire. Then he faked a falling-leaf maneuver to create the impression
he was out of control, and his adversaries withdrew, giving him an
opportunity to land at an advanced field where French mechanics
made a temporary repair of the aileron bracket and Victor received
emergency medical care.

Later that afternoon Victor flew back to the Lafayette field, and
although his head was swathed in bandages, he laughed off his close
call and refused to go to a nearby hospital for further medical attention.

This gives some idea of the general discipline enjoyed in the Lafayette Escadrille. This happy-go-lucky attitude was to have tragic
consequences.

"I'm quite all right," Victor insisted. "You know how a scalp wound bleeds, but unless you suffer concussion or skull injury there's no real damage. I tell you, I'm fine."

Bill Thaw, then commander of the group, suggested that Victor take his headache to Paris for a few days.

"I'm not doing anything of the sort," Sergeant Chapman said to Lieutenant Thaw.

"Well, you're not flying for a few days," Thaw said flatly. "There is no plane available for you. Take it easy."

"Me—just sit around?"

"You must have a large headache. Why not try to get some sleep?"

And so it was decided, but when Clyde Balsley was shot down near Verdun the next day, June 18, and taken to the hospital at Vadelaincourt where his condition was considered to be critical, Victor rushed over to Clyde's bedside. Although still swathed in bandages, he wanted to see if there was anything he could do for Clyde.

As they grinned at each other, Clyde mumbled, "You can get me out of here. I'm not really too bad, am I? It's just that I'm thirsty all the time. All they let me have is a wet bandage to suck on."

Victor then knew how serious Clyde's condition was, but he kept a cheerful tone.

"Don't worry. Tomorrow I'll be back and I'll bring you some oranges."

"That would be wonderful," Clyde breathed.

"Wonderful? That's nothing. I'll even get you some champagne when the doctors say you can have some real liquid."

Thus assured, Clyde dropped off to sleep.

Victor Chapman made some concession to his head wound by sleeping a little later than usual, but by June 20 a new Nieuport was flown in and Victor busied himself adjusting the compass and the machine-gun sight. The weather was not too good, so he countered his boredom by making several circuits around the field just to work out a few control or engine bugs.

Late that afternoon an advanced post reported some German planes intruding into the French lines. A handful of Escadrille pilots, including Victor Chapman, went up to welcome them but the tip proved to be too vague and too late.

During all this time Bill Thaw and other members of the group worried about Victor and tried to induce him to take a proper rest.

His bandages were so bulky it was impossible for him to wear a helmet, but he insisted on doing a few test flights, refusing to take things easy.

The morning of June 23 was one for the poets and Victor insisted on flying a regular patrol. Fortunately, they ran into little or no opposition, and on returning Victor remembered Clyde Balsley. After lunch he gathered a basket of oranges and was taking them out to the hangar when he saw Thénault, Prince, and Lufbery warming up their Nieuports for an afternoon patrol. Chapman insisted he was well enough to take his place with them.

"Look!" he explained. "I have a small basket of oranges for Balsley. I'll wrap them carefully and shove them behind my seat. I'll go up the lines with you and if there is nothing hot going on, I'll break off, fly back and land near the hospital. Clyde's just dying for some fresh fruit."

"Go deliver your oranges," Thénault ordered. "You've flown enough for today."

"Take it easy, Victor," Raoul Lufbery pleaded.

But there was little discipline in the American squadron in those days. Their engines were ticking over, and on a signal from Thénault, all three rumbled away for their take-off. Plainly annoyed, Victor called a mechanic, ordered him to prepare his Nieuport, and soon roared after them.

The rest of the story can be put together quickly. Thénault's flight climbed into enemy territory and found two German planes on which it immediately dived, and while they were thus engaged three more came down from a cloud formation above, so Thénault prudently withdrew and carried out a routine patrol, still believing Chapman had flown over to visit Clyde Balsley.

When they returned to their own field, they wondered how their wounded comrade was, and whether he would be permitted to enjoy Victor's oranges. In fact no concern was felt until later that day when a Farman pilot who had been in the same area reported he had seen three Nieuports in combat with five German planes, and that in the middle of the engagement he had noted a fourth Nieuport diving at full speed to join the fight. The Farman pilot was positive that this plane had, for no apparent reason, crashed with its engine full on. That was Victor Chapman.

But as usual, there is another version to this story. The German planes concerned were two L.V.G. observation machines, and as soon as Captain Thénault had signaled for the attack he spotted three Fokkers that were sitting above waiting to pounce. Realizing they were too far over to engage that many, Thénault pulled out and headed back for his own lines. In the meantime Chapman, who had followed them, nosed down to give what aid he could. No one in the Nieuport formation saw him and he was left to fight his way out of the Fokker trap. Whether any of the Germans actually fired on him is not known. What might have happened is that after his first attack, noting he was alone, Chapman went into a number of wild aerobatics, and his desperation may have tried his machine to the limit, and the wings ripped off. A later report from Germany indicated that Victor had been shot through the head, and this may have been closer to the truth. But the French Farman pilot and his observer insisted that Chapman simply went into a full-power dive from which he never recovered. If so, we may assume that as a result of his recent head wound, he had fainted and never knew what was happening to him.

In conclusion, a typical wartime misunderstanding resulted when Chapman's body was pulled out of the crash. Besides the package of oranges Victor had a couple of letters in his pocket that were addressed to Clyde Balsley. When these letters were found it was presumed that the dead pilot was Clyde Balsley and such information was forwarded to the International Red Cross. With that, it was reported that Clyde Balsley, who was recovering from his wounds in a French hospital, was at the same time presumed to have been shot down and killed in German territory.

The Escadrille Américaine lost one of its most popular members, a victim of his own obstinate determination.

HAMILTON COOLIDGE

The military career of Hamilton Coolidge of Brookline, Massachusetts, presents a fairly complete outline of the training program set up by the old Aviation Section of the Signal Corps. Coolidge was a first-class airman who was credited with eight confirmed victories, but his career came to a tragic end when his Spad received a direct hit by a German antiaircraft shell, and he fell to his death in the village of Chevières. His squadron mates removed his body from the wreckage, and buried it in the little French settlement.

Ham Coolidge, as he was popularly known in the 94th Aero Squadron, was born September 1, 1895. He entered Groton School where he captained the football team and played on the baseball nine. From there he went to Harvard where he played varsity football. During the summer of 1915 he joined the Reserve Officers' Training course at Plattsburgh, and following that bought flight training at the Curtiss Flying School, then located at Buffalo, New York.

Shortly after the end of February 1917 Ham left Harvard and joined the Aviation Section at Key West and received his preliminary training at Miami. He was sent from there to the Massachusetts Institute of Technology for further ground school instruction. He went to France in July 1917 and was bogged down for a time in Paris doing staff work. His commission came through in September of that year and a week or so later he was assigned to the 3rd Aviation Instruction Center at Issoudun to help organize the school. After gaining his wings he was retained as the commander of a school squadron, and over the next seven months acted as a test pilot, carrying out as many as fifteen to twenty flights a day.

Finally, on June 16, 1918, Coolidge who was now a captain was assigned to the 94th Aero Squadron, at that time located near Toul on the French front. He proved to be a most aggressive fighter and had downed five enemy aircraft and three kite balloons by October 27.

On that fateful Sunday, only two weeks before the end of the war, Ham went to the aid of several American DH.4s that were heading into enemy country to bomb a concentration of German troops in the vicinity of Grand Pré. These troops had been unloaded from trains the night before and their movements were being covered by a number of German Fokker fighters. Coolidge saw the bombers fighting their way to the enemy concentration, so he buzzed in to give a hand. He spotted two DH.4s being attacked by six enemy fighters, and as he roared in to give aid an antiaircraft shell scored a direct hit and exploded directly under his Hisso engine.

Coolidge's Spad seemed to break up in midair from that million-to-one shot, and as there were no parachutes as yet available for Allied airplane pilots, the New England youth went down to his death. He was posthumously awarded the Distinguished Service Cross for this action.

ELLIOT COWDIN

Elliot Christopher Cowdin, a native New Yorker, has been presented in most histories of the Lafayette Escadrille as a bombastic character. Those who knew him were not overawed by this flamboyant man, and although he was credited with but one enemy aircraft, he was awarded the Médaille Militaire and the Croix de Guerre with two Palms and a Star. James Norman Hall stated that Cowdin must be credited with an important role in the initial concept of the American volunteer force.

The son of a Tuxedo Park, New York, silk-ribbon manufacturer, Cowdin attended Harvard. His father was a fairly wealthy socialite who was considered to be a good polo player. In the early months of the war Elliot joined the American Field Service as a volunteer ambulance driver. In February 1915 he met a college companion, Norman Prince, who had been working on the idea of forming an all-American aviation squadron to serve with the French but up to this point had had little success. Elliot was intrigued with the idea and learned that there already were enough Americans serving with various French outfits to form a squadron. He arranged an interview with a Colonel Barrés, then Chief of French Aeronautics at the front. Colonel Barrés promised to lend his support, and Cowdin advised Prince of his success. This aroused new enthusiasm, and the Escadrille Américaine eventually came into being.

Meanwhile Cowdin, Thaw, and Prince had completed their training and had served some time with various French squadrons and by December 1915 these three men were given a month's leave and sent home to the United States for the Christmas holidays. They immediately created a furor although all three had discarded their French uniforms for modest business suits, Melton overcoats, and derby hats.

When they landed they were recognized by the harbor reporters; Bill Thaw, in particular, attracted their attention as he had been a college playboy prior to the war and was a cousin of the notorious Harry K. Thaw, the Pittsburgh millionaire who in 1906 had shot and killed Stanford White, the famous architect, over the affections of Evelyn Nesbit, a popular show-girl model. In consequence the newspapers took varied viewpoints concerning the volunteers' service with the French. George Sylvester Viereck, then editor of the pro-German newspaper *Fatherland,* protested to Secretary of State Robert Lansing, arguing that these three men should be interned—chiefly to prevent their returning to the front. He cited the legal aspect of the situation as he saw it and pointed out that Thaw, Cowdin, and Prince had forfeited their American citizenship. Thus, any German submarine could intercept the vessel on which they sailed and remove them forcibly without infringement of American neutrality.

While being shaved in the Ritz-Carlton barber shop in New York, Bill Thaw encountered a man he had met socially before the war. This was the German Ambassador Johann-Heinrich von Bernstorff who chided the American for what he considered to be a breach of international law. The Pittsburgh man refused to be drawn into an argument, and as soon as his haircut was finished, he rose from the chair and walked out.

Von Bernstorff also took the question of violation of America's neutrality to the State Department, but before any official action could be made, Thaw, Cowdin, and Prince slipped aboard a French liner and sailed for Le Havre. A short time later the plan to group all American pilots into one squadron was approved, and on April 20, 1916, the original Escadrille Américaine was placed in force.

It will be appreciated that Elliot Cowdin did have a role in the basic organization, but why he was considered for the American volunteer group is a mystery, for up to this time he appears to have been a most boisterous type and did not stay very long with any of the four French squadrons to which he was assigned before joining N.124. He was aggressive, always seemed to be in trouble, and even his American companions found him difficult.

On July 4, 1916, Cowdin was involved in an incident that has been questioned time and time again. Elliot claimed on this occasion to have engaged the famous Oswald Boelcke in a long drawn-out duel, and would sometimes produce an extract from the German airman's diary to prove his point. From all accounts, Boelcke and Cowdin were referring to two different incidents.

For instance, Boelcke claimed to have talked with another German pilot who stated that his two-seater had been attacked by a French Nieuport that was boldly "flying an American flag." Boelcke went up in a new Albatros to investigate and ran into six Nieuports, but after his first attack on one of them his gun jammed after about seventy rounds. Boelcke makes no mention of seeing an American flag and of course there is no record of any Nieuport of the Escadrille Américaine carrying such an insignia. This Boelcke-Cowdin "duel" has been picked up and revamped a dozen different ways by each new crop of aviation writers.

In August 1916 Cowdin's health broke down and he was found to be suffering from stomach ulcers. He spent six weeks in a hospital and was then discharged from the French service, and in turn attached to the British Aviation Headquarters in Paris. He was released early in 1917 and returned to the United States. In June of that year he was commissioned a major in the United States Air Service, and worked with the Board of Aircraft Production.

EDMOND C. C. GENET

One of the most picturesque characters to represent the United States in the early days of the Great War was Edmond Charles Clinton Genêt of Ossining, New York, a direct descendant of Citizen Genêt who had been the first French minister to the United States in 1792. Edmond Genêt was born in November 1896, the traditional youngest son predestined to achievement. He grew up completely ignoring his three older brothers, seeking his pleasures and interests by himself.

He had an unco-ordinated schooling, and felt an unending love for the sea and ships. He was skilled in music, could paint in oils, and kept an interesting diary. He applied for admission to Annapolis but failed the entrance exams, so he enlisted as a seaman in the United States Navy. When he was denied a role in the Mexican Border affair, he lost all interest in ships and the sea and made plans to desert.

He jumped his ship January 8, 1915, and went aboard the S.S. *Rochambeau,* obtaining passage for France. By coincidence, Norman Prince was aboard the same liner, and it was from him that young Genêt first heard of the plan to raise a squadron of American volunteers. Following the accepted routine, Edmond enlisted in the Foreign Legion February 3, 1915, and was sent to the front after two months of training. He was a small youth, hardly big enough to wear the greatcoat or carry a rifle, but he soon won the admiration and praise of his superiors. In the deadly Champagne offensive fought through September and October of 1915 Edmond's battalion attacked the enemy in the Bois Sabot and during one charge he was stunned and hurled into a crater by the explosion of a large-caliber shell. When he regained consciousness he saw a regiment of Zouaves continuing on in support of the Legion, and asking no questions he joined them and fought manfully. Three days later he rejoined his comrades who had mourned him for dead.

On another occasion he took part in a bayonet charge that carried his company into a storm of machine-gun fire until he was the only man left in the advance, all the others having been killed, wounded, or driven to shelter in nearby shell holes or abandoned trenches. Genêt found another member of his regiment, and together they decided to work their way back. Edmond made it because he kept cool; his companion lost his head in the excitement and was cut down and killed.

Edmond put in fifteen long months of this kind of activity, but never forgot Norman Prince and the talk of a possible American air squadron. Eventually, one of his many applications for a transfer was acted on and he arrived at Aviation Headquarters on May 24, 1916. He was happy and cheerful as a lark, although by now he knew that war flying was more dangerous than general infantry action. "Still," he pointed out in a letter home, "if I am killed while flying you will know about it almost immediately. If one is killed in the trenches there are a dozen chances no one will ever know what actually happened."

Along with Genêt went another American, Herman Lincoln Chatkoff who had served in the Foreign Legion and been in the thick of the ground fighting since late August 1914. On transferring to the French Aviation, Chatkoff, however, never managed an assignment to the Escadrille Américaine or the Lafayette Escadrille before it was taken over by the American forces. After gaining his brevet, Chatkoff requested permission to go back to the trenches where he spent two more months with his old comrades until an opening was found for him with the French C.11 Squadron, flying Caudrons. It was while serving aboard a Caudron that he was injured during a flying accident near Soissons that incapacitated him for the rest of the war.

During his flight training Edmond Genêt began to worry about his desertion from the U. S. Navy, and from his letters home it was evident that his concern at times bordered on hysteria. He suffered an accident aboard a Blériot that put him in the hospital for several days where he continued his fretting. He was certain this minor accident would cause him to be sent back to the Foreign Legion, but on the contrary, his training period continued to go smoothly and he soon passed out on Nieuports, being posted to the Lafayette Escadrille on January 19, 1917.

He was a popular member of that squadron, being musical, artistic, and most enthusiastic. He decorated the walls of their bar-lounge with murals depicting air battles between French and German planes. He also painted replicas of their famous Indian-head insignia in prominent places on the walls.

Shortly after he began his active-service flying, young Genêt was wounded in the face by a German bullet. Then while the Escadrille was working out of Ravenel, he put in some extra training time taking courses on engines and machine guns. This was the period when the Germans were staging their "planned withdrawal" to their new Hindenburg line, and the French squadrons were preparing to keep the enemy off balance as much as possible.

On St. Patrick's Day, with a threatening storm moving in, Edmond Genêt, Jim McConnell, and Ted Parsons were alerted for a 10:00 A.M. patrol. All but Ted Parsons' engine started with little trouble, and shortly after take-off, Ted had to return to his field to have an obstinate Le Rhône attended to. Genêt and McConnell went on alone.

They crossed the enemy line northeast of Ham and then headed for Saint-Quentin. Over Douchy they were intercepted by two Albatros two-seaters, and though both Americans were short on experience each took on an Albatros. A typical wild melee followed, and once more there were vague reports of "explosive" bullets, but they probably were light-cased tracers that broke up on impact with anything. At any rate, one of these bounced off Genêt's main spar and splinters spattered his face and cut a gouge in his cheek. The wound put him out of the play for a few seconds, and he started to head for home, not certain how badly he was hurt. As a result, he lost track of McConnell, and though he circled about over Ham for more than a quarter of an hour, Jim never turned up.

Some time later a French cavalryman out on patrol near Petit-Detroit that had recently been abandoned by the Germans, came upon a crashed Nieuport. Jim McConnell's completely stripped body was beside it. A farm woman came out of a cottage nearby and explained that she had seen the air fight and that the French machine had been engaging a German airplane when a second enemy plane dived on him from behind. Whether this was the one that had previously engaged Genêt could not be confirmed, but it was discovered that Jim had received several bullets in his body, any one of which could have killed him.

Edmond Genêt was awarded the Croix de Guerre, and cited in the Order of the Army. James McConnell was the last American, wearing a French uniform, who was killed while fighting the enemy before the United States entered World War I. Edmond Genêt was to be the first American to fall after America declared war on Germany.

He was killed on April 16, 1917—not by an enemy airman, but by a direct hit by an antiaircraft shell, another of those million-to-one shots that seemed to happen so frequently. In this case it was young Edmond Genêt who had made so many sacrifices.

On this memorable morning he and Raoul Lufbery were sent on a patrol between Saint-Quentin and La Fère. By this time the Lafayette Escadrille had moved up to Ham to keep pace with the German retreat. Luf led the flight, of course, and he reported later that once they were in the vicinity of Mouy, German antiaircraft batteries started to shell them. They had been in the air for about thirty minutes when Lufbery noted three shells burst uncomfortably close to Genêt's Nieuport, and though it was accurate shooting, Luf who had been through this a hundred times, took little notice of the bracket. However, when he again glanced over at his companion, he saw that Edmond had turned and was apparently heading for the French lines. He followed to make certain Genêt was flying in the right direction for Ham, and once convinced that he was safe though his aircraft may have received some damage, Luf turned back to their original patrol area.

Then Luf suddenly remembered that Edmond had not been feeling well, but when his name came up for the patrol he had refused to be excused—another example of volunteer discipline. He had been out earlier that morning, but on his return had gone back to bed. Recalling this, Lufbery decided to go back to see that Genêt had crossed the line safely, but because of a sudden overcast of low cloud he could not find him.

Raoul learned later that Edmond might have fainted in the air, or died from a wound inflicted by one of the shell bursts, as he tried to get back to his field. A group of soldiers said that they had seen this particular Nieuport go into a corkscrew spin at about five thousand feet, and as it continued down a wing ripped away and the aircraft crashed just a few hundred yards from where Jim McConnell had piled up. The Nieuport was a complete write-off, having gone in with its engine full on, which indicated that Genêt had either fainted or died some time before the crash.

He was buried at Ham during a blinding snowstorm, and at the funeral service it was announced that the plane Edmond had attacked on the day McConnell was killed, had been shot up so badly it had had to land in French territory. The captured crew had made statements that indicated that Genêt had fought well and that McConnell's death in no way reflected on him. When his loss was officially announced at home, Woodrow Wilson sent his sympathy to his family, but it was not until November 1919 that Josephus Daniels, the strictly abstemious Secretary of the Navy, formally absolved Edmond Genêt of all charges of desertion; chiefly through a generous interpretation of the facts and in consideration of his service and sacrifice.

BERT HALL

Bert Hall, who claimed to have been born in Higginsville, Missouri, "or somewhere in Kentucky," is the outstanding "character" of the Lafayette Escadrille. Depending on your point of view, he was either a comic or a complete phony. But whatever, his history certainly enlivens the records of America's contribution to World War I.

This Hall—not to be confused with James Norman Hall—must have been a clown, a mystery man, and a lovable rogue. On his arrival in the ranks of the French Foreign Legion in August 1914, he stoutly declared he had been fighting in the Turkish-Bulgarian War (1912). Depending on his audience, or the potency of the grape, he had flown as a military airman for one side or the other. He may have put in some time with Lord Kitchener's army, either prior to or following the retreat from Mons. And then we find records of his service with the French Legion in the early days of the very same war. No question, Bert Hall was a character.

According to some records, Bert had never seen either Turkey or Bulgaria. He had first arrived in France in 1912, acting as a chauffeur for a Fort Worth, Texas, cotton broker. His antics in Paris soon ended that sinecure, and he next drove a taxi, but it is strange that he never claimed to have headed the famous taxi-transport service that took French soldiers out to stop the Germans along the Marne.

He must have been with the Foreign Legion in some capacity, for we find him following in the footsteps of Bill Thaw and the others. He was accepted by the French Aviation on December 28, 1914, and despite his long list of "glorious air battles" for the Turks—or the Bulgarians—he showed no evidence of having encountered an airplane before. Some of his early adventures aboard the Penguins, and later on Blériots, were epics that would fill a good-sized book. But he managed somehow to stumble and flounder through the Pau, Avord, and Buc training routine and eventually won his wings on August 19, 1915, and was assigned to MS.38, a Morane-Saulnier squadron where he carried out routine observation missions through the late summer and autumn of that year. From all accounts he earned his pay and rations, and was accepted for the new Escadrille Américaine in April 1916.

Once in association with his own countrymen, Bert again came under the attention of the French intelligence service which was certain he was an enemy agent. Previously, while training at Avord he had been under continual surveillance by the French Secret Service when two Army intelligence men, posing as student pilots, occupied beds on either side of Bert's, and he was seldom out of their sight. But he apparently never proved to be anything but a happy-go-lucky, garrulous, ne'er-do-well adventurer. He had few manners, no cultural qualities, and was overly shrewd with cards, dice, and the art of signing mess chits with other pilots' names.

His service with the Escadrille Américaine lasted from April 28 to November 1, 1916, in which time he was credited with three enemy aircraft and had been awarded the Médaille Militaire and the Croix de Guerre with three Palms, although his pals argued that none of his reports could be believed and that he rushed back to report a victory every time he saw something burning on the ground. His worst act was when Kiffin Rockwell was killed, and he hurried to Paris to try to peddle a firsthand story of Kiffin's death to Paris newspapers.

His behavior grew steadily worse. He cheated at cards, did some queer things with checks, would promise to chip in to make squadron purchases and would renege when the time came to pay up. There were reports that he was a bigamist, that he was in some way involved with Mata Hari, the strip-tease spy. Finally everyone was certain that he was faking many of his combat reports. In a body, the

volunteers requested that he leave the squadron and take his pecul-
iar charms elsewhere.

On November 18, Hall was transferred to N.103, a French Nieuport squadron, where he flew well for about a month and picked up
another citation for his energy and courage. By this time he had
reached the rank of adjutant, but a month was all the French pilots
could stand, and for some unknown reason we next find Bert Hall
acompanying a French aviation mission to Romania, although some
reports state that Adjutant Hall went to Russia. Shortly after this
assignment, Hall requested and received permission to return to the
United States, ostensibly to join the United States Aviation Service.
He did nothing of the kind, but is said to have appeared on the
vaudeville circuit giving lectures on the art of air fighting, while
wearing all his medals *and* the Legion of Honor that had not been
awarded to him. To this day, Bert Hall is listed as a deserter from
the French Aviation.

But Bert Hall was just getting into the swing of things. In a short
time he mystified his critics by writing two books, *One Man's War*
and *En l'Air,* that attempted to prove how one man can be in several
places at the same time.

With the coming of peace, Bert, like so many soldiers of fortune,
found it difficult to get back into action, but by scanning the newspapers carefully he decided that Nationalist China might be a fertile
field. Once there, he promoted a contract to train Chinese airmen.
To teach anyone to fly, one had to have an airplane or two, so
Bert next induced the Chinese authorities to entrust him with $34,-
000 for a shipment of American aircraft that oddly enough never
arrived on any Chinese field. This brought him under the eye of the
United States Consular officials, and for the first time Bert was unable to wriggle out from under, and was sent to the Federal Peni-
tentiary at McNeil Island, Washington, where he spent the next two
and a half years. On December 6, 1948, Bert Hall was killed in an
automobile accident while driving between Chicago and Castalia,
Ohio.

After his death his tangled domestic life was revealed. A Hollywood syndicate with which the author was associated, planned to
film a documentary of the Lafayette Escadrille, and the producers
first had to obtain full clearance from all concerned. In delving
into Hall's background—and one or two others who served in that
organization—it was obvious that it would be impossible to "clear"
most of Bert's adventures, since, in one form or another, they had

been parceled out to survivors of his several marital affairs to compensate for his alimony commitments. This is one of the chief reasons no motion picture company has been able to present a complete history of the Lafayette Escadrille; too many survivors with delusions of importance concerning their rights in the presentation of its history.

Few Boswells of the Lafayette Escadrille have given Bert Hall much space in their chronicles, which is unfortunate, for he must have been a most provocative character.

JAMES NORMAN HALL

Here is another American volunteer whose wide career and adventures would make a major film. Strangely enough, the tycoons of the silver screen have instead seen fit to film several books on the adventures of other men that came from his pen. This hero, James Norman Hall, was born in Colfax, Iowa, in 1887. He graduated from Grinnell College in 1910 and later did postgraduate work at the University of Chicago. After a vacation trip to Scotland he took up social service work in Massachusetts. He made another trip to the British Isles in 1914, and shortly after his arrival World War I broke out, which seemed to promise an interesting experience, so he joined the 9th Battalion of the Royal Fusiliers on August 18, 1914. After a stretch of infantry training in England he was sent to the front in May 1915. From all accounts Jimmy served with some distinction in the early days of trench warfare and was promoted to lance corporal and placed in charge of a machine-gun team. He served through the Battle of Loos, and on one occasion every man in his gun team was killed save himself. However, he was relieved of duty and discharged in December of that same year.

Hall's release apparently came about when he requested an emergency leave to visit his father who was seriously ill in Iowa. This was a military consideration totally unknown in the British Army of those days, particularly where noncommissioned soldiers were concerned. However, influential friends in the United States added their intercession and Hall was given a definite discharge.

After visiting his father in Iowa, Jimmy returned to Boston where he spent the early part of 1916 lecturing on the war and writing a book detailing his experiences with the Royal Fusiliers. This work, titled *Kitchener's Mob,* enjoyed some financial success, and the editors of *The Atlantic Monthly* suggested that he return to Britain and write a series of articles about the war. This appealed to Jimmy Hall, and he made plans to return to England and rejoin his old regiment, but before he left the same editors brought up the subject of the Lafayette Escadrille, and added that it might be a good idea if he wrote two articles about the American fliers before he again tied himself up with the British regiment.

So Hall returned to Europe with this general plan in mind and first made a contact with Paul Ayres Rockwell, brother of the ill-starred Kiffin. Paul was working in Paris and acting as historian of the Lafayette. Paul introduced Hall to Kiffin, Bill Thaw, Raoul Lufbery, and Jim McConnell. This association in turn brought in Dr. Edmund L. Gros, one of the heads of the American Field Service, who was interested in the idea of publicity for the American fliers and offered to provide every assistance possible.

A short time later it occurred to Dr. Gros that Hall might do better by joining the Escadrille, thereby seeing the whole story first-hand. This proved to be a logical inspiration, for a few years later James Norman Hall, in collaboration with Charles Nordhoff, completed the famous two-volume history of the Lafayette Flying Corps.

Although the idea interested him, Jimmy felt he was a little too old to learn to fly. He was pushing twenty-nine, and wartime fliers were supposed to be harum-scarum schoolboys—at least those he had encountered in the British service seemed to be scarcely out of their teens.

But Dr. Gros brushed aside Jimmy's protests, gave him a medical examination and assured him he would have no trouble at all. With the ways greased in this manner Hall, the correspondent, found himself taking flying lessons at Buc by October 11, 1916. By the following April he had progressed through Avord, and the G.D.E. (Groupe des Divisions d'Entrainment) to take his brevet on a Caudron. He was posted to the Lafayette Escadrille and arrived at Ham on June 16, 1917, but after serving with his countrymen for a few weeks, he was, for some reason, transferred to the French Spad 112 Squadron with which he served until October 3 of that same year.

By this time it occurred to Jimmy that he was supposed to write a couple of articles about the Lafayette Escadrille, but while he was with Spad 112 he had little or no contact with the Americans.

Dr. Gros was consulted and in October 1917 he was transferred back to Spad 124. (The Lafayette by this time had been equipped with Spads.)

Hall fitted the picture beautifully; all his patrols were exciting and colorful, and his articles written for *The Atlantic Montly* reflected his experiences. Later they formed the basis of his book, *High Adventure,* published by Houghton Mifflin in 1918.

Paul Ayres Rockwell, official historian of the Lafayette Escadrille, wrote: "Jim Hall was one of the finest all-around persons I have ever known, and an honorable man in every way. He had just about everything, intelligence, courage, appearance, talents of many sorts, and was most modest and withdrawing. We all liked him, but he did not give his friendship and consideration to everyone."

When Hall returned to the Lafayette he was given a war-weary, beat-up Spad that was about ready to end its days at a training school. This was routine procedure. The veterans took over the new aircraft as fast as they arrived, and the newcomers had to take what was available. But Jimmy made no complaint. He accepted the hulk and flew several patrols aboard the battle-scarred veteran.

On one occasion his name was up for a late afternoon patrol to be led by Bill Thaw. Lufbery, Ted Parsons, Ray Bridgman, and Bill Dugan were also assigned, and it was agreed that they would rendezvous at 12,000 feet over a nearby reservoir.

Thaw and the rest got away with no trouble, but Hall's coffee grinder refused to start, so he was left behind with the agreement that, if possible, he would take off and try to make the rendezvous. Within ten minutes or so Hall's bus finally opened up and off he went for glory. Thaw's formation had gone on, but Jim decided to cross over on his own and tool about until he came upon a Spad element and then join them.

All well and good, but unfortunately Hall mistook a formation of German scouts for Spads, and blithely banked over to fill out the unit. As he moved to get into position he suddenly noticed there were six of these machines—not five—but he was so pleased with finding his squadron mates he assumed some lone-eagle type had joined them.

By the time he was properly settled Jim finally saw that these Spads had very narrow lower wings, and that they also employed the Nieuport-type Vee strut. All very interesting, but on taking a closer look he realized that none of these airplanes carried the official Indian-head insignia. Nor were there any red-white-and-blue cocardes; instead these "Spads" were decorated with black-barred crosses.

They were Jerry Albatros planes, and there *were* six of them. The pilots wore black helmets and massive goggles. One or two of them glared at him in amazement, others in grim anticipation. By this time Jimmy realized he had joined the wrong mob, and he sat there wondering how he could get out of this ticklish spot. For an instant he felt the urge to bow, salute, and withdraw as a gentleman should, but these black-helmeted ruffians had other ideas, and Jim had to depart unceremoniously.

He nosed down like a dart, followed by streams of Spandau fire. Knowing this tactic could be very unprofitable, he eased out, and went into a wild display of aerobatics, but every turn or twist somehow brought him into a new cone of enemy fire. Bursts of lead slapped through his wings and peppered the fuselage. One slug creased his forehead, another cut a gash across his groin, and a third pierced his shoulder, paralyzing his whole left side. These three bullets knocked him unconscious, and he fell against his belt, carrying his stick well forward. This put him into terrific speed, and his enemies could not keep pace.

With the engine screaming and all flying wires strained to the limit, Hall's Spad continued its plunge, but he finally came out of his stupor. Instinct caused him to yank the throttle back. He also drew back on the stick, and saw he was still heading for the French lines. With that effort he again passed out.

By some freak stroke of luck the wings had stayed on, and by now the Spad had wabbled into a sloppy glide. It then swung into a number of flat turns; at times it was heading toward the enemy lines, only to turn back for the French area. Hall was still unconscious when his ancient machine finally plopped down with its wheels deep in a communication trench and its wings scraping along sandbag buttresses.

When Jimmy came to he found himself on a stretcher that was being hauled away from the trench area. At the advance dressing station it was discovered that the crash had not inflicted a scratch and that the three Spandau wounds were not too serious. He was soon back flying Spad patrols again.

✳

While he was with Spad 124 Jimmy had a number of wild adventures involving kite balloons and German two-seater aircraft; though none of them brought outstanding rewards they added materially to his stature as a front-line airman. When the Lafayette Escadrille personnel was taken over by the U. S. Aviation Service, Sergeant Hall was assigned to the 94th (Hat-in-the-Ring) Aero squadron. It was while serving with this unit that Hall's military career came to an end.

On May 7, 1918, while flying a Nieuport scout near Pont-à-Mousson, he dived on an Albatros single-seater and was startled to see the upper fabric covering of his right-hand wing tear free. This was typical of the Nieuport under diving stress, but even worse Hall next took a heavy burst of machine-gun fire that finished his Le Rhône engine. He went down out of control near Pagny-sur-Moselle in the enemy lines and was taken prisoner. Some reports have it that Hall's engine was knocked out by an incendiary shell.

James Norman Hall was, of course, to become a world-renowned author who eventually wrote the famous trilogy, *Mutiny on the Bounty*, *Men Against the Sea*, and *Pitcairn's Island*, with Charles B. Nordhoff, another American who had served with the French Aviation.

LLOYD ANDREWS HAMILTON

Lloyd Hamilton will be something of an unknown to most air-war enthusiasts, but he is credited with eight enemy aircraft, and was awarded the Distinguished Service Cross. He was killed on August 24, 1918, after successfully attacking an enemy kite balloon.

Hamilton was one of the finest scholars lost to the war. Born in Troy, New York, in 1894, he graduated from Pittsfield (Massachusetts) High School with high honors. From there he went to the Jacob Tome Institute in Maryland where he won the school's chief scholarship prize. He graduated from Syracuse University in 1916 where he had been on the football and track teams. He then entered Harvard University's School of Business Administration, but when the United States declared war on Germany, Lloyd went to the Officers' Training Camp at Plattsburgh, New York. He requested aviation training and was sent to the Massachusetts Institute of

Technology for his ground course. By mid-September 1917 he was in Britain taking the Royal Flying Corps courses at Oxford, Tadcaster, Turnberry, and Ayr. He went out to Number 3 Squadron, RAF, flying Camels, where he scored his first victory, a German two-seater.

In June 1918 Hamilton was transferred to the United States Air Service and made a flight commander of Number 17 Aero Squadron. He proved to be a redoubtable performer over the next few weeks, and had many engagements on the difficult front ranging from Amiens to the Channel. His Distinguished Service Cross, awarded by General Pershing, came as the result of an action carried out on August 13, 1918. While leading a bombing attack against a German airfield some thirty miles behind the enemy lines, he went to a very low level, and with machine-gun fire and Cooper bombs destroyed at least five German planes. On turning away, he spotted a château in which the enemy pilots would probably be quartered. He made several dives on it, pouring machine-gun fire into the windows and doors. An enemy report, made available after the Armistice, stated that twenty-six Germans were killed in this particular attack.

Hamilton came to his end eleven days later, after destroying an enemy balloon. While making his getaway, machine-gun fire from the ground inflicted severe wounds and he crashed about three miles inside the German lines. A few months later his grave was found, and Lloyd Hamilton was reburied with full military honors at Bomy, France.

HAROLD EVANS HARTNEY

Harold E. Hartney was born in Packenham, Ontario, Canada. He was trained by the British and served with an F.E.2b squadron in France, but for some reason, never fully explained, was transferred to the U. S. Air Service, commissioned a major and given command of the 27th Aero Squadron. A few weeks later he commanded the First Pursuit Group. How this was contrived is a mystery, for Hartney did not become a citizen of the United States until 1923.

After graduation from the School of Practical Science in 1906 and from the University of Toronto in 1911, Hartney took up law, and while working for his brother became an officer in the Saskatoon

Fusiliers. In October 1914 this regiment was mobilized as part of the 28th Canadian Infantry which was shipped to England in May 1915. While completing his training there, Harold put in for a transfer to the Royal Flying Corps. He received his training at Norwich and was then posted to Number 20 Squadron of the R.F.C.

Flying with F.E.2b squadrons provided plenty of thrills and excitement. The old pusher-fighters were called on to do everything from bombing to escort fighting. Hartney learned a lot with Number 20 Squadron, particularly on the bombing and reconnaissance raids of that period. On February 14, 1917, his aircraft was badly shot up while he was carrying out an important photographic mission. Hartney managed to crash-land in British territory although he had suffered painful injuries and had to be hospitalized in England. What happened to his aerial gunner has not been recorded.

Hartney was available for duty by September 1917, and then, for some reason, was transferred to the U. S. Air Service and took command of the 27th Aero Squadron that was being trained in Canada. The 27th later went to Hicks Field near Fort Worth, Texas. They then sailed from Hoboken for England and finally went to Issoudun, France. On June 1, 1918, the 27th, 147th, 94th, and 95th squadrons became the First Pursuit Group, and were later joined by the 185th Squadron which had been trained as a Night Pursuit squadron.

Harold Hartney, who had commanded the 27th, was next appointed Commanding Officer of the First Pursuit Group, a post he held until after the Armistice. From 1919–21 Hartney served in the office of the Chief of Air Service, Washington, D.C. His son James also signed up with the U. S. Air Force, and became a captain, flying F.100s in a tactical squadron.

WILLIS B. HAVILAND

This American airman was born in St. Paul, Minnesota, and during 1915 served with the American Field Service. He transferred to the French Aviation in January 1916, and finished his training by May 20 after which he was posted to the Lafayette Escadrille with which he served from October 22, 1916, until September 18, 1917. After his time with the Lafayette Haviland flew with Spad 102 from October 1, 1917, to January 1, 1918, ending his long active service with the French with the rank of adjutant.

In February 1918 he was promoted a lieutenant in the United States Naval Aviation, becoming the chief pilot at the U. S. Naval Air Station at Dunkirk. He also flew for about three months with the British Royal Naval Air Service, and was then made commanding officer of the U. S. Naval Air Station at Porto Corsini, Italy, serving there until the Armistice. Few Americans saw as much active service in so many theatres as Willis Haviland.

DUDLEY LAWRENCE HILL

Dudley Hill of Peekskill, New York, was one of the most engaging personalities to grace America's effort in World War I. He was so unusual, some readers believe he is nothing more than the figment of some romance-writer's imagination. Although he put in twenty-eight months of active-service flying, few World War I buffs could identify him. He not only served with the Lafayette Escadrille from June 1916 to February 1918, but he also put in time with five different squadrons of the U. S. Air Service. Unquestionably, Dudley was the most self-effacing airman on the Western Front.

How he got into any military service is a mystery, for he was really unfit. He had one very defective eye, but like the famous Mickey Mannock he tricked the medical examiners. He was practically a semi-invalid when he joined the American Field Service, but proved to be reasonably adept with a motorcar. He tried for the French Aviation, and Dr. Gros gave him a few breaks, and he started his training. French service doctors thought him more suitable for a wheelchair, and he was proposed for a medical discharge several times—his eyesight was so bad he could not read the order to go home. He just kept taking his various tests. By the time one medical discharge had caught up with him he had moved on to the next training base. The consensus of opinion was that Dudley would never become a pilot, but by that time he had passed all requirements of the aerobatic course, and before more papers could be drawn up, he had wangled his way into the Lafayette Escadrille.

Dudley Hill never missed a mission during the next nineteen

months, and time after time volunteered for dangerous assignments. He wore no regular uniform but turned out daily in an old French infantry jacket with no decorations, insignia, or rank. Whenever American correspondents arrived on the field looking for heroic deeds, Dudley would sneak away, or hide behind a three-week-old newspaper until the newsmen had cleared out. Once, he was awarded the Croix de Guerre with a Star, but he never wore the medal or the ribbon.

When the Lafayette was transferred to the U. S. Air Service it was discovered that Dudley was indeed completely blind in one eye, but he was taken, nevertheless. He served with the 103rd Pursuit Squadron for a time, and from there went on to the 139th Pursuit Squadron and then the 138th. He finished his war as CO of the Fifth Group, a post he held for only eleven days. The Armistice closed out his long, but modest, career. We can find no official, or unofficial, report stating whether Dudley Hill ever destroyed an enemy aircraft. If we could, he probably would deny any such accomplishment.

JOHN W. F. M. HUFFER

Another American who had an important role in the development of our military air arm, but has been ignored in most pages of history, is John W. F. M. Huffer, listed in some records as Jean Huffer. Yet he served a lengthy period with the French and American Air services, contributing greatly to the development of the U. S. Air Service after America entered the war.

John Huffer was born in Paris of American parents, and prior to 1919 had not been to the United States or, in fact, any English-speaking country, but he had traveled extensively, and spoke English like a Bostonian. It was he who first suggested the Hat-in-the-Ring insignia for the 94th Pursuit Squadron.

Huffer joined the French Foreign Legion in September 1915 and some four months later transferred to the French Aviation. He completed his pilot training April 1, 1916, and was assigned to Escadrille N.95, a Nieuport squadron. During the next two years he served with three other French squadrons and for a time flew in Italy, but he never checked in with the Lafayette Escadrille. John Huffer ended his service with the French as a sous-lieutenant, and before transferring to the American forces was awarded the Médaille Militaire and the Croix de Guerre with three Palms and two Stars. He was credited with seven victories, four of them scored while serving with the French.

On November 7, 1917, Huffer was commissioned a major in the Aviation Section of the Signal Corps, and on March 17 of the next year was named commanding officer of the newly formed 94th Aero Squadron. He held this post for about two months, leading many of the patrols, and was then transferred to the 1st Air Depot at Colombey-les-Belles as assistant operations officer. On July 25 he returned to the front to take command of the 93rd Aero Squadron, a post he held until some time after the Armistice when he finally set foot on the soil of his native land to be formally discharged from the service.

FRANK O'DRISCOLL HUNTER

This well-known American is credited with downing nine enemy aircraft, and is one of the few wartime airmen who stayed in and made a career of the military service. Born in Savannah, Georgia, in 1894, he graduated from Hotchkiss School in Connecticut in 1913. In 1917 he volunteered for flight training with the Signal Corps, and after some instruction in the United States, he finished his courses in France. On May 22, 1918, he was assigned to the 94th Aero Squadron, and four days later was transferred to the 103rd Aero Squadron with which he served as a pilot and flight commander until the end of the war.

After the war Frank, by then Captain Hunter, attended the Air Service Observation School, and later the Air Service Tactical School. In 1936 he was promoted to major, and had become a full colonel by World War II. In 1943 he was promoted to the rank of major general, and retired with that rank in 1946.

DAVID SINTON INGALLS

The only U. S. Navy ace of World War I was David S. Ingalls, a native of Cleveland, Ohio, where he was born on January 28, 1899. He attended public schools in his area, and entered Yale University in 1916. While there he first took up flying by joining the university's flying club in which wealthy young students bought their own aircraft and paid for their tuition. So well was this organization run that before the United States entered the war, moves were made to incorporate the club into a military organization. Eventually, through the Appropriations Act of 1916 the Yale Unit, as it was listed, became part of the U. S. Naval Reserve, and finally the whole membership was ordered to Pensacola for further training.

Though only seventeen, Dave Ingalls was one of the club's best pilots, but he was not supposed to take part in any active duty with the original unit. However, he continued to fly whenever possible, and when a second unit was formed he proved that he had reached his eighteenth birthday, and he was accepted for active duty. He graduated from flight training as Naval Aviator Number 85.

After a series of training courses on both sides of the Atlantic young Ingalls was assigned to an Allied naval base at Dunkirk in the middle of the summer of 1918 with practically nothing to do. There were no U. S. Navy squadrons, and certainly no aircraft for anyone to fly, but now and then he managed to keep his hand in, flying some old bombers. To whom they belonged, or what they bombed, has not been clearly explained.

But eventually his luck changed, and Ingalls was assigned to Number 213 Squadron of the RAF that previously had been Number 13 Squadron of the Royal Naval Air Service. He was given a Sopwith Camel and put in a week or more flying on regular patrols with the British, but the Germans were having no part of these lads who flew Camels. Becoming bored with the routine proceedings, Dave requested permission to stage a lone-eagle patrol, and to teach this young man a lesson the British CO gave his consent. Dave took off and flew straight into a small swarm of Fokker D-VIIs that had come down out of a cloud to welcome him.

Realizing that caution was the better part of valor, the young American dived and headed for home, but three Fokkers had other ideas. For what seemed hours, they took turns shooting snap bursts at this singleton target. One by one they went in and poured Spandau lead into the Camel. All Dave could do was to keep in a tight right-hand turn—and pray.

Eventually, when the enemy planes must have run out of ammunition, the game came to its close and the Fokkers went home. The young pilot brought what was left of the Sopwith Camel down to a landing, and the best that could be said for him was that either the Camel was the greatest defensive ship in the war, or Dave was the most evasive pilot on the front.

A few days later David Ingalls gained a sweet revenge when he found a German observation plane near the line, and, ignoring the wild spraying by the observer, calmly put his twin Vickers on the two-seater and shot it down in flames.

A short time later he encountered another two-seater, a Rumpler, in the vicinity of La Panne, and without taking much notice of the sky in general, concentrated on putting his Aldis sight on the rear cockpit. Later Ingalls admitted he had become very careless. He should have checked the gunner first, for this one wasted no ammunition. When he fired, he knew where he was putting his shots. The Camel was sprayed time and time again. Ingalls tried other tactics and approaches from different angles.

He nosed down with the idea of coming up from below in a sharp zoom, but in his anxiety overshot. The German pilot simply put on a jab of rudder and the gunner had a beautiful target. Tracers and armor-piercing rounds sizzled all around Dave's head, and ripped great holes in the fabric of his plane. The two aircraft passed each other, and Dave threw the two Germans a friendly wave, and then set about making another attack.

He made a feint to attack from the left, and the German pilot swung around to meet it. Dave then pulled a half roll and went in with both guns blazing. Two full bursts did the trick, and the enemy plane went down in flames.

Checking his position Ingalls saw that he had been carried far across the enemy lines by the prevailing wind, so he turned his bullet-scarred Camel and headed for home, whereupon enemy antiaircraft gunners put up a display. The young American decided it would be much safer at a lower altitude, so he nosed down to risk machine-gun fire rather then the explosive three-inch stuff the big guns were hurling at him, and headed west at full throttle.

But machine guns can be as deadly as high-angle artillery. There was an ominous *plop!* and the rotary engine coughed and finally stuttered to a complete halt. Gasoline squirted from a punctured tank and flooded Ingalls' cockpit. The guns below continued to chatter, and Dave was sweating out a very difficult situation. He reasoned that the end of his war was at hand, and decided to make as decent a landing as possible, but he still had sense enough to switch on the gravity-feed tank, hoping for a miracle.

As the enemy landscape rose to welcome him, the gravity fuel began to trickle through. The Le Rhône engine spluttered and popped several times, and then suddenly raised his hopes by bellowing into full power. Once again, David Ingalls returned with a Camel that had been shot to junk. Only a few flying wires remained intact, and there wasn't much taut fabric left to bear the weight of the fuselage, but Dave got back, and for the second time reported a victory over a Hun two-seater.

✳

The RAF boys were delighted with this young fire-eater and kept him on, particularly since Number 213 had been assigned to give fighter escort to a formation of DH.9s that were to bomb a German aerodrome located at Varsensere. The enemy was concentrating fighters there to annoy the British and their bombers which were staging night attacks on vital strong points. The U. S. 17th Aero Squadron, flying Camels, was also assigned to this mission. All the Sopwiths were armed with 20-pound Cooper bombs.

On the morning of the attack the weather was generally dud, but not too much so. The bombers and their escort flew above a low cloud layer and roared on through a clear sky without being annoyed by antiaircraft fire, but the minute they went down through the clouds, antiaircraft shells, machine-gun fire and flaming onions came up to greet them.

The big ships flattened out and roared at their targets. In no time the field was a blazing inferno. Not to be deprived of the fun, Dave Ingalls nosed down sharply and headed for a lineup of aircraft. Then, just as he was about to reach for his bomb-release toggle, he looked up and gasped. Not ten feet above him were the wheels, undercarriages, bomb racks and muddy bellies of the DH.9s. He had but a fraction of a second to kick his rudder and whip his ailerons into action, hoping to clear the deluge. Even so, he saw two blue-banded 100-pounders slip past his wing tip as he turned away.

1. Frank L. Baylies of New Bedford, Massachusetts, destroyed twelve enemy planes while flying with the French. Son of a New England doctor, he was one of the most modest heroes although he put on an astounding career. He was shot down while engaging four Fokker Triplanes. *(U.S. War Department General Staff)*

2. Victor over four enemy aircraft, Charles J. Biddle contributed much more to the cause by becoming an expert on tactics, maneuvers and aircraft maintenance. He was able to lecture on aerial combat and on his return to the United States he wrote a memorable book titled *Way of the Eagle. (U.S. War Department General Staff)*

3. Although he is seen here wearing the Distinguished Service Cross, the Legion of Honor and the Croix de Guerre, Thomas G. Cassady is almost unknown in American war-air history. He is credited with nine victories, serving on the front from July 1917 to Armistice Day. *(U.S. Air Force)*

4. The home-grown products. Douglas Campbell, left, and Alan Winslow of the 94th Aero Squadron each downed an enemy plane on April 14, 1918, the first victories to come to an all-American squadron on the Western Front. A short time later Winslow was shot down, taken prisoner and lost an arm as the result of his injuries. *(U.S. Signal Corps)*

5. Reed McKinley Chambers, victor in seven enemy combats, turned out to be one of the finest flight leaders in the American service. With him is Captain E. R. Cook, who is credited with five enemy planes. *(U.S. Air Force)*

6. An architectural student, Victor Chapman was the first American to die as a member of the Lafayette Escadrille. He had been a machine gunner in the Foreign Legion and after three months of trench warfare was wounded. After convalescence he volunteered for the French aviation service. *(U.S. Air Force)*

. Elliot C. Cowdin, who contributed much to the organization of the Lafayette scadrille, was a flamboyant, playboy character who added considerable color to the American volunteer group. He downed only one enemy plane but was awarded the Médaile Militaire and the Croix de Guerre. *U.S. War Department General Staff)*

8. The Peck's Bad Boy of the Lafayette Escadrille. Bert Hall of Higginsville, Missouri, was the outstanding "character" of N. 124 Squadron. He claimed to have flown in the Turkish-Bulgarian War but could never prove it. He may have served in the Foreign Legion and in Kitchener's Army. A comic or a complete phony—depending on your point of view or sense of humor. *(Paul A. Rockwell photo)*

9. A million-to-one shot finished the career of Captain Hamilton Coolidge of Brookline, Massachusetts. With the Armistice only two weeks away He was downed by a direct hit by an anti-aircraft shell. Prior to that he had downed eight enemy aircraft. *(U.S. Air Force)*

10. An American volunteer whose career would have made a motion picture epic. James Norman Hall fought with the British infantry, the Lafayette Escadrille and the U.S. Aviation Service. Years later he became an internationally known author of South Pacific adventure and romance. *(U.S. Air Force)*

11. A native of St. Paul, Minnesota, Willis B. Haviland had an extensive war career. He began driving ambulances with the American Field Service, transferred to the Lafayette Escadrille, put in a few months with the British Royal Naval Air Service and completed his war with the U.S. Naval Air Service in Porto Corsini, Italy. *(Paul A. Rockwell photo)*

2. Major John A. Huffer who commanded the 93rd Aero Squadron was born in France of American parents, and he did not see his native land until some time after the Armistice. He served in both the French and American aviation services. He was credited with seven victories. *(U.S. Signal Corps)*

13. A former Canadian who flew two-seaters with the British, Major Harold Hartney eventually became commanding officer of America's First Pursuit Group. *(U.S. War Department General Staff)*

14. David S. Ingalls, the only Naval ace of World War I, put in considerable time with the British, flying everything from ancient bombers to Sopwith Camels. After the war he became Assistant Secretary of the Navy during President Herbert Hoover's administration. *(U.S. Air Force)*

15. One of the most picturesque characters in the Lafayette Escadrille, Edmond C. C. Genêt of Ossining, New York, was also ill-fated. He deserted from the U. S. Navy, joined the Foreign Legion, served fifteen months in the trenches and then transferred to the Lafayette Escadrille. He was the first American to die in France after America declared war on Germany. *(U.S. Air Force)*

16. Trained by the Royal Flying Corps and sent on to the 148th Aero Squadron, Field E. Kindley, an Arkansas boy, shot down twelve enemy aircraft. Killed in a flying accident after the war, he was honored by having the U.S. Air Force base in Bermuda named after him. *(U.S. Signal Corps)*

17. This airman from Girard, Illinois, Howard C. Knotts, destroyed more enemy aircraft while a prisoner-of-war than he did as an active service pilot. While being transferred from one prison camp to another he managed to set fire to a German freight car that was loaded with seven Fokker aircraft. His story reads like a movie plot. *(The Smithsonian Institution: National Air Museum)*

18. A son of Judge Kenesaw Mountai[n] Landis, Reed G. Landis served th[e] greater part of his war career with N[o] 40 Squadron R.F.C. and received h[is] fighter training under the famed Maj[or] Edward C. Mannock and Captain M[c] Elroy. Later he commanded the U.[S.] 25th Aero Squadron. He is credited wi[th] ten enemy aircraft. *(U.S. Air Force)*

19. Frederick Libby, a native of Colorado, was the first American to become an ace in World War I. A member of No. 23 Squadron R.F.C. he first downed ten Germans as an NCO aerial gunner. Then as a commissioned pilot he downed fourteen more, but to this day he is credited only with the fourteen he destroyed as an officer pilot. This is how it was. *(Arch Whitehouse photo)*

He cleared off long enough to get his breath and then nosed about until he spotted a repair shed. He could see the big bombers re-forming and turning back, but he still had four Coopers in his rack. He zigzagged about until he was sure of his target. The whole area was festooned with smoke and flame, but he managed to release his Coopers and saw them spatter among some sheds and stacked supplies. He then nosed up for some altitude but by the time his altimeter needle was showing one thousand feet his engine quit cold. He rammed the stick forward to avoid a stall and a spin, and then found he was sliding back toward the burning aerodrome.

He juggled with the switch, and manipulated the two levers of the rotary's primitive carburetor. Gradually, three cylinders picked up, others backfired. Then some semblance of a proper sequence opened and the Le Rhône gradually burst into full power. A few ground guns sprayed him with machine-gun fire, and Dave had to screech for cloud cover. He worked his way into the clear above and was joined by another Camel pilot, who, it turned out, had come back to see what had happened to the young American.

So together they headed out over the North Sea, hoping to turn inland later and land at Dunkirk, but just when they were enjoying a sense of relief a German two-seater came out of the murk over Ostend. They knew they should have been satisfied with their day's work, but the two Camel pilots thought they would have no trouble with this "sitting duck."

Ingalls put in the first burst just as the two-seater darted back into the murk, and he followed it with both of his guns sparkling and spitting at the faint outline of the enemy plane. Then the mist suddenly thinned and both planes came out into a clear area. Dave exchanged shots with the observer, and then saw the two-seater fall off on one wing and disappear into another bank of clouds, drag-ging an oily streamer.

All the Allied aircraft used in the attack miraculously returned to their fields. A large gasoline and oil dump was destroyed, six Fokker biplanes were set on fire on the ground and two totally destroyed by direct hits by bombs. One large Gotha hangar was set afire and another seriously damaged, and many living quarters were set afire by phosphorous bombs, and burned for hours.

Following this raid David Ingalls was promoted to flight commander, and to celebrate he took a six-ship flight across the lines to look for enemy balloons. Three were found, two on the ground in their beds and one aloft. Ingalls took the one in the air and set it on fire while his flight mates attacked the two on the ground.

Over the next few weeks Number 213 was busy escorting DH. bombers on raids aimed at Zeebrugge, Ostend, and Bruges, and, generally speaking, the Camels had little trouble, but on one occasion when Ingalls had his flight at 15,000 feet he saw four Fokker D-VIIs heading in, looking for trouble. He watched them carefully, and then noted that they seemingly were holding off, apparently waiting for stragglers. Ingalls wanted to hare off and engage, but his orders were to stay with the bombers.

This cat-and-mouse act went on for several minutes, but when the Fokker leader made a move to edge in closer, that was all Dave needed. He nosed over sharply, and saw that the German leader intended to dare him to keep coming on, but as the two machines headed for each other, it was the Fokker pilot who gave ground, taking his D-VIIs with him. Back they went to their original position well away from the Sop Camels.

Ingalls obeyed the instructions, and watched the bombers drop their eggs. He also saw one of the DH.s hit by antiaircraft fire and realized that no matter how bad the hit, the bomber would have to relinquish its position in the formation, and that would be all the Fokkers were waiting for.

Two of the Fokkers nosed down toward the cripple, but the aerial gunner in the DH kept his head and held the Fokkers at bay with a bracket of twin-Lewis guns. Ingalls then dropped away to give a hand, leaving his flight to carry on without him. He moved in close and caught one Fokker before the pilot knew he was in the area. The second D-VII was so busy trying to get past the aerial gunner's fire, Ingalls was smack on its tail before he was spotted. But he became anxious with this second target and missed. The Fokker went into a half roll, nosed over and wound into a tight spin. There was no chance to catch up, and Dave cussed his luck and overanxious maneuvering.

He stayed with the faltering DH.9 although three more Fokkers came down to pick it off. This was difficult as it entailed a savage rearguard action until the British bomber was safely across the line, but though he did not down any of the new attackers, Dave did have the satisfaction of seeing the bomber wallow into its own area.

✳

Ingalls' flight was continually in action, and on another occasion knocked down three of the much-vaunted D-VII Fokkers. After that the Camels of Number 213 Squadron were assigned to low-level attacks in support of the Belgian offensive that began on September 28, 1918. This historic push was staged between Ypres and the North Sea and resulted in an advance of more than four miles along that front.

During this advance Ingalls' flight spent hour after hour, attacking with 20-pound Cooper bombs and then harrying the enemy along the roads with machine-gun fire. During one of these forays an interesting incident was logged. Ingalls had been harassing road transport when he came upon a German wagon driver whose vehicle had become stuck in a mud hole. Dave had dropped his bombs along that road, driving marching troops to cover, and then went to his guns, firing on troops and motor transport, but when he returned he saw that the same lone driver was still doing his best to get his wagon to high ground. As the Camel roared over Dave saw that the two horses were frantic with fear, so he held his fire and circled the spot. He watched the driver carefully unhook the team from the whiffle-tree of the wagon and then guide them away from the road. When Dave looked again, the driver had his horses under some trees and was stroking them, trying to calm their fear. Dave passed over once more, but his guns were silent; he just waved to the man under the trees and roared back to his field.

On October 1, 1918, Ingalls was sent back to England where he was to help organize a squadron of U. S. Naval pilots, but the work was unrewarding and seemingly wasteful. However, while he was in London, King George V awarded him the British Distinguished Flying Cross, and later American authorities pinned on their Distinguished Service Medal, but while all this took place, the war ground to a close and the Armistice was signed. In the six short weeks in which Dave had been at the front he had downed five enemy planes and one kite balloon.

When he returned home Dave went back to Yale to study law and play on the varsity football team. He took a post-graduate course at Harvard and then practiced law for two years. In 1925 he became a member of the Ohio Legislature, and in 1929 was appointed Assistant Secretary of the Navy for Aviation by President Herbert Hoover, and for a number of years he personally flight-tested every plane adopted by the U. S. Navy.

Now there was a man who paid his way.

CHARLES CHOUTEAU JOHNSON

A picturesque figure, known to his associates as Chouteau Johnson, has never been overly publicized in American aviation history, and though he could not be listed among the high-ranking aces, this particular Johnson contributed more than his share to the tradition of the American volunteers. He was steeped in the lore of the Lafayette, and willingly dispensed history and information whenever he could collect an audience at the old Chatham Hotel in Paris.

Chouteau Johnson was born in St. Louis, Missouri. Shortly after the outbreak of war, he joined the American Field Service as an ambulance driver early in 1915, and transferred to the French Aviation in September of that same year. He first served with V.97 (Voisins) through February and March of 1916, and was among the vanguard of Thaw, Lufbery, Chapman, Norman Prince, Kiffin Rockwell, and James McConnell that helped establish the Lafayette Escadrille. Between May 29, 1916, and October 31, 1917, he flew fairly regularly with the volunteer group, but was never an outstanding performer, except for the fact he managed to stay alive and be available.

Johnson's one and only victory came on April 26, 1917, during a pitched battle among a collection of cumulus clouds. The Lafayette flight, led by Bill Thaw, encountered a number of Albatros fighters over the old Somme battlefield. Because of the clouds, the ensuing melee became just that. Aircraft of all types were darting in and out of the clouds, appearing now, and then disappearing, only to come out in the clear, either on someone's tail, or being shot at by a machine of the opposite breed. Johnson came out of one bundle of cumulus, and found himself riding directly behind a lone Albatros. He pressed his trigger release, scoring his first and only victory of the war. Willis Haviland downed another under exactly the same circumstances.

When other Lafayette pilots were being selected for transfer to American squadrons, Chouteau decided to stay with the French, and between November 1917 and January 1918 he acted as an instructor at Tours. He was taken over later by the U. S. Air Service, commissioned a first lieutenant, and continued as an instructor. In the summer of 1918 he was promoted to captain and sent to the United States for Staff duty.

Charles Chouteau Johnson died in 1939.

FIELD E. KINDLEY

The U. S. Air Force base in Bermuda, established during World War II, was named for Field E. Kindley, a native of Gravette, Arkansas, where he attended school. Later his family moved to Coffeyville, Kansas, and there Field became a motion picture projector operator. He enlisted in the Aviation Section of the Signal Corps in May 1917 and took his ground courses at the University of Illinois. Along with a number of others, he was sent to Great Britain where he received the standard Royal Flying Corps training courses, after which he was assigned to the U. S. 148th Aero Squadron with which he served until the Armistice. Kindley was quickly named flight commander of "A" Flight, to relieve Lieutenant Bennett Oliver who was taken ill and had to be sent to a hospital. Kindley destroyed the first enemy machine credited to No. 148 and over the next four months raised his score to an even dozen, tying Elliott White Springs. The British were the first to recognize his ability and awarded him their Distinguished Flying Cross. Later his own country honored Kindley with the Distinguished Service Cross. Before the Armistice he was made a squadron commander. Early in 1920 Kindley was killed in a flying accident at Kelly Field, Texas.

HOWARD CLAYTON KNOTTS

Howard C. Knotts came out of the war with the distinction of having destroyed more enemy aircraft while a prisoner-of-war, than as an active pilot. His story reads like a movie plot.

Knotts was born at Girard, Illinois, in 1895. He graduated from Blackburn College in 1915, and during the following year took a postgraduate course at Knox College. When he signed up with the

Aviation Section of the Signal Corps, he was sent to Toronto for his initial training, and early in 1918 was assigned to the 182nd Aero Squadron that was being formed at Fort Wood, New York, and trained later at Fort Worth, Texas. He went overseas in August 1918, was assigned to the 17th Aero Squadron, and flew Sopwith Camels. Over the next two months Knotts was credited with destroying six enemy aircraft, but on October 15, he himself was shot down and taken prisoner.

While he was aboard a train that was taking him from one prison camp to another, Knotts discovered that seven Fokker aircraft, loaded in a freight car attached to the train, were being transported to a German aerodrome. He requested permission to get down from the passenger coach in order to stretch his legs, and while pretending to light a cigarette, he set fire to some refuse used in packing the aircraft. After again settling down in his compartment with his guard, he learned that the goods car was burning merrily under the forced draft of the moving train. The seven Fokkers were completely destroyed.

A short while later the guard remembered the ruse Knotts had used, and reported his testimony to the authorities concerned. There was a quick investigation and a summary trial. Knotts barely escaped being executed for his sabotage, but his captors, realizing the war was already lost, decided to be lenient. Knotts was clapped in a nearby prison camp where he languished until the Armistice.

After his repatriation and return home, he entered the Harvard Law School, graduating in 1921. In 1929 he was Secretary to the Illinois Aerial Navigation Commission. From 1930 to 1942 he served as Aviation Supervisor of the Illinois Commerce Commission. He became editor of the *Journal of Air Law and Commerce* in 1937, and in that same year was a consulting expert on aviation to the United States Bureau of Air Commerce, and the Civil Aeronautic Authority.

Howard C. Knotts died on November 23, 1942.

FIORELLO HENRY LA GUARDIA

La Guardia Field, the municipal airport in the Borough of Queens, New York, was named in honor of a Mayor of New York, Fiorello

H. La Guardia. It was fitting, not only in memory of a respected politician, but as a memorial to this man's service to American aviation.

La Guardia was born in New York in 1882. As a young man he accompanied his mother to Europe, and was employed in several American consulates. He returned to New York in 1906 and studied law while working for the U. S. Immigration Service. He was admitted to the bar in 1910, and ran for Congress in 1914, but was defeated. After waging a bitter campaign against the Tammany Hall machine, he was successful in 1916. In 1917 he resigned his Congressional seat to take command of the American Aviation Group then serving on the Italian-Austrian front. Because of his linguistic background and his ability to handle diplomatic situations, he was most successful, although his record as a pilot may not be particularly impressive. It is said that he "wound up flying Caproni bombers," leading a detachment of eighteen American pilots.

After the war Fiorello La Guardia became president of the New York City Board of Aldermen, and in 1933 ran successfully for mayor of the city of New York. He was re-elected for three successive terms, but in 1945 refused to run again.

GORMAN DeFREEST LARNER

Another American ace with a score of eight enemy aircraft is Captain G. DeF. Larner, a native of Washington, D.C. In 1917 he attempted to join the Aviation Section of the Signal Corps, but was turned down because of his youth. So he bought passage to France out of his own pocket, and was accepted for action with the French Aviation in July 1917. He passed through the usual routine at Avord, Tours, Pau, and Le Plessis-Belleville, and took his ticket on a Caudron trainer.

On December 3, 1917, Larner was posted to Spad 86, and flew routine missions aboard Spads until April 1918. By that time the U. S. Air Service was searching for experienced pilots, and Larner was given a first lieutenancy, but continued to fly with Spad 86 Escadrille. Not until June 16 was he assigned to the U. S. 103rd Aero Squadron and made a flight commander. Between that date and the Armistice Larner was credited with downing eight enemy aircraft.

Three days before the end of the war he was promoted to captain.

On his demobilization, Larner entered Columbia University from which he graduated in 1921. For a number of years he served as general manager of the National Aeronautic Association. When World War II broke out, Larner went back into the Air Corps, and had become a colonel by 1945. He lived for a number of years in Englewood, New Jersey.

REED GRESHAM LANDIS

The well-known Reed Landis, who is credited with nine enemy aircraft and one kite balloon, received the bulk of his training and front-line experience with the Royal Flying Corps' Number 40 Squadron, the same squadron that produced Mickey Mannock and Captain G. E. H. McElroy, and from all accounts, Landis' complete score was run up while he was a member of this famous organization.

The son of Judge Kenesaw Mountain Landis, the first commissioner of professional baseball, Reed was born July 17, 1896. By the time he was twenty years old he had enlisted as a private in the 1st Illinois Cavalry and served on the Mexican Border. Early in 1917 he transferred to the Aviation Section of the Signal Corps, and on completing his ground school tests was sent to England for flight training.

Because Landis' career with Number 40 Squadron has never been widely publicized, we know little of the actual details, but it is obvious that most of his active service flying was aboard S.E.5s with the British. Following this service, Landis was sent back to England and assigned to the U. S. 25th Aero Squadron which was then being formed. On its arrival in France it became part of the new 4th Pursuit Group, and Landis was promoted to the rank of major, but whether he took part in any front-line patrols as a member of the 25th Aero Squadron has not been made clear in any available history. However, he did receive Great Britain's D.F.C., and his own country's D.S.C.

After the war Landis was associated with American Airlines, and became a regional vice-president in 1940. For a time he was a consultant to the Director, Office of Civil Defense, and by 1942 was recalled to active duty with the Army Air Force where he attained the rank of colonel. He again retired at the end of hostilities.

FREDERICK LIBBY

This may come as a surprise to many readers, but the first American airman to become an ace in World War I was a little-known adventurer, Frederick Libby, a native of Sterling, Colorado. The interesting feature of Libby's career is that though he actually shot down twenty-four enemy aircraft he is credited officially with only fourteen. The first ten Germans to fall before Fred's gun, though completely eliminated from further combat, are not recognized by members of the august American Fighter Aces Association, because the man from Colorado was *only an NCO observer* at the time. Later, after being given a commission and becoming a pilot, the British credited him with fourteen "kills," and Libby is so recognized in the lists of fighting airmen.

The writer went through much the same experience, which accounts for his name seldom appearing in any "authorized" list of Allied aces.

The author has had some lengthy correspondence with Libby who now lives in Los Angeles, and it has been shown that our war trails ran parallel, but not over the same period of time. Fred was more fortunate in managing to transfer from the front to the R.F.C. early in the spring of 1916, whereas it was almost a year later that I attained my release from the line. Consequently my active-service pilot time was very limited, and the victories I had scored as an aerial gunner and observer were not officially credited until many years later.

Fred Libby, an ex-cowboy who had enjoyed a free and easy life until the outbreak of World War I, was in Canada that summer of 1914. He immediately joined the Canadian Army and after about a year of regimental training was sent to Britain, eventually landing in France where, like so many others, he soon sensed there was little future in trench warfare. When the Royal Flying Corps sent out a call for machine gunners to man the so-called battle planes, Libby was among the first to be accepted, and was posted immediately to Number 23 Squadron which was flying F.E.2b two-seater pushers.

Libby was very lucky on his first patrol, managing to shoot down an enemy plane in flames, and on his return to his field was greeted by his wing commander, a Colonel Shephard who was waiting on the Tarmac to congratulate him. This brief association in no way hampered Fred's climb to the heady atmosphere of a commission and eventual pilot training.

Although I put in almost a year as an aerial gunner, I never once met my wing commander, Colonel Robert Loraine, and although my squadron adjutant gave me credit for sixteen aircraft and six kite balloons, I was just another cadet novice when I began my pilot training late in January 1918.

Fred Libby, unquestionably, was an excellent aerial gunner for he downed ten enemy aircraft in a very few weeks. By August 27, 1916, he had racked up his fifth, which certainly made him the first American ace in that war, but you know the hair-splitting of the Fighter Aces Association, and the British Air Ministry. Considering his record and length of service, he can claim to be the least known of all American aces.

Another American, Captain Alan M. Wilkinson, who was commissioned with the R.F.C. on June 14, 1915, downed his fifth enemy plane on August 31, 1916, exactly four days after Libby had scored his fifth. Have you ever heard of Captain Alan M. Wilkinson? He ended his career as a major with the R.F.C. with nineteen victories to his credit, but he never transferred to the American forces, so has never made the glamorous list of American aces. Wilkinson is also one of the few airmen who won Britain's Distinguished Service Order—twice!

When Libby received his commission and finished his pilot training, he was posted to a British single-seater (Number 43) fighter squadron with which he served from May until September 1917. In that period of time he was credited with fourteen "kills" and awarded the Military Cross.

In a recent communication Fred Libby wrote, "I am ten times as proud of my observer's wing as of my pilot's insignia. Anyone can be taught to fly a plane, but not everyone could be a good observer and live through those days when a pilot's life depended entirely on his observer. Take a look around and you'll find very few observers who flew from 1915–17. You should certainly know, considering how many months you flew as an aerial gunner with Number 22 Squadron."

General Billy Mitchell manipulated a few strings, and had Fred transferred from the R.F.C. to the U. S. Air Service as experienced pilots were much needed, but to Fred's concern he was not welcomed warmly in Washington where he was sent to contribute his wide knowledge. In the first place the question arose as to whether he was still a citizen of the United States, although this question was never raised about those who had volunteered and served with the French. Next, it was questioned whether he was entitled to wear U. S. Air Service wings. With that Fred was ready to give up and return to the R.F.C. Only Mitchell's support kept him with the American forces. This may explain why so many Americans who were flying with the British felt no compelling desire to transfer to their own air service. In the case of Raoul Lufbery, a French-born, naturalized American citizen, it was explained that he was a fitting figure to enrich Franco-American traditions. His citizenship was never questioned.

GERVAIS RAOUL LUFBERY

Possibly the outstanding figure in the Lafayette Escadrille was G. Raoul Lufbery. As explained above, he was born in France on March 14, 1885, and was therefore somewhat older than the average World War I airman. His mother died one year after his birth, and his father remarried in 1890. Shortly after, Lufbery senior took his new wife to the United States, leaving young Raoul and two of his brothers with their grandmother while their father sought his fortune in the New World.

When in his teens Raoul had a job in a chocolate factory and for nearly four years sent his father most of his earnings, money that helped Lufbery senior to set up a flourishing stamp-collector's business in Wallingford, Connecticut.

When Raoul was nineteen he decided to see the world, eventually arriving in the United States to look up his father. On the day he landed, however, his father had left Connecticut, and had sailed from New York for Europe. As events turned out they never did meet again, although Raoul stayed in Wallingford for nearly two years, picking up a smattering of English. Next, he moved on to Cuba, then swung back into the United States, and after holding various jobs joined the U. S. Army in 1907. He was immediately shipped to the Philippines, and his military service entitled him to make a claim for American citizenship. After completing a two-year hitch, he pocketed his savings and headed for Japan and China. It will be seen that this young man was not held by deep roots of nationality or home ties.

In 1912 Lufbery was in Indochina where he struck up an acquaintance with Marc Pourpe, a noted French aviator who was giving exhibition flights with a Blériot monoplane. Raoul took over the task of bossing a group of coolies who were erecting a canvas hangar for the monoplane, a job that led to his agreeing to travel with Pourpe, handle the heavy work, and learn some of the skills of the aviation mechanic.

These two men barnstormed around Europe and Africa for the next two years, and when Marc attempted a flight from Cairo to Khartoum and return, it was Raoul who made the attempt possible. Without his superhuman efforts to keep his pilot supplied with fuel, spares, and mechanical service the epic event could not have taken place. As a result of this flight Marc Pourpe became one of the outstanding airmen of that period and was in demand everywhere.

In the early summer of 1914 they returned to France to buy a Morane Parasol with the intention of returning to the Far East, but war broke out and Pourpe offered his services to the French Aviation.

Contrary to popular belief, Raoul Lufbery did not enlist with his companion. He was now an American citizen and was not sure he could serve with a "foreign" force. Instead, he wished Marc good luck and wandered about Paris where he met a number of Americans who were volunteering to enlist in the French Foreign Legion. Sensing that his national status was in no way at stake, he also joined the Foreign Legion as an infantryman.

Whether Pourpe exerted any influence, or whether Lufbery's mechanical skill had something to do with it, he was transferred within a week to Pourpe's squadron as an aviation mechanic. Three months later Marc was killed in action. Raoul remained with the squadron for several months, servicing the aircraft. He did his work, made no comment about Pourpe, but his superiors, ignoring his boisterous ways, his hard drinking, and the fact he took his fun where he found it, saw that deep within him Raoul had been badly shaken by Pourpe's death. Someone suggested that he be transferred, or better still, given pilot training, and this Lufbery gratefully accepted. There were no dramatic resolutions, no theatrical declarations of revenge; he was not capable of such paltry histrionics. He simply packed his gear and strode out of camp.

Lufbery received his early training at Chartres, and earned his wings on a Farman. Later, he had some bombing instruction on a Voisin, and his first war flying was with VB. 106 where he proved to be a workmanlike performer, carrying out his duties with stolid complacency. He won a few citations, and then volunteered for *chasse* training. His commander tried to dissuade him, and then used every means available to keep him on bombers, but Lufbery won his point and moved on to Plessis-Belleville for training on the Nieuport scout.

There he showed no particular skill or promise for he was heavy-handed, seemingly lacking the touch for such work, and there was a time when his instructors feared he would have to be sent back to the Voisin group. But Raoul persisted until he finally picked up some proficiency, and in due course found his way to the Escadrille Américaine.

When he arrived at Luxeuil where the squadron was formed, he was a total unknown and did not create a pleasant impression with the American youths, most of whom were ex-collegians from good homes. Raoul was a small, chunky man, not much over five feet tall. He had broad shoulders, a perpetual scowl, crude speech, and apparently no emotions of any kind. He seldom laughed, and when he did it was a hearty tavern roar, his eyes sparkling like polished brilliants. He made few friends at first, and seemed inscrutable to his companions. Only Ted Parsons seems to have gotten under his skin, or fully understood him.

None of this is any reflection on his skill or daring. Lufbery had the makings of a great fighting airman, and had fate been kinder, had history been more favorable, had he remained with the French after the United States entered the war, he might have become an outstanding airman, one in the same class as Mickey Mannock, or Jimmy McCudden, both of whom came up from the dregs of poverty.

To most readers of air-war history, Lufbery remains a mystery, and very little is actually known about him. No flying field has been named in his honor, although an ancient defensive maneuver known as the Lufbery Circle bears his name. But it is debatable that Lufbery conceived it, any more than Max Immelmann devised what is generally known as the Immelmann turn. The trick of a number of planes latching on to one another's tail and flying in a tight circle as a defense against an enemy moving into that critical position was known on all fronts from the time aircraft worked in elements, and used as a protective measure long before Raoul Lufbery had made his first solo flight.

This man of mystery joined N.124 on May 24, 1916, after the air war had been on for almost two years, but he did not score a victory until July 30 when he downed an enemy singlehanded on the Verdun front. However, his second victory came that same afternoon, and from that time on Raoul became a relentless stalker, prowling the sky hour after hour, never returning to his field until his fuel was exhausted or his ammo containers empty. He kept up this good work all through August, flying innumerable hours over the line. On August 8 he came upon an Aviatik near Fort Douaumont and shot it down in flames. Another Aviatik fell before his guns on October 12 during a raid on the German Mauser works. This was his fifth, which made him an ace.

From this point Luf became a changed man. He was quietly pleased with the renown that came to him on both sides of the Atlantic, and was proud to be accepted by such stars as Georges Guynemer and René Fonck. Once the adulation died down, he too settled down to make himself worthy of the position he had gained, and became the fighting mainstay of the Lafayette Escadrille. He probably was the proudest airman on the Western Front.

When the American squadron was broken up to be distributed throughout the new U. S. Air Service, Lufbery's situation became tragic. He made no official request for the transfer, and there are many reasons to believe he dreaded making the change. Ethnologically, he was more French than American. In the short time he spent in the United States he could have absorbed little of the American spirit or background. He had had no schooling in the United States, and English was his second language. Those who remember him in the early days of the Escadrille insist he was far more comfortable when speaking French. When he wrote in French he was especially lucid and expressive.

The historian of the Lafayette Escadrille, Colonel Paul Ayres Rockwell, once told the writer: "Lufbery was a solitary soul. Had he lived I think he would have made his mark in civilian life; I doubt if he would have remained in a United States uniform. He might have become a good test pilot. He never would have become a 'bum' or in any way a disgrace to the Escadrille, of which he was the greatest ace. There were phases of the higher social life that left him uncomfortable. Whenever he was shipped to Nice to recuperate from the pain of his periodic rheumatism, he was unaccustomed to the pattern of life in a swank Mediterranean hotel, or as a guest at any of the palatial rest homes that were made available to convalescent servicemen. Because of this Lufbery often returned to the front before his leave period was over."

But fate was unkind, and Raoul Lufbery was among the first selected to join the new American Air Service. In fact, he was given a major's commission, although he had been only an adjutant (warrant officer) most of his time with the Lafayette. He was immediately posted to the 94th Aero Squadron.

All this reads fine on paper, but there was no 94th Aero Squadron to command. It was simply a cadre organization, and to occupy his time Raoul was sent to the American instruction center at Issoudun where he was placed behind a desk, given some pencils and paper and told to make himself comfortable and allow the nonflying specialists to organize the Aviation Service. Luf knew nothing about paper work, and cared less about forms, figures, and routine organization, but even worse it was insisted that he wear a complete United States uniform that made him feel and look like a dressed-up tailor's dummy. All the old free-and-easy glamour of the front-line airmen had been stripped from him, and it is not difficult to sense how unhappy he must have been.

Lufbery knew he was not earning this new money. He felt that in this silent office he was of no use to anyone. He was a combat leader, not an administrative officer. He yearned to be back with a fighting organization. Front-line flying men know the dangers of these periods of let-down, particularly if the rests become too prolonged, or worse still, if they do not afford a complete change from the daily routine of war. Short breaks from daily patrols are ideal and most valuable. Periods of pleasant country homes with good companionship, walks along a lake shore, or quiet heather-strewn hills of Scotland were more likely to revive the spirit and nervous system than all the artificial hilarity of wartime capitals.

But Raoul Lufbery enjoyed none of these simple pleasures. He was withdrawn from the line, deprived of most of his companions, and placed in a position where he could do nothing but sweat and fume. The big German push of March 1918 had just hurled back the British and French troops for many miles. The Channel ports were threatened again, and only the airmen were holding their own, attempting to stem the tide. Just when the experienced pilots were most needed, the men of the old Lafayette Escadrille were enduring the bitter dregs of enforced idleness.

*

Finally, Lufbery was sent on to Villeneuve in the Champagne sector where the United States' 94th and 95th Squadrons were being organized. He was not given command of the 94th, as has been so often stated, but he did act as a special instructor. Major John Huffer was the actual commander. The 94th had a few decrepit Nieuport-28s but no machine guns. On the other side of the field the 95th had Nieuports *with* machine guns, but none of their pilots had yet been given machine-gun training.

Lufbery's service with the 94th has not been clearly defined, but apparently he gave impromptu lectures, took small formations on training flights, and undertook to bring the newcomers along slowly. It is known that he destroyed only one more German plane, and his war career ended with seventeen victories, sixteen of which were scored while he was a member of the Lafayette Escadrille.

Something went wrong during his short service with the 94th Aero Squadron, and Lufbery became moody and irritable. He repeatedly spoke of his fear of fire in the air. He fussed over the newcomers and worried about the structural qualities of the Nieuport-28. He never really felt at home. He missed the old freer days with the Lafayette Escadrille. Time after time, particularly on rainy days, he would harp on the fear of fire in the air. (The Italians were experimenting with the Paulus parachute, and it had been reported that a number of German airmen had been given such life preservers, but as yet none was available to the French or British.)

The bitter end came on May 19, 1918. About ten o'clock that morning a German two-seater Albatros photography plane was seen snooping about and actually heading for the Hat-in-the-Ring squadron's field near Saint-Mihiel. A Lieutenant Gude was the only pilot available, and he was sent aloft to intercept the German. It was Gude's first combat flight, and just as he was well airborne and heading for his quarry, French antiaircraft guns nearby apparently scored a hit. The enemy plane began a long series of spirals, and seemed to be heading for the ground. Then, as Lieutenant Gude and everyone else thought the photography plane was about to crash, it was seen to pull out suddenly, recover and turn toward the German lines, flying at not more than 200 feet from the ground. Gude continued on, determined to finish it.

But this young man was inexperienced, and he fired all his available ammunition at a ridiculous range—or so Major Huffer reported later—and had to return to his own field. The Albatros, daring another barrage of antiaircraft fire, continued on toward Nancy.

Meanwhile Major Lufbery who had been watching Gude's airplane from a nearby barracks, jumped on a motorcycle, roared out to the field, and because his own Nieuport was out of commission, took one that had been assigned to a Lieutenant Davis.

Lufbery went on this flight with the great hope that at last he would down an enemy plane within the Allied lines. None of his victories had taken place where the victim could be examined or stripped for souvenirs. He keenly wanted to get this two-seater Albatros.

The speedy Nieuport soon caught up with the Albatros, and Lufbery had about 2000 feet to work with. He fired several short bursts on his first dive, and was then seen to swerve away, possibly to remedy a gun stoppage. He circled the Hun, cleared the jam and once more went down for the kill. With that, those who watched to see The Master perform held their breaths as Luf's machine suddenly burst into flames. He continued on and passed close to the Albatros.

It was discovered later that an incendiary bullet had hit the Nieuport, passed through the fabric, clipped Raoul's right-hand thumb that grasped the joystick, and somehow pierced the fuel tank.

The watchers saw Lufbery climb from his blazing cockpit, and then leap clear. It was figured that he had jumped from a height of 200 feet. He fell on a low picket fence that protected the small flower garden of a villager and was impaled. A woman and her young daughter lifted Lufbery off tenderly, and one of them pulled a length of fence picket from his body before they laid him out and covered him with flowers.

Ironically, there are two stories about Luf and fire in the air. According to Eddie Rickenbacker, Lufbery had said that in case of fire he would *always* get out on the wing and try to ride it down. On other occasions, and to other comrades, he had sworn he would never roast in a burning cockpit; he would immediately jump and get it over with.

There is still more to the story of Lufbery's end. A French ace from a squadron across the field had also taken off after Lufbery's plunge, and he too managed to catch up with the dawdling Albatros, but during his first attack the German observer put a bullet through his heart and he piled up only a mile or so from where Lufbery had fallen. But another Frenchman was luckier. He finally caught the two-seater and brought it down inside the Allied lines, and both the pilot and gunner were captured. Doug Campbell also took off, but could not catch up with the Albatros. However, he did find a two-seater Rumpler over Beaumont, and after a brisk exchange killed the gunner and wounded the pilot. This plane also fell inside the Allied lines.

FRANK LUKE

Frank Luke of Phoenix, Arizona, will always be known as the Balloon Buster, for his speciality was enemy kite balloons, and before he met his end he had downed no less than fifteen, as well as four German airplanes. He was the epitome of the brave, brash, undisciplined two-fisted Yank so popular in the pulp-magazine field. This savage, unreasoning air fighter was the first American flier to win the Congressional Medal of Honor, and the only one to be awarded that decoration during the course of the war. Seven others were thus honored, but only after their records had been considered by Congressional boards years after the end of hostilities. Luke was also awarded the Distinguished Service Cross, but he did not live to wear either medal, and had he returned from his last patrol he would have been court-martialed for taking off on that flight.

Few readers will believe the figures or details of his meteoric career, but for the record they are offered here.

Although Luke's combat missions took place in a period of only nine days, logging less than thirty hours of air time, when he was through he was America's leading ace. Only Eddie Rickenbacker overtook his score later on. Flying a 120-horsepower Spad biplane he destroyed fifteen enemy balloons and shot down four German planes in ten combat patrols. Some records insist that Luke downed five planes, but his official record of nineteen enemy aircraft in thirty hours of flying time should be good enough for anyone.

This contrary youth had wanted no part of the war, and in fact had to be taunted into joining by his sister Eva who was serving as a Red Cross nurse. A brother also had enlisted in the artillery. With little enthusiasm Frank finally volunteered for the Signal Corps, and indifferently requested aviation training. This took place in the fall of 1917, nearly five months after the United States had declared war. He finished his various courses and sailed for France March 4, 1918.

He was definitely the Mickey Mannock type, employing the tactics of the dock-walloper, the bar-brawler, and the everything-goes code of the gutter fighter. There was nothing personal in his animosity. He did not hate the enemy, he simply resented the situation in which he found himself. Military life was absurd. It deprived him of the sunshine and the simplicities of life in his native Arizona. In France he was given a new Spad, posted to Number 27 Aero Squadron and expected to live up to the traditions established by such men as Quentin Roosevelt, Raoul Lufbery, Jerry Vasconcelles, Harold Hartney, and the paragons of the Lafayette Escadrille.

But Frank Luke showed no awe or respect, and after two unfortunate preliminary patrols, he was grounded for a month to teach him that rookie airmen were expected to stay in formation and obey the orders of their superiors.

Luke was tall, lithe, hawk-featured, without a spot of humor in his whole 170 pounds. Sparing of speech he hated the wind of words. Deep thinking was a tedious detour; only action paid its way.

At the front everything was new, each day a flipped page in an unfamiliar book. He made few friends, and so short was his stretch of glory, few people remember him. The only close flying companion he attracted was Lieutenant Joseph Wehner, who, like Luke, had a German background, and had come under suspicion. These two outcasts became firm friends for as long they both lived, which was only a few weeks.

Major Harold Hartney, then CO of the 27th Aero Squadron, was the first person to meet Luke on his arrival at the Saints field in the old Aisne-Marne salient. Major Hartney wasted half an hour explaining to Luke that it was important to go slow, take things easy, and stay in formation. The next afternoon the major took a small flight of Spads up the line. Luke and another fledgling were included, but once they were safely inside the element of experienced airmen and cruising up and down the front line, Luke pulled out and went hunting on his own. He returned to his field a few minutes after the other fliers had landed.

"What happened to you?" Major Hartney demanded when Luke walked into the operations shack.

"I had engine trouble," Luke replied and reached for a form.

"Engine trouble? But you stayed out longer than the rest of us. What sort of a line is that?"

Luke did not bother to explain.

Two days later Frank Luke was again assigned to a familiarizing patrol under another leader, and again he disappeared the minute the front line was reached, but this time he had peeled off into trouble. He was attacked by a Hun he had not seen. There was a jangle of metal, the scream of torn plating, and the clatter of engine parts. He was lucky to get back to his own field, but when he arrived and pointed out the damage, he stoutly declared he had shot down an enemy aircraft.

"What kind?"

Frank Luke did not know.

"Where?"

He had no idea. Only Major Hartney and Joe Wehner believed him, but, unfortunately for Luke, Hartney was promoted the next day and given command of the new First Pursuit Group. Captain Alfred Grant, a keen disciplinarian, took over Number 27 Squadron. The squadron moved up to the Verdun front and settled in at Rembercourt where Luke was appointed an engineering officer and ordered to make the new camp shipshape. The records disclose that following his patrol on August 16 when he claimed to have destroyed some kind of an enemy plane, he did not fly again until September 12.

During this time Luke listened to the messroom gossip about kite balloons. A hundred things could happen to a man who tried to attack a Jerry balloon; there always was a five-ship fighter formation up to protect them. Luke made a bold boast he would get a balloon on his next show.

"You couldn't get a YMCA hut if it was tied down," someone said. It was still believed that Luke had lied about the Hun he had claimed the previous month.

The next morning Frank "borrowed" a Spad and went up toward Marieulles, and over Lavigneville spotted three German biplanes. He gave chase, but they disappeared in the mists over Metz. Turning back for his own lines he suddenly saw a kite balloon and went in hell-for-leather. His first burst produced nothing, so he went up into a loop, came down, and fired again—but nothing happened. By this time the enemy balloon had been drawn down almost into its bed, but

Frank persisted, and on his last dive the big gray kite went up in flames. Its observer, Willi Klemm, died in the basket. It was Willi's first day as a balloon observer.

✳

Captain Grant accepted Luke's report, and decided to give him all the balloon shows he could take. "There's a Jerry Drachen up over Buzy. It's all yours, but I suggest you take one man with you."

"O.K. I'll take Joe Wehner."

Joe apparently had no choice, but he went along. While Frank had almost immediate success with the observation balloon, Joe proved to be bait for eight Jerry planes that came in to guard the kite. Frank tried to help but his guns jammed, and he had to clear out until he could remedy the stoppages. Meanwhile, Joe hung on, the Jerry fighters drew off, and went north to protect another bag.

Joe and Frank joined forces once more and tried to find a flight from Number 27 Squadron, but instead Luke found an enemy balloon. He attacked and the observer returned the fire with a light machine gun. However, he was finally forced to go over the side of the basket and take to the silk. This time everyone was convinced that Luke had indeed been in action. He had Wehner to confirm his fights, and his Spad was bullet-slashed from engine to rudder.

Two offensive patrols—three balloons!

The next day, September 12, Luke and Wehner took off to attend to a balloon up over Boigneville. This time they had incendiary ammunition, and after crossing the line together they broke up and went off on their own. Luke downed two more balloons, and Wehner destroyed a balloon and two German planes!

Late that afternoon Luke went out again, and just north of Verdun found another balloon that he attacked boldly, and soon destroyed. He took a severe beating from German antiaircraft guns, however, and had to make a forced landing in a French wheat field near Angers. His balloon was quickly confirmed, but Number 27 had another Spad on the "unserviceable" list.

The next morning Joe and Frank went out again, but all the enemy balloons seemed to have been hidden away behind the lines, so they decided to try another early evening patrol, and this time Luke made quite a dramatic show, advising Major Hartney that he would down three known balloons in quick order.

"We'll take the first at 7:10," Luke is said to have explained, "the second at 7:20, and the third at 7:30 . . . right on the nose."

Hartney left his office and went out to a nearby rise to watch this boastful exhibition.

The first balloon went up in scarlet flame, exactly on the dot. The second was one minute late in catching fire, but the clock had reached 7:36 before the third went down, dragging a long streamer of black smoke. Colonel Billy Mitchell had arrived at the field to witness the climax of this fantastic show.

*

Because of bad weather there was no more flying until September 18, but on that day Wehner and Luke went out again and headed for the Saint-Mihiel sector where two balloons were up. Luke took the higher one first, and it went down in a great gout of flame. Then he turned and headed for the second, flying through a heavy barrage of antiaircraft fire and had to go down as low as 70 feet before it flaunted a scarlet streamer.

In the meantime Wehner had become embroiled with a flight of Fokker D-VIIs and Luke went to his assistance. He knocked one down and it spun in. Then he found himself in a cone of fire from another Jerry. He made a tight climbing turn and caught a Fokker pilot cold, but realized he was being sucked in well over the line, so he turned for home. He looked for Joe but he was nowhere to be seen, so Frank joined some Cigognes Spads that were harrying a German Halberstadt observation plane. Ignoring the fact that the Frenchmen considered this target as their own special prize, Frank tore in and finished the Hun, sending it down in flames.

To recapitulate: in that blistering ten minutes Luke had destroyed two observation balloons, two Fokker fighters, and one two-seater observation machine. He was now short on fuel, so he pulled out and went home, hoping to find Wehner and compare notes, but Joe failed to turn up.

Although Luke now was America's Number 1 ace with a total of fourteen victories—four planes and ten balloons—whereas Rickenbacker had only nine confirmed at this time, he found no satisfaction in the situation. He had to accept the fact that Joe was missing. He didn't touch a meal for the rest of the day, but just sat around the mess, staring into space. He showed no interest in flying the next day, so Major Hartney decided to send him to Paris.

His orders were typed out, a leave warrant filled in, and Frank was given extra money. Hartney himself drove Frank to a railroad station and made certain he got aboard the train. That was September 19. On the afternoon of September 25, less than a week later, Frank returned from Paris, still silent and morose.

"What are you doing back so early?" Major Hartney demanded. "You have four more days left."

"There wasn't anything to do."

The gayest wartime city in the world had nothing to offer him. Apparently Luke had sat around the Hotel Chatham, and instead of mixing with the boys and girls, had thought up a new plan to down enemy kites. He importuned Hartney for permission to form a special balloon flight that would work out of an old advanced field closer to the line. The major didn't like the idea, but he went along with it, and assigned Jerry Vasconcelles to take a balloon-busting flight up to the field.

Then, on September 26, while these plans were under way, Luke took young Lieutenant Ivan Roberts of Lee, Massachusetts, on a show. Luke went after a balloon, but they ran into five Fokkers. One went down after a short burst from Luke's guns, and when he looked around for Lieutenant Roberts he was nowhere to be seen. Later, American balloon observers reported that they had seen Roberts crash inside the German lines, but that was all that was ever heard of him.

Once more, Luke went into surly seclusion, and the next day left the field without permission which drew a scathing reprimand from Captain Grant. Boldly defying his squadron commander, Luke again took off and torched a partly inflated balloon that was resting in its bed near Bantheville. This one must have been a thriller, for Luke had to go down to 30 feet to torch the bag, and when he pulled out, he nosed into a barrage of wicked antiaircraft fire. He finally took refuge at a French Cigognes field where he spent the night without advising his commanding officer. When he returned to Rembercourt the next afternoon, Captain Grant naturally inquired where he had been all night, but all Luke would say was, "I was over at the Cigognes."

When Grant insisted on knowing more details, Luke added, "Oh, and I got another balloon near Bantheville."

Grant, nevertheless, resented this insolence, and told Luke he was grounded until further notice. Actually, he was just trying to save this young firebrand from himself, merely intending to settle him down.

Frank did not answer him. He just flicked a salute, went out the door and headed back for the hangars.

"I'm taking off again," he said to a mechanic.

"But, holy smoke, Lieutenant, she needs gas and oil!" the enlisted man argued.

"I'll fill her up at Vasconcelles' flight up the line," Luke said. "Swing that prop!"

Captain Grant soon sensed what was happening, and he shouted to his adjutant, "Tell Vasconcelles to put Luke under open arrest and return him here by sidecar. We'll send up another pilot to fly his ship back."

"Then what?" the adjutant said, probably shielding a grin.

Captain Grant frowned and considered. "First, I'm recommending him for the Distinguished Service Cross, and then, by God, I'm going to court-martial him!"

*

Luke landed at the forward strip, and Vasconcelles started out from his dugout office to carry out Grant's order, but at that moment Major Hartney circled the field for a landing, so Jerry wisely delayed Captain Grant's order.

Frank charged up to Hartney the minute he stepped from his Spad. "Major, there're three balloons up beyond Verdun. I can get all three if you let me go now."

Hartney looked at his watch. "Too early. The sun will go at 5:22. You can take off then, not before."

At 5:20 Luke was in his cockpit and had his engine started.

The major bellowed, "I said 5:22, Luke! Shut that engine down."

Hartney said later, "That's the last I remember of him. He was sitting there laughing at me while I bawled him out. In fact, it was the only time I ever saw Frank laugh."

By 5:22 Luke was in the air again and heading for the American Balloon HQ in Souilly. He banked over wildly and flipped a message to a group of waving observers. It read:

Watch those three Hun balloons along the Meuse.
                                                    Luke

Frank climbed away and headed for Dun on the far bank of the historic Meuse River. His guns raked the first kite and it exploded as he went into a half roll. Then he cleared and headed for Brière Farm where another enemy sausage lolled in the evening twilight. He started down with it dead in his sights but looked around and saw an element of Hun fighters moving into position above him. A hornet trail of tracers smacked into his tail assembly, and he nosed down hard, heading for the cover of the ground smoke.

This was a new Luke. Now he was making the most of protective cover. The Germans veered off, probably figuring he had piled up somewhere below. Instead, the Balloon Buster headed for the balloon over Brière Farm and stitched it with short, uneven bursts of incendiary ammunition. The second bag of the day went up in a cloud of oily smoke.

As he swung for Milly where the third balloon was aloft the ground observers saw the Spad flutter and hesitate. Luke seemingly blundered on toward the bulbous target but the Ack-Ack fire was now a veritable curtain. The Spad staggered on, finally brought its nose in line and two streams of sizzling lead laced into the balloon's sides.

Luke's third of the day, and the last of his wild career, went up in smoke and flames.

From this point on what happened is mere conjecture. We know he made no effort to scramble for altitude or head for smoke cover. Perhaps he was too tired to drag the stick back. Instead of making a 180-degree turn and heading for his own line, he turned toward the village of Murvaux that huddled on the north bank of the Meuse.

Why? No one knows. The available records state that Frank Luke was seen over the village where, according to some villagers, he spotted a number of marching troops. He is said to have nosed down and raked the street with his guns. Others stated that he was flying like a drunken man. The most reliable report is that Luke was seriously wounded while attacking the balloon over Dun, and that several antiaircraft guns had scored heavily, and from that point on he must have been flying by blind instinct.

At any rate his end came at Murvaux, where, after he had finished the third Drachen, he floundered about, only just missing the spire of the village church. He was then seen to go into a sideslip landing, and pancake into a meadow that provided a grassy carpet all the way to a churchyard wall where, according to some reports, he tried to make a stand against a platoon of German infantrymen. Others claimed that he staggered about and headed for a small stream where he presumably quenched his thirst or bathed a wound. The most popular version is that Luke climbed into the graveyard of the church and tried to fight it out with his enemies. When German voices ordered him to surrender he answered with automatic fire. Perhaps he did not know what they were saying. The enemy deployed, and then fired at him again. Luke was found dead among the gravestones.

His body was carried out to the street and someone brought out a farm cart. The villagers wanted to lay some clean straw in the bottom of it but the German area commander refused this last token of respect. Frank Luke was quickly buried nearby, but just exactly where, no one is certain.

JAMES R. McCONNELL

Jimmy McConnell came from Carthage, North Carolina, and was one of the first Americans to do something about the invasion of Belgium and the German march into France, for he always felt he was "a citizen of the world at large." He put his personal affairs in order as soon as possible and sailed for France in January 1915. He signed up with the American Field Service and drove ambulances all through the spring and summer of 1915, and was so inspired with this service he wrote a number of letters detailing this life that were published by *Outlook* magazine, and graced with an introduction by Colonel Theodore Roosevelt. These gay reports stimulated much interest in the A.F.S., and particularly in France's cause.

In October 1915 he transferred to the French Aviation, and completed his training February 6, 1916. By April 20 of that year he was posted to the new Escadrille Américaine, and was, in fact, included in the first formation flight made by that squadron, May 14, 1916.

Jimmy had never flown above 7000 feet and when Captain Thénault took them up to patrol height, Jimmy went a few hundred feet higher, "simply because I had trouble keeping the other aircraft in sight." As a result he encountered clouds and became lost, but with some luck, and time, he finally caught up with them again. Luckily, they were operating on a quiet front and were not molested.

Jim McConnell was a big man, a good companion, and had plenty of courage, but at the time was not the world's greatest pilot. He was always willing and ready for any mission, and, in fact, was overly industrious, and on several occasions overstayed his fuel time. Once, when he had remained out too long he piled up with a dead engine, suffered a back injury that plagued him for weeks, and was forced to go into a hospital for treatment.

He was not released and permitted to return to the squadron until two days before Christmas 1916, and his friends noticed he was far from tiptop. He insisted he was well enough to take his place in any formation, and although his back still bothered him he felt that the best remedy would be routine work. Because it was the holiday season and there was a jovial spirit of good fellowship everywhere Bill Thaw and Georges Thénault acceded to his pleading and agreed that he might pick up where he had left off.

There was considerable moving back and forth about this time, and the escadrille was just settling down at Ravenel where a new ground offensive was in the making, so all through the month of February 1917 the Lafayette Escadrille was advised to limit its flying to practice formations, and put in time improving its knowledge of engines and machine guns. By St. Patrick's Day the regular work was resumed with renewed spirit for it was learned that the Germans were carrying out their "planned withdrawal" to the Hindenburg line, and French aviation was called on to counter this activity with many observation and photography patrols, all of which required close fighter escort.

A patrol composed of Jim McConnell, Ted Parsons, and Edmond Genêt was sent out, and, as previously related in Genêt's history, Jim was shot down.

Once his companions knew his loss was certain, they opened a letter Jim had left that was to be read in case he was killed:

My burial is of no import. Make it as easy as possible for yourselves. I have no religion and do not care for any service. If the omission would embarrass you, I presume I could stand the performance. Good luck to the rest of you. God damn Germany, and *vive la France!*

J. R. MC CONNELL

KENNETH MARR

Kenneth Marr of San Francisco, California, served in France from August 1914 to October 1, 1918, most of which time he spent in the French or American Aviation services. He was credited with only one enemy aircraft, but his contribution to Franco-American amity was immeasurable.

Affectionately known as Si or Siwash, Ken had spent some time in Alaska where he had a number of varied jobs, but specialized in the training of Eskimo dogs. He was, in fact, a typical adventurer of the early 1900s.

At the outbreak of war Ken went to France in charge of a large shipment of Husky dogs that were to be trained for military use in the Vosges by the Alpine Chasseurs. While thus engaged, Ken picked up a bewildering patois of what he believed was French, but it only puzzled or astonished the natives. In fact, because of his weird linguistic ability he became something of a character throughout that sector of the war front.

Once the dog deal was completed, Ken took his linguistic act into the American Field Service with which he served through 1915 and until July 20, 1916, when he transferred to the French Aviation. He finished his training on January 7, 1917, and joined the Lafayette Escadrille on March 29, 1917.

When America entered the war Kenneth Marr was commissioned a captain in the U. S. Air Service and served with the 103rd Aero Squadron, and as a flight commander, and later as commanding officer of the 94th Aero Squadron. In June 1918 he was sent back to the United States, promoted to major, and undertook important staff duties in Washington, D.C., where his ability with the French language was quietly discounted.

Kenneth Marr died in 1965.

DIDIER MASSON

Here was another American with a distinct French background. Born in Los Angeles of French parents, Didier enjoyed a most adventurous life before he had reached voting age. He actually learned to fly as early as 1909 while visiting in France. He took his ticket on an Antoinette monoplane, and although his early flying career was marked by a number of painful crashes, he continued to fly, and from 1911 to 1913 did considerable flying in California in a Curtiss biplane. One of his early exploits was to carry Los Angeles newspapers to smaller cities in all parts of the state.

Then late in 1913 Masson volunteered to organize an air service for Mexican General Alvaro Obregón who at the time was attempting to establish democratic rule in his troubled country. Obregón's chief opponent was General Victoriano Huerta who was in complete command at the time. This uprising was not important internationally; there were few massed battles, neither side had much in the way of artillery, rifles, or transport equipment, and international gunrunners were furnishing both factions with anything that would make a loud bang.

However, someone had suggested to General Obregón that a modern military airplane in the right hands could have an important role. Didier Masson was approached, and through devious channels was engaged. He took his Curtiss biplane and a British soldier of fortune, Tommy Dean, as his mechanic. Sporting a Mexican major's commission, Masson created a Mexican Air Force, but his was the only airplane in the country and Masson was the only pilot south of the border.

The sea lanes were General Obregón's chief trouble, for General Huerta's "navy" was in full command bringing in guns from all points along the Gulf of Mexico and the islands of the Caribbean. The "navy" consisted of one slab-sided gunboat that was powered with a wheezy engine and managed about four knots. It was manned by a crew of beachcombers and sailors of fortune, all of whom claimed to be admirals.

Didier was ordered to sink this enemy warship in any manner he saw fit, and since his rank and pay depended on his success, something outstanding had to be done. So Tommy Dean devised a num-

ber of aerial bombs, using empty syrup cans that were filled with
bolts, nuts, nails, and even discarded Gillette razor blades—and a
charge of explosive. These deadly missiles were rigged with wire
handles and hooked to a primitive bomb rack fitted with a release
mechanism that was controlled from the pilot's cockpit.

This arrangement might have done the trick, but after some consideration both Masson and Dean thought these dangling projectiles
might be swept off the rack by the scraggy brush that grew on their
airstrip and blow the airplane to bits before it could take off. Didier
then decided that because Dean had devised the bombs it was his
duty to see that all would go well. Tommy was persuaded to perch
on the lower wing, clinging to an interplane strut, in which position
he could peer below to see if the bombs were clear of the brush and
cactus as the pilot slowly taxied the plane.

Dean had never been off the ground before and was not too keen
to risk his neck in such a manner, but he willingly made this ground
test with no consideration for what would happen if one of the
bombs was knocked off while he was so mounted. But once it was
fairly evident they would have no trouble, Masson turned the ship
around, rolled back to their starting point, and instead of letting
Tommy crawl down, quickly opened the throttle and roared away
with the astounded Englishman still clutching the interplane strut.
In a few seconds they were aloft to make what was probably the
world's first ground-strafing patrol.

In a few moments Tommy's courage and sense of the ridiculous
were restored and as they roared out across a desert that was said
to be infested with enemy troops they saw an adobe shack that may
have sheltered a platoon or so. With Tommy still hanging on for dear
life, Didier nosed down, swept over the enemy concentration and released the bombs. Two made direct hits, setting up a roar that rolled
across the hot sands. There was a great puff of white smoke, and
chunks of structure, furniture, window frames, and slabs of adobe
twirled through the blast.

As the thrill of triumph dissipated, Tommy looked down and saw
that one big bomb was still clinging to the rack. It was a special
one, devised for some vital target, and Tommy knew there was a
good chance this hung-up bomb could be bounced off the instant
their wheels touched down on their own field.

He had no choice but to leave his hazardous perch on the leading
edge of the wing, forsaking his grip on the interplane strut. The next
thing the pilot knew the bombardier was doing a wing-walking act

inching along the main spar, and clutching at crossbracing wires until he was where he could lie flat on the wing and reach under for the recalcitrant bomb. This drama then went into high gear. The ancient engine spluttered as Tommy struggled with the load dangling from the rack, and Masson searched for a landing strip. Wild-eyed from the slipstream, Tommy was stricken with fear to see the ground coming up fast and finding the bomb well hooked. In savage desperation, he managed to untangle the wire-and-hook device, letting the bomb fall free an instant before the wheels of the plane touched down. The old Curtiss surged on, and received a terrific "nudge" from the exploding missile, but they landed safely. Tommy was half-frozen with cold and fright. Didier tried to laugh off their experience, but in truth he was the more frightened of the two.

The airplane engine was rebuilt within days and Tommy had devised a few more bombs, so General Obregón requested that they make an attack on Huerta's navy. This was an even more thrilling occasion that saw Masson chasing the comic-opera gunboat all around a tropical lagoon. He had come upon it just as the freebooters were about to unload a new shipment of Mausers and blunderbusses. According to some versions of this episode the enemy seamen had never seen an airplane before, and on its first approach shoveled on fuel hoping to make for the open sea. But Masson roared down, pulling his bomb releases whenever he flew through the gunboat's funnel smoke. He scored several hits, but, sad to relate, the bombs refused to explode. The only effect registered was the terror on the faces of the men on the gunboat.

Military matters proceeded in this manner for almost a year, but when the action became too one-sided, Didier switched allegiance, flying for Venustiano Carranza against Francisco "Pancho" Villa. There were several airplanes in the Mexican conflict by this time, one of which was flown by Edwin Parsons who had signed on with the opposition. By a stroke of fate these two fliers never met in the air. Later on both men abandoned this hopeless campaign, and volunteered to fly for France. In fact, they both wound up in the Lafayette Escadrille and worked together on many occasions.

As was to be expected, Masson was a worthy addition to any air squadron, and was one of the American Nieuport pilots selected to fly cover for the first big bombing attack on the Mauser munitions plant at Oberndorf.

This famous operation, staged on October 12, 1916, was a French-British attempt to destroy the German Mauser plant. It was carried out by a number of R.N.A.S. Sopwith 1½-Strutters and a mixed bag of French multi-seat planes. Masson, aboard a Nieuport scout, flying as an escort fighter, found himself in a tangle of three Fokkers and a lone Bréguet, with bullets flying in all directions. He nosed down for speed and then came up in a sharp zoom to get below a Fokker, but just as he was attempting to draw a bead, his engine spluttered. He glanced at his fuel gauge and was amazed to find his tank was empty. This could only mean he had taken a bullet that had pierced the container.

Clambering into a stall, he next found himself the target of the Hun he had been sighting on. There was no choice but to nose down and hope to glide into his own lines. Meanwhile, his Jerry opponent was firing short accurate bursts. One shattered his small windscreen and another peppered his instrument panel. Hoping for the best but expecting the next would slam into his back, Masson sat it out. Then his opponent misjudged his speed and overshot Masson's plane. The tables were reversed and the German now appeared full in Masson's sights. Making the most of the opportunity, he pressed his Bowden trigger and put twenty rounds where they did the most good. The Fokker machine spun away and disappeared from the scene.

But Didier was still in trouble and he had to flatten his glide considerably in order to skim into friendly territory. He crossed the barbed wire with about 150 feet to spare and finally pancaked in for a crash landing amid a pattern of shell holes and wound up straddling a communications trench. He scrambled out, dropped down and made the most of the cover. Five minutes later German artillery shells had blasted his Nieuport to splinters.

This was probably Masson's most exciting front-line experience, but he continued on, flying his regular patrols until he went down with a severe cold. On recovery he became something of a Mess President and put in much time finding good cooks, extra food and suitable nourishment for the squadron bar. He is probably best remembered for the quality of his mess than for the length of his victory score.

JAMES A. MEISSNER

Another popular member of the U. S. 94th Aero Squadron was James A. Meissner from Brooklyn, who is credited with eight confirmed victories. When the war bugles rang out in 1917 Jimmy was an undergraduate at Cornell University, and he dropped college to enlist in the Aviation Section of the Signal Corps. He received the bulk of his training in the United States, and finished it at Issoudun. He was then posted to the Hat-in-the-Ring Squadron on March 17, 1918. While flying with Rickenbacker's group he downed six enemy planes, and by July 24 was appointed commanding officer of the 147th Aero Squadron, a post he held until November 18, 1918. While leading flights of the 147th he gained two more victories and was made a major. Jimmy flew through the bulk of America's air action, and turned in a very creditable performance. After the war he went into business in Birmingham, Alabama, and while there organized the Alabama National Guard.

Meissner is perhaps best remembered for his near accidents while flying Nieuports. When acting as escort for a photography machine he was attacked by two Albatros fighters, and he went into a quick zoom hoping to get above them. He was successful, for the two fighters continued their attack dives and Meissner went down after them. He fired long bursts at one Hun, so the pilot immediately went into a spinning nose dive. It was an old trick, and Jimmy thought his adversary was playing "possum." He gave his engine throttle and increased the speed of his dive, and managed to get in a burst that set the Albatros on fire. It was his first victory for the 94th.

But Jimmy was dangerously low, and the enemy back area could be plainly seen, so he pulled out fast, but, to his consternation, saw the fabric of the upper side of his left wing strip away. He was spellbound for a second or so, and then realized he had a very serious situation with which to cope. He eased out more, and then cut back on his speed, hoping to keep the aircraft together, but once he had crossed into Allied territory, he put the Nieuport down on the first open stretch he spotted. The machine rumbled through a number of shell holes and was cracked up beyond repair.

A short time later when Meissner had become a flight leader he experienced this Nieuport wing-stripping frailty again, but this time he managed to keep her flying, and brought her safely back to his field.

WILLIAM MITCHELL

The career of Brigadier General William Mitchell is more than a record of an American military hero. His life presents a lesson for the people of our nation, and offers high adventure, leadership, heroism, and great attainment. Although he came from a family of wealth and social standing, Billy Mitchell possibly was the most democratic figure in modern military history. What rank he attained, he earned in the field. He combined leadership with personal example to an extent no present-day hero has attained. He asked for and received no favors. He was awarded many decorations for valor, and his courage was recognized by our Allies, as well as by our own government. Nevertheless, Billy Mitchell is one of the "unknowns" of United States history. The general public vaguely remembers that Billy Mitchell was a military firebrand who was court-martialed for his outspoken criticism of military aviation. Few have any idea what he did, where he came from, or how he ended his fabulous, but tragic career.

Billy Mitchell, one of America's greatest patriots, was born in 1879 in, of all places, Nice, France. His parents were relaxing on the French Riviera at the time and stayed in France for the next three years. When they returned to the United States their son spoke better French than English. In fact, by the time he was ready for school his playmates were calling him "Froggie," a nickname that so irritated him, he refused to speak a word of French for many years.

The Mitchell home in the United States was spread over acres of fine Wisconsin ground. There were ponies to ride, cows to be cared for, barnyard fowls to feed and pet. The place had a pond on which Billy and his brothers played many games, from high-seas pirates to jungle explorers. They sailed rickety rafts, fished from leaky rowboats, and fought from war canoes that were built to capsize.

In 1898, ignoring the advantages of his birth, Billy, then nineteen, enlisted as a private in the 1st Wisconsin Infantry, chiefly to get into the promised action of the Spanish-American War. He saw little of the contest, but did learn a great deal of the new means of communication—telegraphy. This skill earned him a commission in the old Signal Corps, and in turn took him to the Philippines and across Alaska.

In 1907 an Aeronautical Division was organized within the Signal Corps, but Mitchell, now a married man, was ineligible for flight training. He, however, believed in the modernization of the U. S. Army, and eventually paid for and took flight training at the Curtiss School at Newport News, Virginia. The cost—$1470—included thirty-six instruction flights and twenty-five hours of flying time.

Between 1914 and 1916 the war in Europe had introduced the armored tank, poison gas, flame throwers, the submarine—and the modern fighting aircraft. But even as late as the spring of 1917 the United States had none of these modern items of warfare. Mitchell, who had made a survey of American aviation needs, soon found himself the chief spokesman for the Aviation Service, and in that role secured an assignment from the War Department to go to Europe as a military observer. A week after he had landed, the United States entered the conflict, and once he was able to make his way to the war zone, Mitchell was astonished to find that air power had passed through its embryo stage and become a full-fledged military arm.

This was not a period of "crates" and ragtime pilots flying Curtiss Jennies. In early 1917 the aircraft were beautifully built machines, powered with the finest available engines. They were equipped with modern armament, machine guns, bomb racks, and camera fittings; all tremendous improvements over the equipment used at the start of the war in August 1914. Billy Mitchell could not believe what he saw. There were airplanes he had not dreamed of, and missions were being carried out that seemed fantastic to his eyes. His limited training in no way fitted him to fly any of these warplanes, and he begged French and British pilots to give him instruction, and eventually check him out on their modern equipment. He flew on observation planes as a gunner. He went aloft in kite balloons to carry out artillery "shoots" to direct the fire of the ground guns. Week after week, he raced from one battle front to another, regardless of the risk, so as to absorb as much campaign knowledge as possible.

For his willingness to share their many hazards, the French awarded him the Croix de Guerre.

❄

World War I had been stalemated for three years. Neither side could claim any outstanding victory. Month after month grim losses and setbacks had been the rule. Mitchell sought the reason for this state of affairs, often consulting high ranking officials who also had searched for the evasive solution.

The front was a muddy tracing of irregular lines. The front and rear zones were marked by the white festers of shellfire. The zigzagging lines were the communication trenches through which men relieved other men every few days. It was the pattern of trench warfare, and in those deep slots, crouching from the artillery, mortar fire, and the choking fumes of poison gas, men had fought and held on for three long, weary years.

The trenches were also marked in another manner. Every few miles, on both sides of the lines, Colonel Mitchell could see large, bulbous, kite balloons swinging from steel cables. Skilled observers in the baskets slung beneath the balloons watched the ground activities of their enemies, and telephoned down the same cable to the men on the ground what they saw. They in turn relayed the information to those most concerned.

But with all the advance in military tactics, the new weapons, and the skill of the men assigned to use them, never before had so many men fought so long for so little success. By now nearly 8,000,-000 men had been killed on both sides, and more than 20,000,000 wounded. Seven million more were either missing or prisoners of war.

On every Allied front Mitchell searched for a solution. He was positive trench warfare was not the answer. He had great hope in the airplane, but not in the dogfight at great altitudes. The answer was not in artillery cooperation, or low-level attack. He was beginning to believe that the war could be shortened by mass bombing.

Soon after his arrival in France, Colonel Mitchell had gained the friendship of General Sir Hugh "Boom" Trenchard, former commander-in-chief of the Royal Flying Corps. Like Mitchell, Trenchard was a forthright man with unorthodox views concerning the use of military aircraft; views that were gradually forming in Mitchell's mind. Both men were to experience stormy careers before their lives had run out.

Colonel Mitchell's task was no sinecure. In the first place his ideas were too far advanced for the office-bound staff in the War Department in Washington. Practically all his suggestions or requests were ignored. In fact, while he was working to organize a headquarters in

Paris for the new U. S. Aviation Service, the powers-that-be along the Potomac sent over a complete staff, headed by Brigadier General Benjamin D. Foulois, that moved in and nudged Mitchell out of the spotlight. In order to quell the uproar that followed, General John J. Pershing soon appointed Major General Mason M. Patrick of the Corps of Engineers to head the whole American Air Service. General Foulois was given command of the Service of Supply and Schools in the rear, and Colonel Mitchell, who did not become a brigadier general until 1920, was given charge of all fighting squadrons at the front. This seemed to satisfy all concerned, and Billy went to work to justify America's entry into the war.

Echoing General Trenchard's phrases, Mitchell made his stand: "The airplane is an offensive weapon, not a defensive weapon. Air power, properly organized, will make it possible to attack and to continue to attack, even though the enemy is on the offensive. We have been using the airplane improperly. No number of flying machines can prevent an enemy aircraft from crossing the lines. The sky itself is too large to defend. We must plan military aviation to attack the rear areas of any enemy and destroy all means of supply."

Just before the war ended, Mitchell had gone to Pershing with a most advanced idea of air-infantry cooperation. He was determined to capture Metz, and proposed using sixty squadrons of British Handley-Page bombers, and fill them with one of America's crack infantry divisions. He had no idea where these planes were to come from, but he believed Boom Trenchard would get them for him.

Inspired by Trenchard's views, Mitchell had actually gathered a force of 1500 Allied aircraft that he used in mass strikes during the battle for the Saint-Mihiel salient, and in the Meuse-Argonne offensive he sent more than six hundred American aircraft into the attack. Great bombers, escorted by fighters, flew deep into enemy territory, broke supply lines, entangled transport, and cut important communications. Some losses were suffered, but heavy critical damage had been inflicted.

Meanwhile in London, Trenchard had convinced the War Office that some form of independent aviation should be established, a force designed to attack important industrial cities deep inside Germany to hamper their manufacturing potential. Oddly enough, the greatest opposition to the plan came from British humanitarians. Although they had suffered for years from bombings by German Zeppelins and Gothas, they refused to condone the bombing of German cities. Trenchard won out in the end and in May 1918 was sent back to France to organize the Independent Air Force.

Billy Mitchell had also put on a show, despite heavy opposition from various quarters. By November 11, 1918, there were 740 American-flown aircraft at the front, or about 10 percent of the total aircraft strength of the Allies. Our bombers had carried out 150 separate bombing attacks in which 138 tons of bombs had been dropped. Some of our airmen had penetrated as far as 160 miles behind the enemy lines. American losses in combat amounted to 289 planes and 48 balloons, and of this number 57 were aircraft piloted by American officers who flew with the British, French, and Italians. American pilots claimed 781 enemy planes and 73 kite balloons shot down. Mitchell's fighter squadrons boasted of 71 pilots who qualified as aces, and this gallant company shot down 450 aircraft and 50 kite balloons.

PAUL H. NEIBLING

Paul H. Neibling was awarded the Distinguished Service Cross for downing a Fokker fighter. "So what?" one may inquire. A D.S.C. just for shooting down one Hun? There were many airmen in World War I who were credited with half a dozen Jerries, but not all of them were decorated for their successes.

But the interesting feature concerning the award is that the Fokker in question was shot down by a balloon observer who used only a Colt's automatic pistol. It is one of the most intriguing stories to come out of that war, and whether or not one believes it, the fact remains that Lieutenant Paul Neibling was decorated for such a feat.

According to his own report he started out as a second lieutenant with the 1st Minnesota Field Artillery on the Mexican Border, but by the time the United States had switched from Pancho Villa to Kaiser Wilhelm, Paul had reached the rank of first lieutenant and was finishing training at Camp Mills as a member of the renowned 42nd (Rainbow) Division.

One morning his CO stomped into a gathering of young officers and asked why no one had volunteered for training in kite-balloon observation. It seems that the French had made such an appeal for American officers to undertake this "interesting" work.

So, for no especial reason, except that perhaps he was bored with the dreary routine of training, Paul put his name down—and promptly forgot the incident. A month later he sailed with the 42nd aboard the SS *President Lincoln* and subsequently arrived at Coetquidan, France. There was another spell of training that was broken up by an unexpected order to report to the training depot of the French Balloon Corps. The next day he reported to the 73rd Balloon Company located at Maix in the Lunéville sector. By this time some reservations had set in. Paul was certain there were hundreds of AEF men better fitted for kite ballooning than he, but all that was forgotten during the next week or so when he was taught to plot distances from the air, give instructions to artillery batteries, and keep a balloon log of what was going on in the German area ahead.

He received no particular instruction in how to pack a parachute, or what to do should he need to use one. He was simply told that if things "got hot" to go over the side and drag the parachute with him. Everything would be all right; or so he was told. He did make an effort to find out more about this life-saving device but was put off with the explanation that all that would be taken care of when he went up to the front. It seems there was still another move to be made—one much closer to the scene of action.

On his arrival at the new base he again probed for some details on parachute jumping, and this time was given a complete demonstration on how to pack the folds of silk into the leather cone that held it. The instructor did not make a demonstration jump to give his pupils the required confidence. He just sent the balloon up, and when it had reached about 1800 feet another instructor shoved a large sandbag filled with 200 pounds of sand over the side. It was strapped into the parachute harness.

"Now watch," the French instructor explained. "You will see the sandbag carried safely to earth. It is a marvelous invention!"

Paul Neibling leaned back against the balloon winch, lit a cigarette, and watched the proceedings. The sandbag went over the side with no trouble. It yanked on the harness and shroud lines, and the silken canopy finally came out of the leather cone.

"It's a great invention," Lieutenant Neibling agreed.

But as the sandbag tumbled clear, nothing else happened. It simply fell in a beautiful straight line, hundreds of feet per second. The harness was properly buckled, and the shroud lines glistened in the sunlight, but the silken canopy failed to open. That is, it didn't until the sandbag was about 500 feet from the ground. It opened eventually, and it was a beautiful canopy, but the sandbag hit with a thump, burst its seams and threw sand high into the air.

One of the American volunteers walked back to his cubicle and scribbled out a request for a transfer back to the Rainbow Division.

The next day Lieutenant Neibling was shunted to a front-line balloon company hidden behind Brouville opposite a large German rear area. He was advised that this was a comparatively quiet front and there would be time to put all his training into action with little, if any hindrance.

It was quiet—for about fifteen minutes. Paul went to his quarters, hung up his gear, and walked outside to stare at the balloon sent up to watch the German rest area.

"Boche! Boche!" someone yelled as a Fokker fighter came down out of nowhere. The winch began to scream, and the drum twirled in its effort to haul the bag down to its shelter bed, but not in time. A stream of incendiary bullets torched the bag and it fell blazing to earth. The two observers aboard it went out of the basket head first, and this time their canopies opened quickly, and they dangled there for minutes, prime targets for the intruder. The Hun pilot ignored them, however, and instead sprayed the whole camp with Spandau fire to warn the newcomers this area wasn't as quiet as had been stated.

Lieutenant Neibling frankly wished he was back at Camp Mills teaching rookie artillerymen how to fire a French Seventy-five. In fact he would have settled for a nice muddy gun pit somewhere in the Argonne sector. He had even better ideas the next morning when he learned that he was posted for his first active-service balloon show.

In the next few weeks Paul did routine observing with nothing untoward happening. The weather was generally good, and he picked up considerable experience directing planned barrages on enemy strong points, harrying marching troops and moving transport. During this time he was never forced to jump, or had a balloon burned over his head, but by September 1918 the weather deteriorated and the clouds and murk gave the enemy better opportunity to move in close and attack before being properly identified.

On September 2 Paul was up alone with low-hanging clouds pressing in on all sides. Visibility was very poor, there was little chance of working any reliable "shoots," and he spent most of the time flapping his arms to keep warm. Then just as he was resenting this waste of time he heard the roar of an airplane engine, and as he pondered the situation two German planes came up through the cloud layer, and turned quickly to put several long bursts into the gasbag.

Lieutenant Neibling wasted no time. He went over the side of the basket at once. By the time he was clear and the 'chute had opened he saw that the balloon was already on fire. As he settled in his harness he remembered a small vest-pocket camera he had brought out with him, and with commendable coolness took three quick snapshots of the enemy planes as they continued to fire in his direction. Satisfied with that accomplishment, he then decided to use his Colt's .45, blazing off several shots at one of the attacking planes.

Apparently nothing happened, but during that mild offensive the camera slipped out of his pocket and fell to the ground. When he landed the instrument was found, and the three pictures on the film proved later to be of excellent detail, but as so often happened, the prints were stolen and never recovered.

Two days later Neibling, along with eight other American balloon observers, was sent to operate near Fort du Marre at Verdun to act as eyes for the Meuse-Argonne drive.

Twenty-two days later, September 26, 1918, Lieutenant Paul Neibling and Lieutenant C. Carroll of Garrett, Indiana, were ordered to direct artillery fire on Sivry-sur-Meuse. They first went aloft at 3:30 A.M., and continued routine work for most of that day. At 2:30 that afternoon they both spotted a plane approaching from the enemy side of the line. It was dodging Archie fire and antiaircraft defense, and as it approached Neibling identified it as a Pfalz. By that time there was no mistaking its goal and intent.

The German pilot selected a balloon somewhat to the left of the one manned by Neibling and Carroll, and after one long burst of incendiaries that bag went up in flames and the two observers jumped clear and floated safely to the ground. Inspired by this first "kill" the enemy pilot selected a second, and the incendiary storm made two more American observers take to the silk. Then, as the enemy seemed to be considering Neibling's and Carroll's basket, an American Spad swept into the picture and for a few minutes the two machines staged a classic air fight, but neither one suffered any real injury, and finally, obviously short of fuel, the Pfalz put its nose down and roared for home.

One hour later, after a long and anxious study of the area ahead, a Fokker pilot turned up and began a number of menacing moves. First he warmed his guns, and the two lieutenants could see his tracers sparkling across the sky. Then he nosed around and headed for their balloon. As the two observers crouched in the basket they could see the spatter of incendiaries racing toward them.

"Go ahead, jump!" Neibling ordered Carroll who was his junior.

Lieutenant Carroll wasted no time, and went tumbling away as lighthearted as a kid bouncing on a feather bed.

Neibling watched the proceedings and waited to see if the bag would catch fire. The Hun circled and zipped off short bursts whenever he could get his nose on the target. Neibling climbed outside the basket and hung there with one arm, and once when the Fokker pilot came in dangerously close, he triggered several shots from his automatic pistol. The pilot nosed up sharply and tried to put another burst into the bag, and with that Neibling let go and floated earthward. The balloon above him burst into flames.

The Fokker then turned away, and as there was no Allied plane in sight, it made the most of its field day by going after a fourth balloon. Meanwhile Neibling was still floating slowly to the ground, angry, frustrated, and wondering how long this Fokker clown would stay in this area. Then he saw his enemy turn back toward him, and another burst of tracer zipped across the sky. Two of Neibling's shroud lines were clipped and air began to spill from the section of the canopy that was left fluttering. Neibling slipped to one side as the Fokker approached to pass by as close as possible.

Again Neibling drew his Colt's and blazed at the Fokker. "He was so close to me I could have touched him with a fish pole. I simply had to let him have it."

Actually, while hanging in his parachute harness, Neibling pumped five shots at the passing Fokker, and, as in all good air stories, his gun jammed and while he struggled with the mechanism he watched the German, knowing he might turn back and finish him. But the enemy plane began to stagger about the sky. Gradually the nose went down, and with the engine full on the plane started a wild, tight spin until at last, to Neibling's amazement, it nosed in at full speed. The engine went in deep enough to bury the pilot and what was left of the D-VII.

The impact was such it was impossible to learn what had actually put an end to the Fokker's four-balloon triumph. Neibling never made a claim for the kill, but to the groundlings his Colt's was the only weapon in the area that challenged the German, and it was admitted generally that in this particular instance an attacking airplane had been shot down by a balloon observer using only a Colt's .45.

It is unfortunate that in Neibling's report, and in stories of his experience published later, the name of the Fokker pilot has not been disclosed.

EDWIN C. PARSONS

Ted Parsons, as he was known to his associates, came from Holyoke, Massachusetts, and was probably the most colorful figure in the Lafayette Escadrille in that he not only ranked with the most successful fighter pilots of his day, but was a most striking figure in uniform. He served from 1915 until the close of the war. During World War II Ted elected to join the United States Navy, and finished his career as a rear admiral.

Born on September 24, 1892, he was educated in the public schools of Springfield, Massachusetts, and at Phillips Exeter Academy, and put in two years at the University of Pennsylvania. Unlike most of the American volunteers Ted was not a great athlete, nor was he an outstanding physical specimen. As a schoolboy he smoked like a tar factory and his respiratory system bewildered examining medicos. There were times when he was color-blind; he was always plagued with enlarged tonsils, and one eyelid tended to droop producing a piratical leer.

"If ever I had tried to get into the U. S. Aviation in those days I would have been booted out on my ear," Ted once explained. However, after wangling his way past the French medical authorities, he eventually learned to fly and joined the Lafayette Escadrille on January 25, 1917. He flew in the dreariest pair of breeches, a ragged mackinaw jacket, and an outmoded crash helmet provided by some amused Britisher. Since this leather monstrosity was decorated with a Death's Head Hussar insignia, it gave him a terrifying aspect. On the ground he was a fashion plate, a veritable Scarlet Pimpernel, wearing a smart kepi, an Ascot stock, a neat French tunic, snappy breeches, and glossy field boots. When he displayed all his decorations—the Médaille Militaire, the Croix de Guerre with eight Palms, and the Croix de Leopold, topped off with a natty *fourragère,* he would have stopped General Billy Mitchell in his tracks. Just a few years ago, the French decided to complete his outfit by belatedly awarding him the Legion of Honor.

Ted Parsons contributed more than his share to the cause, not only fighting long and well, but proving to be a lively historian. His book *The Great Adventure,* written in 1937, is one of the more engrossing volumes on the history of the Lafayette. It has recently been reissued under the title *I Flew with the Lafayette Escadrille.*

Despite his many infirmities, Ted sought adventure early in his life. Leaving the University of Pennsylvania in 1912 he bought flying lessons at Dominguez Field in California, and with that skill in hand took a captain's commission in the Mexican Aviation Corps. From various sources, it is apparent that he may have led his aerial armada against General Obregón's legions, but Ted has wisely kept his counsel on this facet of his career.

Once that musical-comedy campaign came to an end, Ted returned to Massachusetts where he learned there was a much better war going on in Europe. This was a real production with men flying real airplanes, shooting machine guns, and a lot of people were being killed or wounded. Ignoring the fact that he was a physical wreck, he decided to look into this campaign, and as a first test of his frailties, he thought he would become an ambulance driver. He tried to borrow passage money from his father, but Dad Parsons was too wily a bird to waste money in that manner, so Ted had to work his way over on a cattle boat. The author took the same pungent route to the war.

Once in Paris, Ted joined the American Field Service where he built up his muscle and brawn to a point where he was able to command a complete ambulance section, and served with Mrs. Whitney Warren's hospital near Juilly behind the Soissons front. With this behind him, Ted next wangled his way into the French Aviation and was set for a three-year stint as a flying man.

The United States entered the war in April 1917, and by the following September some moves were being made to entice the Americans serving with French squadrons to transfer to the U. S. Aviation Service. Billy Mitchell was all for it, and Dr. Gros was prodding U. S. Army men in Paris to show some initiative, but matters moved with dreary uncertainty. Days became weeks, weeks ran into months. Then it was Christmas 1917, and still no activity by any American squadrons. Ted Parsons wrote:

"Just when we were on the point of believing we would never hear from the American brass hats, the U. S. Army finally sent out another delegation of top rankers to make an examination of the Lafayette Escadrille pilots.

"After comprehensive physical examinations, which, much to the dismay of some of the boys, included urinalysis and blood tests, we were put through a long series of ridiculous physical demonstrations which weren't helped by frequent visits to the bar to bolster our courage.

"Then the awful truth came out.

"In solemn owlish conclave the board decided that not one of us, despite hundreds of hours in the air, many of us aces, all thoroughly trained war pilots with many victories to our credit, could ever be an aviator. Their tests showed definitely that physically, mentally, and morally we were unfit to be pilots. It was truly pathetic.

"Dud Hill had one blind eye. Bill Thaw's vision was hopeless and he had a crippled arm. Raoul Lufbery couldn't walk a crack backwards. Dolan's tonsils were past all redemption. Hank Jones had flat feet! All this was revealed in the light of pitiless publicity. We were simply a broken-down crew of crippled misfits. There was hardly a man on whom they didn't have to ask waivers.

"However, while we were waiting to hear the outcome of these tragic examinations, and while Paris was filled with American aviators and YMCA men—with the bars, theaters, and night spots doing a capacity business—the Escadrille continued to carry on with the war. It was the only American outfit on active service, but, of course, not allowed to wear the uniform of its own country. At the same time the Lafayette was again cited by the appreciative French who allowed us as members of a twice-cited organization to wear the fourragère in the colors of the Croix de Guerre. It was the second escadrille in the French Army to be so honored; the only one preceding being Escadrille Spad 3, commanded by the famous and beloved ace, Captain Georges Guynemer."

Ted Parsons gave up, and between November 1917 and January 1918, he took leave to go home. On his return to France he elected to stay with his French comrades. Actually, he hoped to organize a new Lafayette Escadrille, but this was not possible, so Ted was posted to Spad 3 of the famous Storks Group, and while serving with them downed seven more planes making his final score eight. He rose to rank of *sous-lieutenant,* and preserved the splendid spirit of affection that had been revived by the American volunteers.

PAUL PAVELKA

Another colorful, if tragic, figure among American fighting airmen was Paul Pavelka of Madison, Connecticut, a man who ran up an amazing career until he died from injuries received while attempting to ride a savage horse. Unlike most of the other American volunteers, Paul was brought up on a farm, but left home at the age of fourteen after some differences of opinion with his stepmother. He had little formal education and during his teens he worked as a cook in a sheep camp, as a cowboy, as a male nurse in a hospital in San Francisco, and finally became a seaman, visiting ports all over the world.

When the war broke out Paul was living in a seaman's home in New York City from where he made an effort to join one of the Allied armies. He first accepted an offer of a British recruiter who took a number of volunteers to Halifax, Nova Scotia, from where, it was pointed out, they might work their way over to England by feeding and watering horses intended for the British Army.

I can vouch for this arrangement, having also worked my way over, possibly on the same vessel that carried Paul Pavelka. She was the RMS *Etonian* which sailed from Halifax early in October 1914. I first enlisted in the British Army, later transferring to the Royal Flying Corps, but Paul appears to have joined one of the most mystifying organizations to emerge from that conflict. It was known as the Army of the South American Republic of Counani, a fictitious government invented to arrange the transfer of a number of these volunteers across to France. Paul enlisted in the Foreign Legion at La Rochelle on November 28, 1914, and served with distinction until October 19, 1915, when he was wounded during an attack on German positions north of Arras. It was Paul who in fact had given Kiffin Rockwell first aid when he had been wounded five weeks before. Paul's wound was received during a bayonet attack at Givenchy-en-Gohelle.

Although still limping, Paul applied for transfer to the French Aviation and was accepted in October 1915. He completed his training by August of the next year and joined the Lafayette Escadrille when it had settled down on the Verdun front. One of his first experiences on patrol was almost his last. While flying a Nieuport his engine caught fire, and he had to retain complete calm and make a series of falling-leaf sideslips to keep the flames away from his cockpit. He managed to keep the aircraft together in this manner, and finally pancaked safely in a swamp.

Paul who seemed to have "cat's eyes" showed great skill as a night flier. He always was willing to take off after dark whenever enemy bombers came over during the shelter of night. On the evening of December 9, 1916, German planes sneaked over and dropped eight bombs on the Cachy field to which the Escadrille had been transferred. One of the bombs scored a direct hit on a hangar of Number 3 Squadron of the Storks, inflicting considerable damage.

Noting that the enemy planes were still circling to see the effect of their bombs, Paul took off. Once above the ground he realized he had no navigation or cockpit lights, possibly owing to defective wiring. Instead of returning, he continued on as Allied ground guns, as well as the enemy bombers, fired at him because he had no navigation or signal lights.

Boring into a light cloud layer he finally evaded the explosives and shrapnel and went looking for the bombers. They were up there somewhere but it was difficult to spot them in the glare of the rockets, searchlights, and explosions of antiaircraft shells. After a few minutes of this Paul saw he was on a hopeless quest, so he headed for Amiens on the assumption other raiders might be there. German airmen seemed to strike at Allied hospitals in that area.

Paul found the city in complete darkness and no bombers in sight. As he gained night sight he realized he was in a ticklish situation. There were no lights to identify friendly areas, and he had none with which to identify himself. He cruised about, hoping for an early dawn, but as soon as he glided down anywhere near the ground Allied guns opened up to drive him away. The gunners evidently could not identify his plane or the familiar sound of his Le Rhône engine.

Paul knew he had just so much fuel, and the dawn seemed hours away. He sought a familiar area but could not tell flat land from plowed fields, shelled sectors, or even woods. He reset his air valve and slowed down his engine so it was just ticking over, and managed to cling to his safety altitude. Time went by and there was little promise of the dawn's early light. Finally the engine conked out for good, and there was nothing to do but take a long, wild chance and go down. Fortunately he was rewarded with a minute or two of visibility, and he put the Nieuport down inside the British lines at a place called Martainville. No sooner had his wheels stopped rolling than a bank of fog rolled in shrouding everything. Some British officers took him in at a nearby château where he had to stay for four days.

During the rest of his service with the Lafayette, Paul Pavelka became so fascinated with night flying, he made twenty or more such flights, contributing much to the new art. A short while later a call was made for volunteers to serve on the Salonika front in Greece, and Paul offered to go, arriving there in February 1917. He seems to have enjoyed himself doing scout flying aboard the Nieuport, and carrying out many artillery shoots while flying an Italian A.R., a Caudron-like two-seater. He was mentioned in dispatches several times, and awarded the Croix de Guerre.

On November 12, 1917, Paul met an untimely, and unnecessary death. While taking a walk in the Salonika area he met a British cavalry officer whom he had known in the Foreign Legion. He was invited to visit the British regiment for a drink and a meal. During his stay Paul, who was an excellent horseman, asked permission to ride a remount that had just been sent to the regiment. The beast was a vicious devil, and did its best to unseat Paul. Failing in that, it suddenly reared up and rolled over on its back, crushing its rider beneath it. Pavelka's neck was broken in the mishap, and he died a few hours later.

DAVID McKELVEY PETERSON

Another Lafayette volunteer, who was to contribute much to Billy Mitchell's American Air Service, was David McKelvey Peterson of Honesdale, Pennsylvania. Dave had a memorable characteristic that endeared him to many of his comrades. Unquestionably he was the world's most toneless and tuneless whistler. From the day he signed up in Paris until the bugles rang out signaling the Armistice he trilled what he sincerely believed was *The Girl I Left Behind Me*. His friends thought he was tootling *Onward, Christian Soldiers*.

Peterson started off with a fine family background. One uncle was a general in the United States Army, but Dave was far from the accepted professional soldier. In fact, he was another Dudley Hill who found no thrill in his adventures. No event of the Great War elated, depressed, or frightened him, and perhaps because of this immunity to excitement he lived to see the end of the conflict. Unfortunately, he was killed in a postwar flying accident at Daytona Beach, Florida, on March 16, 1919.

In the late summer of 1916 Dave made his way across the Atlantic and enlisted in the French Aviation on October 9 of that year. He had completed his training by April 16, 1917, and joined the Lafayette Escadrille, along with James Hall and Douglas MacMonagle.

Dave served with the Escadrille and was soon selected as a regular patrol leader by Bill Thaw and Captain Thénault. In truth, the records show that Dave led more patrols than any other member of the Lafayette; always alert, always in control of the situation, and always retaining the confidence of his comrades. He was a smart fighting pilot who usually spotted Huns or trouble long before any of the others knew what was going on. He concentrated on anything that belonged to the enemy; trains, transport, kite balloons, enemy aircraft, or concentrations of troops. But he usually completed his patrol report with the French cliché, *Rien à signaler*—Nothing to report.

Pete, as he was called by his pals, had a worthwhile hobby. He was a fair amateur carpenter, and made his cubicle as snug and comfortable as any on the field. He put up shelves, built a decent washstand, nailed a table together, and scrounged material for comfortable chairs. So his room became the unofficial headquarters of the squadron.

When the American volunteers were finally taken over by the U. S. Air Service, Peterson was immediately commissioned a captain, and served at various times with the 103rd, 94th, and 95th Pursuit Squadrons. He was promoted to major on August 29, 1918, and by October 8, 1918, was sent back to the United States to take on an executive position. By the end of his wartime flying Dave had racked up five enemy aircraft and been awarded the Distinguished Service Cross with a Bronze Oak Leaf, and the Croix de Guerre.

NORMAN PRINCE

Norman Prince of Prides Crossing, Massachusetts, unquestionably was the first to conceive the idea of forming a squadron of American volunteers to fly with the French. The scion of a distinguished New England family, he had traveled widely, and before the war had spent several hunting seasons at Pau in the Basses-Pyrénées. During these holidays he had made many friends and spoke the language fluently.

Norman was a small, compact man with powerful shoulders. His hair was blond and his blue eyes were far from the 20/20 standard, but like so many of his ilk he felt compelled to offer his services, having grown to love France and her people. He did not take up the cause via the American Field Service or the Foreign Legion. He had felt the lure of aviation from the hour the guns began to boom. For a few days he dallied with the idea of volunteering for French Aviation, but on consideration, he decided first to become a pilot, and then offer his services.

He returned to the United States and entered the Burgess Flying School at Marblehead, Massachusetts, where he met Frazier Curtis, a thirty-year-old enthusiast who also had ideas of doing something in the war. But Curtis did not speak French, so decided it would be better to volunteer with the British.

Both men completed their training on hydroplanes and were fairly proficient—as civilian fliers. By that time Curtis had made a bid to join the British Army, but gave that up when he learned that by joining this particular foreign force, he would lose his American citizenship, although Americans who joined the French were not so penalized. Perhaps it was a matter of interpretation of the international nomenclature. At any rate Curtis decided not to risk his national status, and went to Paris to see what could be done there.

By March 1915 Norman Prince had enlisted in the French Air Service and then had to hang around for nearly five weeks awaiting an opening at the Pau flying school. During that time he and Curtis worked mightily to bring their plan of an American squadron to fruition. They sought the aid of several Americans who were living in Paris, and won the interest of some French military officials, but real progress was slow, and then when everyone was ready to give up the idea Norman Prince, Frazier Curtis, Elliot Cowdin, William Thaw, Bert Hall, and James Bach were accepted for the international experiment.

Curtis trained with the volunteers at Pau and Avord, but he was plagued by accidents. One time his plane caught fire at 2000 feet, but he managed to get down without too severe an injury. On another occasion, while making a routine landing, his undercarriage collapsed sending him to a hospital for a week. Following this Frazier was given forty-five days' sick leave, and when this time was up, he asked to be assigned to a fighting squadron. Instead, he was given an honorable discharge, the French authorities explaining that he was unfit for further flying duty. After four months' rest in England, Curtis returned to his homeland and organized the Harvard Flying School, but again his health broke down and he had to go to California to recuperate.

In the meantime, Norman Prince's older brother Frederick had caught the volunteer bug and put in a bid for acceptance by the French Aviation. By January 1916 he too joined the new American squadron that was to become the Lafayette Escadrille, but he remained for only a few months. He then served for a time as an instructor at Pau and eventually had a desk job with the U. S. Quartermaster Corps, holding several such positions until the close of the war.

Norman became a devoted airman, and despite his poor eyesight proved to be a good performer, and was soon promoted to sergeant. Some records state that he downed five enemy planes, but the Lafayette historian credits him with only three.

On October 12, 1916, French-British officials decided to bomb the German Mauser arms plant at Oberndorf about one hundred and fifty miles inside the enemy lines. Some eighty bombers were assigned to the mission, most of them Royal Naval Air Service Sopwith 1½-Strutters—a name indicating the splayed center-section struts that appeared to be composed of one and one-half struts, the inner short, the outer long. These machines were also the first to be fitted with trailing-edge flaps, and when flown solo could carry four 100-pound bombs. The French contributed a number of Bréguets and Farmans to this mission.

The available scouts of that period could stay in the air for only about two hours, and so could not accompany the bombers all the way to the target. As a general rule, they did the next best thing. They covered them as far as possible, turned back at the last moment, and refueled at an emergency field at Corcieux in the Vosges. Then, timing their take-offs so they could pick up the returning bombers as soon as possible, they furnished escort cover over the rest of the journey home. Needless to say, this kind of cooperation demanded courage, devotion to the cause, and accurate timing if it was to be executed successfully.

The American squadron could provide only four machines and pilots so the most experienced airmen were selected; Lieutenant de Laage, the French liaison pilot, Raoul Lufbery, Didier Masson, and Norman Prince. The raid itself was more successful than had been hoped, since the Germans were caught unaware, and the important arms factory was damaged considerably. Of course, there were several versions of the results. The Germans claimed that no bombs were dropped on the works. Neutral visitors declared that two complete plants were destroyed and that the officials had put a high fence all around the works' area. The Germans said that dozens of Allied planes were shot down with no loss to the defending airmen. Actually, the cost was 27 percent of the bomber formation, mostly Farmans and Bréguets. It was believed generally that the Mauser plant had suffered widespread and severe damage.

No real opposition was met on the way to Oberndorf, and all fighters returned to their refueling fields. The bombers found their targets with no trouble, and reported that a good pattern was delivered. Then, so as to evade any enemy aircraft sent up to intercept them, they took a circuitous route home, and were a long time in making contact with the escort planes. It seemed hours before the Nieuport pilots could find the bombers, and when they did, they appeared just in time to engage a formation of determined Fokkers that were bent on beating them down. The result was a wild melee staged in light that was fast fading. It was difficult to distinguish friend from foe, but in one of these tangles Norman Prince shot down a Fokker.

Once the bombers had been escorted across their own lines, the N.124 pilots broke off and made for the same emergency field that had furnished the additional fuel and ammunition. While making his approach to this unfamiliar strip, Norman Prince must have become confused in the uncertain light, for as he circled and S-turned for his final glide-in that carried him over a small patch of woods, he failed to notice a high-tension cable stretched just over the tree tops. The wheels of his landing gear caught the trip wire, and the Nieuport was snubbed so it nosed down and hit hard. The aircraft rolled itself into a ball, and the safety belt that might have saved Norman broke as the plane hit. He was somersaulted from the cockpit.

The shock of the double impact multiplied Norman's injuries. He suffered two broken legs, and had serious internal injuries, but despite his agony he made a brave effort to make sure no one else made the same mistake. When ground crewmen rushed up to help him, he waved them away, and gasped, "Light some gasoline to make a flare. We don't want anyone else to hit that cable."

Lufbery who had landed a few minutes before, hurried over to console his friend. "Don't worry, Norman. You're going to be all right," he said cheerfully. "We'll get you to a hospital fast. A good night's rest . . ."

But Prince was critically hurt, and although the best skill and care were provided, there was no hope. Captain Happe, who had been in command of the bombers, took a group of Lafayette Escadrille pilots to see him, and Prince was promoted to second lieutenant as he lay in bed. Later, he was awarded the Legion of Honor, but he knew nothing of all this. He died three days later. In May 1937 the remains of Norman Prince were brought back to the United States and entombed in a memorial chapel in the National Cathedral, Washington, D.C.

DAVID E. PUTNAM

According to those who knew him, David E. Putnam from Brookline, Massachusetts, was one of the most inspiring figures who represented America in France. A son of Frederick Huntington and Janet (Halowell) Putnam, he was a direct descendant of General Israel Putnam of Revolutionary War fame. He attended Newton High School, and eventually entered Harvard where he became president of his class, and excelled in swimming, football, baseball, and hockey.

From the time he had read of the high-altitude deeds of the aviators along the Western Front, David had wanted to fly and during his freshman year, he took and passed an examination for the U. S. Aviation Service. He was too young to be accepted, so he left Harvard in his sophomore year, worked his passage to Europe on a cattle boat, and made his way into the French Aviation. By December 12, 1917, he was on the front with Spad 94. He was never assigned to the Lafayette Escadrille, but still ranks as one of the most colorful and impetuous members of the group that came to be known as the Lafayette Flying Corps.

Young Putnam did not get over the enemy lines until December 22, but he downed his first Boche on January 19, 1918. On April 11 he endured one of his longest and most dangerous conflicts while fighting four enemy aircraft for more than thirty-five minutes. He downed one of them, and the others withdrew. The next day he engaged what he termed a German "circus"—actually eight enemy planes, and succeeded in destroying two of them. On April 23 three more fell before his guns, and then on June 5, while a member of Spad 38, he roared into what was his greatest battle. He charged into a formation of ten German Albatros fighters, and when he had dispersed them, claimed to have shot down five. Full official confirmation was withheld, however, and Dave's claim was never accepted. He was credited with three; the other two apparently were downed so far over the line it was not possible to check them.

Dave made no complaint, accepted the decision with good grace, but seethed inwardly for boylike he wanted that record of shooting down five enemy planes on one patrol. "You can't shoot them all down in your own backyard," he said in good humor, but never gave up trying to prove his original claim.

Putnam's records were next switched to the U. S. Aviation Service, and on June 10, 1918, he was commissioned a first lieutenant and assigned to the 139th Aero Squadron, and appointed a flight commander.

This responsibility appears to have shackled the spirit and dash he had shown with the French, for he added only one more victory to his score before he was killed on September 12, 1918. There was a new grade of discipline in the United States service, and Putnam seemed to chafe under the restraint. Like so many more, he was an individualist, not a member of a tight team. He could take care of himself, but he was not geared for command.

His last patrol was in company with Lieutenant Wendel A. Robertson, who downed seven enemy planes in the war, and became a colonel in World War II. They were attacked by at least fifteen German aircraft that caught them by surprise. (Another version has it that there were eight enemy planes in the pack.) Putnam shot one of them down in flames before he was himself shot down, and Robertson managed to disengage and get to his own lines.

Another story states that Dave went down with two Fokkers shooting him to pieces, while still another relates that he too disengaged, and then saw an Allied two-seater being attacked by eight Germans, so he roared in to the rescue. The two-seater scuttled clear, but in that melee Dave went down with two bullets through his body. His Spad fell at Limey, and he was buried with full military honors beside Raoul Lufbery near Toul.

These versions of Putnam's last fight show how difficult it is for anyone not involved to trace out the details of any fight in the air. Three pilots engaging the same group of opposition, will have three distinctly different versions of the fight. It was always difficult to get any two to agree on the nunber of enemy planes engaged, who was trying to save whom, or how So-and-so was shot down.

In the final assessment David Putnam was credited with twelve victories, and was awarded America's Distinguished Service Cross, the French Legion of Honor, the Médaille Militaire, and the Croix de Guerre.

EDWARD VERNON RICKENBACKER

Captain Eddie Rickenbacker, as he is still known, would have been the last person to be selected as America's outstanding air ace, or even a candidate for the Air Service. He was twenty-eight years old when he first flew on the Western Front. A sober, mature man, he seemed at times to be out of place among the young daredevils of his squadron. A complete antithesis of Frank Luke, he ran up a victory list that seems incredible when it is remembered that his twenty-six successes were scored in less than two months of front-line action.

As has been pointed out by one British historian, Rick's score for the limited time he spent in action is a record that never has been equaled by any Allied or enemy pilot in either World War I or

World War II. Although many are credited with a greater number of victories, their scores were compiled over many long months of combat. Surprisingly, Eddie never received a scratch in any of his sky battles.

To his great credit, Rickenbacker has never assumed the role of the professional hero, and most historians have had difficulty in presenting his career for popular consumption. He never posed as the two-fisted, intrepid birdman, so popular in postwar fiction.

Daring, but not foolhardy, Captain Eddie fought with the same cool intelligence with which he had handled racing cars on the country's professional speedways. He took over the leadership of the famed 94th (Hat-in-the-Ring) Pursuit Squadron, but never received the majority rank that should have gone with it. The 94th ended the war with the largest number of victories scored by any American squadron—sixty-nine. It was the first American unit to go over the lines, the first to destroy an enemy machine, and the squadron credited with destroying the last German airplane to fall in the campaign. Under Rickenbacker's command the 94th became the greatest fighting squadron the United States sent into the war.

Edward Rickenbacker was born in Columbus, Ohio, October 8, 1890, and grew up with much of the reserve of a Midwestern boyhood and family background. When he was twelve, his father died, and the day after the funeral the youngster's schooling ended. A series of makeshift jobs followed, one of which paid as much as $7.50 a week. During this time Eddie subscribed to an engineering course with the International Correspondence School, and by 1908 was proficient enough to be employed to road-test automobiles for the then famous Frayer-Miller Company. In those days, even more than now, motorcars sold on their reputation for speed with practically every automobile company concentrating on the existing speed marks made in such racing classics as the Indianapolis-500, and the Sheepshead Bay Trophy Race. Rickenbacker drove in three of the Indianapolis contests, and once pushed a Blitzen Benz to a record of 134 miles per hour.

In 1916 Rickenbacker went to Great Britain with the idea of consummating a business suggestion of the Sunbeam Motor Company. Before the outbreak of the war there had been some general talk of Eddie's supervising the makeup of a Sunbeam racing fleet, but by this time the Sunbeam Company had converted to the wartime production of their Arab, Maori, and Cossack engines for aviation and could not consider racing competition abroad. But the trip was not a complete loss, for during his stay in England Rick caught the spirit of the war, and saw some of the activity and training operations of the Royal Flying Corps at Brooklands.

When the United States entered the conflict, Rickenbacker proposed that a special flying squadron composed of American racing drivers be organized at once. The initial plan was turned down, but Army officials suggested that Rick enlist and join General John J. Pershing's staff of drivers. He considered the proposal carefully, and finally decided to accept, using the appointment as a means of getting overseas quickly, and then transferring to the Aviation Service in France, rather than wasting time in the general channels of procedure.

Once in France, however, Eddie found himself shackled by his skill as a driver, and General Pershing's determination to retain this well-trained and most soldierly man. "Look here, Eddie," the general once said. "You are getting on, you know. War flying is for youngsters just out of school. It's not for mature men."

One day Colonel Billy Mitchell, then senior officer of the budding air force, had a motorcar breakdown while on a tour of the front with a Major Armengaud of the French General Staff. Another car carrying Major T. F. Dodd who had been assigned to Pershing's staff as an aviation official, followed and pulled up behind Colonel Mitchell. Dodd's driver hopped out, lifted the hood of the Mercedes and soon located the trouble. Colonel Mitchell was impressed with the man's skill and asked who he was.

"That's Eddie Rickenbacker, one of the Indianapolis drivers. He's been with Pershing's staff for several weeks."

"Seems like a good man," Colonel Mitchell observed.

Eddie naturally made the most of the roadside incident and expressed a desire to get into the Air Service. A short time later Mitchell had persuaded Pershing to relinquish his top driver for aviation pilot training. The decision proved to be most satisfactory for all concerned. In eighteen months Rickenbacker had become America's Ace of Aces.

Because of his racing and repair-pit experience, Eddie was an apt pupil, but since he was an excellent mechanic it was decided that he would make a good chief engineering officer at the Issoudun center. Although this ground job occupied most of his days, Eddie logged flight time on several types of aircraft. He was keenly interested in the planes from an engineering point of view, but hated violent acrobatics in the air, and like so many star pilots, had to force himself to spin and roll the primary trainers of that day, and carry out the required school maneuvers to the satisfaction of his instructors.

Early in March 1918 the tall, slim man from Columbus, Ohio, was posted to the nucleus of the 94th Aero Squadron then based at Villeneuve. The outfit was being formed around Major Raoul Lufbery, but, as explained before, actually under the direct command of Major John Huffer. Other pilots included James Norman Hall, Hamilton Coolidge, James Meissner, Reed Chambers, Douglas Campbell, and Harvey Cook. When Rick joined the 94th the squadron had lots of pilot talent, but no airplanes. In fact, another month passed before a few second-hand Nieuport scouts could be picked up, but once sufficient aircraft were made available, the 94th felt justified in moving up to the Toul sector to begin its great adventure.

＊

Six weeks of front-line flying passed before Rickenbacker scored his first victory. Another month went by before he was again successful. Up to that point he was just another run-of-the-mill war pilot, but a study of his first victory will give some hint of what was to come. Here surprise, and anticipation of the enemy's moves played important roles.

Flying with James Hall, Rick encountered an Albatros over Pont-à-Mousson. He sent Hall up into the sun, and he himself went headlong at the German fighter. Hall took his turn, making the Jerry swing right. Rick anticipated the move and was exactly where he should be and nailed the Albatros cold. The more experienced Hall continued on around and moved in smartly to cover Rick's tail.

Eddie wasn't completely happy with his second triumph. He took off with Reed Chambers, but the two pilots became separated in the clouds. Patrolling Toul, Commercy, and Nancy at 20,000 feet he came upon three Albatros fighters and stalked them, hoping they would cross into Allied territory, but German Ack-Ack pointed him out, so he had to attack over the woods at Mont Sec. He was over-anxious and went in too fast, and when he pulled out, after downing one of the enemy planes, he lost a lot of his upper wing covering and was lucky to make his own lines.

Rick's third victim provided unexpected drama. Along with Reed

Chambers he had agreed to take a newcomer, a Lieutenant Kurtz, on a general acquaintance patrol. Kurtz was slated to become an armament specialist.

They encountered three Albatros scouts over the line, which attacked them immediately, but the Nieuports evaded them, turned the tables, and chased them deep into their own territory. Over Thiaucourt Rick met one that was making a climbing turn and firing wildly. With a quick half-turn Rick got on his enemy's tail and shot him down. The anxiety and excitement of this engagement may have been too much for Lieutenant Kurtz. On the way home he appeared to lose control of his plane, and may have fainted in the air. Unable to help, Captain Rickenbacker had to watch his companion crash after which the Nieuport burst into flames.

On May 30, 1918, Rickenbacker became an ace, and shortly after the 94th turned in their Nieuports for the more rugged French Spad. Once he was well acquainted with the new mount, Rick was made a flight commander. Shortly after he caught a cold that resulted in a serious ear infection that kept him grounded much of the time until September 14, a period of more than fifteen weeks. It was believed he would never fly again.

By June 27 the First Pursuit Group was gathered together at a field twenty-five miles south of Château-Thierry. Rick tried to get back into action, but after leading his flight a few times he had to go to Paris for further treatment. Then, during the Saint-Mihiel drive in September Rick got back into his stride despite inclement weather. Late in that month he downed his ninth and tenth victims. Never a spectacular performer, he nevertheless continued to raise his score. His methods were calm, his attacks carefully planned, and many of his "kills" came after long periods of crafty strategy. He made few mistakes, and never made the same one twice.

Eddie Rickenbacker returned from the war a national hero, but a very humble man, and the spirituality he had gained in World War I stood him in good stead twenty-four years later when he was bobbing about in a rubber raft in the wide Pacific for twenty-one harrowing days.

As did so many others, Rickenbacker found peacetime a difficult period. He was America's Ace of Aces. He had a number of worthy decorations, and a social status many notches above what he had known previously.

What does a man do when his war-hero world topples about him? Rickenbacker took it calmly and went back into the automobile business. Wise money decided to capitalize on his name and background, and a company was formed to manufacture a Rickenbacker car. It was a splendid vehicle but was offered to the public at an unfavorable time, and Rick found himself head of a bankrupt firm.

He joined Tony Fokker who was trying to establish himself in the United States, and some of their early transports gave America a big lead in the aviation field. Whatever contribution Rickenbacker made was soon recognized in the industry and he was taken into the infant Eastern Air Lines. Today that company is a monument to America's greatest air hero, one of the few of his era who made good in postwar aviation. On November 6, 1930, twelve years after the close of hostilities Captain Eddie was presented with the Congressional Medal of Honor by President Herbert Hoover at Bolling Field, Washington, D.C.

And thus America's greatest ace was finally rewarded for his extraordinary contribution to the Allied cause. Previously he had been awarded the Distinguished Service Cross with nine Oak Leaves, the French Legion of Honor, and the Croix de Guerre with four Palms.

KIFFIN YATES ROCKWELL

The first aerial victory scored by the Escadrille Américaine was made by Kiffin Yates Rockwell of Asheville, North Carolina. It came after the squadron had been flying on the front for only four days.

Kiffin Rockwell was the epitome of the idealistic volunteer, and possibly the first American to offer his services to France. He also offered those of his brother Paul in a letter written August 1, 1914, which was sent to the French Consul at New Orleans. It read as follows:

I wish to volunteer to serve in case of actual warfare and wish to know whether I can report to you at New Orleans and go over with the French Reservists, or would it be wiser to go to France before enlisting. I am twenty-one years old and have had military training at Virginia Military Institute. I am very anxious to see military service and would rather fight under the French flag than any other, as I greatly admire your nation. If my services can be used, I will bring my brother who also desires to fight under the French flag.

Interestingly, the following news item appeared in the Atlanta *Journal* of August 4, 1914, alongside a portion of President Wilson's neutrality proclamation:

THREE YOUNG ATLANTANS
WOULD SHOULDER ARMS
IN DEFENSE OF FRANCE

Paul Rockwell and his brother K. Y. Rockwell and their friend R. L. Mock, three young men of Atlanta, have telegraphed to the French Consul in New Orleans offering to enlist as soldiers of France in the war against Germany.

An ancestor of the Rockwells named Rochelle fought in the army which came from France to aid the American patriots in the War of the Revolution.

Wilson's proclamation read in part:

I do enjoin all citizens of the United States and all persons residing or being within the territory or jurisdiction of the United States, to observe the laws of nations in that behalf. That no person within the territory and jurisdiction of the United States shall take part directly or indirectly in the said wars, but shall maintain a strict and impartial neutrality.

The Rockwells had little respect for neutrals or neutrality.

Years later Paul Ayres Rockwell, historian of the Lafayette Escadrille told of Mock's change of heart: "When he realized Kiffin and I were serious about going to France and enlisting for the war, he faded out of the picture. I have never heard of him again."

Unwilling to wait for consular red tape to untangle, Kiffin and Paul sailed from New York on August 7, 1914, and on their arrival in Paris immediately enlisted in the Foreign Legion along with twenty-nine other Americans. Kiffin, who was a rapid learner, was soon sent to the front where his record gleamed with courageous exploits. On May 9, 1915, when the Foreign Legion made a bayonet charge at La Targette he was wounded in the thigh, and though not critically hurt, he had to drag himself across an open field, pulling and clawing at tufts of grass, an ordeal that took most of the afternoon. More than half of his regiment had been wiped out in that engagement.

Kiffin spent some time in a hospital where he chafed with impatience when he heard that his 3rd Regiment had gone into action again and once more had been cut to pieces. He apparently liked this kind of action, and his letters reflected his enthusiasm.

Although his leg wound gnawed and pained, he was sent back to the trenches. By this time he had learned of the moves being made to form an American aviation squadron, and through Bill Thaw he forwarded his request for a transfer. After he had served another month in the trenches, he was accepted for the French Aviation on September 2, 1915, and received his first schooling at Avord and Pau. He gained his wings on an ancient Maurice Farman and became one of the original members of the Escadrille Américaine.

The honor of scoring the Escadrille's first victory came on May 18, 1916, as the result of the typical conditions of the period. Kiffin had decided to make a lone-wolf flight, but shortly after crossing the enemy lines his engine started to miss and sputter. He turned back, hoping to make a corrective carburetor adjustment and continue his patrol, but before he could complete any of this he saw a German aircraft about 2000 feet below that was flying up and down just inside the French lines. He drew back his throttle and nosed down after it, and then saw that he had taken on a German two-seater. The gunner was spattering him with fire and the first burst made the Nieuport rattle from prop to rudder, but Kiffin continued his dive until he was well within range of the two-seater. He pulled the cord that actuated the trigger of the Lewis gun, and fired four rounds. By that time he had to swerve sharply to avoid a collision.

The two-seater fell off helplessly, and turned for the German lines. Smoke was pouring from under the engine cowling, and the plane continued in a sharp dive until more smoke and some flame appeared. As Rockwell circled to make sure of the location, the doomed plane swerved toward its own lines again and piled up amid the wire, shell holes, and debris of the battle zone. It was a complete write-off.

This was Rockwell's first combat, the first time he had seen an enemy plane, and the first time he had fired his machine gun. The squadron armorer later verified the story, stating that only four rounds had been fired from the drum that was still attached to Kiffin's gun. An observation post telephoned the news of the crashed plane to the squadron before he had returned, and his comrades gave him a huge welcome.

On September 23 Kiffin and Raoul Lufbery went over the front lines, both of them flying Nieuports with an improved set of guns, including the new British interrupter gear. They had intended to start together, but at the last minute Raoul's machine gun gave some trouble, and rather than wait while suitable adjustments were made, Kiffin went off on his own.

He headed for the same area over which he had scored his first victory, and as he approached the front he spotted a two-seater observation plane that was working toward the French line. He probably hoped he could bring this one down in Allied territory. Vibrant with excitement, he nosed down steeply, and again a German gunner sprayed him with a steady stream of machine-gun fire. Kiffin ignored the "hate" and continued on until it seemed he must collide with the enemy aircraft. Observers below heard the Nieuport's guns begin their staccato rage, and saw the German plane seem to fall away. Then as they watched for the "kill" Rockwell's Nieuport appeared to falter. It turned its nose down steeply and the wings on one side flipped away from the fuselage. The remainder of the machine started to spin, and the wings that had been ripped off fluttered in the sunshine, their clean, doped surfaces reflecting glints of light until at last they parted and threw away the gleaming V-strut, sending it across the sky like a boomerang.

Meanwhile the rest of the Nieuport tightened its spin and augered down at terrific speed, finally crashing with an unearthly roar in a field of late summer blossoms. The French trenches were only a few yards away. Gunners from a nearby battery raced out and pulled Kiffin's body clear, and it was discovered that he had died from a chest wound caused by an incendiary bullet, the kind used in attacks on kite balloons.

News of Kiffin's death was telephoned to his squadron, and in the ensuing concern someone reported that the area was alive with enemy planes. Lufbery was so disturbed by Rockwell's loss, he took off again and climbed for the area, even ranging deep into the German lines, flying as far as Habsheim where a well-known enemy field was located, but none of the enemy took off to accept his challenge.

While rushing to the scene of his crash, Kiffin's friends remembered he had once stated in a philosophical mood that if he were shot down and killed he wished to be buried where he fell, but in this case his wish could not be granted. German artillerymen were already laying down a box-barrage in an attempt to completely destroy the Nieuport.

This was the saddest blow yet suffered by the Escadrille Américaine, and when the N.124 pilots gathered in their lobby that evening, Captain Thénault said, "We are all saddened. When Rockwell was in the air, no German passed. The best and bravest of us is no more."

Kiffin's brother Paul, who had been invalided out of the service because of a crippling wound, was now a civilian, but was permitted into the war zone to attend the funeral. Airplanes circled the procession, led by a cortege of Royal Naval Air Service pilots from a nearby field. Behind them marched a regiment of French territorials, a battalion of Colonials, and hundreds of French pilots and mechanics. Civilians from the nearby areas banked the grave with flowers, and Captain Thénault read a touching but manly tribute.

QUENTIN ROOSEVELT

Some of the national concern and determination to avenge Germany's invasion of Belgium and France was widely reflected in the number of young men from well-known or important families who volunteered to serve with the Allies. When the United States finally took up the gauntlet, representatives of many of our best families rushed to the enlistment centers, but the aviation service seemed to attract the bulk of them.

One of these enthusiastic young men was Quentin Roosevelt, youngest son of President Theodore Roosevelt. Despite his position in the American society of that day, Quentin was one of the most popular men in the United States Air Service. Youthful, boyish, and outgoing; because of his family background he was made a flight commander before he had ever crossed the enemy lines, but he refused to take the responsibility, arguing that his inexperience would jeopardize the lives of his flight mates. He declined the captaincy, but his superiors insisted that he accept the assignment. Once off the ground, Quentin would give a signal and one of the more experienced pilots would move up into the lead slot. Young Roosevelt insisted on this arrangement right up until the day he died.

Like his illustrious father, Quentin was reckless in action. His superiors cautioned him time and time again, and to the experienced men it was obvious that young Roosevelt would either run up some spectacular success, or go down to his end. Patrol after patrol in which Roosevelt was concerned were hair-raisers, but he always returned laughing, ignoring appeals for caution. He possibly was not particularly skilled as a pilot, for he was heavy-handed, and lacked the touch that made good fighter pilots. He blundered into predicament after predicament, from which only pure luck extricated him.

For instance, a few days before his end Quentin went over the lines with his flight. Somewhere in that cloudland he disappeared, and the assigned leader brought the formation home without him. Young Roosevelt returned a short time later, and reported he had finally shot down a Hun. On making out his patrol report he explained that he had left his flight to investigate a formation of enemy aircraft some few miles away. When he realized that the hostile group consisted of nearly twenty planes, he decided that discretion was the better part of valor, and so flew about on his own. While thus engaged he saw a formation ahead that he took to be his own, and moved into a position behind and tried to catch up.

This went on for ten or fifteen minutes when the leader of the formation gave a signal and all the aircraft banked to the left. As the machines tilted for the turn Quentin caught the Maltese cross on their wings and fins. He had been following a formation of German planes, but obviously the enemy pilots were as unaware of his identity as he had been of theirs.

Making the most of the situation, Roosevelt fired one long burst at an aircraft directly in front of him. The enemy plane immediately burst into flames, and Quentin streaked for home, astonished at his luck. The Germans were too shaken to go in pursuit. It is said that the German Training Command issued warnings about this sort of action, and denounced this American-Indian type of warfare. It must be presumed that they believed every American pilot on the front used these tactics in their everyday performances.

But Quentin Roosevelt's blind luck deserted him on July 14, 1918, when he took off with five other pilots, and crossed the lines east of Château-Thierry where the air was cluttered with Jerry formations. Both sides were working over the roads, railheads, and transport networks, and there were many opportunities for sudden attacks from above and down-sun. Shortly after crossing, this formation of the 95th blundered into a flight of Fokkers. Both were at low altitude and both seemingly were concerned with attacking or defending a body of marching men. The five American pilots, however, went headlong into seven Fokkers.

For a few minutes the sky was graced with these gaudy machines, circling, diving, zooming, and weaving their tracer streaks into the pattern of battle. Suddenly, Quentin spotted the approach of a gaggle of red-nosed Albatros D-Vs that were moving in from above and behind. Reckless as ever, he withdrew from his formation and turned to meet the newcomers. From all accounts the other pilots were unaware of his withdrawal from the original skirmish.

A Lieutenant Buford who was leading the flight saw a Nieuport falling through a light cloud formation, obviously out of control. He had no idea whose aircraft it was, but it indicated there was another enemy force somewhere above. He decided that they were there in numbers, so, tightening up his formation, he led his charges back across the lines. Not until then did he realize that it was young Roosevelt who was missing.

The squadron waited out the rest of the day, and by nightfall American signalers caught a wireless message from the enemy lines that explained that a Captain Quentin Roosevelt had been shot down by a Sergeant Thom, a member of the Richthofen Circus. This message must have been somewhat garbled for it actually referred to a Lieutenant Karl Thom, a member of Jasta 21, commanded by Eduard von Schleich, the famed Black Knight of Germany. Thom was to down twenty-seven Allied aircraft.

Roosevelt's loss became the subject of several legendary tales. His death was played up from many angles because of his family background. One reporter claimed that Quentin was not dead, but was being held a prisoner. Another reporter stated openly that Roosevelt had been deserted, and had his flight mates joined him they might have destroyed both enemy formations. This completely untrue story was published widely, but since the action took place about ten miles over the enemy lines no American could have seen it from the ground. This report also stated that the young man had shot down two Albatros fighters before he himself was downed. Von Schleich who lived out the war, and often visited his old enemies in London, denied that his Jasta had lost any machines on that day.

Young Quentin Roosevelt was sorely missed, for he was a delightful companion, a trusted member of his squadron, and an inspiration to all who knew him. His death, at age twenty-one, was a severe blow to the whole service.

SUMNER SEWELL

On January 25, 1966, Sumner Sewell, former Governor of Maine and a pioneer in commercial aviation, died at his home in Bath, Maine, at the age of sixty-seven. During World War I he was credited with destroying five enemy aircraft and two kite balloons. He was awarded the D.S.C., the French Legion of Honor, and the Croix de Guerre.

While Sumner was a student at Harvard he dropped out in 1916 to serve with the American Field Service. He had put in some time with the Reserve Officers Training Corps at Plattsburgh, New York, and after the United States entered the war, he left the American Field Service to enlist in the United States Aviation Section in Paris. His transfer was completed by August 23 and he went to the 2nd Aviation Instruction Center at Tours. From there he moved to Issoudun, and completed his training and gunnery at Cazeaux. He was commissioned a second lieutenant and assigned to the 95th Aero Squadron that was being formed at Issoudun.

Sewell was a daring flier and a courageous fighter pilot, but on one occasion he needed all the nerve and coolness he could muster. Flying in the rear element of a Spad formation he was startled by the rat-tat-tat of machine-gun fire, and as he glanced back he spotted a German Fokker diving on his tail and firing bursts of incendiary ammunition. Sumner made a quick change of direction, as the rest of his formation continued on for not one of them knew Sewell was being attacked. When he moved out of the cone of fire, there was a sudden puff of smoke and flame, and he realized his gas tank had been torched. At this point he was flying at 16,000 feet—almost three miles above the ground.

With few alternatives, Sewell nosed down steeply, trying to keep the fire from his body, but the Hun had no compassion and continued to fire short bursts at the blazing aircraft. The American looked back and saw that the fire was eating away most of his fuselage and its linen cover. The enemy Fokker still persisted in finishing the job, and Sumner had to take evasive action, which may have contributed toward saving his life. He had now dived and banked to within a thousand feet of the ground, and with that the Fokker pilot withdrew, satisfied that he had scored a "kill." But the flames that had been eating at the Spad's fuselage, suddenly dampened, and Sewell managed to hold the plane together long enough to pancake into some shell holes just inside the Allied line. He crawled out of the wreckage, looked in all directions, and as he stood trying to figure which way to head, he was struck on the arm by some falling wreckage—one of his plane's wheels that had been shot off several hundred feet above and had followed the battered, burning Spad all the way down to earth. The linen covering over the spokes had made the wheel slither and slide like a flying saucer, thus delaying it in joining Sewell and his crashed Spad.

An investigation made later disclosed that the bullet that pierced his tank created such a large hole the fuel gushed away rapidly, and a prolonged fire was not possible.

Sumner Sewell was awarded the Distinguished Service Cross for repeated acts of heroism, and on October 13, 1918, along with two other pilots, attacked a hostile formation of six planes. His two companions were forced to withdraw with jammed guns, but Sumner continued the action for about fifteen minutes, and before he withdrew had sent one of the enemy down in flames. Again, on October 18 while on a voluntary patrol he saw an American observation machine being attacked by a German Fokker. There were eight enemy planes in the vicinity, but he challenged the Fokker and destroyed it. The other aircraft turned on him, but he outmaneuvered them all and brought the observation plane back to the security of the Allied lines.

After the war Sumner Sewell worked in Cuba and Mexico, chiefly in the oil fields, and in 1920 he helped organize the Colonial Air Transport Company and served as its traffic manager for several years. Between 1930 and 1945 he was a director of United Air Lines.

ROBERT SOUBIRAN

The camera bug is a standard character in all gatherings of travelers, but in 1914 the photographic device was still novel. Only a few people had taken up the hobby, for at that time it was still a somewhat messy and odorous process. But fortunately for history, and the activities of the Lafayette Escadrille in particular, a New Yorker, Robert Soubiran went to war with a folding Kodak in his pack. He might have become one of the world's professionals had not the war intruded on his happy-go-lucky life.

An expert mechanic and a better than average driver of racing cars, Soubiran was among the first Americans to volunteer to fight with the French, and was fortunate in being of French descent and able to speak the language fluently. He first joined the Foreign Legion on August 24, 1914, and served in the trenches until February 25, 1916. After he had been wounded in October 1915 and was convalescing, he volunteered to help harvest the crop of wheat. Because he was skilled with tools and understood intricate mechanisms, he ran a threshing machine.

As soon as he heard of the formation of the Escadrille Américaine he applied for a transfer. Again his mechanical skill served him well, for he was quickly accepted and began his training with the French Aviation on February 27, 1916. Robert served with the Escadrille until February 1918. He had been given a captaincy in the U. S. Air Service as early as January 1918, and he flew with the 103rd Pursuit Squadron until the Armistice. This gay, and willing man put in eighteen months as a French infantryman, twenty-three months in the French Aviation, and nearly ten months with the U. S. Air Service.

But Robert Soubiran was hardly typical of the average American volunteer. He had spent so much time with the French infantry he had absorbed many of their active-service characteristics and manners. He could, in fact, have passed for a native-born Frenchman. He hacked his bread with a gleaming jackknife, swilled down his wine from a *bidon* (can), and laughed like a character out of Alexandre Dumas or Victor Hugo. Most of the villagers were astonished to learn that their favorite *estaminet* patron was an American.

Soubiran was never an aerial hero, at least in the lists of aces. In all his months at the front, he was credited with only one victory, but he seemed to be on hand with his camera whenever his squadron made a move. He turned up at every crash or amusing incident, and recorded every ceremonial in which his pilot pals played any role. Had it not been for Bob much of the pictorial history of the Lafayette Escadrille would never have made the pages of the records. Today his many photographs are priceless.

At this writing only four members of the Lafayette Escadrille still live. They are Edwin C. Parsons, Charles H. Dolan, Jr., Henry Sweet Jones, and Lawrence Rumsey.

ELLIOTT WHITE SPRINGS

The most popular, and certainly one of the more personable characters among the American airmen of World War I was Elliott White Springs, son of a millionaire cotton manufacturer. Springs' wartime career reads like a tale concocted by Thorne Smith, for things happened to, or were contrived by him that were presented later by air-story writers as out-and-out fiction. Would there were more like him, for the duty of fighting for one's country would be greatly lightened. He was one of the few who campaigned with joy in his heart and utter contempt for the enemy. While he lived I was more than proud to be included among his many friends.

Because of his personality and natural leadership, Springs was in September 1917 elected to head a small band of American aviation cadets sent across the Atlantic to continue their training in England. With nothing much in hand but a few solo hours on the primitive Curtiss Jenny, this hapless group soon learned they were expected to take over the cockpits of real wartime airplanes. For a short time they were lectured by a number of United States armchair warriors who had never flown a patrol or even heard a shot fired. At best, it was a bewildering situation.

Springs' unit was something of a Lost Battalion. They were neither fish nor fowl; they were not officers or noncoms—just aviation cadets with no real standing. At Oxford where they had been unloaded, they gradually realized they were getting nowhere, so Elliott wired home for money, took his group to London, put them up in a second-class hotel, and outfitted them with uniforms of his own design. For the next week or so they lifted London out of the gloom of war with their antics in the theaters, the hotel lobbies, and the night clubs of that period. Needless to state, Elliott was able to obtain plenty of champagne or whisky, and there is one story that it was he who taught London society the art of making several types of cocktails.

Sergeant (?) Springs made the most of his chances during this boozy crusade, and one evening induced some British staff officers to take over his legion and train them at a special RAF station. In fact, they were soon turned out as first-class war pilots, but their capers during this session would fill a large book. Most of them survived the course and some of them proved to be ranking aces.

As for Springs, he was first noted by Colonel Billy Bishop, the Canadian ace who at that time was organizing Number 85 Squadron. Two other Americans, Lawrence Calahan and John Grider, were also accepted. Bishop's squadron went to France on May 22, 1918, and settled down at a field a few miles below Dunkirk. Springs received valuable instruction from Bishop and scored his first triumph on June 5. Three more enemy aircraft fell before his S.E.5, and then on June 27 he himself was shot down and only just managed to glide into his own lines. He cracked up badly and spent some time in a nearby hospital.

When he was next ready for action he was ordered to report to Number 148 Squadron of the U. S. Air Service. This came as somewhat of a shock to Elliott who by now was quite at home with the RAF, and had almost forgotten that he had originally joined up in the United States. He liked his British companions, and felt, as did many others, that he owed Great Britain a debt for the training that had been provided, but the order stood. He was equipped with the American stiff-collared uniform, and given a Sopwith Camel, instead of his beloved S.E.5. The transfer had some compensations, for he was made a flight commander and promoted to captain. As may be imagined, this squadron was made up of many other Americans who had trained and served with the R.F.C., or the RAF.

Springs took up his new role with his old-time zest, and was soon back in the air battling the Boche. On August 3, while leading his flight, he knocked down his fifth enemy plane, becoming an ace. Eventually, his squadron was as famous as Rickenbacker's Hat-in-the-Ring outfit, and ranked second among American squadrons in the number of victories scored. But the 94th was in action from April on, whereas the 148th did not begin operations until late July.

After the war Springs returned to his father's cotton mill in South Carolina, but he had little interest in the industry and wrote riotous novels set against the background of wartime London and the Western Front. For years the Elliott White Springs' version of frontline flying was the basic idea of many Hollywood air-war epics. Pulp writers lifted his plots, characters, and hilarious situations, and offered them as their own originals. But Elliott only laughed and turned out more. His best novel was *War Birds—The Diary of an Unknown Aviator,* but it is now clear that John Grider was the "unknown" hero.

WILLIAM THAW

On April 22, 1934, William Thaw, one of the leading lights of the Lafayette Escadrille, died of pneumonia in Pittsburgh, Pennsylvania, where he was born. His obituary stated that he was forty years old which would indicate he was born in 1894, although photographs taken of him in 1914, 1915, and 1916 show a man who then looked to be well into his thirties. But he was a mature type who wore a heavy mustache, and he may have adopted this older personality for military reasons. At any rate, war records fail to agree on the actual date of his birth.

Bill's father was a Pittsburgh banker, and his mother a noted art collector. After tuition at the Browning School in New York, the Hill School in Pottstown, Pennsylvania, and two years at Yale, Bill took up flying at the Curtiss School at Hammondsport, New York, in 1913, when presumably he was nineteen. With Steve Macgordon he made a sensational flight from Newport, Rhode Island, via New Haven, to New York, flying under the four East River bridges and around the Statue of Liberty. Thaw also was one of the first pilots to attempt a ship-to-shore airmail service by dropping a package of letters on the German *Imperator* as she left New York Harbor.

In April 1914 Bill received the brevet of the Aero Club of France, and for several months after he flew a Curtiss hydroplane along the resorts of the Mediterranean.

At the outbreak of the war Bill Thaw was trying to interest the French government in an automatic stabilizer for aircraft that he and his brother, Benjamin Thaw, Jr., had perfected, but there was no time for such business, so Bill dropped all his aviation interests and enlisted in the French Foreign Legion.

Trench life soon palled, and Bill made an attempt to take his flying skill into the French Aviation, and after four months of ground warfare he succeeded in being accepted for military flight training. His first active-service flying was with a Deperdussin two-seater squadron where he served as a gunner armed with a carbine and an automatic pistol. Later he was given training on the Caudron G.2, and was employed in taking would-be observers aloft to complete their training.

20. James A. Meissner, a Cornell student, was credited with eight victories. He began his war career with Rickenbacker's 94th Aero Squadron and eventually took command of the 147th. After the war he headed the Alabama National Guard and is still in business in Birmingham, Alabama. (*U.S. War Department General Staff*)

1. America's first Lafayette Escadrille e. Raoul Lufbery, who claimed Walling-rd, Connecticut, as his home, although was born in France, destroyed seventeen emy aircraft before he was killed. A true ldier-of-fortune, he became one of the ar's most colorful flight leaders. (*U.S. Air orce*)

22. Kenneth Marr took a shipment of Eskimo dogs to France for use in the Vosges by the Alpine Chasseurs and stayed on to drive ambulances, fly with the Lafayette Escadrille and finally ended up commanding the 94th Aero Squadron. He is best remembered for his development of fractured French. (*U.S. Signal Corps*)

23. There was always a close association between the American Field Service and the Lafayette Escadrille. Here we see James R. McConnell, left, of Carthage, North Carolina, who became a pilot and Paul A. Rockwell of Asheville, North Carolina, who was to become the official historian of the Lafayette Flying Corps. *(Paul A. Rockwell photo)*

24. Brigidier General William E. Mitchell, the stormy petrel of the U.S. Aviation Service, who did more to create an American air arm than any man in uniform, was among the first to visualize a parachute brigade and support General Hugh Trenchard's theory of strategic aviation. *(U.S. Air Force)*

25. Frank Luke, the Arizona Balloon Buster, first American airman to win the Medal of Honor. Credited with twenty-one victories, he represented the headstrong type who usually come to a tragic end. Luke was killed resisting a platoon of German infantrymen who were trying to capture him. *(U.S. Air Force)*

26. Norman Prince, the true founder of the Lafayette Escadrille, bought his own flight training in the United States and spent much of his own money setting up the organization. Like so many patriots he came to a tragic end on October 18, 1916. (*Smithsonian Institution: National Air Museum*)

27. The all-American boy of school book stories, David Putnam of Brookline, Massachusetts, more than lived up to that role. A descendant of Israel Putnam, an outstanding athlete at Harvard, he flew with the French and U.S. Air Service with dash and daring. Before he was killed he had downed twelve enemy aircraft. (*U.S. Signal Corps*)

28. Edwin C. Parsons of Holyoke, Massachusetts, was awarded the French Médaille Militaire, Croix de Guerre, the Belgian Cross of Leopold and the Belgian Croix de Guerre. A few years ago the French then added their Legion of Honor. He served his complete war career with the French but in World War II he joined the U. S. Navy and reached the rank of Rear Admiral.

29. America's ace of aces, Edward V. Rickenbacker, was credited with twenty-six victories during a camparatively short career on the Western Front. Rickenbacker had considerable difficulty in getting into the aviation service; then, harassed by a painful ear affliction, flew actively for only two months. (*U.S. Signal Corps*)

30. Kiffin Yates Rockwell, the most beloved American in the Lafayette Escadrille, was probably the first citizen of the U.S.A. to offer his services to the Allied cause. He downed the first enemy plane credited to the American volunteer group. (*Paul A. Rockwell photo*)

31. Destined for tragedy. Four immortals of the Lafayette Escadrille and their French leader. From left to right: James McConnell, Kiffin Rockwell, Captain Georges Thénault, Norman Prince and Victor Chapman. Only Captain Thénault survived the war. *(Paul A. Rockwell photo)*

32. The famous Bill Thaw stands in the center of a Lafayette Escadrille group taken on the Aisne in 1917. Left to right: Robert Soubiran, Courtney Campbell, Kenneth Marr, Thaw, French mechanic and David Peterson. *(Paul A. Rockwell photo)*

33. One American ace who went a long way. Sumner Sewell of Bath, Maine, dropped out of Harvard to serve in France. He destroyed seven enemy aircraft and was awarded the D.S.C., the Legion of Honor and the Croix de Guerre. After the war he became Governor of Maine and for a time Director of the Military Government in Germany. He died in 1966. *(U.S. Army)*

34. America's playboy ace, Elliott White Springs, whose postwar literary work contributed much to the legend of the bar-fly war pilot. He is credited with destroying twelve enemy planes while serving with the Royal Air Force and the U.S. Air Service. He died a few years ago a millionaire textile manufacturer. *(National Archives)*

35. America's second-ranking living ace, Lieutenant George Vaughn. A Brooklyn boy, a product of Princeton along with Hoby Baker, Jesse Creech and Lansing Holden, George first served with a British S. E. 5 squadron and then transferred to No. 17 Aero Squadron during which time he accounted for thirteen enemy aircraft. *(National Archives)*

36. Another Massachusetts volunteer who died while flying with Frank Luke. Joseph F. Wehner, son of a German shoe manufacturer, endured many bureaucratic indignities because of his name and background, but he proved to be a true-blue American observing the traditions of team-play to the end. *(U.S. Air Force)*

37. The boldest of them all. Captain Albert Ball, the first of Britain's great aces. Bold, impetuous, he put on one of the wildest fighting careers in all war history. He destroyed forty-three enemy aircraft before he himself was shot down by a machine gunner lurking in an old church tower. *(Arch Whitehouse photo)*

38. Major George Barker, a Canadian airman, fought the greatest air-battle of all times. Flying a new Sopwith Snipe, he took on more than sixty enemy aircraft and downed five of them before bowing to the strength of the opposition. He landed in his own lines, badly wounded, and on his recovery was awarded the Victoria Cross. *(Imperial War Museum, London)*

39. Canada's air hero, Major William A. Bishop, stands before his Nieuport scout. He was credited with seventy-two victories. In one period of twelve days he shot down twenty-five aircraft, twelve of them in his last three days on the front. *(Imperial War Museum, London)*

It was not until late March 1915 that Bill learned of Norman Prince's efforts to organize a squadron of Americans. But Bill had little interest in this project. Instead, he completed his own pilot training, and then requested an assignment with a French squadron, and, in fact, actually served with C.42 (Caudrons) and N.65 (Nieuports) before he was finally induced to join the American group. By that time Bill had flown every available French military type and had fired at enemy machines with everything from rifles, revolvers, and rockets to machine guns. Few men in any service at the time had had as much in-air experience.

Once he joined the Escadrille Américaine N.124 with the rank of *sous-lieutenant,* he devoted all his time to training his companions, and particularly to their leadership. He was not an outstanding ace, for he was more interested in the safety and training of his pilots. In other words, he was an ideal squadron leader. He was credited with five enemy aircraft.

When N.124 was disbanded and sifted into U. S. Air Service squadrons, Thaw became a major, and for a time headed the 103rd Aero Squadron. On August 10, 1918, he was made a lieutenant colonel and given command of the Third Pursuit Group. By the time of the Armistice, Bill Thaw had been awarded the Distinguished Service Cross, the French Legion of Honor, and the Croix de Guerre.

After the war Bill Thaw went prospecting in Baja California, but by 1921 had returned to aviation, also becoming interested in some lighter-than-air projects. In 1923 he engaged in insurance, which he continued until his death. In 1928 Bill and Captain John P. Morris entered and flew a Lockheed Vega in a transcontinental air race, but en route they crashed, and Bill was painfully injured.

One of Bill Thaw's brothers, Lieutenant Alexander Blair Thaw, commanding officer of the 135th Aero Squadron, was killed in an airplane accident in France in 1918.

CHARLES TRINKARD

Another refugee from a cattle boat was Charles Trinkard, a comical character from Ozone Park, New York, who was known to many American volunteers as "Tiny Trink." He arrived in France shortly after the declaration of war and joined the Foreign Legion on August

24, 1914. He received his wound stripe during an action in 1915 and served with this organization until March 1, 1917.

Trink transferred to the French Aviation March 13, 1917, finished his training by July 24, and was assigned to N.68, a French Nieuport squadron, on September 1.

This young American was a great storyteller. His reputation preceded him wherever he went, and he always was willing to oblige at any dinner or café. He joined the French Aviation Service in March 1917 and on completion of his flying course, was offered a month's leave because of his long service as an infantryman. He could have gone home to the United States, but instead decided to stay on and get in some front-line flying time. He did log several routine patrols, but there is no record of his having downed any enemy airmen.

On Thanksgiving Day (November 29, 1917) while returning from a patrol with two other airmen he decided to entertain his old pals by staging some wild aerobatics over a village where his old regiment was billeted. The show was a thriller, but somewhere in the program Trink lost control of the Nieuport and stalled at low altitude. He was killed instantly as his plane spun in.

Many fine lives were sacrificed in this form of pointless showmanship.

GEORGE VAUGHN, JR.

An American ace, still alive, is often ignored by aviation historians. He is George Vaughn, Jr., a native of Brooklyn, and another Princeton student who served with distinction. His name can be found with those of Hoby Baker, Jesse Creech, and Lansing Holden. He ended the war with thirteen confirmed victories, seven of them scored while serving with Number 84 Squadron of the newly formed Royal Air Force.

After some primary ground instruction at Princeton, George was sent to England where he came under the instruction of several British airmen and by May 1918 was assigned to Number 84 that was flying over the Amiens sector. He worked for three busy months with seasoned veterans. They were flying the S.E.5a, and because of his leader's insistence on tight formations and a general taboo on free-lance excursions, George learned a great deal under excellent circumstances. He was soon considered to be one of the most dependable and experienced fighters in the squadron.

Since teamwork was the rule in the British service George absorbed every skill required, and learned to handle his machine under all combat conditions, particularly in crowded engagements. The man who can stunt and grandstand over his own field is often chilled stiff with fear if he is suddenly attacked from behind. Vaughn was a cool operator and exceptionally skilled in all battle maneuvers.

On his second trip over the lines he was attacked by an enemy Pfalz that poured in a wicked round of fire that riddled his tail. Recovering quickly from the surprise attack, George zoomed hard, and the Boche went on through with his dive. George then heeled over and went after his man, triggering two short bursts that caused an explosion in the enemy's fuel tank.

The next day Vaughn went on a balloon-busting show and succeeded in destroying one. As it went down in flames, he pulled away and met an enemy two-seater patrolling at 500 feet over Méricourt. George roared through a storm of enemy ground fire, emptied a drum of ammunition, and the two-seater plunged to a shattering finish in a back area.

On another occasion he found an enemy plane over Villers-Carbonel and chased it into the ground where it smashed and burned.

When he had run up seven victories Vaughn was transferred to the newly formed Number 17 Aero Squadron of the U. S. Air Service, and like Elliott White Springs, had to switch from S.E.5s to Sopwith Camels. The S.E.5 was faster and could climb to greater heights, but the Camel was much more maneuverable, and once Vaughn and his mates became adjusted to the rotary-powered gadfly they found they could outfight any German mount.

The Camel was a small, very chunky biplane powered with a Le Rhône, Clerget, or Bentley rotary engine that gave it one important factor of maneuverability. The rotary power plant had its nine cylinders set on a circular casing and turned on a master crankshaft. The heavy engine, whirling about this central point, exerted a strong pull or torque in the direction of rotation. Because the Camel was comparatively small, stub-winged, and short in the fuselage, it whipped over startlingly fast on right-hand turns. By using this feature in fighting maneuvers, Camel pilots could outfly most of their adversaries. They simply right-hand-turned them to death.

George Vaughn had mastered the Sopwith within a few short

weeks and added six more kills to his total. On one patrol, which he was leading, an upper-level flight of fifteen Fokkers was seen nosing down on another flight of five Camels. George outmaneuvered one Fokker, and sent it down out of control. Zooming out of that action he came out just above another; a short burst, and Number Two went down minus a wing. By this time the sky was swirling with single-seaters and crisscrossing tracer fire. Two Fokkers nosed at Vaughn, but he flipped over into a tight spin. The enemy pilots tried to get a bead on this corkscrewing target, but George held to the twirl until he could see barbed-wire entanglements below, and knew it was time to pull out. One Fokker tried a long burst, but George evaded the fire and tried to switch on his engine. Nothing happened, and he decided he was out of gas. Thinking he was in for a pile-up somewhere near no man's land, he suddenly remembered that the Camel had a small reserve tank, and he switched over to that. The engine picked up immediately. On the way back to his field he sensed that his back was wet and cold, and concluded that in the melee he had been hit; the dampness of his shirt and jacket was blood, but it could only be a flesh wound since he felt no serious damage to his bone structure.

George has told this story for many years with great glee, explaining he was certain he had a real "Blighty" wound that meant a spell in a hospital, and probably a month's leave, a reward he felt he was entitled to.

He landed safely, and confided to his mechanic that he thought he had been wounded by a bullet that had grazed his back. The mechanic inspected, sniffed at Vaughn's sodden jacket, and then examined the Camel.

"No luck, Lieutenant." The mechanic let out a hilarious howl. "That 'blood' is only gasoline that sprayed out of one corner of your tank while you was in that spin."

Instead of a leave to London, George was given a new Camel and recommended for the Distinguished Service Cross for his gallant attempt to save the Camel flight below. He lost one of his mates on that show, but the remaining three were credited with two more kills.

JOSEPH F. WEHNER

Joseph F. Wehner was born in Everett, Massachusetts, of German parents, and was one of the unfortunates who was burdened with a German background. How he managed to enlist in the old Aviation Section of the Signal Corps and obtain flight training is somewhat of a mystery, considering how many young men of German ancestry were harried and haunted by the United States Secret Service.

Joe attended Everett High School and Phillips Exeter Academy, but before he joined the American forces there were reports that he had served in German prison camps with a YMCA unit; apparently he resigned after the United States entered the war. There are many such stories concerning Joe Wehner, few of which are reliable. In some reports he is the son of a poverty-stricken cobbler, yet after he left high school, he entered an academy. It is possible that Joe's father was the owner of, or an executive in, one of the many shoe factories in the Massachusetts area, in which case the family income was in what was then considered the upper middle-class bracket. The term "cobbler" sounds too much like a pat phrase used by a pulp writer. Another yarn has Joe as the son of a German delicatessen store owner; a canard, if ever there was one.

The German prison camp story may be true, for after diplomatic relations were broken with Germany, Joe returned to his homeland and enlisted in the Signal Corps at Kelly Field, Texas.

Almost immediately Joe came under the eye of an overzealous intelligence officer who was prepared for a wave of sabotage and top-level espionage. Wehner was a German name. This son of a poverty-stricken cobbler had paid his own way from New England to enlist in Texas. There had to be something sinister in that. It was amazing how far the long arm of the Kaiser's agents reached in this war. This Joe Wehner would have to be watched.

He was. His every move was observed and reported. Fantastic reasons were invented for his going to church, to the YMCA, to a movie, or even a late call to the latrines. Every letter he wrote was steamed open and studied. Secret codes were seen in every mark he made on his examination papers.

Joe would have to have been a complete idiot not to realize he was under surveillance. Eventually the hunt became intolerable, and Joe lost his temper. He spoke his mind, accused his trackers of childish persecution, and taunted them with the unimportance of their role in the war.

Then the sleuths were certain they were on the right track. Now he was getting desperate and would make a break for it any day, and to forestall such a move Joe was picked up and placed under close arrest. Meanwhile, the real enemy agents were blowing up munitions factories, placing time bombs in coal bunkers, plotting with Mexico, inciting strikes and work slow-downs, and rewriting the Allied role in the Great War.

When the nucleus of the 27th Aero Squadron left Texas and headed for the New York Port of Embarkation, Joe was still under arrest. Then a mature-minded court absolved him of all suspicion and he hurried east to join his squadron, only to be arrested again by Secret Service agents in New York. Joe talked himself out of that situation and finally was permitted to sail with his organization. However, on landing in France he was again shadowed, detained, and questioned by various groups of military officials.

None of this helped Joe's morale, his determination, or heightened his patriotism. He felt he was an outcast, and by now the growing suspicion was poisoning his own mind. He distrusted everyone around him, and found himself doubting the genuineness of the snores that came from the cots on either side of him.

There was little time to absorb the lectures, the in-air training, or the patient advice of men who were experienced in this new art of war. As a result, Joe Wehner, like Frank Luke, decided to become a hellcat in action. He wanted to show off in the air, display his skill as a stunt pilot, his marksmanship against ground targets, and his recklessness against the enemy.

Is it any wonder that when most of the squadron discredited Frank Luke when he claimed his first Hun Joe welcomed Frank's approach, and eventual companionship? He responded like a blood brother. A bond was forged, and for a few raddled days they were the deadliest duo on the Western Front. Unreasoning, wild, senseless; both were determined to show they were on the up-and-up. There were many pilots with greater scores, long careers, and with chests agleam with medals, but most of them were run-of-the-mill squadron fighters. They stayed in formation and adopted the team game because all around them were others who respected—even worshiped—that doctrine. But to be lone-handers, a pair of outcasts determined to show up the whole system of formation, that was something else entirely. Joe Wehner plunged to his death while protecting Frank Luke. The Arizona lad went to his end, avenging Joe's death, neither realizing that in the true sense they were playing the game, employing team play, and backing up the formation to the last.

ALAN WINSLOW

Alan Winslow, one of America's first air heroes, and the second member of the 94th Squadron to bring down an enemy plane, had to endure the indignity of prison camp after being shot down at the height of his wartime popularity. He was a native of River Forest, Illinois, although often listed as a Chicagoan. He began his service with the French Aviation, finished his training on a Caudron on October 12, 1917, and was assigned to Escadrille Spa.152 by December 24, 1917. He remained with this French squadron as a sergeant until February 12, 1918, when he was commissioned a second lieutenant and eventually joined the 94th Aero Squadron.

We have related previously how Alan Winslow and Douglas Campbell marked the United States Air Service's entry into the war by shooting down two enemy planes near Toul on April 14, 1918. On June 13 Winslow, along with Jimmy Meissner and Thorn Taylor, came upon a German Hannoveraner CL-III, a two-seater fighter-reconnaissance plane, and after a combined attack spreading over ten minutes, these three pilots finally sent it down in flames, and the hulk fell just north of Thiaucourt.

While Rickenbacker was away receiving treatment for his troublesome ear, Winslow was one of the stalwarts who kept the squadron intact. Douglas Campbell was on leave, and it was Alan Winslow, Reed Chambers, Jimmy Meissner, and Thorn Taylor who bore the brunt of the daily patrols.

On July 31 the Americans tangled with several Jagdstaffeln of the German Air Service, and a number of first-class pilots were lost in the whole First Pursuit Group. Lieutenant John McArthur of Buffalo, New York, who had racked up five enemy machines, was leading a flight of six Nieuports of the 27th Squadron in a sortie against enemy airdromes believed to be occupied by squadrons of the Von Richthofen Circus. In this instance it was the field north of Fismes.

Only one of the American formation returned from this action. What happened was learned later. It seems that all six Nieuports spent considerable time roaring up and down the area, and probably forgot that they were attacking a target that was twenty miles over the enemy line. This gave the enemy time to put up interceptor flights to engage the Americans when they tried to head for home. Mc-Arthur put on a magnificent show, but the opposition was too much, and one by one the Nieuport 28s were downed, or ran out of gas while trying to find a soft spot through which to battle their way out.

That same day the 94th lost Alan Winslow. Late that evening he was seen by another member of his flight, engaging a Fokker. The two machines continued descending lower and lower with each circuit until they both disappeared in the dusky glow below. Winslow never returned from that combat, but his squadron mates remained out on their field until well into the night, firing Very pistol flares to guide him home. When all hope had dissipated they returned to their quarters convinced that the most popular member of their squadron had "gone west."

Then, about a month later, Paul Winslow, Alan's brother who at the time was a member of Number 56 Squadron, RAF, received a letter from the missing Alan. He had written from a German hospital saying he had been wounded in combat. A bullet had shattered the bone in his left arm, and the German doctors had had to amputate his arm above the elbow. From all accounts Alan accepted his fate, and seemed content to be out of the war. After five months in hospitals and prison camps, Alan Winslow was repatriated back to France, one of the last of the American fliers to regain his freedom.

For some time after the war he was an aide to Brigadier General Billy Mitchell, and lived in Washington, D.C. for many years. When last heard of he was writing a book relating his experiences.

FREDERICK ZINN

Among the Americans serving with the French Aviation was one man who, because of his particular talents, was eagerly sought by the U. S. Aviation Service in 1917. This was Frederick Zinn of Battle

Creek, Michigan, a volunteer who had served in the Foreign Legion from August 24, 1914, and remained a soldier in the trenches until February 1916 when he was severely wounded at Champagne. After a spell in a hospital, it was decided that his days as an infantryman were over, but instead of returning home Fred volunteered for the French Aviation to which he was transferred in the spring of 1916.

He started his training at Etampes and went through the complete routine. He became a *mitrailleur-bombardier* by August 29, and first served with F.24, flying as an observer aboard Farmans and Sopwith two-seaters, work in which he was engaged for almost a year. In that period of time he learned a great deal about reconnaissance aviation. He was an excellent cameraman and carried out dozens of long-range patrols to gather important information. He was bold in the air, and fought his way home from many dangerous missions. Once back on the ground, Zinn would complete his task by developing his negatives and producing first-class prints in a short time. He also became expert in interpreting his photographs for his superior officers.

It was small wonder that Frederick Zinn was the first man the United States mission requested. He was soon commissioned and attached to the United States Air Service headquarters at Chaumont. He had been a sergeant in the French service, but was soon promoted to captain, a rank he retained until the Armistice. After the war Zinn was sent into Germany as Chief of the American mission for locating the graves of his countrymen who had fallen in German-held territory.

PART TWO

Belgian

BELGIAN

The opening battle of World War I was the German assault on Liège, during which the Belgians made one of the most heroic stands of that conflict. Historians do not agree as to the actual military value of this defense and resistance from the forts that surrounded the gallant city, but many have stated that if there had not been this long-forgotten stand, the German armies would have swept on and overwhelmed France before it could have established any effective opposition; that the British Army would never have had a chance to fight.

Of military value, or not, Liège's resistance was an event of rare moral and spiritual worth. Belgium's brave stand was proclaimed throughout the world, and the depravity of Germany's aggression highlighted in a manner no professional publicist could have matched. The great heart of the Belgian people equaled the honor which the German government had declared to be an empty word. The stand at Liège inspired the ringing phrase, "Brave Little Belgium."

Belgium also contributed considerably to the air war. Her aviation history is particularly noteworthy. Because she is joined with France over so wide a border, she naturally absorbed much of the aviation pioneering carried out by French aeronauts in the early days. French airmen went into Belgian towns and presented their daring displays, and eventually Baron Pierre de Caters and Professor Emile Allard engaged in the sport, both men becoming pilots. The Chevalier Jules de Laminne, a young, well-to-do engineer, gained his wings at the Farman flying school at Mourmelon, and was the first airman to fly a royal passenger when he took King Ferdinand of Bulgaria aloft at Kiewit. De Laminne became the founder of the Belgian Air Force.

Two civilian airfields were established in Belgium in 1910, one at Kiewit where De Laminne was housing his new Farman H.F.3, the other at Antwerp. During July of that year the War Minister, General Hellebaut, stopped at Kiewit to watch the flying activity there. A few days later he returned and risked a flight, and became so enthusiastic about aircraft he decided to form an air arm. He asked De Laminne to train a number of military officers which the young engineer agreed to do, but all these good intentions came to naught because certain staff officers were determined that all military pilots should come only from the ranks of the military balloon sections.

In the meantime two young officers, Lieutenants Baudouin de Montens d'Oostenryck and Alfred Sarteel, had been flying as a hobby at Baron de Caters' flying school at Antwerp, although they were supposed to be training under De Laminne on a form of powered glider. When General Hellebaut heard of this new interest, he ordered the purchase of an airplane and told De Laminne to establish the proposed training course. The general had good intentions, but other officials managed to delay the proceedings. Some young officers ignored regulation channels and hired De Laminne to train them at his Kiewit school, and all this fringe activity eventually lit a bonfire under the Belgian military staff so that in due course normal training procedures were established, with the officers taught piloting, and enlisted men given courses in the mechanical features of the airplane.

The progress of military aviation in Belgium endured many misfortunes and hardships. Prior to the start of war progress was slow, but one interesting incident was worth all the tribulation.

An American armament expert, Colonel Isaac Newton Lewis, was in Europe in May 1912 trying to interest some government in a new machine gun he had invented. As had been the case with the Wright brothers and Hiram Maxim, he had been ignored at home, so he requested permission in Belgium to display his weapon and explain how it might be used aboard an airplane. At the time no one saw the necessity for arming an aircraft, but Colonel Lewis was allowed to have his gun taken aloft by a Lieutenant Nelis, with a Second Lieutenant Stellingwerff acting as his gunner. A Farman F.20 Jero pusher was used. In this model the observer sat behind the pilot and the gun was mounted on a metal peg bolted to the side of the fuselage.

A white bed sheet was laid out on the ground for a target, and held down at its corners with large stones. Lieutenant Stellingwerff was a good marksman, and after two or three runs over the target, the sheet was slashed to ribbons. The field quartermaster was enraged and suggested that the two flying men be court-martialed for destroying government property, but the field commandant arranged to have the sheet written off by the equipment officer and so satisfied the quartermaster.

Colonel Lewis was rewarded with a small contract from the Belgian government for the manufacture of his gun, and a short time later Nelis and Stellingwerff flew their "battleplane" that mounted a Lewis gun to Great Britain where they staged another performance.

After two in-air demonstrations, the British were delighted, and soon adopted the American's remarkable weapon with the result they had a large number ready when the war began. Although the Belgians had early appreciated its value and nicknamed it the Belgian Rattlesnake, they had none available and had to rely on British manufacturers for their supply when German troops violated their neutrality.

In March 1913 a new Minister for War, Comte de Charles M. P. A. Broqueville, signed a decree making Kiewit a military airfield; and officers who volunteered for flying duty were given two months' leave with pay to take the course. On completion of their training they were presented with an additional allowance of six hundred francs to cover incidentals. Later, a royal decree set up a heavier-than-air division consisting of four squadrons, and it was hoped that two more could be added as soon as pilots could be trained.

But at the outbreak of war Belgium had only one Depot Squadron, and three service squadrons available, only two of which could be considered up to full strength. There were thirty-seven pilots flying a mixed bag of Voisins, Farmans, Blériots, and Maurice Farman-14 biplanes. Eight civilian pilots volunteered their services and brought their personal planes, but within three days there was little left of the Belgian Air Service; much of the country and the airfields had been overrun. When Namur was threatened Number 2 Squadron flew to Buc near Paris to reorganize, and a month later moved up to Ostend just in time to encounter a storm of gale proportions that wiped out many of their aircraft.

Meanwhile, Number 1 Squadron fought on with its six Maurice Farmans, and a Nieuport scout for the use of the commander, until France could re-equip them with Nieuport Baby scouts. Over the months and years eleven squadrons were organized by the Belgians who in the course of events took over Sopwith Camels, Hanriots, Spads, Bréguets, and various other types. Their Second Lieutenant Willy Coppens was credited with thirty-seven victories. Adjutant André de Meulemeester downed eleven enemy machines, and Second Lieutenant Edmond Thieffry became a ten-plane ace.

WILLY COPPENS

This mysterious young man who became Belgium's Ace of Aces has a history that is as fascinating as any found in World War I. The son of an artist, he was born in 1892, and was called up in 1912 and joined a Grenadier regiment. He fought as an infantryman in the early months of the war, and when his battalion was converted to an armored car squadron to be sent to Russia, Willy somehow evaded that duty and transferred to Belgium's Air Service.

This evasion required money enough to buy flying lessons in England. In fact, Willy Coppens checked in at the Ruffy-Baumann school at Hendon where he met another refugee from the infantry, a young English subaltern named Albert Ball.

Willy gained a school certificate by December 1916, and on returning to Belgium picked up more school training, eventually learning enough to be posted to a front-line squadron. He made routine reconnaissance patrols aboard B.E.2s and various Farman types with Number 6 Squadron, and it was not until May 1917 that he finally flew something warlike. This was the Sopwith 1½-Strutter, a two-seater fighter, and with this he set out to open up his score.

He had little luck, but many close escapes aboard the Sopwith, and then by mid-July 1917 he was transferred to Belgium's Number 1 Squadron which was flying Nieuport scouts. In this same unit were Fernand Jacquet, André de Meulemeester, and Jan Olieslagers who were to provide the inspiration for Belgium's air-war effort. However, the Nieuport proved to be no better than the Sopwith, so Coppens turned to the Belgian Hanriot HD.1, a splendid little machine that could be mistaken for a Sopwith Camel, except that it carried but one machine gun. Strangely enough, no other Belgian pilot of Number 1 Squadron wanted any part of the Hanriot, but Coppens accepted it immediately. Since the machine was painted a giddy mixed color that offended his artistic nature, Willy had his scout painted a striking blue, and eventually started his lengthy run of victories aboard this plane.

During March 1918 the Belgian Staff decided to follow the German trend, and it organized a fighter group of three squadrons, which disturbed Willy Coppens for he was the free-lancer of all free-lancers. Since he was still only a warrant officer, he had to obey orders, and in fact was made a flight commander. In all this time, though he had had from twenty to thirty air fights, he had not yet destroyed a German plane.

On April 16, 1918, Coppens finally scored, torching a German plane that fell near Ramscapelle. Then, like Frank Luke, he suddenly worked up a hate for enemy kite balloons. He seemed to have particular luck in the Houthulst Forest area, and almost daily put on a balloon show that entertained the Belgian troops who were holding the line there. In the next few months he destroyed thirty-six enemy aircraft—twenty-six kite balloons, and ten planes.

His fighting career came to a close on October 14, 1918, less than a month before the Armistice was signed. On that day Willy rose early to go in search of a balloon said to be up near Thourout. At 6:00 A.M. he first encountered a kite up at Praet Bosh which he attacked and quickly sent down in flames. Then he went after the bag at Thourout that was tethered at 2000 feet. During his dive on this target he was hit in the leg by a piece of shrapnel and lost control of his plane for a time. He went into a dangerous spin but was able to get into his own lines, finally crashing in a field. Local troops removed him from the wreckage and he was taken to the hospital at La Panne where his leg was amputated.

His government made him a Chevalier of Honor, and he became known as Willy Coppens de Houthulst. He stayed on in the Air Service, despite his amputation and continued to fly until May 1940 when the German invasion again overwhelmed his country. Willy then retired to Switzerland, and when last heard of was still living there.

FERNAND JACQUET

World War I aviation buffs quite possibly will recall the names of Willy Coppens and Edmond Thieffry, but that of Fernand Jacquet will leave most of them puzzled. He was never high among the aces, but he flew from 1914 until the end of the war, and must be considered the "spark plug" of the Belgian Air Service.

The son of a wealthy landowner, Jacquet spent most of his early life in idle luxury, but in 1907, for no ostensible reason, he joined the Brussels Military Academy, and three years later was commissioned a lieutenant in the Belgian infantry. While serving in the Bruges area he became an expert in Flemish painting and sculpture, and made many friends among the artists of that period.

But the infantry held little interest for him, and he next became an aviator, taking his training at the Military Aviation School, and in May 1913 was assigned to Number 2 Squadron equipped with Henri Farmans. This squadron was thrown into the defense of Namur, but their 80-horsepower Gnome engines were not equal to the task, and very little flying was accomplished. So Jacquet mounted a Lewis gun on an Opel racing car, and using Prince de Caraman-Chimay as his driver, drove through the Belgian rear-guard troops to harry German cavalry. During one of these forays Jacquet trapped a troop of Uhlans, killed their leader, two other officers, and twenty-six troopers. Those who escaped this Belgian Rattlesnake galloped into the Belgian rear guard and suffered further casualties.

When his squadron had been furnished with new Farmans, Jacquet took over the command, and they went back to an area south of Antwerp to do artillery-spotting in the hope of neutralizing the big German guns that were pounding the seaport city. When the British and Belgians were finally driven out of Antwerp the aviation units moved back as far as Saint-Denis, and erected their hangars on the racecourse at Ostend. The fortunes of war eventually carried Jacquet's squadron back to Saint-Pol where he and his pilots took part in the Battle of the Yser.

Aboard these ancient Farmans, Jacquet carried out escort patrols, low-bombing, and other requirements until early 1915 when a few Lewis guns were at last available. On April 17 this Belgian aristocrat met and destroyed his first enemy plane when he downed an Aviatik that fell in flames over the village of Beerst. This was the first victory scored by any pilot of the Belgian Air Service.

When by late 1915 the first fixed-gun Fokkers were appearing on the front, Jacquet realized that air fighting would become a standard feature, so he daubed his Farman in gay colors, adding a white skull to the nacelle. He then set out on a new program, flying alone in the manner of a high-seas corsair. He worked out the art of joining up with unsuspecting Jerries, and then when he could move within range his gunner would pound the nearest enemy plane to wreckage. They downed seven planes in this manner in a very short time, but because the gunner handled the weapon the score was apparently credited to neither. As Fernand explained, "We do not fly and fight for decorations and awards, we fight to shoot down enemy planes, and that should be enough," he added proudly.

Fernand Jacquet enjoyed a charmed life, and although he flew continually he was not wounded until September 8, 1916, when he was hit by an antiaircraft burst while flying over Birchoote. He was credited with his fifth success on February 1, 1917, when he—still flying Farmans—shot down two Rumplers off the sea front at Lombartzyde.

During the summer of 1917 Jacquet's squadron was equipped with Spad S.11 two-seaters, and he handled these questionable machines so well, it was decided to organize three full squadrons of Spad two-seaters. Jacquet was put in full charge of this new escadrille, and he boldly attacked any Von Richthofen Jagdgeschwader that entered his domain. He downed two of their planes before the Armistice put an end to his "corsair" operations.

After the war Fernand Jacquet founded a civilian flying school near Charleroi where dozens of new pilots were trained. When World War II broke out he joined the resistance movement but was soon captured by the Nazis and imprisoned at the Huy fortress. When peace was secured, Jacquet returned to his estate at Beaumont where he died in 1947 at age fifty-nine.

ANDRÉ DE MEULEMEESTER

This son of a wealthy brewer of Bruges racked up eleven victories as a sergeant pilot, and before the war ended was known widely as the Eagle of Flanders. André, a small, slim youth, volunteered for the Air Service shortly after the start of the war, and was fortunate to be assigned to the Belgian school at Etampes rather than having to buy his training in England as Willy Coppens had.

By late 1916 de Meulemeester, still a reedy man with a shock of unkempt hair, was assigned to Belgium's Number 1 Squadron, and given a Nieuport scout. For a time it was felt that André would be of more use as an entertainer, for he was an excellent pianist, but once he found himself with such stars as Captain Jacquet and Jan Olieslagers, he soon displayed excellent flying ability. He downed his first enemy plane on April 30, 1917, nailing a two-seater just inside the German lines. On June 11 he destroyed a second over Beerst.

Ever the languid type, de Meulemeester was not too enthusiastic about piloting, but paid much attention to his guns, and like so many others who became ranking aces, was a skilled sharpshooter. On July 21 he intercepted an Albatros pilot who had been making life miserable for Belgian troops in the trenches. Although the young Belgian was slightly wounded, the Albatros was shot down between the lines.

On his return from a hospital, André was made a flight commander although he still held the rank of sergeant. He and Willy Coppens flew together, one aboard a Nieuport, the other a Hanriot, and eventually André was converted to the Belgian machine which he had painted a canary yellow. The British fliers who were not permitted to take such liberties with their aircraft looked on this yellow and blue display with deep suspicion. Finally, de Meulemeester had to take his yellow Hanriot on a familiarization flight to visit all nearby R.F.C. squadrons and assure them it was an Allied plane. He then selected two other Belgian pilots, Kervyn de Lettenhove and Custo de Mevius, as his wing men and continued his forays against the German Air Service.

In time de Meulemeester's Yellow Flight became a fixture on the Flanders front, and the young man from Bruges gradually added to his score. There was one period when he was Belgium's leading ace, but he could not keep pace with Willy Coppens. He carried on, however, and finished the war safe and sound. When last heard of he was back in Bruges managing the family business, but he is still remembered as the Eagle of Flanders.

JAN OLIESLAGERS

This Belgian hero began life in a poverty-stricken family that lived in a dreary shack hidden in an alley near Antwerp Cathedral. His childhood was typical of any boy brought up in a dockyard area, and young Jan apparently enjoyed himself playing truant from school, roaming the streets, and making the most of the seaport's romantic background. His father wanted his children to attend the local schools, but, unfortunately, he died when Jan was eleven years old. Deciding to get a job young Jan joined a local bicycle firm, became a skilled mechanic, and later turned to bicycle racing. He competed on many tracks, was a sales manager, and with the advent of the powered cycle, switched to motorcycles. By 1900 Jan Olieslagers was one of the crack riders of his day and was known all over Europe.

By 1909 he was famous and had made a lot of money. He became interested in flying, and after Louis Blériot flew the Channel, Jan bought a Blériot monoplane for 12,500 French francs, about $3125 in that day. He entered a number of meets with this machine but had little success, and he finally made a tour of Algeria where he gave exhibitions until he cracked up the monoplane. At the Air Display in France in 1910 Jan set a new endurance mark by staying aloft for more than five hours. Between 1911 and 1913 he flew in air meets all over Europe, and "even learned to loop-the-loop." His native city renamed one of its streets in his honor.

When the war broke out, Olieslagers put himself, his airplanes, and staff of mechanics at the disposal of his country. He was immediately made a corporal and ordered to report to the Aviation Headquarters at Brasschaet, and from there was sent off to fly a reconnaissance mission, using his own Blériot-11. After that, he retreated to Saint-Pol. In the following months Jan flew a number of observation missions, and then was posted to Number 1 Squadron, and listed as a fighter pilot.

In March of 1915 Jan was commissioned a second lieutenant, relieved of his Blériot monoplane, and given a Nieuport scout. By this time much of his earlier enthusiasm had been burned out, and he spent most of his war commanding his flight, inventing new firing systems, and tending the officers' mess flower garden. He came through unscathed, and is credited officially with six victories, although he was very desultory about filling out his combat reports. Most of his companions swore he must have downed triple that number. They pointed out that he was on the front for more than four years, flying practically every day, generally operating well over the enemy lines.

Once the war ended, Olieslagers gave up aviation. He was now over thirty-five years of age, and peacetime flying had no appeal for him. He died in 1942.

EDMOND THIEFFRY

Another colorful figure in the Belgian Air Service was Edmond Thieffry who was studying to become a lawyer when he was drafted for national service in 1912 and assigned to the 14th Infantry Regiment. He managed enough furlough to pass his university examination, and then went to the 10th Infantry Regiment to fill out his time. Unfortunately, war broke out and Edmond was taken prisoner in the first week, but in the following confusion he escaped. He picked up an old motorcycle and chugged toward the Dutch border. Switching to civilian clothes, he next used his legal training to get a border pass from a German officer, and on arriving in Holland was interned. Again, his legal training stood him in good stead. He talked himself out of Holland, taking his battered motorcycle with him. He rejoined the 10th Infantry Regiment near Coxyde on the Flanders coast.

There were several Allied flying fields nearby, and, having already had his fill of the infantry, Thieffry put in for a transfer to the Air Service. He managed to get his "wings" and was soon posted to an observation squadron that was equipped with Farmans and Voisin Canon biplanes. From this point on he seemingly went to work for the opposition, for his log book relates nothing but crash after crash, and it was decided that no observer should be risked when Thieffry was piloting. So he was sent to school again to learn to fly single-seater fighters. Here, he piled up three or four more trainers, but by December 1916 he was considered capable enough to join Number 5 Squadron that was equipped with Baby Nieuports. He soon crashed two of these 80-horsepower Gnome machines, but his superiors kept him on as the squadron was about to move to a new airfield.

Thieffry's luck did not turn until March 15, 1917, when he was on a lone patrol. He saw a German two-seater making a reconnaissance over the Belgian trenches, so he moved up into the sun, dived, and crashed the snooper in front of the Belgian lines. A few days later Edmond found a Fokker, and again a German airplane piled up in the Allied trenches. The next morning the tables were turned when he was spotted by two German fighters who sent him crashing into no man's land.

In the spring of 1917 a few of the early type Spads were made available to the Belgians, and Thieffry was given one of the first three to be delivered. The next day he caught an Albatros by surprise, and racked up his third victory. It had been making a submarine-protection patrol. Late in June he came upon a flurry of British scouts and Albatros machines circling about at 18,000 feet. Moving up into the sun he went down on a German who was stalking a Britisher. His first burst caused the Albatros to break off and flutter away, but the next day he himself was shot down once more, but fortunately crashed inside the Belgian lines.

He returned to his field at Houthem, and during dinner that night a flight of Gotha bombers passed overhead. Thieffry took off in another Spad, and in one short lesson learned the trials of the night fighter, but downed no Gothas. On July 3, 1917, he was assigned to escort an observation ship that was carrying out a photorecon-naissance patrol between Bruges and Ghent. During this show Thief-fry and his flight mates barged into a number of German planes and there ensued what was called a dogfight. Edmond managed to knock down two Albatros fighters, upon which King Albert personally rec-ommended him for a commission. This promotion came through on July 24.

Thieffry went on leave to London, and shortly after his return an amusing situation arose when he found that his Spad had been fitted with a new type propeller. He decided to make a test flight, and while circling his area made a practice dive on an observation balloon. Unfortunately, it was a British bag, and the ground crew not knowing this was simply a test flight, sent up a fighter machine to drive him away. The Belgian flier was given a bad time until it was seen that he was a member of the Allied forces. To salve any injured feelings the British pilot invited Thieffry to have lunch with him, and when he left he was given a case of whisky and a pair of field boots. From that day on Edmond flew in suitable footwear. Up till then he had flown in a pair of old carpet slippers.

In mid-August Thieffry checked the Zeebrugge submarine base again and found two Albatros planes on patrol. He engaged both of them, and shot one down. For the rest of that autumn he scored consistently, and had ten enemy planes to his credit. When winter set in, air action was curtailed by the weather, but Edmond was in the air whenever possible. On February 23, 1918, he teamed up with de Meulemeester and Kervyn, and the threesome flew off to act offensively. They found a couple of German aircraft moving in and out of a low layer of overcast. Thieffry went after one, and when last seen was in a steep dive with smoke billowing from his Spad. He had selected a German two-seater, and the observer scored first. The Belgian ace managed to land safely, but was captured and clapped in a Stettin hospital.

Once his slight wound had healed Edmond made several attempts to escape. In fact he managed to break out four times, but was always captured before he could cross the enemy lines. After the Armistice was signed he was in the Ingelstadt Fort, and when he felt that the repatriation machinery was moving too slowly, he broke out again. This time he had no trouble in reaching Switzerland, and was back in Brussels by December 6, 1918.

Edmond Thieffry returned to the profession of law, but eventually established an air line in the Belgian Congo. In 1929 while making a survey flight over a proposed route, he was caught in a tropical storm and killed.

PART THREE

British Empire

BRITISH EMPIRE

All reliable records disclose that the military airmen of the British Empire contributed more sound tactical and strategic effort to the Great War than those of any other service. With the inheritance of the sea as a background, most of them seemed born to the cockpit, and the new element—the air—while their traditional spirit of sportsmanship prepared them for the all-or-nothing dueling in the skies. British designers and manufacturers provided the best military aircraft of that day. Their leaders who lived through the 1914–15 engagements quickly learned the required application of aircraft to ground problems with greater skill than the staffs of any other nation involved. Great Britain's magnificent effort and sacrifice is probably the finest and most appealing story of the whole military campaign.

Entering the fray with a handful of aircraft, a few pilots, and no doctrine to guide them, they carried out the first reconnaissance missions under the most difficult conditions. There was little hope, and certainly no glory, in flying in those days; that Great Tradition had to be created. There were tremendous handicaps, plenty of hard work, and reams of criticism. The enemy had struck the first blow and had taken the initial offensive, gobbling up miles of Allied ground long before the British Army could put a force into the field. The flying men were the pawns of any service that demanded their aid, for they had no central command, no guide lines to follow, no precedent to carry out their many tasks.

But in seventeen short months the Royal Flying Corps and the Royal Naval Air Service had proved themselves, and had won their crests. The R.F.C., in particular, had learned how to bomb, to observe, and to fight in the air, and by November 1916 this new military arm was holding a line that stretched from Calais to a point well east of the Somme. Their reconnaissance machines had revolutionized artillery fire, and their bombers had saturated 298 military targets with 17,600 bombs. They had even begun to bomb at night. Their greatest stride, however, was in the field of air fighting. Though they had started the long battle with inferior equipment, they never relinquished their offensive spirit.

Their true fighting history began shortly before the Battle of the Somme in the summer of 1916. On the opening day the R.F.C. had 426 pilots available to their front-line squadrons, and when that grisly campaign was over by mid-November it could still boast of 585 pilots standing by their machines. Between those two dates 308 airmen had been killed, wounded, or were missing. Another 268 had been struck off strength for various reasons, other than direct action. Nearly 200 observers were lost or seriously wounded, but over that same period British airmen had taken 19,000 photographs, registered 8612 targets for the artillery, destroyed 164 German aircraft, and damaged 205 more. All this action was, of course, carried out deep within the enemy lines.

The Royal Naval Air Service that had taken responsibility for the defense of Britain eventually created the world's first true naval air service. They developed naval air operations to a fine point. They worked with naval architects to design the first aircraft carriers, and solved the many problems of deck flying. They fought the common enemy from seaplanes and flying boats, perfecting the torpedo attack, antisubmarine tactics, and long-range naval reconnaissance. A number of R.N.A.S. squadrons went to the Continent and shared the burden of fighting the enemy over France and Flanders.

When the Royal Flying Corps and the Royal Naval Air Service were combined in April 1918 to become the Royal Air Force, it was soon realized that this new air arm not only was an amalgam of land and sea fighters, but included the best of Great Britain's colonies; her sons who had swarmed from all corners of the globe to fight for her cause. Canada and Australia had contributed generously. New Zealand and South Africa were well represented as were many of the lesser-known territories. Australia had four complete squadrons in action at the Armistice, while hundreds of individual Australians were still serving in British squadrons.

There are no reliable figures to indicate how many Canadians flew in World War I, but of the 7589 flying men lost in the British air services, about one quarter were Canadians. Of the twenty-seven British fliers credited with thirty or more "kills," ten were Canadians, and as a group the Canucks accounted for 438 enemy aircraft.

These and other figures are often used by critics of the British effort to bolster their argument that Britain's air war was fought chiefly by men of her colonies. This is a distortion of fact and circumstance. It should be pointed out that it was comparatively easy for Canadians—and Americans in particular—to apply for and be accepted for the British service. It is easy to ignore the fact that British young men were just as eager and willing to fly as any representative group, and that they volunteered continually in great numbers.

But transfers for the British were difficult. By mid-1916 the cream of Great Britain's youth was already in other arms of the military service. They had been trained for the infantry, the artillery, the engineers, machine-gun sections, and by 1916 for the new Tank Corps. As they were most valuable to the ground or sea arms, it was almost impossible for them to obtain transfers to the flying services.

My own experience illustrates this point. I joined up in 1914 and became a member of a British mounted-infantry regiment. By 1916 I saw the attractions of the Royal Flying Corps, and, along with thirty others of my squadron, applied for a transfer. I was the only one permitted to make the change, and I can only assume I was the one who would be missed the least.

During the same time Canadians and Americans, across the Atlantic, were volunteering for R.F.C. appointments and flight training in North America. As soon as they were capable of flying a primary trainer they were given their commissions, and awarded flying pay, long before they reached Britain or France. We, who were active-service volunteers, started to fly as aerial gunners on the Western Front with the same rank we had held in our previous regiments. In my case I was a cavalry trooper (private), and flew as an aerial gunner for months before I was promoted to corporal, and I had to put in many more months before I was commissioned and given an opportunity to become a pilot.

This was typical of the treatment accorded British volunteers who sincerely wished to fly. What openings were available in the training schools were filled by Canadian and American volunteers.

This aside in no way detracts from the splendid records of the many British colonials. They contributed enormously in all phases of military flying. This happy blending of Anglo-Saxon blood and spirit no doubt accounted for the glorious esprit de corps we enjoyed in that memorable service.

When the Armistice bugles rang out the Royal Air Force had written a magnificent chapter of military history. It boasted a force of 291,175 officers and men, quite a growth from the 2073 who had been mobilized in August 1914. More than 16,000 officers and NCO airmen had given their lives while fighting over France, Flanders, Italy, Macedonia, Syria, Palestine, Arabia, and Africa. Many had died over the North Sea, the Mediterranean, and the Indian Ocean. Of the 50,000 planes built and flown on all fronts, nearly 36,000 were lost or written-off. At times the enemy did gain technical superiority, but never long enough to dominate any battlefield, or to ensure victory. It was a campaign that proved once more it is men— not machines—that win wars.

Here are the histories of some of the men who made Great Britain's effort so successful.

ALBERT BALL

This young Englishman dominated the Western Front between the summer of 1916 and the spring of 1917, and had British officialdom permitted him to be publicized in relation to his deeds, he would have been the most fabulous character of World War I. Strangely enough, he has never attracted American interest, despite the fact he downed forty-four enemy aircraft. For wild, uncontrolled pugnacity, he had no equal on any front.

He was the true maverick, a devil-may-care type, who had no regard for his own safety, rules, or discipline. He had the tenacity of a bulldog, and the views of a poet. He liked music, books, paintings, and wrote with the touch of an essayist. Aflame with sincere patriotism, and buoyed by what he considered his bounden duty, Albert Ball's war career reads like that of some pulp magazine hero. Dead by the time he had reached his twentieth year, he had won more honors for heroism than any man his age. Besides the Victoria Cross, he was awarded the Distinguished Service Order three times, the Military Cross, the Russian Order of St. George, and the French Legion of Honor.

Albert Ball was born at Lenton, Nottingham, the son of Alderman Ball who became Mayor of Nottingham. Albert was an ardent member of the Boy Scouts, was devoted to his mother and adored his sister Lois, a delightful tomboy who matched Albert stride for stride. He attended the Nottingham High School and Trent College in Derbyshire where he majored in engineering. By the time he was seventeen he had set up a small plant he called the Universal Engineering Works. His business cards proclaimed that the firm was

On Admiralty and War Office Lists, giving the impression he was turning out dreadnoughts and 16-inch guns for the government.

The war put an end to that project, and he signed up as a private in the 7th Battalion of the Sherwood Foresters; the Nottingham company was known as the Robin Hood Rifles. Albert had won his sergeant's stripes within a month. When he indicated a keen desire to get to the front, he was made a second lieutenant, and trained other recruits in England.

In May 1915 he learned that a certain Lieutenant Rhodes-Moorhouse had won the Victoria Cross while flying in France. At 3:00 A.M. the following day, he straddled his motorcycle and roared over the sixty miles from his base at Luton to a private flying school at Hendon. Making a quick deal, Albert paid for a series of flying lessons, and before he returned to his base he had a few minutes of dual instruction aboard an old French Caudron. He then chugged back to Luton just in time to make his early-morning parade. It would be difficult to imagine anyone today buying his own instruction in any weapon so as to be accepted for a fighting role in a global war, but that is exactly what young Ball—and dozens of other British lads—did in those halcyon days.

＊

Ball eventually earned his "ticket" despite two hair-raising crashes, and by October 1915 he had put in sufficient time to warrant a transfer to the Royal Flying Corps. This entailed more weeks and months of comparative inaction, for once the R.F.C. tutors took him over there were many new things to learn. However, by early 1916 Albert Ball was given the opportunity to go to France—but not as a pilot; the R.F.C. was short of observers and aerial gunners. Albert who had bought most of his training felt he was entitled to fly as a pilot, so he disdained the offer.

His luck took a turn for the better by February 1916 when he was posted to Number 13 Squadron where they were flying the B.E.2c (the Quirk). Compared to the ancient kites he had been trained on in Britain, the B.E.2c was a rip-roaring battleplane, and for a time it was too "hot" for him to handle. In fact, there was a period when his commanding officer considered sending him back to England for further training, but Albert made such a scene, he was allowed to stay on.

In order to show his determination to fly on the front, Ball volunteered for a number of "secret" missions, flights that carried British intelligence agents over the line and deposited them in enemy territory. He did an excellent job of getting them in safely, but on several occasions had to use his limited authority to make them disembark. These agents usually were Belgians or Frenchmen who had some knowledge of the German language. They were well paid, and most of them enjoyed their work, but on two occasions Ball took off from Izel-le-Hameau with one of these reluctant operators, and twice had to turn around and fly him back. It was a spirit of behavior the Nottingham lad could not understand. If a man agreed to do a job, he should do it. He finally settled the issue by forcibly booting one of these reluctant passengers out of his cockpit, pointed to a nearby hedge, and took off again. He never had any trouble with an intelligence man after that.

There also were other jobs for Ball. Regardless of the weather, he took his turn in carrying out artillery shoots, daring the German fighters, and now and then doing the odd photography show. In all this he increased his skill as a pilot, but at best he was only a journeyman apprentice as far as Army cooperation work was concerned. He found it difficult to work with other airmen, and it was soon evident that if he was to be used to his full capability he would have to become a single-seater pilot.

It was the practice in those days to have certain two-seater squadrons assigned one or two single-seaters that could be flown in support of the cooperation machines. Number 13 Squadron had two Bristol Scout single-seaters for such sorties, and Ball began to fly one of these aircraft regularly. It was soon seen that he was finally earning his keep in this manner, and he agreed to fly escort for the two-seaters of both Number 13 and Number 11 squadrons that were on the same field.

Ball spent most of the early summer hacking about the sky, chasing enemy formations, or diving pell-mell into Fokker groups, but none of these forays resulted in any official confirmations. Then, through a routine distribution of new aircraft, Ball was furnished with a new Nieuport scout, but victories still evaded him although he coursed far and wide.

✳

After a short leave he returned to the front early in June in time to take a leading role in the Battle of the Somme. This famous campaign gave him plenty of opportunity to work hard, and he made the most of it. Hour after hour, he was out attacking enemy kite balloons, chasing enemy transport, peppering enemy trenches with machine-gun fire, and providing some cooperation for the advancing British troops. During all this he finally downed a kite balloon for which he was awarded the Military Cross. While working with a flight of F.E.2bs he downed a Roland two-seater, but paradoxically admitted that it made him feel ill to see two brave men go down in flames.

While the Battle of the Somme continued all that summer of 1916, Albert Ball still worked with Numbers 11 and 13 squadrons. He also dug and planted a small flower garden behind his hangar, and at nights would entertain his flying mates with a few violin solos. Some airmen remember him as a splendid musician, while others felt he was only torturing strings of catgut. He still disliked anything resembling routine formation, and his superiors decided that he was only happy when he was flying alone, so he was shifted to a single-seater squadron (Number 60) and told to work out his own routine. This is not to imply that Ball never flew in flight formation; he did, but he was permitted to fly lone-wolf patrols as often as he wished.

After a week or so adjusting to scout-squadron life, Ball began to show his true mettle. He also developed a new style of air fighting by making the most of a Lewis gun mounted on the upper wing of the Nieuport that could be tilted and aimed up at the underside of an enemy plane. Combined with daring skill, Ball used this tactic in stalking an enemy and getting below him without being seen. On one occasion he stalked his CO, Major Smith-Barry, all the way from the front line to their airfield without the major having any idea there was another plane within five miles. Ball was particularly adept in trapping German two-seaters in this manner.

His score began to increase, and his exploits were common talk all through R.F.C. squadrons, but none of his victories were published in British papers. Now and then the French correspondents managed to insert the latest Ball exploit, but little was known of him in his own country until he himself was shot down. When he went on leave in September 1916, the *London Gazette* mentioned that Captain Albert Ball had been awarded the Distinguished Service Order but without relating for what the high honor had been bestowed.

Ball's unorthodox method of attacking two-seaters may have induced German designers to devise "tunnel guns" that fired down through open ports cut in the fuselage floors of their Junkers J-I, the Gotha G-V bomber, the Friedrichshafen G-III bomber, and, in particular, the famous A.E.G. two-seater bomber that appeared early in 1918.

On October 3, 1916, Ball was suddenly posted to Home Establishment. He had scored thirty-one victories, but these figures were not made available to the British press, although at the time Germany was flooding the world with detailed reports of her leading aces, and American newspapers were giving these stories wide promotion. The French, who had unwittingly created the "ace" category, found that to counter this German propaganda they would have to record and distribute detailed accounts of their own fighting airmen.

All that the people of Britain knew of Captain Albert Ball's amazing career was that a young man, son of Nottingham's Mayor, had been awarded the D.S.O. and the Military Cross . . . and it seemed that he was in the Royal Flying Corps, or some such organization. Only uncommunicative officialdom had any idea what young Albert Ball had accomplished.

In England Ball was sent out to give lectures at flying schools, but he was too young to present any enlightening information. Next, he was given a refresher course in aerial gunnery at some fighter school. "What a fool's game!" he complained.

While on this leave he persuaded the Austin Company to build a single-seater fighter of his own design. This machine had some good features, including a fixed machine gun that fired through the hollow crankshaft of the Hispano-Suiza engine and out through the center of the prop boss. It had fairly good speed, but never went into production, since the new S.E.5 was by then ready for mass manufacture and it was considered wiser to concentrate on that memorable type.

By February 1917 Ball was permitted to return to France and was posted to Number 56 Squadron, at the time renowned for a number of star pilots including Major G. J. C. Maxwell, Captain James B. McCudden, Lieutenant Arthur P. F. Rhys-Davids, Captain R. A. Mayberry, Lieutenant H. K. Knaggs, Captain R. T. C. Hoidge among others. After his long period in England Ball found the Western

Front an enigma. He was unable to comprehend what had happened to the war. He discovered he was an "ace" and was expected to act the role, but he had no idea how an ace was supposed to act. For a time he was homesick, missing the affection of his family. Then, too, he had fallen in love with a girl who was serving in one of Britain's women's uniformed services, and he spent every spare minute writing letters to her.

As he resumed his war flying he was so dissatisfied with the S.E.5 he was given a Nieuport for his lone-wolf forays. As a captain he did lead his flight on routine patrols, but carried out his personal prowls in his favorite scout. Between April 22 and May 7 he shot down and destroyed eleven enemy aircraft, and with the thirty-one credited to him previously, he again led the Allied field with forty-two victories. Maturity came fast, and Ball forsook his Nieuport and accepted the S.E.5, realizing that he had to acknowledge progress, and the fact that this machine was better equipped to engage the new German fighters.

As happened in so many cases, Ball's finish furnished a mystery that has been refurbished many times. It may never be known just how he died, or by whose hand, but this is how the final chapter of his life began:

Officials of 9th Wing, R.F.C., decided that a formation of Spads, Camels, and S.E.5s should patrol over the Douai-Cambrai sector throughout the day of May 7, 1917. Another Battle of Arras was in progress, and the British were concentrating on the village of Bullecourt. At 5:30 P.M. that day a three-element formation from Number 56 Squadron, headed by Captains Ball, Crowe, and Meintjes, set out for that area. All pilots rendezvoused as arranged, formed up in three tiers, and crossed into enemy territory through heavy clouds and rain. Ball and Knaggs broke away from the group during these unpleasant conditions, and prowled about together at 7000 feet, while Meintjes and Crowe took their little packs up through the clouds to the 9000- and 10,000-foot levels. Over Bourlon Wood just west of Cambrai they met even worse conditions and were widely dispersed. Meintjes' flight came upon a German Albatros and one of them shot it down.

Gradually, the whole S.E.5 formation collected itself, and came roaring out of clouds—nose-on to a circus of red-and-white Albatroses. Everyone went into action with no particular order. Meintjes had to spin out when two Huns got on his tail. Cecil Lewis was Meintjes' wingman and found himself in the same trouble, so Ball and Knaggs had to go to their rescue. Meintjes then returned to the fray and shot down a red fighter that fell east of Gouy-sous-Bellone. Hoidge knocked down an Albatros smack into the streets of Cambrai.

When this melee became unmanageable, the British fighters turned and re-formed over Arras, after which more intensive fighting occurred until most of the S.E.5s began to run out of ammunition or fuel. Ball, Crowe, Hoidge, and Knaggs were widely separated, but Crowe reported later that he had seen Ball fire two red lights, indicating he had spotted more enemy aircraft. Crowe looked around but could see nothing at which to shoot, so he followed Ball who was heading for Lens.

Then Ball suddenly went into a dive, and Crowe saw him firing at an Albatros single-seater below. Crowe joined in the fight until Ball took full command and followed the German eastward into a heavy cloud. That was the last Crowe saw of Captain Ball.

❋

What seems to have happened was reconstructed later by military and civilian officials in the area.

Ball continued on to finish what is now credited as his forty-fourth victim. Then, finding himself out of ammunition he dropped through the clouds and came out in the clear just east of the village of Annoeulin. He recognized the hamlet, and following an old habit decided to check on the time. Although he wore a wrist watch and had a small clock in his instrument panel, Albert, a Sunday school lad, implicitly trusted church clocks. Whenever he was in that area, and on his way home, he usually sped past the Annoeulin church and glanced at the time-encrusted hands of the tower clock.

The villagers knew this, and the Germans occupying the area eventually learned of his habit. They recognized the British scout with the scarlet nose spinner, and the habit was an invitation. Early in May the Germans put a machine gun in the church tower—and waited.

On the evening of May 7 Captain Albert Ball sped past the church clock, and a few seconds later crashed just outside the village of Annoeulin. A spray of bullets from that sanctuary had accomplished what the whole German Air Force had been unable to do.

At the end of that month—more than three weeks later—German newspapers announced the death of Captain Albert Ball, and reported that he had been shot down by Lothar von Richthofen, brother of Baron Manfred von Richthofen.

But the villagers of Annoeulin knew better; the British soon learned better, as Lothar von Richthofen stated in his combat report that he had been victorious over Captain Ball, and had shot down his Sopwith Triplane near Annoeulin. He had somehow produced the engine number of Ball's S.E.5, but was unable to produce the aircraft's number. When he was charged some time later with the mistake of calling Ball's biplane a triplane he said offhandedly that in the excitement of air action he often made an error of that nature.

But Lothar von Richthofen could not explain this victory over Annoeulin on May 7, 1917, because, if German records can be relied on, he was on sick leave on that date.

Here was another slip-up in the German propaganda machine. When an Allied star was shot down, his defeat usually was credited to one of the Von Richthofens. Details were of no concern. Facts could be woven and twisted into a required pattern. All that mattered was the development of a new tale of glory to bolster the sagging morale of the German Air Force. By the same token when Max Immelmann was shot down by a British aerial gunner, it was explained in Germany that Max had died in an aircraft accident; that he had shot his propeller off and chunks of the blade had smashed through the main bracing wires of his wings. Another version was that he was shot down by a direct hit from antiaircraft cannon. British records disclose that Lieutenant G. R. McCubbin, flying an F.E.2b of Number 25 Squadron engaged Immelmann, a Sergeant Prehn, and two brothers named Heinemann well inside the German lines. McCubbin's aerial gunner, Corporal J. H. Waller who was just out of the trenches, put a long burst of twenty-five rounds into Immelmann's fuselage, and the Eagle of Lille went into a spin and his Fokker broke up in midair. But it was McCubbin, of course, who received credit for the victory, not the aerial gunner.

Albert Ball's death has been rehashed for years, but it should be evident that neither of the Von Richthofen brothers was in the air that day. The Baron was in Berlin on leave, and his brother was still convalescent as the result of a bullet wound in a leg. Years later, Albert's brother Cyril talked to a peasant woman in Annoeulin who stated that she had pulled Albert out of the crash. He was still alive at the time, but died shortly after as she held him in her arms. Some years after that, Albert's father bought the field on which his son's plane had fallen and had the actual crash spot concreted over. Albert Ball, however, was buried in a nearby German cemetery.

On June 3, 1917, less than one month after his last flight, Ball was honored with the Victoria Cross. It was the tenth V.C. to be awarded a flying man in nearly three years of air fighting. Of those gallant ten, six had died in winning it.

WILLIAM GEORGE BARKER

In these pages of World War I history the lives and deeds of fighter pilots make up a considerable portion. At one time the careers of air aces claimed world-wide interest. This was a new art of warfare, and the jousting was carried out in full view of thousands of earthbound spectators. Such battles will never be seen again, which possibly explains the continuing interest in World War I air adventures.

The cast of characters in these deadly dramas were household names for many years, and all of these names had a certain cadence, a certain tang, all producing an immediate picture of spectacular war flying. But who of all these players was the greatest, the most renowned, the top air-fighter of them all? It is simple to pick such a man from the list of the highest-ranking aces, but this would not produce the greatest. We are all prone to chauvinism or personal prejudices in such matters. Perhaps we would select Baron von Richthofen who is credited with eighty victories. Some would prefer the two-fisted, wide-legged type so popular in standard adventure stories. There is a school of thought that visualizes the Celtic character with a bucko name and manner for that championship belt. The conservative group would select the quiet, modest man whose history is a series of understatements. We may argue that a man who lived through it is certainly more skilled than one who went out in a blaze of glory.

As an example of the higher type of air fighter, let us consider for the moment Colonel William G. Barker, one of the greats who came out of Canada. A native of Dauphin, Manitoba, Billy Barker, as he was widely known, first joined the Canadian Mounted Rifles and became a member of its machine-gun section, known lugubriously as the "suicide squad." By 1915 the Mounted Rifles had reached Shorncliffe, England, and by September of that year had crossed the Channel where they had to do what most mounted regiments did—give up their horses and saddles and serve in the infantry. As did so many other cavalrymen, and particularly the Canadians, Barker soon saw the advantages of the flying men and wrote out a request for a transfer to the Royal Flying Corps.

The request was granted, and because of his skill with the machine gun, Billy first served as an NCO aerial gunner in the back seat of a B.E.2c with Number 9 Squadron. During the Battle of Neuve-Chapelle in March 1916 he scored his first victory, and a couple of weeks later was awarded a commission, and he went to London for a change of uniform. He returned to France on April 7 and joined Number 4 Squadron and continued as an observer-gunner.

On one occasion, while serving as an observer during the Battle of the Somme, Barker was hit by a chunk of antiaircraft shrapnel that caused a painful wound in his leg. On landing, the squadron medical officer prepared papers that would have sent him to a hospital and perhaps back to Britain. But Barker sensed he was needed at this crucial time, and persuaded the doctor to do a special job of bandaging, and retain him on strength of the squadron. The next day he limped to his cockpit, but was able to carry out a very important reconnaissance patrol.

He served with three different squadrons before he applied for pilot training, but by November 1916 he was in Narborough, England, taking dual-control instruction. Skilled by his many hours as an observer, Billy Barker needed only one hour of such training, after which he was turned loose to run up the required solo time. "There's nothing much I can teach you," his instructor said. "I think you're a born pilot."

By January 1917 he was back on the front flying as a pilot with Number 15 Squadron where he was immediately made a flight commander because of his long experience. Over the following months he logged considerable time on the B.E.2c and R.E.8, and by the following October was probably the best-trained Canadian airman on the Western Front. His ability to spot trouble and report it clearly brought him his first British decoration, the Military Cross, and his fine work with the artillery batteries soon added a Bar to that award.

His broad knowledge of the Western Front was noted by his

superiors and he was returned to England to become an instructor, and in that manner pass on some of his knowledge to others who would replace him. While there, Billy did his best to be selected for fighter training, but Staff decided to keep him on Army cooperation work, so back he went again, this time to serve with Number 28 Squadron. To his great joy he found they were flying, not R.E.8s or B.E.2cs, but Sopwith Camels that had been modified for low-flying tactics, bombing, and such Army cooperation duties. Their field was laid out at Droglandt in the Ypres salient.

By the time Number 28 was well settled down, the Third Battle of Ypres had slogged to its close and there was comparatively little to do, but Barker made the most of his chances, flying the Camel at every opportunity. He particularly stressed contour-flying, or low-level sweeps over enemy territory. During one such sweep Barker and two of his lieutenants went over and ran into a flight of Albatros scouts. Barker shot two down, and his wingmen downed one apiece.

During this hiatus Barker worked on tactics and strategy. He made the most of the maneuverability and performance of the Sopwith, and insisted that his pilots use the fast right-hand turn to their every advantage. Undoubtedly, he contributed much to the manner in which other British pilots eventually showed that the Sopwith Camel was the greatest fighter ever sent out to the Western Front.

Late in October 1917, with only three weeks of Western Front experience, Number 28 Squadron was rushed to Italy where the Austrian Army, reinforced by several German divisions, had smashed the Italians at Caporetto, and was pouring unchecked over the plains of Lombardy. The Italians had lost 800,000 men in this headlong retreat, and the country faced a grim defeat. Number 28 Squadron was part of a newly formed VII Brigade made up of five squadrons selected to make a stand along the Piave River.

Italy was a rare contrast to the Somme. The aircraft were sheltered in canvas hangars, and the personnel lived in bell tents. Before them spread the broad panorama of the Alps above which Austrian airmen skimmed at will. Barker went aloft alone to look over the situation and encountered an enemy plane that he immediately shot down.

By November 28, 1917, Numbers 28 and 34 squadrons were well set up at Grossa and carried out their first offensive patrols from there. Barker led the first patrol and found five Albatros fighters high above the Austrian lines. One was sent down in an out-of-control glide, and a second had its wings shot off. A few days later Barker downed his first kite balloon, and on Christmas Day torched another.

On that December 25, 1917, they learned that an Austrian formation was raiding an Italian airfield a short distance to the south, so Barker took an element of Number 28 Squadron to intercept. They caught up with twenty-two two-seaters, and were joined by a number of Italian scouts. This was the greatest melee ever seen on the Italian front. The Sop Camels and the Italian Ansaldo scouts downed twelve of the Austrian raiders in as many minutes; the remaining ten were lucky to get back home.

Just as Barker was re-forming his unit he noticed another formation of Austrians climbing up from behind the Piave River. He moved so fast he left his flight and was soon tackling ten German Gotha, twin-engined bombers. Sensing that these new planes carried two gunners, he knew they would have to be tackled in a more careful manner.

He circled them first and then went in under the nose of one that seemed to be leading the pack. He pressed his trigger control and watched his tracers zip into the big fuselage. He next treadled his rudder bar until his cone of fire spattered into another, and this bomber staggered under the beating. With that Barker zoomed slightly and came up close under the long fuselage, triggered another burst and the second Gotha went up in flames, crashing on the Italian side of the Piave. After this bewildering attack the remaining bombers turned back, for by that time the rest of the Allied scouts were coming into the picture. A short running battle ensued, but no more Gothas went down. No more mass raids occurred, either.

With the coming of the new year Barker and his lads settled down to add to their scores. Barker downed two more and was awarded the D.S.O. British divisions had dug in along the Asiago Plateau, awaiting reports from their observation squadrons. The Sop Camels helped in all this, and Barker continued to harry enemy kite balloons, shooting two down, and keeping the Austrians off balance until plans could be made for a counterattack. On one occasion Barker piled into eight Austrian planes, causing two to crash in flames, and at another time he found seven in beautiful formation. He downed one of these which brought a Bar for his Military Cross.

❋

After studying R.F.C. aerial photographs, Barker decided to make a raid on the Austrian Army Headquarters located at San Vito al Tagliamento about fifty miles east of the Piave. Leading a flight of Camels, he made a diversionary move by flying toward the sea north of Venice and then suddenly turning inland. By this ruse his planes were able to make their initial dive against the headquarters with no opposition of any kind. They machine-gunned all the buildings, shooting out most of the windows, then they curled back and took turns dropping their four 20-pound Cooper bombs. Before any air opposition could be put up the Camel pilots had blasted the area to wreckage. The trip back produced some mild action when a few Austrians tried to intercept them, but Barker brought every plane safely home.

Following this exploit Barker was taken from Number 28 Squadron and given command of Number 66 Squadron, another R.F.C. unit which was equipped with two flights of Camels, and one of Bristol Fighters. The two-seaters were intended for reconnaissance and observation. Number 66 worked closely with several French squadrons that had been rushed out to Italy, and this association operated so well Barker soon found himself accepting a Croix de Guerre.

As the air opposition faded, Barker decided to introduce the British practice of dropping intelligence agents into the enemy lines. This had never been attempted on this rugged front but Barker was convinced it would be profitable.

He first selected an Italian S.V.4, a big twin-engined biplane built by the Caproni company. This was modified for the trip by cutting a trap door in the lower part of the fuselage. An Italian who had been trained in the use of the Paulus parachute and the handling of homing pigeons was selected to make the intrusion. Barker and Wedgwood Benn (later a noted Labour peer, Viscount Stansgate) decided to pilot this unusual machine on a night intrusion.

They got off successfully, flew across the enemy lines and dumped their man, and his basket of pigeons, safely, and then staged a fake raid by dropping a number of bombs on Austrian emplacements, giving the intelligence agent a chance to get down without being spotted. A few days later the first pigeon reported in with its little tube of information. Another followed a few hours later, and within days Barker and Benn had to fly over again to deliver another crate of pigeons.

This scheme was so successful King Victor Emmanuel III of

Italy awarded Billy Barker the highest medal that country could bestow on anyone—other than an Italian soldier—the Silver Medal for Valor.

*

Early in June 1918 one of Barker's favorite Camel pilots, Lieutenant E. G. Forder, was shot down by an Austrian airman who flew an Albatros D-III that was marked with a classic eagle insignia. Barker sensed that this airman could be Austria's crack ace, Frank Linke-Crawford.

This airman with the perplexing name was born in Poland, but early in his career joined an Austrian Dragoon regiment that by 1915 was fighting the Russians. Cavalry was no better off in the eastern theater of war than in the western, so Linke-Crawford transferred to the Austrian aviation service. Over the months he was posted to a number of squadrons where he flew anything from Brandenburgs to Albatros scouts. He ran up a remarkable score during the Italian retreat, and was given command of Number 60 Squadron of the Austrian Air Force.

Barker lined up a formation of Bristol Fighters which he himself led with a Camel, and set out to search for this Austrian ace. They encountered a ten-ship formation being led by an Albatros daubed with a checkerboard design and a gay eagle. Though he was outnumbered, Barker took his flight into action, and soon selected the gaudy Albatros as his own. Meanwhile the Brisfit boys took on the rest.

Barker and Linke-Crawford staged a duel that lasted several minutes, and while the Austrian was clever, he could not solve Barker's method of attack, so he finally tried to clear out and head for home. But Barker persisted, and just as Linke-Crawford was reaching his own field, he shot him down in flames.

This fight and victory has at times been credited to Captain J. Cottle of Number 45 Squadron, RAF, or to three Italian pilots, but British records would seem to indicate that it was Billy Barker who finally downed the renowned Austrian ace.

By June 1918 the Austrians set up another offensive against the Italians, but they hadn't reckoned with the RAF squadrons—and the now Major Billy Barker. It was Barker who, flying alone over the Piave, first spotted Austrian troops crossing the river on a series of pontoon bridges set up east of Treviso. He turned sharply, and dropped messages on other Allied aerodromes warning of the attack, and then continued on to his own field.

Number 66 Squadron loaded up with everything their Camels and Bristols would carry. The other squadrons, British and Italian, joined in the defense and in no time there was a wild dogfight over the pontoon bridges as the Austrian airmen attempted to head off the attackers. Barker led the Allied thrust, keeping his machines in the air for more than twenty-four hours, leading patrol after patrol, until at last the Austrians were driven back, their bridges cut adrift, and their air components battered and burned. The King of Italy had to find another medal to pin on Barker's chest.

But the Austrians still continued to attempt to get over the river, despite the opposition. On one day the four British squadrons made seventy-two offensive patrols—an average of six patrols per pilot. Amid all this Barker, aboard his Camel, sought out the Albatros D-IIIs, and his score mounted. At one point the British sent out another Bristol Fighter Squadron, the 139th, that was turned over to Barker to command, but he still led this new fighter force from the cockpit of his Camel, though on occasion he would pilot a Brisfit over the line.

Early in September Barker was finally relieved of his strenuous command and ordered to return to England to head a new school of instruction for fighter pilots. He left Italy with some regret and returned by ship, but on his arrival in England he suggested that he be allowed to return to France to serve some time with an active-service squadron so he could brush up on the latest tactics being used along the Western Front. This request was granted and Billy went out to Number 201 Squadron that by then was flying the new Sopwith Snipe. He found this machine to be even more maneuverable than the Camel, and in a short time had run his score to forty-six before it was insisted that he return to England to take up his new post.

So on October 27, 1918, Major Barker took a Sopwith Snipe and headed back for Hounslow where his new school was to be set up. It was a beautiful day as he climbed for sufficient altitude for his flight across the Channel; in fact, he suddenly realized he had reached 22,000 feet and was still on the French side of the Channel. So, appreciating that no other plane of the period was likely to be that high, he turned and crossed into the enemy lines, instead of heading for Britain.

Over Bois de Marmal he spotted a Jerry two-seater and he decided to intercept. The German pilot took little notice of him, but the observer poured a couple of bursts at Billy, so he nosed down, picked off the observer, and then put another burst into a wing root. The two-seater broke up in midair and slithered to earth. During this aside a Fokker triplane moved into the picture and put a bullet into Barker's leg with its first burst. His right thigh was shattered, and flying with one leg, Billy outmaneuvered the triplane and soon set it on fire.

As he turned away, somewhat chastened, to make a landing to seek medical attention, he was surrounded by a complete German Circus composed of about sixty Fokkers and Albatros single-seaters. Spandau guns opened from every direction, and the Snipe took a severe beating. Another bullet smashed into Barker's left leg, but he fought on.

Flying as best he could he quickly destroyed two Fokkers, making his score four for the two bullets he had received. He watched his victims spin down, and then he fainted and was spinning down himself. Fortunately, the spin started with plenty of height, and by the time he had lost several hundred feet he regained consciousness again. He soon discovered that the Circus pilots were attacking once more. He must have given up all hope of reaching his own line, but he decided to stick it out and take as many as he could with him. He even tried to ram one Fokker, but he was using his guns without knowing he was pressing the Bowden control, and another Fokker went down in flames.

Amid all the confusion, smoke, and tracer design, he finally found an opening and tried to push his stick forward to nose through but his arm would not respond. He stared down and then saw that at some time he had taken an incendiary bullet in his elbow. He tried to take over with his left arm, but before he could make any progress he fainted again.

Seeing that the Britisher was badly hurt, the opposition nosed in for the kill. The Snipe went into a flat spin, and once more the rush of air revived the Canadian, so he rammed his stick forward, went pell-mell for another Fokker and somehow shot it down in flames. As he tried to evade that wreckage, another Hun poured a burst into the Snipe that literally shot the fuel tank from under Billy's seat.

Reacting only by instinct, Billy managed to nose through another covey of Fokkers into the clear. He switched to his reserve tank and headed for the British lines. How he remained conscious all that time is a mystery, but realizing he was somewhere near safety he finally nosed down and tried to make a landing in a shell-torn area. He wiped off the undercarriage, skidded sideways, and then the plane went over on its back.

He had piled up in an area held by a Scottish regiment, and when a group of Jocks pulled him from the wreckage they were amazed to find him still alive. As a result of the crash he had suffered only a broken nose in addition to his wounds received in the air, but he had shot down six enemy planes, running his score up to an even fifty. Some records indicate that William Barker downed fifty-three enemy aircraft; other reports indicate that Barker downed five German Fokkers in his epic battle, making a final score of fifty-two, but whatever his record, this, unquestionably, was the greatest air fight in the history of World War I.

Billy lay in a coma for two weeks. Only his amazing physique saved his life, and whether his unauthorized combat was worth the effort is debatable, for his wounds left him with permanent, painful disabilities. When he finally regained consciousness he learned that the war had ended, and he had been honored with the Victoria Cross. He was promoted to lieutenant colonel and finally returned to Canada where he bravely tried to continue as a flier. He walked with canes, and carried his arm in a special sling for some time, but in 1923 he helped organize the Royal Canadian Air Force. Also, with Billy Bishop's help, he founded Canada's first major air line.

This man who had lived such a fantastic and almost legendary life met his end in a manner that resulted in many odd stories. In March 1930, when all of us believed he was finally relieved of his torture and pain, he was carrying out a routine test flight of a new service plane at Uplands Air Station, Ottawa. For no apparent reason the aircraft suddenly nosed down with the engine full on and crashed in the middle of the airport. A very detailed examination of the machine revealed no possible malfunction, but this is the way in which Lieutenant Colonel William G. Barker died.

In his end can be noted the first of a number of strange deaths that came to Canadian airmen, after they had served so valorously through a long, harrowing campaign.

FRANKLYN LESLIE BARNARD

Few military aviation enthusiasts will recognize the name of Franklyn L. Barnard, but he was one of the outstanding airmen of World War I, though you will not find his name in any list of air aces. Believe it or not, this man began to fly at ten years of age! Young Barnard had made the acquaintance of Colonel S. F. Cody who, years before the war, had built a monster biplane that actually flew. In fact, Colonel Cody (no relation to the famous Buffalo Bill) won the first Military Trials contest held in England, though he was an American citizen at the time. Master Barnard had a winning way, and as he was not too tall Colonel Cody would take him along whenever he was testing out his famous Cathedral biplane. As might be expected, young Barnard learned a great deal about heavier-than-air machines long before most Englishmen had seen a plane in the air, or believed such things could be.

Franklyn Barnard enlisted early in the Royal Flying Corps and eventually went out to France to pilot F.E.2bs of Number 18 Squadron. One day in October 1916 while flying escort to a photoreconnaissance plane in the Bapaume area he had to fight off several enemy machines that were harassing the camera plane. While escorting his charge back to the Allied lines the Fee was attacked by three Albatros fighters, and while his observer, F. S. Rankin, used the front gun, Barnard somehow managed to fly the plane and use the rear weapon well enough to shoot down the Jerry leader. He then relinquished the gun to his observer who raised it on its telescopic mounting, and climbed up on the nacelle locker in order to fire over the top plane at another Albatros that was getting on their tail. This was routine defense aboard F.E.2b pushers.

When he was in this precarious position Rankin was struck in the head as he downed a second Albatros. Barnard was so engrossed in maneuvering the Fee and watching the activity of the third Jerry, he was unaware of what had happened to his observer until he saw Rankin topple from his perch and appear to tumble over the side of the nacelle.

Barnard unsnapped his belt, relinquished the joystick, and made a grab for Rankin, just managing to grip the observer's leather flying jacket. The tussle to haul him back to safety almost yanked Barnard out of his seat, but after a minute or so of tugging and hauling, the pilot finally pulled Rankin back into the nacelle. The observer was unconscious, for several bullets had gone through his helmet.

In the meantime the remaining Albatros was pouring burst after burst into the British biplane, and when Barnard was finally settled in his seat he found he had no aileron control, and the elevator cables were suspiciously slack. He took the long chance and dived until the German pilot gave up the chase. He then headed for the shell-torn area behind his own lines. Rankin died shortly after their landing, and Barnard was supposed to have been recommended for the Distinguished Service Order, but the decoration never came through. Several months later he was awarded the Air Force Cross for special services rendered.

Shortly after he had lost Rankin, Barnard was over the lines again, and during an air action his propeller was shot up and two of the four blades broke off and cut two of his four tail booms. This time it was a gamble whether the tail of the Fee would stay on, but luck flew with him, and he managed to put the hulk down in his own lines. The plane hit hard, rolled over, tossing the observer clear, but trapping Barnard for some time in the wreckage. He spent almost a year in a hospital recovering from his injuries, but as soon as the medics said the word he was back flying again. After the war he won the King's Cup air race twice, but died in his thirty-first year. Still, for a man who had begun to fly when he was ten years old, he probably had experienced more masculine pleasures than many men who live beyond the allotted three score and ten.

A. WEATHERBY BEAUCHAMP-PROCTOR

This British ace with the aristocratic name was a South African, but is seldom recognized by aviation historians, though he is credited with fifty-four victories, and was awarded the V.C., the D.S.O., the M.C., and the D.F.C. for his courage, determination, and general all-around effort. I was most fortunate to meet this amazing pilot shortly after he had been decorated by King George V at Buckingham Palace.

I remember him as a chunky man about five feet, two inches tall, rather swarthy of complexion. Before joining up he had studied law in South Africa, and after his preliminary flight training he was assigned to Number 84 Squadron being organized at Lilbourne, England. In no manner was he the typical colonial, nor did he appear to be greatly interested in flying. He was pleasant, but shy, and spent most of his free time poring through law books. In the mess he was generally popular, but few of his mates believed he would ever get to France because, like so many young birdmen destined for greatness, Beauchamp-Proctor was an absolute dud as a pilot, and seemed incapable of making a simple landing. He wiped off an S.E.5 undercarriage at least twice a week. Why he didn't kill himself long before he went on active service is a puzzle.

When the famed Sholto Douglas, who became an Air Marshal in the Second World War and was eventually elevated to a barony, took over Number 84 Squadron he wanted to dismiss the South African, but everyone else found him so likable he was allowed to stay on. However, when Number 84 flew across the Channel to take over my old field at Estrée-Blanche, he was not permitted to go by air but had to cross by boat, and was then held on the ground for more than a week after he arrived.

But once Beauchamp-Proctor was given his head, the feathers began to fly. On his first flight over the line he downed two Huns in as many minutes. There was no holding him after that, and overnight he became the fireball of Number 84 Squadron. When he eventually was awarded the Victoria Cross the following citation was read to the assemblage:

For conspicuous valor and devotion to duty between August 8 and October 8, 1918, this officer proved himself in twenty-six decisive combats, destroying twelve enemy kite balloons, ten enemy aircraft and driving down four other enemy aircraft completely out of control.

Between October 1 and October 5, 1918, he destroyed two enemy scouts, burned three enemy kite balloons and drove one enemy scout completely out of control. On October 1, 1918, in a general engagement with about twenty-eight machines he charged one Fokker biplane near Fontaine and a second near Flamincourt; on October 3 he drove down completely out of control an enemy scout near Mont d'Origny, and also burned a hostile balloon; on October 5 he destroyed a third hostile balloon near Bohain. On October 8, 1918, while flying at low altitude after destroying an enemy two-seater near Maretz, he was wounded painfully in the arm by machine-gun fire, but continued on and landed safely at his aerodrome, and, after making his report, was admitted to hospital.

In all he proved himself conqueror over fifty-four foes, destroying twenty-two enemy machines, sixteen kite balloons and driving sixteen enemy aircraft completely out of control. Besides these, his work in attacking enemy troops on the ground and in reconnaissance both during the withdrawal following the Battle of Saint-Quentin from March 21, 1918, and during the victorious advance of our armies commencing on August 8, has been almost unsurpassed in its brilliancy and as such has made an impression on those serving in his squadron and those around him, that will not be forgotten.

Despite his devotion to law Beauchamp-Proctor stayed in the Royal Air Force after the war, but, tragically, his old landing problem caught up with him. While practicing for an air demonstration at Upavon, England, in 1921, he apparently flew into the ground while attempting to land an S.E.5. Some people leaned to the theory that he had strained his eyes in his study of law books, but, presumably, this is a conclusion reached by a group of nonreaders.

WILLIAM A. BISHOP

Heading the list of Canadian air fighters is Lieutenant Colonel William A. Bishop, one of the outstanding figures of the war in the air. Much has been written about Billy Bishop, most of it penned by enthusiastic, but careless, authors who have allowed their hero-worship to exaggerate the details of his career. However, there is sufficient material of a high order to fill several volumes, for Bishop was an airman's airman, and a great aviation warrior.

Again, we have a man who was far from a skilled pilot, but like so many others of his gallant company was a deadly marksman and zealously interested in his guns, rather than the joystick.

William Bishop was born at Owen Sound, Ontario, Canada. He was educated at the Owen Sound Collegiate Institute and the Royal Military College, Kingston, where he was completing his second year when World War I began. He immediately obtained a commission with the 4th Canadian Mounted Rifles, and went to England with that unit a few weeks later. That first winter on Salisbury Plain caring for horses under conditions that were less glamorous than those found in the gay lithographs of cavalry tradition, prompted many of these Canadians to a more realistic attitude. One morning Billy

Bishop glanced skyward and suddenly saw that other military men were carrying out their war duties under more enchanting conditions.

So Second Lieutenant Bishop applied for a transfer to the Royal Flying Corps, and learned that if he wanted action on his request it might be good policy to volunteer as an observer, which he did. He spent four months manning a machine gun aboard the R.E.8s and B.E.2cs of Number 21 Squadron based at Fienvillers. He must have put in considerable time carrying out routine reconnaissance patrols; certainly long enough to obtain his observer's wing. This dreary toil was brought to a close when Bishop was involved in a crash-landing on his own airfield and had to stay in a hospital for several months with a knee injury. Afterward, in his autobiography *Winged Warfare,* Billy declared that during his period as an observer he never once fired his gun at an enemy aircraft.

When he was released from the hospital late in 1916 he was assigned for pilot training, and on completing his course appears to have spent some time with a Home Defense squadron on anti-Zeppelin patrols. There were few Zeps to chase and little opportunity for glory, but this interim period afforded him a chance to improve his piloting. After Christmas 1916 he was given a short course on the Nieuport scout and prepared for the real war in France.

Bishop was astonished to learn that he was to be posted to Number 60 Squadron, then one of the crack fighter outfits of the R.F.C. Number 60 had Albert Ball on its rolls, and Bishop was determined to learn all young Ball could tell him, but when Bishop arrived Ball was home on leave, so he had to gain his information secondhand from other pilots and Ball's mechanic, a lad named Walter Bourne, who did his best to explain Ball's tricks and tactics. He insisted that Ball was daring to the point of recklessness, and that he liked to attack large formations on the assumption that a single machine is more difficult for an orderly formation to handle than that of a small, loose element. Bishop also adopted Ball's phobia concerning ammunition and the mechanism of his machine guns. There was a time when Bishop personally examined every round that went into his drums and ammunition belts, and then loaded them himself.

Bish arrived in France just in time to take part in the so-called Bloody April of 1917. He was assigned a Nieuport scout and told to get in a few days of practice flying up and down inside his own lines, mainly to become accustomed to his machine and the details of his operations area. There is one report that on his arrival at Number 60 Squadron the CO immediately had him lead a flight to carry out a low-level attack on the enemy front line. This is ridiculous in the light of the caliber of the pilots already with that famous squadron. His service as an observer can be discounted as he had been away from the front for many months, and certainly he had no experience to justify his being selected to carry two streamers.

But his chance came at last, and he was taken over the line on his first patrol. He remarked afterward that he could see other formations in the air but for the life of him could not tell friend from foe. He was terrified by the Archie fire and had difficulty in staying in formation. In other words, he reacted like the typical novice.

Bishop had been on the front for nearly three weeks before he was involved in a real air fight. Along with a small formation of Nieuports he encountered three Albatros single-seaters, and his leader brought the element through the opening moves that gave Bish his first shot. He poured a short burst into one and then saw it go down in a tight spin. Completely engrossed with this success, he nosed down, and chased his quarry to give him another squirt and then found himself down as low as 1500 feet before he saw the Albatros crash behind the German lines.

The thrill of this first victory was soon dampened by the shock of finding himself alone and deep inside enemy territory. He had also acted the duffer in allowing his spark plugs to oil up during his dive after the Albatros. Retribution set in as he thought of the possibility of being taken prisoner, but he turned hopefully for home, trusting he had sufficient height to glide a few miles to safety.

He was lucky. After stretching his glide and trying to restart his engine, he finally slid into a sheltered area that by great good fortune was just inside the British lines. Soldiers helped drag his Nieuport into the shelter of a ridge where it remained overnight. He stayed with the infantrymen until a repair crew arrived and hauled his machine away. The young Canadian had scored his first victory, but the experience had drained every ounce of vitality, and he was several days recovering from it.

This initial triumph seems to have impressed his superiors for when he was again ready for action his CO suggested that he lead the patrol, and apparently Bishop held that honor for the next few weeks.

*

It must be said that Bish proved to be an ideal replacement for Ball; at times wildly reckless, but always daring and when given an assignment he aimed to complete it as quickly as possible. In those first weeks of his career he willingly attacked balloons, strafed enemy trenches, or went to various altitudes to engage enemy fighters. He dived on pillboxes, road transport, and enemy troop concentrations. In a short time his logbook read like an installment in a thriller magazine.

He was the ideal hero for the publicity mills, and by now Canadian officials were as publicity conscious as their American counterparts who were moving into the war with suitable fanfare. In a short time Billy Bishop was more widely known than Ball, McCudden, Warneford, or Leefe Robinson, and it is quite understandable that some London newspapers were publishing editorials to the effect that "Canadians showed special adaptability and initiative in the air." Bishop's name was recognized all through Canada and the United States, and as his story was repeated many other Canadians were encouraged to seek careers in the Royal Flying Corps.

But fame is fleeting. Forty years later when a British-Canadian syndicate had a motion-picture scenario written that presented Bishop's colorful career, Hollywood tycoons who were approached to make such a picture, responded with, "Who is Billy Bishop?" The scenario was never filmed.

Although he spent many hours in carrying out the demands of tactical aviation, Bishop continued to score in the air. He flew many lone patrols, and worked himself into a frenzy whenever anything went wrong with his machine or his guns. Then he heard that Albert Ball was returning to France—but not to Number 60 Squadron. He was being sent to Number 56 Squadron, unquestionably the finest British squadron on the front. Instead of flying Nieuports, Ball would be flying S.E.5s, or so Bishop believed. It was this news that seemed to trigger Bish into a new frenzy for it was obvious by now that he intended to match the young Englishman's score. When Bishop went on leave Corporal Bourne scrounged from somewhere a nose spinner such as Ball had had fitted to his Nieuport, and put it on Bishop's scout. Billy liked the idea, but ordered the mechanic to paint it blue instead of red, the color Ball had favored.

Early in June 1917 Bishop suggested that he make a predawn raid on a German aerodrome. He thought he could destroy a whole flight, and perhaps a whole squadron of enemy planes before they could be put into the air. It was not a new idea for such an intrusion

had been conceived by Albert Ball, and there were reports that
Bishop had heard of this and suggested that they carry out such a
raid together. From all accounts Ball was delighted with the idea
but, unfortunately, he was shot down at Annoeulin while Bishop was
on leave. Actually, such an attack should have been made in a Camel
since the Sopwith had racks to deliver four 20-pound Cooper bombs.
Bishop set out to make the raid with a plane that was armed with
but two machine guns.

Corporal Bourne who had been let in on the plan, had Bishop's
Nieuport trim and ready early, and the young Canadian, wearing
his long flying boots and a leather coat over his pajamas, took off
just as the first streak of dawn appeared. He headed across the line
at hedge-hopping level most of the way, and as he proceeded faint
flicks of flame spit and splintered, indicating where the enemy guns
were opening up with their daily contribution. Here and there larger
conflagrations erupted, and with the increasing light came the first,
faint details of the ugly trenches, the white chalk mounds, the great
scars of shell holes, and the dull glint of tortuous rivers. The woods
and forests provided black patterns as the thin line of gold gradually
widened to a splintered rampart that spread across the inky horizon.
A few Archie bursts threw a spatter of gold and black against the
dull blue that was becoming the sky.

Bish reduced his power as the light brought out details of the
countryside below, and eased his nose down. Framed in the center-
section struts was the indistinct outline of an aerodrome. There were
a few square, wooden sheds, some smaller huts, and the colorless
spread of landing turf, but little ground activity. Bish continued his
descent and circled the layout, but no activity responded. There was
not one man or an airplane to be seen. He climbed slightly, curled
away, and hummed across a wooded area. Still searching with his
keen blue eyes, he finally saw another layout where there was activity
aplenty.

"This must be it. I'm about fifteen miles inside the Jerry lines," he
said to himself. "Let's see. There are seven planes on the line and
the mechanics are huddling together in small groups, evidently waiting for the pilots to appear."

He nosed down and made his first run over the lineup of aircraft.
His guns spat and screamed, as tracers flicked into the flat tops
of the wings. The men scattered wildly, and he saw several of them
fall and flounder helplessly. As he reached the end of the line a machine gun arched tracers across the field from a weapon mounted on

a wagon wheel. Bish looked up and saw three telltale rents in the linen of his upper wing. He curled away and prepared to line up for a second run, this time over the row of hangars. As he started down he saw a Fokker D-III crawling away from the line, so he ruddered slightly, nosed down at the bobbing insect, and pressed his trigger control. The Fokker was just getting its tail up when it suddenly burst into flame and stood on its nose.

Billy eased up and attempted to get back toward the hangars, but spotted another Fokker moving for a take-off, so he banked sharply and cut across at an acute angle, triggering off another spattering of fire. This D-III screwed around wildly and headed for a small stand of trees just outside the field where it finished up minus its wings and undercarriage.

Bishop had to claw for a little altitude, and as the Nieuport responded he glanced down and noted two more Fokkers taking off, but in slightly different directions. One got its wheels clear and came around in a fluttering bank, heading straight for him. Bish held his Nieuport in the climb but decided finally to take a shot at the climbing Jerry. He fired a general burst, and his antagonist staggered, stalled, and then bored straight down to crash on the airfield. Another Fokker, well up to Bishop's level, made a tight turn and came roaring at the intruder, who had no intention of engaging any more Jerries at this altitude, so he fired one long burst that made the Fokker pilot pull away, and went into his climb again determined to start for home.

During these brief engagements two more German scouts had come into the picture, probably from some nearby aerodrome, but the Canadian had no intention of pushing his luck. He nosed down slightly for speed, and headed back for the lines. The enemy planes made no concerted effort to head him off, and Bishop reached the Allied area with only spotty opposition from the antiaircraft guns.

Bishop should have been relieved, but he admitted later that he suddenly felt exhausted and nauseated. He had to fly for a while with his head clear of the windscreen so as to revive himself. He tried to remember exactly what had happened. He was positive he had shot down at least three planes that were airborne, but how many he had damaged as they stood on the line was difficult to determine. Still, he felt justified in claiming three, which, were they confirmed, or accepted, would bring his score to twenty-six.

By the time he was gliding in for his landing, he had regained some of his composure. Corporal Bourne who was still standing by simply said when Bish had run the Nieuport up to the cab rank, "How did it go, sir?"

"Good! For the first time both guns worked beautifully. They never missed a round. Not one stoppage. Thanks!"

"You look very tired, sir," Bourne replied. "You should get some rest. You're down for a midafternoon show."

⁎

The raid on the German airfield became the high point of Bishop's career, although he continued his wild attacks on enemy aircraft and ran his score up to forty-seven. British agents inside the enemy lines eventually confirmed that three Fokkers had been shot down; several of the single-seaters had been damaged seriously, and a two-seater so shot up it had to be completely rebuilt. It is interesting to note that after the war German officials said that no such attack had been made on any of their aerodromes on that date. The British, however, were more than satisfied, and by August 11, 1917, Bishop was awarded the Victoria Cross for his effort.

He was withdrawn from the front, sent home to Canada for a long leave during which time he married his prewar sweetheart, the daughter of a noted Canadian department store tycoon. His story was published all over Canada and the United States, and *The Saturday Evening Post* carried it in serial form. At the time he probably was the best-known Allied airman.

Eventually he returned to Britain, determined to go back to the front, but British and Canadian officialdom kept him in England, ostensibly to form a new squadron. This became Number 85 that was equipped with S.E.5s. Bishop personally selected his own pilots and included many Americans who were being trained by the British. When this outfit finally crossed the Channel it was with the understanding that Bishop was to act as its administrative head, but not to fly war patrols.

Ignoring the restriction, Bishop flew every day, and during twelve days of operations he downed twenty-five more enemy aircraft. When this became known, officialdom took a stand and ordered Bishop back to London where he was given a post on a Canadian committee that was to set up a new Royal Canadian Air Force. Before this project could be completed the Armistice was signed, and the basis of the present R.C.A.F. was not laid down until 1923.

Bishop wound up his war with every British decoration for valor, a total of seventy-two victories, and his full share of pages in British aviation history.

GEOFFREY HILTON BOWMAN

Major Geoffrey Hilton Bowman, who had a very distinguished career and is credited with thirty-two official victories, spent much of his time with Number 56 Squadron, yet despite all this he, like so many other British stars, is comparatively unknown. He was awarded the D.S.O., the M.C., and the D.F.C., but seems never to have attracted the attention of the war correspondents or air historians.

Therefore little is known of Bowman's early life, but he began his military career as an officer in the Royal Warwick Regiment, but made a transfer to the R.F.C. in June 1916 and came under the instruction of James B. McCudden, with whom he was later associated in Number 56 Squadron. At another period Bowman and McCudden were in the same flight in Number 29 Squadron.

Geoffrey Bowman was particularly adept aboard the D.H.2, the single-seater pusher that filled in until Britain could provide single-seater tractors with synchronized machine guns. On October 23, 1916, Bowman came upon a German kite balloon that had snapped its cable and was drifting across the British lines. He made several unsuccessful dives on it, but finally the big bag went up in flames, and the wreckage fell inside the British lines. Bowman was so anxious to alight nearby and inspect his prize he made a bad landing, wrote off his D.H.2, and banged himself about.

The records are not clear what Bowman accomplished over the next eight months, but he became a flight commander with Number 56 Squadron. During the Messines-Wytschaete Ridge battle in June 1917 the S.E.5s of Number 56 were heatedly engaged in low-level flying so necessary in that campaign. On one occasion twelve Albatros D-IIIs attacked Bowman's flight, and he himself accounted for two while Lieutenant H. Rogerson downed another. Half an hour later this same flight was attacked by a large formation of Jerry two-seaters. Captain E. W. Broadberry shot down two, and Bowman chased another all the way to the ground, but never claimed it as a direct kill.

On the last day of the battle, June 14, Bowman scored another "double," starting with an L.V.G. two-seater that crashed at Le Quesnoy. He then downed an Albatros over Roulers. Three days later he torched a D.F.W. that fell near Lille. Then the squadron was sent back to Britain to cope with the renewed German air attacks on London, but by July 5 Number 56 was back at Estrée Blanche where it was to make its long and most fruitful stand.

During the month of July, Bowman downed eight more enemy aircraft but took credit for only four since the others were not seen to crash. The bag included D.F.W. two-seaters, an Albatros, and a Fokker that was seen to lose a wingtip, although no one saw it actually crash. During this period Bowman lost Lieutenant R. G. Jardine who had to land in enemy territory, but he and H. T. G. Hoidge each downed an Albatros in reprisal.

While the ground forces were preparing for the Third Battle of Ypres Number 56 Squadron was in the thick of things, and Bowman continued to add to his score through that August, and was awarded the Military Cross and one Bar. Late that month the squadron lost Lieutenant A. P. F. Rhys-Davids who had been credited with downing the German ace, Werner Voss, but Bowman made up for that loss by scoring another "double" on August 29.

In one period of "train-jumping" which consisted of machine-gunning every train that came into view near the Moorslede station, Bowman downed an Albatros that tried to interfere with the diversion. It fell smack in a railroad cutting, and blocked the line for some time. Zooming out of that action with the intention of searching for an enemy balloon, Bowman next found a D.F.W., and piled in. The German observer shot his windscreen away, but Bowman carried on, and in trying to zoom the two-seater ripped off its wings, and the fuselage nosed into a shell hole.

Early in November Number 56 Squadron was moved to Lavieville to take part in the British attack on Courtrai. Bowman destroyed another Albatros while British infantry were fighting at Bourlon Wood. During this action Number 56 destroyed eight enemy machines, although they were supposed to be engaged in very low-level ground attacks. Bowman downed three more after engaging a formation of Pfalz and Albatros scouts. Backing up a flight led by McCudden, he shot an L.V.G. to pieces, and covered Jimmy who was floundering home with a bullet-plugged radiator.

Bowman remained with Number 56 until February 1918 when he was given command of Number 41 that destroyed 124 enemy aircraft before the Armistice halted operations. He was awarded the D.S.O., and credited finally with thirty-two victories.

A. ROY BROWN

Captain A. Roy Brown was possibly the most tragic figure in Canada's list of fighting airmen. A pawn of fate, he never attained the height of popularity that was his due, and though he figured in one of the most memorable events in World War I, he was never able to enjoy the fruits of his part in it. A short time ago a noted Canadian historian compiled a new volume of Canada's fighting pilots but Roy Brown's name is not in its index, nor is there any mention of his part in downing Baron Manfred von Richthofen.

Roy Brown was born at Carleton Place, Ontario. At the outbreak of war he is said to have gone to Dayton, Ohio, to purchase a course of flying at the Wright school there. With this primary training Roy gained a commission in the Royal Naval Air Service, and in December 1915 he arrived in Britain to continue his flight training at Chingford. Here, ill luck began to dog him. While carrying out a solo flight aboard a military trainer he crashed and seriously damaged his spine. This setback kept him in and out of hospitals until the early months of 1917.

Finally Roy was posted to Number 9 Naval Squadron that on the formation of the Royal Air Force in April 1918 became Number 209 RAF. This squadron was assigned to an area along the Belgian coastline, and at times escorted bombing formations deep into enemy territory. Roy Brown performed some good work over this period, and in some records is credited with twelve enemy planes. He is remembered for his contempt for airmen who made claims for victories when the engagement could not be substantiated, and many of his own were first claimed for him by his flight mates.

On April 1, 1918, Brown was promoted to captain and given a flight with Number 209 Squadron which was flying Sopwith Camels. Whether this was a wise decision could be debated, for fourteen months of active-service flying had taken much of his limited vitality. He had been on patrol regularly, and the memorable month of March had made great demands on all British airmen in stemming that famous 1918 Push. Sleep had been curtailed, meals gulped at

irregular hours, and the weather was sullen, sodden, and treacher-
ous. The patrols were particularly terrifying, being flown at very low
altitudes amid great storms of shellfire, and against swarms of enemy
aircraft. The standard routine was discarded. Anything that would
fly, carry a rack of bombs, a machine gun, or a camera was sent off
with only intervals to refuel, rearm, or make minor repairs. Instead
of flying four or five hours a day, these airmen put in as much as
twelve hours, most of it deep inside the enemy lines at frighteningly
low altitudes.

The low-level patrols took much from both pilots and observers.
The nervous system was outraged, stomachs were unable to take
normal food or liquids, but as long as engines would turn the propellers these airmen were expected to crawl back to their cockpits.

Roy Brown was especially affected and spent most of his time on
the ground curled up on his bed. He tried to soothe his war nerves
with brandy or warm milk. By right he should have been under treatment at some quiet hospital, or sent back to Canada for a long
rest. But such considerations were out of the question, for the German Flying Circus was being driven equally hard to try to break
the stalemate on the Western Front and drive the British Army out
of France and Flanders. The Von Richthofen formations of gaudy
Fokker triplanes that were the chief mount of the German fighting
squadrons were kept in the air, swarming up and down—very impressive to watch, and difficult to defeat when engaged. But the Circus
theory proved to be a great mistake, for while the massed formation
might dominate one particular area, Allied squadrons were carrying out broad programs of tactical aviation, serving the big guns,
bombing the important dumps, photographing the vital areas, and
keeping German tactical squadrons from fulfilling their assigned
duties.

The Flying Circus feature was widely publicized, however, and
the young men selected for its squadrons became famous within the
limited scope of their operations. A Flying Circus could not cover
the whole Western Front.

Nevertheless, this opposition had to be recognized, and the Camel
squadrons, in particular, were assigned to this task whenever the
Von Richthofen group appeared in the vital area. Otherwise they
were down low Cooper-bombing the road transport, enemy supply
dumps, and troop concentrations. All through the first three weeks of
that memorable April that followed the halting of the enemy push
Brown and the others of Number 209 Squadron continued to put

the pressure on the German ground troops. There were few so-called
dogfights, but there were dozens of short, violent engagements that
involved small units of aircraft, and once these were brought to a
conclusion, the Camel pilots would return to the assigned duties,
bombing, trench-strafing, or searching for the ground panels laid out
by the infantry to note the progress being made in one direction
or another.

By mid-April Number 209 was located at Bertangles and was co-
operating with Britain's Fourth Army on the Amiens front. Baron
von Richthofen's personal Staffel was hangared at a small village
known as Cappy, and it was from this field, on April 20, 1918, that
the Red Knight took off to score what he claimed as his eightieth
victory. Why the German Air Service had not pulled him out of the
line at this time is one of the mysteries of the war, for the Baron, like
Roy Brown, was a war-weary man. He had been awarded the Pour
le Mérite, the Order of the Red Eagle, the Iron Cross, First and
Second Class, the Order of the House of Hohenzollern, the Bul-
garian Cross, and some twenty-six other citations for valor. True,
there was a report that Von Richthofen would go on leave by April
24 to enjoy a hunting foray in the Black Forest, but why was he not
withdrawn immediately after scoring what still stands as his eightieth
victory? He was grumpy, disturbed, a far from pleasant companion or
Staffel leader.

About 11:30 on the morning of April 21 Von Richthofen led his
Staffel 11 on a routine patrol. He headed two elements of five
planes each. At the same time on the opposite side of the line Major
C. H. Butler, a skilled air fighter who had won the Distinguished
Service Cross with the Royal Naval Air Service, took Number 209
Squadron, made up of three flights of five planes each, out for a
midday patrol. Brown led one of these flights and was considered
second-in-command.

One of the first items of interest was when Von Richthofen
sighted two R.E.8s of Number 3 Australian Squadron that were
photographing enemy movement near Hamel. Four of the Fokker
triplanes nosed down to pick off these ancient but sturdy photography planes. The Australian crews made a good show of defense,
and then British antiaircraft guns came to their rescue as they raced
for their own lines. The white bursts caught the eye of Roy Brown

and he ruddered slightly to get a better look. That inspection disclosed that a pack of Fokker triplanes were trying to molest two R.E.8s as they headed for the Allied lines.

Brown felt he should go to the rescue of the photoreconnaissance planes, but knew he had some responsibility for his flight. He made sure his pilots sensed what he was up to, and after wagging his wings to signal an attack he nosed down and went to the rescue of the Australians. The contact required a long dive for by then the photography planes were down to the 3000-foot level, and their gunners were still holding off at least four gaudy triplanes.

One of Brown's pilots was Lieutenant Wilfred R. ("Wop") May of Edmonton. This was the first time May would see any real air action. He had been ordered to stay in formation, make no attack himself but to keep on the fringe of things and watch how air fighting was carried out. By the time Brown and his flight were anywhere near the triplanes the German formation had been strengthened by a number of additional Fokkers and a few Albatros ships.

When Brown started his dive he saw that he had eight Camels, instead of five, a point that cheered him considerably. The R.E.8s, still intact and probably carrying boxes of important plates in their cameras, headed for home, leaving the opposition to the Camel contingent.

The Camels and enemy planes went into an aerial fandango. All engines were set at their highest speed, for tight maneuvers were the order of the day. The British pilots had to use their trick of turning sharply while the Germans made the most of their triplanes' ability to climb quickly out of danger. At the height of the foray about thirty planes were engaged, and during the various feints, attacks, and moves to elude opposition fire, the mass of aircraft gradually drifted lower and lower; so low in fact an Australian division holding the line at this point could clearly see every individual engagement. Those in the Morlancourt area were particularly favored, and farther back Aussie artillerymen crawled out of their gun pits to watch this extravaganza.

Baron von Richthofen who was flying a gaudy, scarlet triplane seemed to be in the thick of things, but his guns found no target of any kind. Then, moving through an outer fringe of activity he noted a Camel whose pilot seemed to be taking no active part in the melee, and he sensed this was a novice who was obeying orders and keeping out of the fighting.

Seeing an easy kill, or perhaps going after this rookie to get out of the swirling maelstrom, Von Richthofen went down on Wop May. The young Canadian must have seen he was in real trouble. Instead of heading into the center of the action, he made a pointless turn and found himself in the center of a cone of machine-gun fire. Frantic, he nosed down sharper to increase his get-away speed, and the Baron naturally went in full pursuit.

Brown, who had been darting in and out of the melee, concentrating on avoiding a midair collision rather than attempting to eliminate an enemy plane, suddenly saw a red triplane in full pursuit of one of his Camels. He may have realized this was the rookie May for he stated so in his patrol report, although he may have learned this after he returned to his field. What must have impressed him more was that a German was chasing a British pilot over into Allied territory, a risk seldom taken under these circumstances. Brown went to the rescue and saw his flight mate wildly zigzagging, rather than banking into a tight right-hand turn, as he had been taught.

It should be pointed out here that Brown had no idea whom he was chasing. That he was about to engage Germany's ace-of-aces, a man who had claimed eighty British planes, the leading killer of the air war, never entered his head. In fact, the name Von Richthofen meant little to him. He had not been interested in the publicity about German air heroes. There had been many such names bandied about in the many months he had been out at the front. A few British intelligence officers may have known about Von Richthofen, but the everyday pilot had little time or interest in such vague individuals. What they were concerned with was the capability of enemy planes, their firepower, their blind spots, and weaknesses in certain maneuvers. Their pilots were just other men who wore black leather helmets and flying coats.

It would be convenient from the storyteller's point of view to state that Roy Brown knew he was going down to save one of his flight mates from an attack by the Red Knight of Germany, but he had never heard of that popular soubriquet, for it was not conceived until 1937 when Floyd Gibbons wrote the Baron's history under that title. Variations of the phrase may have been used in Germany, such as the Red Flier, but to the war-weary Captain Brown this was just another encounter in a very risky adventure.

In the battle that Von Richthofen had left, a Lieutenant Taylor sent an Albatros down in flames, a Lieutenant MacKenzie sent a triplane fluttering out of control, and Lieutenant J. F. W. Mellersh nailed an all-blue triplane that went into a spin and crashed. Following this, Mellersh found himself in front of the guns of two triplanes and was lucky to get down safely inside his own lines. This forced landing also furnished an interesting feature of the Von Richthofen incident.

As the Baron worked to get on May's tail, Brown continued his rescue dive. Frantic with fear, May still zigzagged, staring wildly over his shoulder until he saw Brown's Camel coming to his rescue, and with that took heart and started calmer maneuvers that prevented the Baron from drawing a clean bead. At the same time both pilots were sacrificing much altitude and by the time Brown was within shooting distance all three planes were down to the 1000-foot level.

As May floundered about in frantic jerks and twists, the threesome gradually moved into an area held by a Royal Garrison Artillery battery not far from the Bray-Corbie road. Looking at the drama being staged above were a Gunner Brue, a Sergeant Popkins, George M. Travers, and Donald L. Frazer. Bombardier R. H. Barron was in charge of a Lewis-gun post that was supposed to provide antiaircraft defense for the 13/18-pound field guns. Bombardier Barron saw a Camel come from inside the German lines, flying very low. According to his later report another Camel followed immediately, *and behind these two* came a red triplane that was firing at both in turn.

Another version is that Von Richthofen was making his final move to put a killing burst into May when the Lewis gun team fired a long burst at the red triplane. Some observers claimed to have seen splinters fly from the woodwork, and to add to this confusion, a noted British historian, Hilary St. George Saunders, states that an Australian Vickers gun team also fired a long burst at the German machine.

It was at this point that Brown finally reached a position where he was justified in firing a burst at May's attacker. In his story of this action Floyd Gibbons stated that Brown had just put his last drum of ammunition in place. This is mystifying as the Camel carried two Vickers guns that were belt-fed, not drum-fed. The point, however, is whether the Lewis or Vickers guns fired from the ground hit Von Richthofen, or the burst from Brown's twin guns. We do know that from that point on the Fokker wavered, stalled, and fell off out of control. It crashed into a shell hole after thumping over rough ground, not fifty yards from where Lieutenant Mellersh, who had had a forced landing, was standing. May hoiked away in grim relief, but Brown, who did not wait to see what actually happened, went into a climbing turn and returned to the main action. In his combat report he stated that he did not see the German aircraft crash, but was told that it had some hours later when he talked to May and Mellersh. At the time Brown probably forgot the incident for he was soon engaged in two more short fights, both of which ended with no damage to either side.

✳

Meanwhile Von Richthofen's triplane lay piled up in an open area, said by some to be two miles from the front line; others reported that it was only a quarter of a mile away, and that German kite balloon observers could clearly see it. The artillerymen watched to see if the pilot would crawl out, but when no figure appeared, an Australian soldier, moving from shell hole to shell hole, finally tied a rope to the wreck, and willing hands hauled the triplane to an area where it would be behind a ridge out of sight of any German balloon observers.

Mellersh who was accepted as a knowledgeable official was asked to look at the pilot who obviously was dead. He went through the man's papers and checked what identifying items were available. Although the machine was a gaudy red triplane no one had any idea who the dead pilot was, but military papers and an engraved gold watch revealed that he was a Baron Manfred von Richthofen. The name meant nothing to the ground men, but may have triggered some response in Mellersh who is said to have cried, "My God, it's Richthofen!"

In reconstructing this scene a dozen years later, historians usually fell into the error of putting words, phrases, and situations into the picture that could not have been in existence. For instance a number of Australian-Cockney ejaculations were supposed to have been made to prove that everyone who was drawn to the crash knew what famous German airman had been shot down. But most of these statements would not have been uttered as the speakers could not have known anything so personal about the German nobleman, nor would artillerymen have been so conversant with the military-aviation idiom.

Mellersh ordered the body carried to a nearby advanced dressing station where a medic made a cursory examination of the obvious wounds, and it is at this point that the Von Richthofen story becomes totally bewildering.

On the first inspection it was reported that the Baron had been killed by two bullets, one *entering* the right breast, the other the left. If this was correct, it would appear that Von Richthofen was killed by one of the machine guns set up on the ground. Then there are newspaper clippings bearing what is said to be an actual photograph taken of the Baron's body in the advanced dressing station, and pointing out that there is unquestionable evidence that a bullet struck the pilot just to the right of his nose, and continued on through the back of his head. This, too, must have come from the ground.

Other reports have it that a number of bullets went through the side of the fuselage and entered the lower part of his body. If so, these must have come from Brown's guns, and it is on this pattern of fire that Brown is credited with ending Von Richthofen's career, but it should be noted that he was awarded no decoration for the victory, whereas two of the Australian machine gunners were given the Distinguished Conduct Medal for their role in the action.

Surgeons who later made an extensive examination of the body declared that the German ace had died from a single bullet that had traversed his breast from the right to the left side, and added that this slug could not have been fired from the ground. Thus, from all the conflicting reports and opinions it will be seen that the manner in which Manfred von Richthofen met his death will forever remain undecided.

Brown never went to see the body of the dead pilot, nor did he paw over the wreckage, examine the engine or the guns as is so popularly believed. The next day he led his flight over the line, but on his return he was so exhausted he could not climb out of his cockpit without help. He was taken to a hospital in Amiens where he lay semi-delirious for three weeks. A short while after he returned to England where he assumed the duties of an instructor, but once more fatigue overcame him. He fainted in the air, crashed, and went to a hospital again. This time tender care, a long rest, and relief from war flying helped him make a successful recovery. Before he returned to Canada he was given a Bar to his Distinguished Service Cross, but the citation made no mention of the Von Richthofen action.

On his return home he was just another Canadian from the war, and there were many in those days. Little was made of the half-forgotten exploit. After all, Canada still had three outstanding airmen who had been honored with the Victoria Cross—Barker, Bishop, and McLeod—and Canadians were newly engrossed with the activity of Major Raymond Collishaw who had taken a British air wing up to Archangel to fight for the White Russians.

Roy Brown tried many jobs and businesses, and after Floyd Gibbons returned him to some temporary fame with his book, *The Red Knight of Germany,* in which much of Brown's career was outlined, he became president and general manager of General Airways Limited of Canada that operated through the gold country and had bases at Rouyn, Quebec, and Amos. But this position was not secure and during his later years he drifted from airport to airport, and job to job, searching for the respect and financial security that always eluded him. He passed away a few years ago in London, Ontario.

KEITH L. CALDWELL

A popular New Zealand airman, often encountered in histories of World War I, but never clearly identified, is Major Keith "Grid" Caldwell who commanded the famous Number 74 Squadron of the R.F.C. Caldwell earned his nickname because he called all aircraft grids, possibly owing to the fact that early versions appeared to be a mass of grid-like flying wires and cable supports. But it may have been a New Zealand phrase.

A big man with a massive cap of black curly hair, Caldwell had a swarthy complexion and deep-set eyes. His prominent chin was a clear indication of his determination and leadership. He began his flying career with Number 60 Squadron, and his CO swore that Grid had taken part in more air fights than any man on the front. When the war ended he was credited with twenty-five enemy planes, and had been awarded the Military Cross and the Distinguished Flying Cross. During World War II he was back in action again, and became an air commodore.

Caldwell, however, was more important as a leader than a man who went out to knock down Huns. During the eight months in which he commanded Number 74 Squadron his pilots destroyed 140 enemy aircraft, and sent 85 more down out of control. In that same period he lost but 15 pilots killed or taken prisoner. The S.E.5 was their mount.

Number 74 Squadron was reactivated for World War II and was known far and wide as Tiger Squadron, and is still considered one of the greatest fighter squadrons of all time.

ALBERT DESBRISAY CARTER

This gallant gentleman, another great Canadian airman, is credited with thirty-one victories, but Canadian historians seemingly have never found the material to give him his rightful place in his country's aviation records. Like his bosom pal, Francis Grainger Quigley, he has never attracted the attention of the men who have spent so much time compiling Canada's contribution to the Empire's first air war. Interestingly enough, Carter ran up the greater part of his score while flying the Sopwith Dolphin, when the Fokker D-VII was supposed to be at the peak of its career.

Carter was born in Pointe de Bate, New Brunswick, and on the outbreak of the war enlisted in a Canadian infantry regiment, but like so many other Canucks, soon transferred to the Royal Flying Corps. He took the regulation training course and qualified for his brevet by the summer of 1917. For a few weeks he was posted to a Home Defense squadron and carried out coastal patrols hoping to intercept either Zeppelins or Gothas, and then late in December of that year was transferred to Number 19 Squadron which had been equipped with French Spads.

Soon after Carter joined Number 19 the Spads were relinquished and the new Sopwith Dolphin was supplied. This machine was an excellent performer, but because of its back-staggered design, was at first considered dangerous to fly—that is, if the pilot suffered a crash-landing and overturned. A safety pylon was supplied and much of this dread was eliminated. The Dolphin, however, was fast, maneuverable and well armed. During the March Push of 1918, Dolphin squadrons carried out many low-level attacks on the German infantry, but by the same token the machine was first-class at high-level fighting. During four and one half months of front-line flying, Carter downed thirty-one enemy aircraft, a remarkable show considering the strength of the opposition.

On May 19, 1918, Carter took on more than he could handle and was shot down. He fell inside the German lines and was taken prisoner. How seriously he was hurt has long been a question. The Germans claimed he was only shaken up, but Canadian authorities reported he was seriously injured.

With the Armistice Carter was returned to England and he was well enough by then to take up flying once more. In the meantime he had developed some sort of wild interest in the German Fokker D-VII and persuaded RAF officials to allow him to fly a captured model. He had hardly taken off and was banking into his first turn when the German biplane broke up in midair and Carter died in the crash.

WILLIAM GORDON CLAXTON

Another high-scoring ace was William Gordon Claxton of Gladstone, Manitoba, who was credited with thirty-seven enemy planes. Claxton also contributed a series of camera-gun photographs, designed to teach aerial gunnery, that were used for years for instruction by the Royal Air Force. He was one of the first fighting airmen to develop the deflection shot—where a pilot aims at his target at an angle to which the aircraft is flying. It requires quick calculation of the "lead" necessary in aiming the weapons. With it he once downed six enemy planes in one day. It should be noted, however, that like so many more high-scoring stars, Claxton put on his show during the latter months of the Great War when British aircraft far outclassed those of the enemy, and the German Air Force had been driven to many pathetic improvisations. This is not to disparage their efforts, but a check of fighter squadron records discloses that many of the high scores were run up by Allied fighters during the last six months of the war. Claxton's score was made in less than three months, and there is no telling how far it might have gone, had not a bullet settled his last air fight on August 17, 1918.

On that day Claxton was flying with Frederick Robert McCall. Both of them at the time had thirty-four victories. They had become separated from their main force and then found themselves cut off by a formation of about forty German aircraft. There followed one of the classic stands of air-war history; both Claxton and McCall shot down three enemy planes as they fought their way toward their own lines. Then, just as safety seemed within reach Claxton was struck in the head by a "grazer" bullet, the kind that finished the famous Major Lanoe G. Hawker, but Claxton recovered consciousness in time to make a landing in enemy territory. He was taken prisoner and held until after the Armistice. German doctors saved his life with skilled cranial surgery.

McCall, who was taken ill a few days later, was sent back to England to recuperate, and so these two noted Canadians ended their war miles apart, but with exactly the same score—thirty-seven apiece. After the war Claxton became a journalist, and his *Financial Digest* was one of the leading magazines of Canada. McCall became involved in the growth of Canada's vast air transportation system.

A. H. COBBY

This outstanding Australian airman, sometimes known as the Kangaroo Ace, was born at Prahran, a suburb of Melbourne, Australia, in 1894. He joined what was listed as the Australian Flying Corps, a little-known unit that began with a small cadre that first served in Baghdad in 1915. Later on, when a number of Australians showed a desire to fly, the unit was taken into Number 67 Squadron of the R.F.C., and committed to the British forces in Egypt. This finally became Number 1 Australian Squadron. Three other squadrons were formed later, all of which ended the war on the Western Front, where they had operated between Soissons and the North Sea.

Cobby first served with a regular R.F.C. squadron, and performed so well he was given command of "A" Flight of Australia's Number 4 Squadron which was flying S.E.5s at the time. In that fateful March of 1918, Cobby, despite low visibility, took his flight out on the twenty-first of that month. They encountered eighteen planes of the Flying Circus over Brway. It was a mixed bag of Albatros and Pfalz fighters, but Cobby ignored the odds and went down on a silver Albatros and killed the pilot with his first burst. He then saw another Albatros holding on to the tail of an S.E.5, and with a quick flip he put a long burst into that one. It, too, went down, piling up 4000 feet below.

Signaling for his flight to re-form, he headed for home where he learned they had downed four enemy planes in the space of eight minutes.

On April 10 Cobby led eleven S.E.5s on a ground-strafing expedition that concluded with a German back area being sprayed with 20-pound Cooper bombs and machine-gun fire. A freight train went up with a roar, and a large section of track was disrupted for hours. A solitary Albatros came up from Estaires to try to stop this foray, but within minutes it was batted back and left burning on the ground. This was Cobby's third victory, and from that time on he was assigned to many of these low-level missions.

Late in May, while leading twelve scouts, his flight started a large fire at the new La Gorgue aerodrome. They then raced along the River Lys and sent three barges to the bottom. When two Rumplers tried to interfere, they were driven to the ground. On their return as they crossed over Neuve-Eglise Cobby spotted a German kite balloon that he shot down with one short burst.

Balloons fascinated the Australian and on May 30 he and Captain G. F. Malley, a New Zealander, each downed an enemy balloon. After leading their flights on a sweep in the region of the Lys they came upon two balloons. These were destroyed within five minutes, while two more were hurriedly pulled down. As Cobby zoomed over the bag he had burned, he saw an Albatros diving on Malley. He arrived just in time, and Malley was startled to see a burning Jerry flash past him. In the next ten weeks Australian airmen downed ten kite balloons in the Estaires area.

On June 1 Cobby caught a balloon in this zone and then came upon a green Albatros that was stalking a lone Camel. Just as the enemy plane started to make its pass, Cobby fired a burst at long range that made the Albatros turn, and then dive for home. The Australian followed and caught up with it over the town of Estaires. A complete burst ripped a wing off and the Albatros went down, tossing away the other wing.

Bad weather put a halt to Cobby's activities for a while, but by June 7 he took out twelve S.E.5s for a general observation show. Another flashy Australian, Captain H. G. Watson, and Captain Cobby became separated from the main force and over Laventie sighted four Pfalz and one Albatros. Cobby shot the wings off one, and Watson sent one down in flames. Watson followed his victim, and as soon as the plane began to smoke, Watson zoomed fast and came up under a Pfalz. He fired a short burst at close range and another Jerry went down.

Meanwhile Cobby chased another down to the ground, and as the pilot made a bumpy landing the Australian fired another burst, causing the unfortunate pilot to smash headlong into a tree.

Three days later Cobby caught a Pfalz that had just shot down two British kite balloons. Then on the evening of June 25, when

Cobby and Watson were returning from a low-level bombing patrol they were jumped by three Pfalz at 3000 feet over Estaires. The Jerries missed in their first dive, and as they went on through Cobby caught one, and saw it break up in midair. Looking for Watson he saw him diving on an A.G.O. two-seater that had been cruising below. Avoiding the gunner's arc of fire Watson went down and came up from under. The two-seater fell near Bac Saint-Maur after it had been riddled by two long bursts.

On June 28 Cobby scored his first triple kill. He dived on an L.V.G. that went down in flames. Six Fokkers and three Albatros fighters then moved in for revenge, and Cobby made a quick pass. He shot down one Albatros and then nosed into a cloud formation. After darting in and out for some time, he was returning home when he spotted a Halberstadt 800 feet below. He went down in a steep dive and first hit the observer, but the pilot made a bold stand, fighting the Australian for several minutes. Cobby finally put a short burst into the cockpit and the Halberstadt crashed on a hill. Cobby managed to get home on the last few pints of fuel and then he discovered that the German pilot had poured many bursts into his S.E.5. In fact he was fortunate to reach his aerodrome as several important controls had been shot away.

Early in July Cobby again turned his attention to the balloon line at Estaires and soon sent one down in flames. Zooming from this success, he saw four Fokker triplanes about a mile away. Using a nearby cloud cover he managed to get close enough to a straggler to put in a long burst that apparently killed the pilot. Three vengeful triplanes turned and chased him all the way home, but were discouraged finally when British antiaircraft guns put up a solid barrage. An hour later Cobby flew back to take a photograph of his triplane victim with an aerial camera.

On July 15 Cobby and Watson were flying over La Bassée at the 6000-foot level when they saw five Pfalz scouts heading toward them. Both pilots darted into light cloud cover and awaited their opportunity. Cobby's first burst set up a flamer, and a split-second later Watson shot down another. While Watson followed his victim down, just to make sure, Cobby turned on a third member of the enemy formation that by now was a most bewildered group. This Pfalz put up a fight, and Cobby had to do his best to get in a telling burst, but it finally went down, throwing away all of its wings and bursting into flames. When a formation of eight Fokker triplanes came into sight, Cobby and Watson decided that discretion was preferable to daring.

Over the next few weeks that included August 8, the Black Day of the German Army, Cobby and his unit bombed transport lines, strong points, and moving troops. On August 6 Cobby again got into the scoring column after bombing an ammunition train. Teaming up with Captain Watson he destroyed a low-flying L.V.G. two-seater. He ended the war with the D.S.O., the D.F.C. and two Bars, and full credit for twenty-nine confirmed victories.

In 1939 Captain A. H. Cobby once more returned to the lists and ended his service as a wing commander in the Royal Australian Air Force.

RAYMOND COLLISHAW

This Canadian airman, a native of Nanaimo, British Columbia, is another of the war heroes who failed to gain his deserved recognition during the Great War. Even more surprising is that he stayed on in the Royal Air Force until late in World War II, gaining high rank and responsibility, but never made the headlines of the free world's press. Today, he is living in active retirement in Vancouver, British Columbia. During World War I he destroyed at least sixty enemy planes, yet seems never to have won the attention of his own country. When he returned from World War II as an Air Vice Marshal he was even less known.

Ray Collishaw was unlike any other World War I airman. He had no phobias, no black days of despair, no fear of death, no particular hate or respect for the enemy, and no personal like or dislike of any type aircraft. He would fly anything on any kind of patrol under any wartime conditions. After he had destroyed thirty-seven enemy aircraft and was awarded two decorations, he was sent home for a leave of two months. He made no fuss about the decision, did not rant about being taken out of action, as high-scoring aces were prone to do. In fact he acted so naturally under all conditions, it is understandable why he was scarcely noticed. True, there were many airmen who went all through the war, taking their turns at everything, and finally getting their discharge papers, but most of them were colorless personalities, contributing little to the eventual outcome.

Ray Collishaw was among the top half-dozen scorers of the war. He was awarded every decoration *but* the Victoria Cross, and it must be added that this high award was given on several occasions for valor and heroism that appear tame by Collishaw's standards. His contribution surely was as important as that of Barker or Bishop, and his career is equally as impressive as that of Mickey Mannock. In fact, in studying Collishaw's complete record, one must admit he contributed more to the fighting history of the Royal Air Force than any man who ever wore that uniform.

Collishaw grew up in an area where the sea had a distinct call, and early in his life he worked on ships that plied between British Columbia and Alaska. Before he was twenty he served as navigation officer for explorations in the Antarctic Ocean.

When war broke out Ray worked his passage to England to join the Royal Navy, but after looking over the general situation he chose the Royal Naval Air Service, as did many other Canadians at that time. He qualified as a pilot by January 1916, and spent the next eight months flying naval patrols along the Channel, or spotting for navy guns off Dunkirk. In late August he was transferred to Number 3 Wing of the R.N.A.S. that was billeted at Ochey, a short distance behind the Allied trenches. Here he began to fly Sopwith two-seaters and was part of the famous raid on Oberndorf, flying as escort for the bombers. It was during this epic raid that Ray scored his first victory when he downed a Fokker. That was on October 12, and on October 25 he scored a "double" over Luneville when he downed two more Fokkers, for which the French awarded him the Croix de Guerre.

In February 1917 he was a member of Number 3 Naval Squadron that was operating with the British Army near the Cambrai front. Over the next two months he shot down another enemy plane and then was moved on to become a flight commander with Number 10 Naval Squadron located at Dunkirk where for a time he did naval reconnaissance and gun-spotting for the Royal Navy. It was during this interval that he downed four more enemy planes.

Number 10 Naval Squadron was next moved down to the British front and both Numbers 8 and 10 Naval squadrons were given the new Sopwith triplane, a machine none of the R.F.C. squadrons liked. They felt that this particular Sopwith was not structurally satisfactory for the heavy air fighting experienced in this section of France, and although it was a fast climber and apparently most maneuver-

able, it was fitted with but one machine gun. The R.N.A.S. boys, however, took to it immediately, and Collishaw personally hand-picked four other Canadian pilots to work with him. They were Flight Sub-lieutenants Ellis Reid of Toronto, J. E. Sharman of Winnipeg, Gerald Nash of Hamilton, and Melville Alexander, also of Toronto. All these pilots were in their early twenties and keen on air fighting.

Collishaw next conceived the idea of painting his flight of triplanes midnight black, a gesture that would not have been tolerated in the R.F.C., but Ray had his way and to add an even more individual touch all five planes were given special names. Collishaw's became *Black Maria*. Reid flew *Black Rodger*. Sharman's was named *Black Death*. Nash's was known as *Black Sheep,* and Alexander's as *Black Prince*. Obviously, they would have to put on a rare show to justify this giddy individuality.

On the Ypres front where the Von Richthofen Circus was supposed to be supreme, the black triplanes went wild. Four enemy scouts went down before Collishaw's single gun in five days, and all his mates racked up victories. By June 6 Ray had registered his sixteenth success. Then on June 26 the Black Flight sustained its first loss when Lieutenant Nash went down during a melee with the Von Richthofen Circus, but he landed safely in the enemy lines and destroyed his machine before he was captured.

The next day Collishaw went out to look for the Circus, and after scouting around he came upon a formation of gaudily painted Jerries. The four black triplanes searched for a German who had flown a green-striped ship. Collishaw spotted him, and with rare skill cut him away from the Circus formation. The two ships were apparently evenly matched, but Collishaw was the more determined, and while they were circling over Lille, he finally sent the green-striped Albatros crashing down on the old fortifications outside the city. While the other members of Black Flight were downing three more pilots of the Circus they noted a blood-red Albatros flying about 2000 feet above the fighting. This pilot stayed up there and apparently did nothing to help the Circus formation.

The man in the red Albatros may, or may not, have been Von Richthofen, but the pilot who died in the green-striped Albatros was Leutnant Karl Allmenröder, victor in thirty contests, and at the time the second highest ranking ace in Jagdstaffel 11. But Ray Collishaw had no respect for any German, ace or neophyte. In the first twelve days of July he added twelve more to his bag, and by July 30 when his score stood at thirty-seven, he was ordered away from the front and sent home on a long leave. Black Flight was disbanded, and the pilots were assigned to other squadrons. By mid-November Collishaw was back again, and given command of Number 13 Naval Squadron. By December first he had added to his score by downing two German seaplanes and an L.V.G. two-seater.

When the Royal Air Force was formed in April 1918 Collishaw was promoted to major and given command of Number 203 Squadron that was flying Sopwith Camels. In the next four months, flying against the best the enemy could put into the skies, Ray accounted for twenty more, ten of which were the vaunted Fokker D-VII. He scored "doubles" on seven occasions, and his decorations now included the D.S.O., D.F.C., and the D.S.C. On October 1 Ray was again taken out of the line and sent to England where, with Billy Bishop, Andy McKeever and other Canadian airmen, plans were being made for a Royal Canadian Air Force.

Unlike most others, Ray stayed on after the Armistice, and took command of an Allied air force that went to the aid of the Czarist cause under General Anton I. Denikin who was trying to oust the Bolsheviki from Russia. It is not known how many planes Ray destroyed in this hapless campaign, but the British government admit that twenty would be a very modest figure, although none were added to his World War I score.

When the Russian White Army collapsed in 1920 Collishaw was brought back to England, given a tropical uniform, and sent out to Persia with Number 84 Squadron where the Bolsheviki were menacing a British protectorate. He was still flying Camels, and by April 1921 was in Mesopotamia for service against insurgent Arabs. Here he was raised to the rank of Wing Commander.

Collishaw remained with the RAF, and was in action again from 1939 on. Now he was in command of a Fleet Air Arm Fighter Group that swarmed off Royal Navy aircraft carriers. He served all through World War II with distinction but little publicity. This is strange as most Canadians, like Americans, were publicity conscious throughout both world conflicts, but they somehow failed to do justice to the man who did so much for his service over so many years. In France and the United States it is not considered bad form to belatedly award the Legion of Honor or the Medal of Honor for service performed many years before, and there would seem to be no logical reason why Ray Collishaw still could not be honored with the Victoria Cross.

STUART D. CULLEY

Another young airman who too might have been awarded the Victoria Cross, had his time brackets been more fortunate, was Stuart D. Culley, an Anglo-Canadian-American. Flying a Sopwith Camel, he took off from a barge being towed by a destroyer, and shot down a Zeppelin in August 1918. Once the gasbag had been disposed of, Culley had to return to his barge and flop down in the sea where he hoped to be picked up and hauled aboard again. Fortunately he was, and though his comrades, and high-ranking British naval officials expected him to be awarded Britain's highest military honor, he was eventually given the Distinguished Service Order.

This epic venture has long been forgotten. At the time only a few eagle minds knew the airplane had become a long-range naval weapon; that the dreadnought no longer was mistress of the seas; and that an amazing vessel to be known as an aircraft carrier would evolve from this historic experiment.

Flight Sub-lieutenant Culley was born in Nebraska in 1895. His mother was a Canadian and his father English. In 1916 he joined up in Canada and was accepted by the Royal Naval Air Service. On completing his flight training in England he was transferred to the light cruiser *Cassandra* and then to a shore base at Great Yarmouth. Until that time his deck flying had been aboard early variations of primitive carrier decks built over the hulls of converted cruisers or liners. In these operations Sopwith Pups had been launched successfully, but no deck landings had been attempted. The planes either landed on the surface of the sea to be picked up, or returned to some nearby land base. Culley had had some experience in taking off from a seagoing platform, but it was something else to fly a more powerful, very tricky aircraft off a flat barge that was only fifty-eight feet long and sixteen feet wide.

This towed-raft idea had been conceived by Commander Sir Reginald Tyrwhitt of the British Harwich Force, and had been attempted once by Commander Charles Rumney Samson, a rather flamboyant officer of the R.N.A.S. But Samson was ham-fisted, and unable to fly a machine as lively as the Camel.

Culley went into the adventure with an open mind, and it was agreed that the destroyer would tow the barge (lighter) at thirty knots, and at the appropriate moment one of the crew would start the engine of the Camel by swinging the propeller. As soon as the Bentley engine was running the airplane was launched through a conventional bomb-release gear operated from the pilot's cockpit. Amazingly, this impractical arrangement seemed to work perfectly.

Culley made his first trial off Great Yarmouth on August 1, 1918. The towing destroyer was *Redoubt* and was worked up to about thirty-six knots before Culley released the Camel. He found himself airborne with scarcely any run over the deck, and once in the air he turned away and landed safely at a shore base.

The Sopwith plane used in this experiment was a type designed to Royal Navy requirements, and was known as the Sopwith 2F.1 Camel. It was shorter in span, had a smaller center-section cutout, and the fuselage aft of the cockpit was detachable for shipboard stowing. The armament in this particular instance was two light Lewis guns instead of the twin Vickers. These weapons were mounted on brackets bolted to the upper side of the top wing. In this arrangement they could not be tilted to change the ammunition drums, and as each drum contained only 97 rounds, Culley went into his historic action with only 194 bullets.

Five days later Commander Tyrwhitt, aboard the light cruiser *Curacoa,* took the whole Harwich Force of four light cruisers and thirteen destroyers out to sea to make an offensive sweep in the southeastern sector of the North Sea. *Redoubt* again hauled the lighter and Camel fighter. Other destroyers towed lighters on which reconnaissance flying boats had been embarked, and cruisers of the force were burdened with coastal motorboats that were to attack German minesweepers operating off the Dutch coast.

At dawn on August 11 the motorboats were put overboard twenty-five miles northwest of Vlieland, and an attempt was made to launch the flying boats, but there was not sufficient wind to get them into the air. They had to be reloaded aboard their lighters, and were finally returned to the harbor waterborne. So six coastal motorboats that were to have been escorted by the flying boats, were intercepted later by German seaplanes, and in the action that followed three of the C.M.B.s were sunk. The remainder limped back to safety areas along the coast of the Netherlands.

While this air-surface action was taking place, Culley and the lighter crew left the destroyer and prepared to launch the Camel. It was reasoned that the Germans would investigate the activity of Tyrwhitt's force, and at 8:00 A.M. the Admiralty monitored a signal that indicated a Zeppelin was cruising over Helgoland Bight. Thus alerted, every man in the force searched the sky, but Culley was the first to spot a great silver cigar cruising at about 10,000 feet. It was the *LZ.53*, commanded by Kapitänleutnant Prölss of the German Naval Airship Service.

Culley jumped into his cockpit, and the *Redoubt* worked up speed. A new factor of naval warfare was about to be introduced. A handsome young man was keeping a rendezvous with destiny. When the speed of the lighter reached thirty knots Culley checked his engine, and gave the conventional "thumbs-up" signal. The pilot climbed straight over the stacks of *Redoubt,* saw the whole flotilla spread out before him, and realized he was the leading actor in this historic drama. Probably no airman ever performed before such a breathless audience, but when he looked up again, the Zeppelin was nowhere in sight.

"Oh, no! Please . . ." the pilot pleaded.

Within a few seconds the airship reappeared, and from that instant, Culley, flying like a robot, never took his eyes off the silver gasbag. At 5000 feet she appeared to have changed very little—a disturbing matter—and the young flier realized that the enemy was climbing fast. He remembered that Zeppelins of this particular period were noted for their ability to gain height rapidly, but he stuck to his task, keeping a discreet distance from the airship. At 15,000 feet the controls of the Sopwith became sluggish. The Bentley gave one disturbing cough, but soon picked up the rhythm. Culley struggled up to 18,000 feet at which time he was positive the Zeppelin had altered course and was heading out to sea.

This dampened his hopes for he knew he would never cut her off if she steered farther out to sea, but he continued to watch and stalk until suddenly the light changed and he saw that the silver raider was heading straight toward him. He thought she was a few hundred feet above his present level, and approaching at a relative speed of fifty knots.

Commander Samson had warned him that he must dive on the airship and avoid any position behind or below the tail. "They are not likely to use a gun mounted on the top of the main frame, and you'll be able to get in closer by going in from above."

But from his position, and judging the speed of the Zeppelin, it was obvious that an attack from above and behind was out of the question. He had no choice but to attack head-on and from below. In a matter of seconds the great bulk of the Zeppelin loomed ahead, and Culley could see the forward control car and the outboard engine gondolas. For a second or so he sat spellbound by the spectacle, but as his eyes searched for some crew activity, his hand instinctively drew back on the stick and the biplane nosed up and almost stalled.

Culley reported afterward: "I can hardly remember the first minutes, and I only came to when I was attacking that great thing. One gun operated beautifully and fired its complete drum without a slip-up, but the other jammed after pooping off about half a dozen rounds. By then I sensed I was about to stall so I leveled off and raced along under the massive belly and saw something either fall or jump from a slit in the framework, and disappear below." (The object he saw was the only survivor from *LZ.53,* and his parachute descent from about 19,000 feet must have been a record for those days. The man was sighted later and picked up by a German destroyer.)

The instant Culley's guns stopped firing, and as the Camel faltered in her stall, she nosed down some 2000 feet before he could ease her out. During that time he lost sight of his target, but when he leveled off again and stared up he saw to his consternation that *LZ.53* was cruising along as though nothing had happened. He turned to make an adjustment to his throttle, hoping to regain the lost altitude, when a glint above caught his eye. Gushers of yellow flame were billowing from three widely separated points of the gasbag, and within a minute practically all of the airship, except the tail section, was enveloped. The savage conflagration burned itself out in a few seconds, leaving a blackened skeleton floundering in the sky. A flag fluttered bravely from a rudder post as *LZ.53* started her final dive. Culley saw the airship writhe, break her back, and finally hit the water. The clock on his instrument panel showed 9:41 A.M., exactly one hour since he had become airborne from the bobbing lighter.

He probed his way through a light coverlet of offshore mist and thought he had spotted a couple of Dutch fishing vessels, but once he had eased down into the clear he was overjoyed to see they were British destroyers, and another look told him the whole Harwich Force was in the vicinity.

Now he could pick and choose, but he selected the *Redoubt* for he saw that they had stopped, and were transferring the lighter's crew and lowering a whaleboat. While these rescue arrangements were being made, Culley circled the rest of the force, enjoying his hour of triumph to the full. He then put the Camel down so skillfully it was soon hoisted out of the water and deposited aboard the lighter. Some time later it was patched up and put on exhibition in the Imperial War Museum where it still can be seen.

RODERIC STANLEY DALLAS

A real mystery man in British aviation was Major R. S. Dallas. Although credited with thirty-nine enemy planes, few of them seem to have been jotted down in any official record book. This was typical of many R.F.C. and R.N.A.S. squadrons through 1915–16, for the British seemed adverse to building up individual stars, and for a long time refused to furnish the actual records of their airmen.

Dallas, who was born in 1892, joined the R.N.A.S. shortly after the start of war and received his commission in June 1915. He became a pilot late in August and was assigned to Number 1 Wing at Dunkirk early in December where he flew Nieuport scouts and various two-seaters. He must have seen considerable action over the ensuing months, but nothing definite is registered until March 21, 1916, when he shot down an enemy plane near Dunkirk. Number 1 Wing was renamed Number 1 Naval Squadron later on, and Dallas seems to have added to his score for by September 1916 he was awarded the D.S.C. and the Croix de Guerre.

On June 4, 1917, he was given command of the squadron, and a few days later a Bar was added to his D.S.C. By this time he had become noted for his skill with the Sopwith triplane. His squadron had fought well all through the period of "Bloody April" 1917 when flights were reduced to five machines because of the lack of pilots.

Eventually the triplanes were replaced by Sopwith Camels, and Number 1 Naval Squadron was gradually brought up to full strength and given a period of familiarization at Dover, after which they were sent again to Belgium and based at Tetghem where they performed many types of missions, including escort duty for heavier units operating along the Belgian coast.

Although he was squadron commander, Dallas led many patrols and continued to add to his bag. Kite balloons were one of the responsibilities, and on one occasion Dallas and another pilot by the name of Rowley shared a balloon that was caught drifting into the British lines. When it fell in flames, it was discovered that the basket contained a dummy of a man. It was presumed that this old gasbag was sacrificed to draw British antiaircraft fire and enable German batteries to pound the British gun positions.

With the formation of the Royal Air Force, Number 1 Naval Squadron became 201 RAF. Dallas was sent to Number 40 Squadron that was flying S.E.5s, and Commander C. D. Booker, who scored twenty-two victories, took over Number 201. Dallas apparently had no trouble with the S.E.5, but while leading a patrol he was wounded in the leg. He must have had a wry sense of humor, for after spending a short time in a hospital, he insisted on being taken back to his squadron on a stretcher. When he was able to hobble on crutches he climbed into an S.E.5, flew across the line, and dropped a pair of slippers on an enemy aerodrome. When some Germans rushed out to pick up what they thought to be a message, Dallas nosed down again and shot at them, leaving several wounded.

Dallas came to his end on June 19, 1918, while fighting three Fokker triplanes. He put up a game show but was shot down and killed near Liéven, an ironic finish for a man who had had to give up the Sopwith triplane, only to be killed by a pilot flying a plane that was a deliberate copy of the Sopwith machine.

PHILIP FLETCHER FULLARD

This seldom remembered British airman destroyed forty-six enemy aircraft in eight months during the peak of aerial fighting in 1917. Typical of the ill luck that seemed to haunt many stars, Fullard was so seriously hurt while playing soccer on his own aerodrome, his injuries prevented his returning to active-service flying for the rest of the war.

Philip Fullard was born at Hatfield and became a distinguished scholar at Norwich Grammar School. He joined up directly into the R.F.C., and after learning to fly was posted to Number 24 Reserve Squadron. In April 1917 he was sent out to Number 1 Squadron where he flew Nieuport scouts and S.E.5s. He was a natural pilot and became a deadly marksman. About a month after his arrival on the front he began his string of victories by shooting down seven planes in two days. As did several other stars, Fullard insisted on servicing his own guns and checking his own ammunition. It is said that although he fired more than 5000 rounds in action, he never had a mechanical stoppage. He was awarded the D.S.O., and M.C. with one Bar. During World War II he held several command staff posts, and at one time headed Number 246 Group of the RAF. He ended his military career as an Air Commodore.

JOHN E. GURDON

The more widely publicized war pilots were single-seater scout fighters, but there were many two-seater stars who ran up remarkable scores though receiving little public acclaim. One of these was Captain John E. Gurdon who fought the good fight aboard the famed Bristol Fighter, putting in his time with Number 22 Squadron, the same one with which the author once served as an aerial gunner.

Gurdon had an excellent military background. On graduating from the famed Tonbridge School in 1916, he went to Sandhurst, and a year later was commissioned in the Suffolk Regiment, but he applied for and received an immediate transfer to the R.F.C. For a time he was kept on home establishment, flying with several Home Defense squadrons in England. A painful crash put him in a hospital for a time, but when he recovered he was given special training at the Central Flying School, and in January 1918 was sent out to Number 22 Squadron.

He was a first-class pilot who knew how to get the most out of the famous Brisfit. He scored regularly, but on June 10, 1918, he got into trouble near Armentières. He received a bullet wound in his arm, and his observer was fatally injured.

In a little over five weeks Gurdon was back on the front as a flight commander, flying with Number 22 for another two months during which time he ran his score to twenty-seven enemy aircraft. He was withdrawn from the front in September and made an instructor at the School of Special Flying, but shortly after was invalided out of the service.

LANOE GEORGE HAWKER

Major Lanoe G. Hawker was Great Britain's first true air hero. Though not an outstanding ace as far as his score was concerned, he was one of the first British airmen to be recognized publicly by Whitehall officialdom. He was of much the same stamp as Oswald Boelcke, the German airman who contributed a great deal to the tactics and strategy used by the German squadrons. A kindred spirit —though officially credited with only nine enemy aircraft—his leadership, determination, and influence on the development of fighting tactics, is still recognized by many military experts.

Somewhat older than the average undergraduate type in the R.F.C., Hawker was born in 1890, and began his service training at the Royal Naval College, but transferred later to the Royal Military Academy. He obtained a commission in the Royal Engineers, and through this association became one of the small group of officers selected for pilot training. He was an ideal pupil, and eventually gained his aero certificate by making his graduation flight aboard a Deperdussin monoplane.

Lanoe G. Hawker was a quiet, shy man of medium build, but his clear eyes and gentle smile covered an iron will, and the heart of a lion. He presented an affectionate nature, and was generous with his friendship.

When war broke out Hawker was assigned to Number 6 Squadron and given an R.E.5, a Beardmore-engined biplane. His group arrived in the war zone early in October 1914 just in time to see the fall of Antwerp. Over the next few months these early war pilots made a gallant stand, taking on a program that would have caused the airman of the later years of the war to feel he was overworked. Some day a dedicated historian will turn out a book that presents fully the arduous routine carried out by these early squadrons. There is no question that the First Battle of the Marne saved Paris and ended Germany's hope for a quick victory, but it could not have been won without the reconnaissance, gun-spotting, and intelligence provided by the R.F.C. airmen of 1914.

On April 18, 1915, while flying a B.E.2c, Hawker made a memorable one-man attack on the Zeppelin shed at Gontrode. He carried three melinite bombs and a haversack of hand grenades. He shot down a kite balloon and destroyed a Zep hangar and a brand new airship. This mission took almost three hours, and when he returned to his field at Abeele he counted thirty-eight bullet holes in his plane. For this wild foray he was awarded the D.S.O.

In June of that year Hawker rigged a Bristol Scout to carry a Lewis gun in much the same manner as the early Nieuport wing mounting, and after testing it out, he established an intelligence warning system by posting a number of mechanics in the trenches who were instructed to telephone him whenever a German machine moved up close to the Allied line. According to the surviving members of his squadron, Hawker soon had the Abeele front littered with skeletons of German aircraft, and some of them state he must have downed thirty or more during this period. In fact, a very reliable historian, Colonel L. A. Strange, has reported that Hawker eventually shot down fifty-five enemy aircraft, but in those days the British kept no records of "aircraft destroyed."

Over the sequent months Hawker became a one-man scourge, being continually in the air, not only as a fighter, but also assuming his share of bombing and reconnaissance patrols. During the poison-gas attack near Ypres he flew at contour height, hour after hour, trying to hold back the German threat. He was finally wounded in one foot but refused to be hospitalized, and was soon back in action, continuing his determined effort to destroy the German Air Force.

He was honored with the Victoria Cross for this display of determination, promoted to major, and given command of Number 24 Squadron which was being formed in England and equipped with D.H.2 pusher-fighters. Hawker whipped his pilots through a stiff training period, and made the most of the gadfly pusher that became the answer to the early Fokker fixed-gun fighter. In fact, it was this unusual machine that gave the R.F.C. its great edge during the Battle of the Somme.

By the middle of 1916 Number 24 Squadron probably was the best known on the Allied side of the line, and under Hawker's leadership registered a long series of victories. During the month of June the squadron had seventeen confirmed scores. In July twenty-three were registered, and in the next three months Number 24 destroyed forty German aircraft.

Then the grim law of averages demanded its price. On November 23, 1916, Major Lanoe G. Hawker was killed by Baron Manfred von Richthofen. This epic fight took place between Bapaume and Albert, and was recorded as one of the most famous air battles of

World War I. It was the Red Knight's eleventh victory and must have given his growing confidence a great boost. That night he wrote to his mother:

Congratulations on your birthday. I trust this will be your last in wartime. My eleventh Britisher was Major Hawker, twenty-six years old, and according to prisoners' accounts, he was the English Boelcke. He gave me the hardest fight I have experienced so far, until I finally succeeded in getting him down . . . Unhappily, we lost our commander three days ago, and eight days ago a plane of our squadron was brought down.

Von Richthofen's mechanics brought him the fabric serial numbers from Hawker's aircraft, and several other souvenirs among which was the Lewis machine gun that for years could be seen over the doorway of Manfred's bedroom in his mother's home in Schweidnitz.

THOMAS FALCON HAZELL

This British airman destroyed forty-three enemy aircraft, but managed to keep out of the wartime limelight. Another product of Tonbridge School, Captain Hazell should have been one of the best known pilots of his period, but he remains another example of Great Britain's aversion to publicizing the individual.

Thomas Hazell began his war as a subaltern in the Royal Inniskilling Fusiliers with which he served in France for nearly two years. He transferred to the R.F.C. in June 1916, but while flying a machine to France he had a bad crash before he crossed the Channel. He finally arrived intact, and was assigned to the old Number 1 Squadron that by January 1917 had become a scout-fighter unit, flying Nieuports. Hazell downed nineteen enemy planes while flying this aircraft, was awarded the Military Cross, and then sent back to England to be an instructor at the Central Flying School. He returned to France in June 1918 to command "A" Flight of Number 24 Squadron that by now had been equipped with S.E.5s.

Hazell immediately went on a balloon-busting crusade, and downed ten Drachens in a short time. He also destroyed twelve enemy planes while serving with Number 24, and as a reward was given command of Ray Collishaw's old Number 203 Squadron, and had to master Sop Camels, but before the Armistice bugles rang out Hazell had downed two more enemy planes, bringing his final score to forty-three.

J. IRA T. JONES

Here is a peppery little Britisher who really began at the bottom of the aviation ladder, went on to become a renowned ace and eventually a Wing Commander in World War II. Ira "Taffy" Jones was a Welshman who, prior to the war had been a member of Britain's Territorial Army, and at the outbreak of hostilities was training to be a civilian wireless operator. He fully expected to be called by the 4th Welch Territorials, and when he seemed to be overlooked, he joined the R.F.C. Because of his wireless training he was selected to be an NCO observer. He was a valuable addition, and was awarded the Military Medal for heroism displayed in moving two injured artillerymen to safety while under heavy fire. (He was acting as a ground wireless operator at the time.) He continued to serve as an aerial gunner and observer until May 1917 when he was sent back to England for a commission and pilot training. He did not get back to France until March 1918 when he became a member of Mickey Mannock's Number 74 Squadron.

Flying the S.E.5, Taffy was soon in the thick of the fighting, and when it was all over his score was exactly forty. When Mannock was shot down, the command of the squadron went to Taffy. He volunteered for the ill-fated Russian campaign, and then received a permanent commission in the RAF with which he served until 1936. When World War II began Taffy Jones returned to his old squadron, Number 74, where he served with distinction, and on occasion unofficially flew Spitfires on offensive sweeps well into Germany.

He died at age sixty-five after a long illness that was brought on by a fall from a ladder.

R. KING

Captain R. King was Australia's second-ranking ace with twenty-two or nineteen victories, depending on which list of "official" scores is accepted. F. M. Cutlack's *Official History of the Australian Flying Corps* seems to go to great length to evade stating how many victories were scored by any Australian airman.

King, who was born in Bathurst, New South Wales, in 1894, became interested in internal combustion engines, and when the war began in 1914 he was the head of a flourishing motor engineering business. He willingly gave it up to volunteer, first serving with the Australian Light Horse, but when the Australian Flying Corps was formed, he was soon accepted, and received his training at Castle Bromwich near Birmingham. He was finally posted to Number 4 Squadron (Australian) and sent out to fly Camels.

As did Cobby, Watson, and Malley, King became a terror in the Estaires sector, particularly along the German balloon line. He was also called on to carry out many low-level attacks on enemy troops and transports, but once his bombs had been delivered, King went aloft to seek out Fokker D-VIIs and Pfalz fighters. He knocked down seven of the vaunted Fokkers in a very short time, but was equally successful against enemy two-seaters. On one occasion he killed the observer aboard an L.V.G., and the bullets must have also severed the man's safety belt, for when the pilot went into a tight turn to get away, the dead observer was seen to fall out. King then put a burst into the pilot and the plane caught fire and augered into the ground.

As did many others, King claimed to have ignored the Armistice order on November 11, 1918, and went over the line loaded with bombs and machine-gun belts. When charged with disobeying orders he explained that he just wanted to see the end of the war from the air, but he had no explanation for the fact that his bomb racks and ammunition boxes were empty.

Captain King returned to Australia, and presumably went back to his engineering firm, though nothing about him has appeared since.

ROBERT LECKIE

Robert Leckie was a noted Zeppelin hunter in World War I, who became Canada's Chief of Air Staff in 1944. He was born in Glasgow, Scotland, but taken to Canada when a schoolboy. At the start of the war Leckie bought his flight training at the Curtiss Flying School in Toronto. With that ticket in hand he went to Britain and gained a commission in the R.N.A.S. From the Great Yarmouth air station he carried out important North Sea patrols aboard flying boats and landplanes. He volunteered for this type of duty for more than two years.

On May 14, 1917, while flying off Texel, one of the West Frisian Islands, Leckie, who was piloting a flying boat, attacked a German Zeppelin, bringing it down. Flight Lieutenant C. J. Galpin, who was listed as the commander of the flying boat, was awarded the D.S.O., and Leckie the D.S.C. How the authorities were able to differentiate between the efforts of these two airmen in this particular action, or what credit was given to the two aerial gunners who were also aboard, is a question.

Leckie later had another encounter with a Zeppelin, this time while occupying the observer's cockpit of a two-seater landplane. The Great Yarmouth air station had been warned on the night of August 5, 1918, that five enemy airships were approaching the east coast of Britain. That night Leckie was C.O. of the station, and he sent out a hurried call for pilots. The first to arrive was Major Egbert Cadbury, and the only plane available was a war-weary D.H.4. In a friendly scuffle Cadbury beat Leckie to the pilot's seat, and they took off at 9:45 P.M. After climbing to about 17,000 feet they finally sighted three of the Zeppelins. Cadbury moved into a position below what turned out to be *LZ.70*. Leckie, acting as the gunner, had brought along a drum of incendiary ammunition, and his first burst set the big airship on fire. It fell, a blazing torch near Wells-on-Sea, Norfolk. Aboard it was Commander Peter Strasser, Chief of the German Naval Airship Service. The Zeppelins never attempted to raid England again.

The remaining two Zeppelins dumped ballast, clawed for altitude, and turned for home with Leckie and Cadbury in hot pursuit. The airships had too much height on the airplane, and though Leckie fired several long-range bursts, the raiders escaped. This time both Leckie and Cadbury were honored with the new Distinguished Flying Cross.

ROBERT ALEXANDER LITTLE

Although only twenty-one years old, Captain Robert A. Little of Melbourne, Australia, destroyed forty-seven enemy aircraft, and won the D.S.O. and Bar, and the D.S.C., and Bar. Somewhat a man of mystery Captain Little has often been listed as a New Zealander, and on several occasions has even been identified as an American.

He volunteered for the R.N.A.S. and qualified as a pilot by October 1915. After a period of flying bombers out of Dunkirk he was assigned to Number 8 Naval Squadron that at the time was a heterogeneous organization equipped with six Sopwith Pups, six Nieuport scouts, and six Sopwith two-seaters. Captain Little registered his first victory while flying one of the Pups when he downed an Aviatik C-I on November 11, 1916. Four more two-seaters went down before his Pup's single Vickers gun, and by March 1917 he had run up a total of nine, and was awarded the D.S.C.

Little was a master in the air with the Pup, not so much for his piloting ability, but for his gunnery and marksmanship. Like Ball and Bishop, he seldom wasted a round of ammunition, but waited until he could move in close and fire point-blank at his personal enemy. On one such occasion he flew so close to an Albatros his landing gear spreader-bar hit the German's tail-plane, and Little landed with a damaged undercarriage. At another time his gun jammed while he was attacking a D.F.W. two-seater, but instead of breaking off he persisted in diving on his enemy until he ran his wheels over the top wing of his adversary's plane and gouged out two great gashes in its fabric.

In April 1917 Number 8 Squadron was equipped with Sopwith triplanes, and with this machine Little really came into his own. On April 7 he singlehandedly attacked eleven Albatros scouts of the Von Richthofen Circus, and though he failed to score he completely outmaneuvered the enemy formation, and escaped unscathed. Later that same month Little, along with three flight mates, attacked twelve

Albatros machines, shooting down five of them. Little was credited with two.

In July Captain Little experienced one of those pulp-magazine hair-raisers when he came upon a D.F.W. and engaged it for several bursts, finally wounding the gunner. The German pilot then raised his hands in surrender, and Little, somewhat suspicious, pointed where he should head to land inside the British lines. For a few minutes the situation had the features of one of those fabulous Kamerad incidents, often discussed but seldom proved. But Captain Little was deprived of his capture for on the way in the tail assembly of the D.F.W. broke up and the rest of the aircraft nosed down out of control.

Between July 1917 and May 1918 Little seems to have been engaged in general instruction assignments, or possibly Home Establishment duties, for we have no record of his adding to his score. Then, toward the end of April 1918, he was transferred to Number 203 Squadron, RAF, and while serving with this unit was killed in a mysterious manner. He is said to have gone aloft one night to intercept a raiding Gotha, and apparently blinded by a searchlight, flew into an area where an enemy gunner could draw a bead on him. He was wounded in the thigh, crashed, and was killed.

FREDERICK ROBERT McCALL

Another renowned Canadian air fighter was Frederick R. McCall, who, it will be remembered, teamed up so well with William Claxton, and like Claxton finished his war with thirty-seven enemy aircraft.

Born in Vernon, British Columbia, in 1896, McCall joined the Canadian Army as a private in 1916, but by the time his 175th Battalion arrived in England he had been given a commission. In March 1917 he made a transfer to the R.F.C., and after finishing his flight training, Freddie, as he is still known, was posted to an R.E.8 reconnaissance squadron (Number 13). McCall was not concerned about the docility of the R.E.8, for he had a fighting observer, Lieutenant F. C. Farrington, and together these two men put on an amazing show. In fact, McCall's first six victories were scored from the cockpit of an old Harry Tate (R.E.8), while he also found time to permit Farrington to carry out their regular artillery shoots.

McCall was next posted to Number 41 Squadron where he was soon joined by Claxton. Their combined operations have been previously related. In August 1918, when his score stood at thirty-seven, McCall was taken ill and invalided to England, and then sent to Canada where he was convalescing when the war ended.

JAMES BYFORD McCUDDEN

No record of World War I aviation would be complete without a comprehensive account of Major James B. McCudden, who became one of the most skilled and experienced airmen of any wartime service. Born in a British barracks to a Scottish father and a French-British mother, a military life was all this handsome young man ever knew. He had little opportunity to obtain much of a formal education. As soon as he was old enough he enlisted as a bugle boy in the Royal Engineers, and when the R.F.C. emerged from the early balloon corps, Jimmy became an engine mechanic and probably learned something of the primary rigging required in the early heavier-than-air machines.

The outbreak of the war found him a member of Number 3 Squadron, and he was among the first to go overseas where he served as a mechanic, lorry driver, motorcyclist—and an aerial gunner. In his association with the officers he cultivated his speech, diction, and broadened his vocabulary. It was easy with his pleasant personality for him to absorb gentlemanly manners, but at the same time he became a master of every available engine, and could rig and true-up any type of aircraft in the service. He studied each machine with intense interest, particularly any captured plane. He gave comprehensive lectures to squadron groups, whether composed of mechanics, pilots, or observers. As a pilot, he was as near perfect as it was possible to be. He flew practically every type of aircraft in the service during his career, but with all his combined skills, fate was unkind to McCudden. He made one tragic mistake—an error that ended his unmatched career.

James flew in action in every year of the war, 1914, 1915, 1916, 1917, and 1918. Before he was twenty-one years old he had served in every possible capacity from bugle boy to major, and had been awarded every decoration for courage his country could bestow. In

April 1918 he was honored with the Victoria Cross for having shot down fifty-four enemy planes, twice scoring four times in one day. He led seventy-eight offensive patrols, and fought duels with practically every noted German aviator.

McCudden and Boelcke booked interesting coincidences in their careers. On October 23, 1916, Boelcke came upon and engaged a formation of Fees. He attacked one, and as it went down the observer fell out and dropped behind the German lines, but the F.E.2b, with a dead pilot at the controls, crashed inside the British lines. It was Boelcke's last victory. Five days later he was killed.

In February 1918 McCudden attacked a Hannoveraner at close range and saw the observer tumble from the shattered fuselage and fall over the British lines, but the Hannoveraner crashed inside the German lines with the German pilot aboard. It was McCudden's fifty-eighth and last victory.

Jimmy McCudden's most memorable days were passed in Number 56 Squadron (S.E.5s). With its record of 200 enemy planes shot down in five and one-half months, it outscored the Von Richthofen Circus report of 200 Allied planes shot down in seven months.

Because of his long months of active service and his splendid achievements, McCudden was sent back to England to conduct a lecture tour in the flying schools. In July 1918 he was returned to France to take command of Number 60 Squadron. He crossed the Channel safely and landed at a nearby field to have lunch with some old friends. When he took off again his brand-new S.E.5's engine quit and he made the mistake of trying to turn back to the field. His engine stalled, and he spun in. His remains still lie near where he fell.

GEORGE EDWARD HENRY McELROY

So far as his background is concerned, Captain G. E. H. McElroy is something of a mystery. In some records he is listed as a Canadian who was born in Windsor, Ontario, but in others he is said to have been born in Donnybrook, Ireland, on May 14, 1893. The more likely version is that he was born in Ireland, taken to Canada at an early age, and then recrossed the Atlantic, and turned up in England some time before World War I. He entered the Civil Service, but at the outbreak of war enlisted as a despatch rider, and in May 1915 was commissioned in the Royal Irish Regiment. He was badly gassed, but after treatment went to Ireland to fight the rebels during Dublin's Easter Rebellion in April 1916.

McElroy was next a member of the Royal Garrison Artillery, but this service soon palled, and he applied for a transfer to the Royal Flying Corps, and was accepted in February 1917. He proved to be a dud pilot at first, and a long series of crashes kept him in hospitals or limping about the training fields. Not until August 1917 did he finally bring a Nieuport back safely, and was then considered for Number 40 Squadron. On his first flight on an active-service field McElroy smashed a brand-new Nieuport—and repeated the performance four hours later. His CO must have wondered about this ham-fisted tyro, but, fortunately, Number 40 Squadron was slated to turn in its Nieuports and take over S.E.5s. As a result, eight weeks after arriving in France, McElroy finally became a member of an offensive patrol.

From that time on Mac went wild, downing dozens of enemy two-seaters, no matter what the odds. During the March Push of 1918 he ran his score to twenty-eight, and then, after another week of wild flying added two more to his list.

When the Germans first put their vaunted Fokker D-VII on the front, there was much talk concerning its merits, and how the enemy would again take command of the air. McElroy soon put an end to that hope, racking up twelve more kills, but on July 31, after taking off in the early morning mists to seek out more D-VIIs, he disappeared completely. No one saw him in a fight. No one claimed to have shot him down. There is no trace of his grave, and there never was even a vague report that might have explained whether he was shot down by ground fire, or finally fell a victim to some unnamed gunner aboard a Hannoveraner. All we have is his record of forty-six enemy aircraft, and the fact that he was awarded the Military Cross, and two Bars, and the D.F.C. and one Bar.

CLIFFORD MACKAY McEWEN

The author has known this Canadian gentleman for many years and has had considerable correspondence with him. To his many friends he is known as "Black Mike," a nickname he acquired while he was training at Camp Borden. "Nothing sinister about it," Mike explains. "I'm one of those people who tan easily—and in 1917 we had a very hot summer." So for this feature Clifford M. McEwen who became an Air Marshal in World War II will be affectionately known as Black Mike, or simply Mike.

McEwen came from Griswold, Manitoba, and graduated from Moose Jaw College and the University of Saskatchewan, so is a true Canuck. He enlisted in the Canadian Army in 1916, and transferred to the R.F.C. in June 1917, and completed his training at Reading, England. He was immediately assigned to Billy Barker's Number 28 (Camels) Squadron.

He went on his first war patrol in Italy on November 29, and by February 18, 1918, had shot down five enemy aircraft, and was a standout as a pilot. When Barker was taken out of Italy and sent back to England, Number 28 was taken over by Captain Stanley Stanger of Montreal. McEwen and Stanger became fast friends, and often went on two-man patrols together with Mike acting as decoy while Stanger was supposed to do most of the shooting. One time they discovered they had attracted ten Albatros scouts and a couple of Aviatiks. Ignoring the circling D-Vs, they concentrated on one of the two-seaters that were presumed to be on an important reconnaissance mission. Stanger nailed the Aviatik, but meanwhile McEwen was being attacked by the fast scouts, and having a bad time. Luckily, the Camels outclassed the Albatros ships, and both Mike and Stanger were able to streak for home.

In the months that followed Mike became champion of Number 28, putting on amazing shows over the peaks of the Alps. His score rose and decoration after decoration came his way. Black Mike's outstanding feature was his ability to take on any type of patrol, high-level fighting, reconnaissance, low-level bombing and machine-gun attacks, or as escort for others who had such definitive missions. In eleven months between October 20, 1917, and November 4, 1918, Number 28 Squadron destroyed 111 enemy aircraft, sent twenty-five down out of control, and dropped a total of 23,400 pounds of bombs. At the time of the Armistice McEwen was the squadron's top-scoring ace with an even twenty planes to his credit.

After the war, Mike, along with a handful of other Canadian stars, made the first definite moves to form a Royal Canadian Air Force, using one hundred war machines donated by the British government. They adapted Bristol Fighters and D.H.10s into peacetime training, and by the time World War II threatened, Canada had the nucleus of a first-class air arm, and Black Mike McEwen was one of its ranking officers.

The Royal Canadian Air Force played an important role in Great Britain's war against Nazi Germany, and McEwen, who became an Air Commodore in command of Canada's Sixth Bomber Group, can take considerable credit for this great contribution. By May 1945 Sixth Group had won 2230 awards for gallantry, including one Victoria Cross, and one George Cross. It had dropped 126,122 tons of bombs, and destroyed 116 enemy aircraft. It sank, or seriously damaged, 438 enemy oceangoing vessels of all sizes during its program of sea-mining operations. Against all this it lost 814 of its own planes, and more than 3500 aircrew were killed.

Air Marshal Clifford M. McEwen retired a few years ago, closing out one of the most impressive careers in the Canadian military service. He still lives in happy retirement in Toronto.

ANDREW EDWARD McKEEVER

There were not too many two-seater pilots who made the high-ranking ace list in World War I, but Captain Andrew E. McKeever of Number 11 Squadron, is credited with thirty enemy aircraft. It should be noted here that McKeever has often been confused with Captain McKelvie of Number 22 Squadron. Their names were similar, both flew Bristol Fighters, and both pilots at one time had gunner-observers named Powell. McKeever, however, had a tragic end when an automobile he was driving in September 1919 skidded on an icy road. He died on Christmas Day. When last heard of, McKelvie, an Englishman, was living in Wiltshire.

Andrew McKeever was born in Listowel, Ontario. After joining the Canadian Army where he was noted as a rifle marksman, he transferred to the R.F.C. in December 1916. He was posted to Number 11 Squadron in May 1917 and discovered that he was fortunately attuned to the memorable Bristol Fighter, and from the beginning he flew it exactly as he would have a single-seater. He quickly ran up an astounding score. His gunner-observer, Lieutenant L. F. Powell, was equally skilled in his particular role, and together these two men made a redoubtable team. Powell is one of the few observers included in Britain's ace list.

These two fliers volunteered for tasks that other pilots refused to consider, and always came home from raids deep inside the enemy lines with astounding stories of fights and encounters that usually ended with new victories for either McKeever or Powell. One time they singlehandedly rescued a flight of S.E.5s that was being browbeaten by a large formation of Albatros fighters. When a crazy Bristol Fighter suddenly appeared out of nowhere and scattered the German pilots to the four winds, the S.E.5 fliers had to admit ruefully that they had been rescued by a two-seater pilot.

Unquestionably, McKeever was the greatest two-seater pilot of the war, and his score only partly indicates his great contribution to the cause. He had no respect for any enemy plane, whether scout or two-seater, and he certainly had little respect for any enemy pilot. His rifle training and marksmanship stood him in good stead, but he also was a sterling stunt pilot, and could put neat bursts of fire into a ground target while flying on his back. Here was the ideal military airman, and it was a grim twist of fate that ended his life just when he was needed by his own country in its bid for its place in aerial transportation.

DONALD RODERICK MacLAREN

This man of unquestionably Scottish descent, was born in Ottawa, Canada, in 1893. Two years later his family moved to Calgary where it must be assumed young Mac grew up on the frontier. There he became familiar with guns and developed the broad viewpoint of the plainsmen. Don has always been a difficult man to interview, and much of his story is still to be ferreted out and told, but there is no question that he was one of the war's greatest fighting airmen, a man who is still remembered and revered in Canada.

Don MacLaren grew up in a trading post in the Peace River country where he was engaged for a time in government survey work. When the war had been on almost two years, he returned from one of these assignments to learn that his brother had enlisted in the Canadian Army. This gesture impelled him to volunteer also, but he selected the Royal Flying Corps, and in the spring of 1917 arrived at Camp Borden where he received his primary flight training. By the following autumn he had gained his ticket and completed the full course.

In November 1917 he was sent to France and posted to Number 46 Squadron (Camels) in the Arras-Cambrai area. By the following November he had become the squadron's commanding officer and was credited with fifty-four confirmed victories. Amusingly, he was eliminated from action as the result of a friendly wrestling bout in which he broke his leg, thus celebrating the Armistice in a hospital.

As did many Allied fliers, MacLaren ran up his score through the midsummer months of 1918 when the British with their wide catalogue of fighting aircraft held the upper hand in the air. His first victory, however, was registered in February, but it was through the German March Push that he began to pile up his score while carrying out the hazardous duty of low-level bombing and trench-strafing to halt the enemy drive.

During this harrowing period MacLaren put on one particular show that is still remembered by the survivors of Number 46 Squadron. During the broad-front enemy attack it was discovered that the Germans had brought in a new long-range gun that was bombarding important sectors of the British line. Heavy salvos began falling on the Saint-Pol rail center and they were striking with remarkable accuracy. The damage began to pile up, but for days no one could figure where this amazing weapon was hidden.

Artillery experts were brought in. Chunks of the shells were studied, photographs of the enemy back areas were made over and over and every type of firing angle was checked out until at last R.F.C. reconnaissance squadrons finally pin-pointed the weapon in the area of Brebieres, some six miles behind the German lines. It appeared to be mounted on a railroad car that had been shunted into a sheltered spur track.

Number 46 Squadron was given the task of blasting the gun out of action. Eight Sopwith Camels, each carrying four 20-pound Cooper bombs went off to put a halt to the storm of steel. They held to a low level all the way in, ducking and dodging the antiaircraft fire until at last they picked out the gleaming rails that bore the big weapon. The great muzzle was poked up out of the low ground mist like the snout of some charging elephant.

The Camels in a tight formation nosed down for the attack. The leader's plane jerked as his rack of bombs went out, but he missed by several yards. MacLaren was next and he tugged his release and put two Coopers smack on the railroad car. The Camel bounced off the bolster of concussion and jerked back into a climb. MacLaren banked over hard and came back with two more bombs and nosed down again. He pulled the release and his last two bombs dropped on the tracks just behind the gun. There was another double blast and the flat-bed truck collapsed and the rails were splayed wide.

That big gun would be out of action for weeks!

MacLaren hoiked back to seek his formation and came out of the smoke and mist to find himself beside his flight leader. The man with two streamers on his tail waved his congratulations, but Mac was on another foray. He had spotted a Jerry two-seater.

The enemy pilot realized what he was in for, and twisted away to give his gunner a chance. The Camel pilot fired one short burst and the German gunner replied with a spread that peppered MacLaren's top wing. Mac took another careful sight and his shots put the gunner out of action, silenced the Parabellum and then tore into the pilot. The two-seater flipped wildly and then went down to crash and burst into flame.

By now MacLaren found himself all alone and he decided that he would be wise to head west and get on his own side of the line until he could round up some companions. He figured he was near Douai, well inside the German lines, so he opened up his throttle and headed west. All well and good, but at this low level he found himself taking considerable ground fire, so he nosed up and climbed for some low cloud cover. It was well he did for he missed ramming a German kite balloon by inches.

Still, the kite had prospects, so he turned back again and with very little trouble, put a long burst into it and saw it explode and go down burning. As he turned away he saw that the observer had jumped for there was a dirty-white canopy drifting down with a human figure dangling in the shrouds.

"This is quite a day," Mac chuckled. "A railroad gun, a two-seater, and a balloon on one patrol."

Checking his fuel gauge he decided he could spare a few more minutes before heading for his field. He coursed up and down and then just when he had decided that his luck had come to a close, he spotted a bright green two-seater flying east—probably heading for home after a reconnaissance show. In fact, the two machines were on a direct collision course.

Mac turned away, hoping to find a blind spot on the Jerry two-seater, but then discovered he was taking on a Hannoveraner, and the pilot had tried a snap burst that splashed through the Camel's left wing panels. The Jerry dived and the gunner was firing up to perforate the right-hand wing panels.

The Canadian snapped into a tight turn, but the two-seater turned with him and then tried to wriggle away from Mac's aim. This circling continued for almost a minute and MacLaren began to worry about his fuel, and the ground was not far below. But the lower they went, the less chance the two-seater had of making risky tight turns. It was during one of these uncertain moves that the Camel was put into one of its tight right-hand turns and the Jerry pilot knew he was finished. A short, deadly burst killed the pilot and the two-seater piled up on the bank of the Peronne-Douai canal.

This was typical of MacLaren's career. He attacked two-seaters, kite balloons and in fact anything that belonged to Germany. He downed thirty-seven aircraft in four and one-half months of combat flying and was awarded the Military Cross and Bar, and the D.F.C. By late October 1918 he had raised his score to fifty-four, which included six kite balloons. It was then his war career came to its close as the result of a wrestling bout.

ALAN A. McLEOD

A very young Canadian, Alan McLeod, wrote a chapter of glory— not aboard a Camel, nor an S.E.5; and certainly not while flying the redoubtable Fee. He obtained honor and renown in a barge-like Armstrong-Whitworth artillery-observation plane. Thus, his story is doubly interesting.

He was born in Stonewall, Manitoba, in the year 1899, and was only fifteen when the war began in 1914. Concealing his age, and gaining the consent of his father who was a country doctor, Alan enlisted in the Fort Garry Horse, a provincial militia regiment. His age was discovered eventually and he was kept in Canada until active-service requirements could be met. Then, in 1917 young Mc-Leod transferred to the R.F.C. He proved to be an apt pupil and soon gained his brevet, but again his age forbade his being posted to a front-line squadron, so he was assigned to a Home Defense unit in England. When there was a shortage of good pilots in the artillery-reconnaissance squadrons, Alan was sent to Number 2

Squadron in France in November 1917 where he tooled a slab-sided Armstrong-Whitworth, known colloquially as the Ack-W.

While on one of his first missions Alan was attacked by three Fokkers, and as his gunner held them off, Alan made a surprise move that found the attackers coming under the front gun of the old Ack-W. Before they realized that the tables had been turned, one of the Jerry ships was sent down out of control.

From this time on young McLeod was positive he could do anything—and he usually tried it.

On January 14, 1918, McLeod carried an observer, Reginald Key, who was even more pugnacious than Alan, and on this day they decided to wind up a patrol by attacking an enemy balloon twelve miles inside the German lines. They were still flying the boxy Ack-W, and no sooner had they made their first move than a barrage of antiaircraft fire spattered all around them. They continued on, however, and McLeod held the old artillery bus dead on and pressed the trigger. The kite balloon burst into flames. Then, as they zoomed for height, three Albatros scouts tried to cut them off, so while Alan flew the bus, Key shot one of them down which seemed to discourage the other two.

"Now he's attacking kite balloons!" Number 2's adjutant wailed when they had returned safely.

The next day Alan went back to the same area and blasted an antiaircraft battery out of commission with two Cooper bombs and a belt of machine-gun ammunition.

This raised some mild concern in Number 2 Squadron, and in an effort to lessen this continued belligerency, Reggie Key was sent to another squadron, and Lieutenant A. W. Hammond, a young Englishman who had already won the Military Cross, was assigned to the back seat of McLeod's bus.

The CO, who tried to adopt a sporting attitude, finally agreed that McLeod and Hammond could do as they liked—once they had carried out their regular artillery-spotting patrols. "Work comes first," he repeated. "If you must go off acting like Camel blokes, please refrain until you have given the gunners their targets."

So McLeod and Hammond studiously carried out their assigned tasks in the mornings, but the afternoons were their own, and during the next few weeks they raised Cain all over the German back areas. In fact, their weeks of frenzied activity would fill the pages of a fair-sized book, but, unfortunately, no one attempted to collect their logbook details.

In the March Push McLeod and Hammond had about all they could handle. On March 27 they were out searching for a special antiaircraft battery when they encountered a Fokker triplane formation. The two young men fought like tigers but one enemy burst wounded both of them and set their fuel tank on fire. This seemed to be the end of their wild career for they had only 2000 feet of altitude and were well inside the enemy lines.

But Alan McLeod refused to be beaten. He turned the Ack-W around and headed for his own lines while Hammond continued to hack away at the triplanes. McLeod had to get out of his cockpit and stand on the wing root, and, as best he could, keep the control stick reasonably dead center. The same flames soon burned out Hammond's cockpit, so the observer had to sit up on his Scarff gun ring, but even from that uncomfortable position he shot down a Fokker triplane.

McLeod finally got the bus into a sideslip to keep the flames from eating out the whole fuselage, and he continued in this manner until their own lines could be seen. The Fokkers made one more concerted attack, and Hammond was wounded again and knocked back inside his cockpit, but he hung on to the seat supports.

Although seriously burned, McLeod managed to keep some control and finally pancaked the Ack-W near the British front lines. It hit fairly hard and the pilot was tossed clear, but Hammond was trapped in the burning fuselage. While enemy infantrymen drilled rifle and machine-gun fire at them, Alan calmly tore the machine apart and dragged his observer out. Then, using a fireman's lift, he crawled in and out of shell holes until he reached the safety of the British lines.

Hammond had been wounded six times, and McLeod five. Young McLeod was in a hospital for months fighting for his life, and was awarded the Victoria Cross. Hammond, who recovered rapidly, was given a Bar to his Military Cross. When Alan was well enough to be moved he was sent home to Canada to recuperate, but in his weakened state he contracted influenza which was then sweeping North America, and he died five days before the Armistice.

EDWARD CORRINGHAM MANNOCK

Major Edward C. Mannock perhaps offers the most bewildering career of any airman in World War I, for he was a complex of paradoxes, and his true life story will never be told fully because of faulty history and erroneous statistics. Although generally listed as an Irishman, Edward's father was a Scottish soldier, a trooper in the famous Scots Greys, and his mother a Liverpool girl whom his father had married while serving on the Curragh in Ireland. Edward was born in the cavalry barracks at Aldershot, and spent most of his civilian life in England.

When Mick—to use his wartime nickname—was twelve years old his father deserted his family, and after weeks of bitterness, months of destitution, and years of dreary toil, Edward signed on as an apprentice lineman with a British telephone company. He worked hard, studied in his spare time, became an expert in the communications field, and, as was to be expected, took up Socialism.

Several months before the outbreak of war, Mannock was sent to Turkey to install a telephone system, and when that country joined the Central Powers, he, along with other Britishers, was interned. As the months wore on the Turks discovered that Mick had but one good eye, so his captors, considering him to be an "old crock" who could not give them any trouble, repatriated him in April 1915 in an exchange of prisoners. Little did they know they were releasing a dedicated man who was to become the greatest of all air fighters. The "old crock" was to destroy the equivalent of several enemy squadrons.

On arriving back in England, Mannock joined a Royal Army Medical Corps regiment, and his comrades nicknamed him "Jerry" because he continually expressed his contempt for and bitterness toward the Germans. Later, owing to his proficiency in telephonic communications, he was transferred to the Royal Engineers. When he read of the deeds of Major Lanoe G. Hawker, he applied for a transfer to the Royal Flying Corps. In order to get past the eye examination, he made a tricky double shuffle. When asked to read the test card, one eye at a time, he raised his right hand and covered his blind eye—and read clearly. Then, changing hands, he covered the same eye, completely fooling the examiner. However, he did not reach a flying school until August 1916.

He was an inept pupil, that is, until he was taken over by Jimmy McCudden who was in England for a period of instructing. Mannock was fairly good in the air, but like McElroy, Ball, and Beauchamp-Proctor his landings were total horrors. He hated to stunt, but it should be explained, that at the time he was thirty-four years old, and very mature. By forcing himself to go through a daily program of practice flights he gradually gained reasonable skill and was finally sent overseas to join Number 40 Squadron that at the time was flying Nieuport scouts.

There he showed little promise, but continued to express his hatred of the enemy. He had no use for so-called chivalry, and when he heard of Von Richthofen's death he refused to drink a toast to him, and growled, "I hope he roasted all the way down!"

When the fortunes of war moved him along to command a flight, Mannock became a martinet, insisting on tight formations, continual gunnery practice, and refused to allow any of his pilots to leave a formation except in the case of obvious engine trouble. He was on the front for about a year during which time he downed twenty-three enemy planes. Later, when he was assigned to Number 74 Squadron he found his stride aboard the S.E.5, and in the next three months added thirty-six more planes to his score, giving him a total of fifty-nine.

After receiving the D.S.O. he was given command of Number 85 Squadron where he continued his scourge of the enemy, running his total up to seventy-three. It should be added that some historians have questioned Mannock's score, and have tried to have it reduced by fifteen or twenty, but these records—being what they are—are generally difficult to verify, and his score probably will remain at seventy-three.

This strange Englishman went to his end in a manner as mysterious as several other high-scoring aces. He was tutoring Lieutenant D. C. Inglis on an offensive patrol, having promised to show him "how to knock down a Hun." While flying at low altitude he came under fire from a German trench and a lone rifle bullet set fire to his fuel tank. According to Inglis, Mannock nosed straight down and crashed just as he had hoped Von Richthofen had. About a year later, July 18, 1919, Mannock was awarded the Victoria Cross posthumously for his "fearless courage, remarkable skill, devotion to duty, and self-sacrifice."

GERALD JOSEPH CONSTABLE MAXWELL

In any group photograph of Number 56 Squadron you usually will find a compact young man in baggy "trews" and wearing a Lovat Scouts Balmoral bonnet. This is Gerald Maxwell, a true Scot who was born at Inverness in 1895. He first served with the famous Lovat Scouts that had been organized during the Boer War by his uncle Lord Lovat. Young Maxwell fought with this regiment with distinction at Gallipoli.

From the Dardanelles, the Lovat Scouts went on to serve for some time in Egypt, but from there Maxwell wangled a transfer to England and eventually a chance to join the Royal Flying Corps. He was first sent to Turnhouse late in 1916 where he was taught to fly a Farman Longhorn and he did so well he was next assigned to the famed Central Flying School at Upavon where he took a special course in advanced flying.

At about the same time Number 56 Squadron was being formed at London Colney, and Maxwell found himself assigned to this outfit and in fact was posted to Captain Albert Ball's "A" Flight.

Once Number 56 arrived in France with their new S.E.5s, Maxwell began his fighting career with no waste of time. On his first patrol he shot down an Albatros single-seater, but four days later he ran into severe trouble after an enemy antiaircraft shell broke up his engine and he had a severe crash landing near Combles.

He was back in action again by May 5, 1917, when he found and destroyed another Albatros. After Ball was killed Maxwell took over the leadership of "A" Flight. He pursued Albatros planes like a demon and by July 20 had raised his score to seven.

Anyone who wanted to stay with Number 56 Squadron simply had to produce Huns, and Maxwell hammered away and in spite of the talent in his own squadron and the stiff competition on the other side of the line, brought his score up to nineteen by September 28. Two days later he provided Number 56 with its 200th Hun when he downed still another Albatros, for which he was awarded the Military Cross.

Late in October Maxwell was given a rest and posted to the School of Aerial Fighting in Scotland, but after a few weeks of this dreary chore, he persuaded the authorities that he himself needed more time in France to catch up with the latest developments in aerial fighting.

The authorities probably scratched their heads at this reasoning, but allowed Maxwell to return to Number 56 Squadron. All this took time, and he did not actually get back until June of 1918. But he proved that he may have learned something at the fighter school, for he downed two two-seaters on June 16, a Fokker triplane on June 27, and an Albatros on June 28.

He was interested in the much-publicized Fokker D-VII and he came upon one on August 1 which he promptly shot down with one short burst. The new machine fell near Albert.

Satisfied that he had at last learned something about front-line flying, the new RAF officials again ordered him back to Britain as an instructor. Before he left he downed still one more Fokker D-VII to bring his score up to twenty-seven. He had won the Military Cross, the Distinguished Flying Cross, and the Air Force Cross.

Maxwell took a permanent commission in the Royal Air Force after the war and on his retirement became a member of the London Stock Exchange. Prior to the outbreak of World War II he joined up in the Royal Auxiliary Air Force and served as the station commander at a famous test depot, and added some 167 varied types to his logbook. In fact he even flight-tested the famous Gloster Meteor, one of the first jet-powered war planes of that day.

Today Wing Commander Maxwell is back in more peaceful commerce.

FRANCIS GRAINGER QUIGLEY

A Canadian airman, Captain F. G. Quigley, who shot down thirty-four enemy aircraft, yet managed to keep out of the limelight, was born in Toronto in 1894. Like Alan McLeod, he, too, was felled by the influenza epidemic in 1918.

Little is known of Quigley's personal life, but he joined the Canadian Engineers and went to England with his unit in May 1915, and crossed over to France a few weeks later. He served two years with the Engineers and then transferred to the R.F.C. After his training, he was posted to Number 70 (Camels) Squadron, and soon ran up a score. During the March offensive he fired more than

3000 rounds into enemy troop concentrations, dropped thirty bombs, and on one patrol downed a kite balloon and four enemy scouts that tried to defend the gasbag.

Early in May 1918 Quigley was wounded in the ankle, and after a period of convalescence in France, he was sent back to Canada to be an instructor at Armor Heights, but soon requested front-line service again. He sailed for England once more, but en route was stricken with influenza, and on arrival was moved to a Liverpool hospital where he died on October 20, 1918.

WILLIAM B. RHODES-MOORHOUSE

The first British airman to be awarded the Victoria Cross was a B.E.2c pilot of Number 2 Squadron. A devil-may-care hero, Lieutenant W. B. Rhodes-Moorhouse had learned to fly prior to the war, chiefly to add to the thrills he enjoyed in motor racing. In fact, he flew various types of planes long before he bothered to apply for a license. He detested officialdom and red tape, but became a first-class cross-country flier, finishing third in Great Britain's first Aerial Derby.

At the outbreak of the war he joined the Royal Flying Corps and eventually went overseas to Number 2 Squadron with which he spent several weeks acting as "The Eyes of the Army," carrying out many important reconnaissance patrols. A few days after the first poison-gas attack by the Germans during the Second Battle of Ypres, a message was received from Air Headquarters that the railroad junction and station at Courtrai were to be bombed at all costs. German reinforcements were being brought up through that town to be sent on toward the two-mile-wide hole that had been opened in the Allied lines by the effects of the chlorine-gas attack.

Four aircraft were assigned to the mission, but only Rhodes-Moorhouse succeeded in reaching the target. In order to carry a suitable bomb he had dispensed with his observer. He went in on the target from 300 feet and dropped his 100-pound missile directly on the signal box. He then could have zoomed into the smoke and low clouds to escape, but he circled the area to gather all the information he could. What he saw convinced him the Allied troops around Ypres were in for a rough time.

During the next few minutes he was peppered with rifle and machine-gun fire. A bullet shattered the fingers of his left hand, so he headed for home. Flying low over the city, he roared past the tower of a Courtrai church where the Germans had set up a machine gun in the belfry. A long burst caught him cold, one slug smashed his thigh and another tore through his abdomen.

His base was thirty miles away, but there were many areas below where he could have landed and requested medical assistance, even though he was well inside enemy territory. However, he felt he should get his information directly to the General Staff. One can only guess what Rhodes-Moorhouse must have suffered over those agonizing thirty miles. Once inside his own lines he could have landed and delivered his message to a responsible official, but, defying his suffering, he flew to the rear area and landed near General French's headquarters. There he huddled in his blood-soaked cockpit and dictated his report to an infantry officer, adding with a grim smile, "I didn't want them to get my old B.E. It's not too badly bashed about, is it?"

Lieutenant Rhodes-Moorhouse died in a hospital twenty-four hours later, not knowing he had been recommended for the Victoria Cross.

ARTHUR P. F. RHYS-DAVIDS

Another airman whose score cannot be fully confirmed, Arthur P. F. Rhys-Davids was one of the colorful figures in the famous Number 56 Squadron. Most records state that he downed twenty-three enemy planes, but others claim that eighteen, twenty, or twenty-two are correct. However, he remains an outstanding figure in aviation history because he is credited with downing Germany's famous Werner Voss.

Rhys-Davids was one of the youngest pilots at the front. He had scarcely completed his studies at Eton when he applied for a commission in the R.F.C. in 1916. A classical scholar and outstanding athlete, he was a breath of fresh air to the service, and when he was assigned to Number 56 he soon was their most popular member.

His first war patrol was almost his last. He became bewildered in a melee, and, obeying orders, was turning for home when some sixth sense warned him he was not alone. He turned and saw a black Halberstadt just above his elevators. Young Arthur then showed how well he could fly for in the next five minutes the German pilot got in only two wild bursts. Arthur tried his own guns whenever possible, but both weapons jammed, and he was not yet experienced enough to remedy the stoppages in the air. For some reason, his tormentor then broke off, and turned back.

His first victory was scored in May 1917 when he shot the wings off a D.F.W. and by the end of the month had racked up five kills. There was a time when it was thought he had shot down Karl Schaefer of the Von Richthofen Circus, but this was clarified later, and the score went to Captain H. C. Satchell, a F.E.2b pilot of Number 20 Squadron.

As the weeks rolled on Rhys-Davids became another Albert Ball, a headstrong, reckless daredevil, and only Jimmy McCudden's concern and control kept this youngster alive as long as he lived. His score piled up, and there was a short period when he led Jimmy McCudden, but he could not keep pace with the quiet, ex-ranker, who planned every patrol hours before he took off.

On September 23, 1917, Rhys-Davids had his great day when his flight encountered Werner Voss who at the time had been credited with forty-eight Allied planes. McCudden's flight had been in action late that afternoon, and on the way back noticed a lone S.E.5 being engaged by a silver and black Fokker triplane. (It was stated later that the machine was a silver-and-blue triplane.) McCudden led his flight to the rescue and for the next ten minutes the triplane made a gallant fight against six of the best pilots of Number 56. Finally, Lieutenant R. T. C. Hoidge forced the Fokker in front of Rhys-Davids' guns and then moved to attack a red-nosed Albatros that had dived to help Voss.

In his report that evening, Rhys-Davids stated:

> The red-nosed Albatros and the triplane fought magnificently. I got in several good bursts at the triplane without apparent effect, and twice placed a new drum on my Lewis gun. Eventually, I moved east and slightly above the triplane and got in a full Lewis drum and a corresponding number of Vickers rounds into him. He made an attempt to turn, until I was so close to him I was certain we would collide.
>
> He passed my right-hand wing by inches and went down. I zoomed. I saw him next with his engine apparently off, gliding west. I dived again and got one shot out of my Vickers; however I reloaded and

kept in the dive. I got in another good burst and the triplane did a slight right-hand turn, still going down. I had now overshot him, zoomed, but never saw him again.

Immediately afterward I met the red-nosed scout who was a very short distance south-east of me. I started firing at one hundred yards. The E.A. then turned and fired at me. At thirty yards range I finished a Lewis drum and my Vickers stopped, so I dived underneath him and zoomed. When I looked again, I saw the E.A. spiraling down steeply out of control.

When the S.E.5 flight landed every machine carried bullet holes, and at dinner that night Rhys-Davids, who was given credit for downing Voss, said, "Oh! If only I could have brought him down alive."

On October 23, 1917, McCudden went home on leave, and Rhys-Davids was appointed to lead "B" Flight, but held this command for less than twenty-four hours. The following day he led his six-ship formation over the lines and was involved with a number of Fokker triplanes. Observers saw one triplane go down out of control, and an S.E.5 completely disappear. No trace was ever found of Rhys-Davids or his aircraft; he had vanished in the smoke of battle, and lies somewhere in an unmarked grave.

WILLIAM LEEFE ROBINSON

The first Zeppelin destroyed over England fell before the guns of Lieutenant William Leefe Robinson on the night of September 2–3, 1916. This youthful Englishman was flying a B.E.2c biplane, an early war machine popularly known as "The Quirk." This unexpected victory was probably the most memorable in the history of the Royal Flying Corps during World War I.

The hero of this spectacular triumph was born in India to British parents, and when the family returned to England William was placed in St. Bee's School in Cumberland, a small institution established in 1583 which produced three winners of the Victoria Cross before the conflict ended.

Robinson apparently enjoyed considerable freedom in his youth as he traveled widely through France and Russia, but by August

1914 had enrolled in Sandhurst Military College. He was gazetted
to the Worcester Regiment, but transferred to the R.F.C. in March
1915. He first served as an observer, and on May 9 of that year was
wounded while on a patrol over Lille. When he recovered he was
given pilot training at Farnborough, and had completed his course
by September.

After various postings he eventually joined Number 39 Squadron,
a Home Defense unit located at Sutton's Farm that became the
famous Hornchurch fighter base in World War II.

At this time Zeppelins were raiding Britain at regular intervals,
and the civilian casualty list was mounting. Though not seriously
hindering Great Britain's war effort, the Zeppelins were causing
many sleepless nights.

Some months before one dirigible airship had been destroyed by
an R.N.A.S. pilot, Flight Sub-lieutenant Reginald Warneford who
came upon it quite by accident over Bruges in Belgium. But the
British public had forgotten about that incident and were demanding action where results could be seen.

On the night in question Leefe Robinson was sent off just after
11:00 P.M. to patrol the area between Joyce Green and Sutton's
Farm. It was a beautifully clear evening. The B.E. climbed to 10,-
000 feet, and the British pilot studied the skyscape, finally spotting
a Zeppelin southeast of Woolwich. He climbed to 12,000 feet, hoping to cut it off, but when antiaircraft guns opened up from the
ground, the Zeppelin darted into cloud cover and was lost to sight.

About 1:50 A.M. Robinson spotted another dirigible that had been
picked out by searchlights. Ignoring the antiaircraft shells that were
bursting at every level, Robinson finally reached a position where
he could fly along below the keel of the big gasbag. His Lewis guns
were loaded with a mixture of Brock and Pomeroy incendiary ammunition, and after several futile attempts and erratic bursts, he
finally put the torch to the *SL.11* (a Schütte-Lanz type), and it fell,
carrying its crew and its commander, Hauptmann Wilhelm Schramm,
to their deaths.

Leefe Robinson was awarded the Victoria Cross and given a captaincy. Some time later he was sent to France as a flight commander
with Number 48 Squadron that had been outfitted with the new
Bristol Fighter. Subsequently in a fight with a formation of the Flying
Circus Robinson was shot down and taken prisoner. He made several vain attempts to escape, and was then clamped in the infamous
Holzminden fortress where he was put in solitary confinement for

a time. His health was undermined, and after being released following the Armistice, he fell a victim to the influenza epidemic and died on January 31, 1919.

WILLIAM S. STEPHENSON

A Canadian ace of rare accomplishment had his remarkable record brought to light only a few years ago when the details of an amazing history were presented in the book titled *Room 3603*. In this work we learned of a career that came to its zenith when Bill Stephenson was knighted by King George VI, and decorated with the United States' Presidential Medal for Merit by General William J. Donovan. Few, if any, airmen of World War I contributed so much to the English-speaking cause as Sir William Stephenson.

Bill grew up in Winnipeg, Manitoba, and graduated from Argyle High School where he excelled in mathematics and many handicrafts. Although a slight youth he was proficient in boxing and at one time was the world's lightweight amateur champion.

When the war began William Stephenson joined the Royal Canadian Engineers, won his commission before he was nineteen, and eventually became a captain. Late in 1915 he was badly gassed and sent back to England, and while convalescing he put in for a transfer to the R.F.C. Late in 1917 he went back to France and was assigned to Number 73 Squadron. He was still suffering from the effects of gas, and no one in the squadron thought he would be able to stand the strain of Camel flying, but as the weeks rolled on Bill became another Canadian scourge, soon running his score to twenty-one. He was awarded the M.C. and the D.F.C. The French, who also appreciated his effort, added their Legion of Honor and the Croix de Guerre.

On July 28, 1918, Captain Stephenson decided to go off on a lone patrol, and quickly found a French reconnaissance plane in trouble. He roared in to the rescue, only to discover he had taken on seven Fokker D-VIIs. He put on a show until he could dive into some cloud. By that time he had torched the leader, broken up a second, and sent a third down out of control. When he returned to make certain the French machine had escaped, the French observer mistook the Camel for a German plane and slammed a burst into the British aircraft. The rotary engine was put out of commission, and Bill was wounded in a leg.

There was no choice but to try to get down safely inside the German lines. He just managed to pancake in some distance short of no man's land. An enemy machine gunner put another bullet in the same wounded leg, and Bill Stephenson was surrounded and taken prisoner. While in a hospital he made several attempts to escape, and was next placed in the Holzminden camp on the River Weser. Here he met Leefe Robinson. Stephenson soon contrived another escape and planned to take Robinson with him. Their first attempt was a failure and the Zeppelin-buster lost all hope, as he himself had tried several times, but Stephenson bided his time, and making the most of the last experience, was able to work his way back to his squadron where he reported in, ready, willing, and able to fight again.

After the war Bill Stephenson went into radio and did very well. He perfected the system of transmitting photographs by radio waves, a device that made him a millionaire before he was thirty. He went into the steel business, and then opened the Shepperton studios where a large number of British films were made. He became interested in plastics, and helped to form the British Pressed Steel Company that manufactured 90 percent of the bodies of English automobiles.

His many interests, particularly in steel, took him all over Europe and he was one of the first to suspect that Adolf Hitler was up to no good in Germany. He was able to give Winston Churchill a very comprehensive report on Germany's prewar planning; information that was to guide Sir Winston in his preliminary moves against *Der Führer*.

With the outbreak of war in 1939 Churchill sent Bill Stephenson to the United States where he set up an anti-sabotage system to protect shipping that carried Lend-Lease goods to Britain. So well was this carried out, not one ship or cargo was damaged in any way in a North American port, and all sailed safely. What the U-boats accomplished in mid-Atlantic was something else, but Bill Stephenson and his undercover team put on a security lid that was later adopted by the United States. In Churchill's words, Bill Stephenson had "pursued his task with cold and silent passion."

LOUIS A. STRANGE

Louis A. Strange is not a high-ranking ace; in fact it is difficult to check whether or not he ever downed an enemy plane, though he seems to have been involved in many incidents in which enemy aircraft were destroyed.

Strange's claim to fame was in his persistence to prove that aircraft could be equipped with machine guns. Although Roland Garros and Tony Fokker have scooped the cream of the fixed-gun philosophy, it was Louis Strange who first fitted a machine gun to an airplane and took it into action. Prior to that it had been considered rank heresy to think of so demeaning a heavier-than-air machine. The airplane, it was pointed out, was "The Eyes of the Army," and to burden it with a noisy machine gun was comparable to equipping troopers of the First Life Guards with entrenching tools.

Louis Strange, the son of a Dorset gentleman farmer, was schooled at Oxford, and true to his breed became a member of the Dorsetshire Yeomanry. But young Strange who had read H. G. Wells, and the flaming editorials of Charles G. Grey in the magazine *The Aeroplane,* soon saw that the classic concept of cavalry was outdated, and to prove his point ducked out of the Yeomanry and started to buy flying lessons at Hendon. As was to be expected, he was among the first selected for the budding R.F.C., and at the start of the war was sent overseas with Number 5 Squadron, by which time the Germans had goosestepped through Belgium and were well on their way to Paris.

Strange flew various types from Avros to Henri Farmans, but always on reconnaissance patrols. The war-in-the-air was to be found only in books. No one did any fighting in the air, just looking. On one occasion, while assigned to a Farman in which the observer squatted beneath the center section while the pilot had a fairly good outlook from a rear seat, he and his observer, Penn Gaskell, considered the possibility of arming the old boxkite with a machine gun. Penn Gaskell agreed to become the gunner.

In poking around a number of boxes piled in the squadron Stores, they found a Lewis gun that they hid in their hangar, and when no one was looking tucked it away aboard their Farman. A short time later a German Rumpler turned up over Maubeauge, and

Strange and Gaskell took off with great hopes, but their machine could not get off the ground with a pilot, an observer, *and* an infantry-type Lewis gun and a stack of drums. That is to say it was not capable of getting off in time to intercept the Rumpler; the enemy plane simply buzzed about some 2000 feet above the Farman, its crew ignorant of the fate that had been laid out for them.

But Penn Gaskell, it should be stated, did try to fire his weapon—when Strange wasn't looking. The Lewis went off with a roar that so startled the pilot he yanked the gasping Farman into a steep zoom and almost flipped the observer out of the nacelle. So they decided to return to earth, each breathing a silent prayer that the aircraft was still intact.

This historic experiment took place on August 22, 1914, and from all accounts was the first time an automatic weapon had been fired in the air.

When their commanding officer learned of this fantastic experiment, he ordered Penn Gaskell to return the weapon to Stores. "If you two must stir up strife in the air," he blazed, "please use a rifle. Machine guns are for the infantry, not aeroplanes!"

Penn Gaskell persisted in his quest to arm the airplane, and on one occasion rigged a flexible mounting. It was flexible in that the machine gun was hung from a rope fastened to a fixture on the top plane, and with this contrivance he often went on ground-strafing patrols. One or two other belligerent types took up this novel idea, and there was a period when Number 5 Squadron was considered something of a bloodthirsty organization.

Louis Strange was next transferred to Number 6 Squadron that had a number of Martinsyde scouts, small fast biplanes that were powered with rotary engines. These single-seaters were available for those airmen who wished to act offensively, and carried a Lewis gun on the top plane in much the same manner as such weapons were mounted on the Nieuport scout.

Early in May 1915 Strange went off on his own to attack an Aviatik that had come up from a German airdrome located outside Lille. As usual, the German outclimbed him, and the enemy observer battered the Martinsyde with his Parabellum gun. Strange responded with his Lewis, but nothing happened, although he wasted a full drum on the two-seater above him.

The gun was firmly fixed, and when Strange decided to change the drum in midair he met with difficulties. First, he loosened his seat belt and tried to hold the joystick between his knees. Then, from that uncomfortable position, he next attempted to get at the release latch on the drum, but in the struggle the Martinsyde nosed up into a stall, and before Strange could get back into his seat, the British scout was over on its back, and he dropped out of the cockpit.

"I felt like an utter fool," he explained later. "I had been swearing because I couldn't get the drum off. Now I was praying it would stay on."

The scout was on its back and Strange was hanging free clinging to the machine gun's ammunition pan. By now the Martinsyde was in a flat upside-down spin directly over the German trenches.

"I finally grabbed a center-section strut and felt more comfortable. Below, I could see the Menin road twirling around, and naturally I was getting dizzier by the minute. I kept kicking upward until at last I got one foot hooked inside the cockpit. I took a second or two to get my breath and finally got the other foot anchored."

Getting most of his body inside the cockpit, Strange then kicked the stick over which eventually righted the machine. He then dropped down with a plop and went straight through the wicker seat and found himself practically sitting on the floor of the aircraft. While he had been outside the plane he had lost his seat cushion, and everything else that was not clamped down. The engine, that had stopped when the machine was on its back, suddenly picked up again, and the Martinsyde went into a wild dive toward Menin Wood. When Strange tried to pull the stick back to level off, he discovered that the broken seat frame had jammed the control, and he spent another few anxious moments clearing away the debris. With the stick finally clear, he zoomed over the tree tops, leveled off and found that in his struggle to get back inside his plane he had kicked out all the instruments in the panel, but was so delighted to find himself alive, he ignored the technical features of flight and made his way home to his field at Abeele.

Some years later, while on a friendly tour of Germany, Strange met a former Staffel leader, a Von Leutzer who remembered this incredible mishap.

"We reported that incident, but no one would believe us when we explained that the pilot had gone down hanging from his wing gun while the plane was flying on its back," Von Leutzer said.

"What about me? I don't think I ever convinced my CO how I had kicked all the instruments out," Strange remarked ruefully.

And that was how it was in the days before the fixed gun was perfected.

Strange ended the war a Lieut-Colonel with the D.S.O., the M.C., and the D.F.C.

REGINALD ALEXANDER JOHN WARNEFORD

This young man with the tongue-twisting name was, for a few days, the outstanding air hero of the British Empire. His photograph appeared everywhere, on motion picture screens, the covers of glossy magazines, and in practically every newspaper published in the English language. He downed only one enemy aircraft, but it was the *LZ.37,* the first German Zeppelin to be shot down by an Allied airman, a feat that inspired British airmen to attain to the heights that finally wiped out the lighter-than-air threat and allowed British manpower to increase the munitions output so necessary to winning the war.

That was on June 7, 1915. Ten days later Warneford was killed in a tragic air accident, and from that date on his deed and memory drifted into oblivion. A year later no one could remember who Reggie Warneford was, or what he did.

Sic transit gloria mundi!

Warneford was a lively composite of the British Commonwealth of Nations. His parents were cheery Yorkshire people who traveled about the empire on various missions. Reggie was born in India, educated at the English College in Simla, and at the Stratford-on-Avon Grammar School in England. His formal education was devoted to the arts and classics, but Reg appears to have shown a marked preference for motorcycles, odorous chemical experiments, and mountain climbing.

The Warneford family was in Canada when war broke out, and Reggie hurried back to England and joined the much publicized Sportsmen's Battalion, but soon found that famous athletic figures are usually physically attuned for sport—not for war. Young Warneford feared the war would end before all these invalids could be whipped into shape, so he transferred to the Royal Naval Air Service, and within eleven months was a first-line pilot with Number 1 Naval Squadron, then located at Dunkirk. He flew a Morane Parasol that was modified for single-seater work and equipped with a light-bomb rack, and a Belgian carbine.

On the afternoon of June 6, 1915, Number 1 Naval was advised that a German Zeppelin, or Zeppelins, had made a raid on Britain, and that with any luck they might intercept one or more as they flew back to their base in occupied Belgium. Their commander, Spenser Grey, had set up a three-ship flight at Furnes just across the French-Belgian border, and assigned Lieutenant J. P. Wilson, and Sublieutenants Mills and Warneford to this out-of-the-way airstrip. Grey had also been advised that a number of Zeppelins were hangared at Evère near Brussels, and he decided that to attack these raiders while they were on the ground, and in goodly numbers, was to be preferred to the possibility of finding one in the sky. So it was decided that the flight at Furnes would attempt that night to bomb the sheds at Evère. Young Warneford was all for trying it, but confessed he had never been in the air at night.

"Good," Wilson said. "There's nothing you'll have to unlearn."

And with that doubtful observation, Warneford was sent off first. With some normal dread he found himself airborne, but with no lights for his instruments. He was puzzled about the bluish glare from his exhaust, but finally realized what it was. He climbed to 300 feet and then looked around for Wilson and Mills, but they were nowhere to be seen. Eventually adjusting to night flying, he risked a turn, and tried to find the Evère airship sheds.

Wilson and Mills had made immediate contact with each other and soon cleared the fog around Furnes and headed for Brussels, seventy-five miles away. Once in clear skies, Wilson decided to head direct for Evère on the north side of the old Flemish city, and together both pilots hit their objective on the nose. Circling the shed once, Wilson went in first, mainly to start a fire to give Mills a pathfinder run-in. He released three of his bombs, but only created a billowing pall of smoke. The German defense began plastering the sky with high explosive, by which time Wilson discovered that his last three bombs had become hung up in their primitive rack.

Mills went in to dare the ground fire, and pulled his bomb plug. All six of his so-called fire bombs slid clear, and he was rewarded with a gigantic explosion that illuminated the sky for miles around. Wilson who had conceived and planned the raid, had to return with little to show for his effort.

(Two weeks later British Intelligence, working out of Antwerp, reported that *LZ.38,* a Schütte-Lanz airship, had gone up in flames as a result of this two-plane raid on the Evère sheds.)

That same night the *LZ.37,* commanded by Leutenant von der Haegen, had been sent off to make a routine patrol between Ghent and Le Havre. The flight had been set up to give a number of airship designers, specialists, and technicians firsthand knowledge of the various problems experienced by the crews on active service.

The *LZ.37* was 521 feet long, and her eighteen gas ballonets carried 953,000 cubic feet of hydrogen. She was powered by four 210-horsepower Maybach engines, and manned by a crew of twenty-eight skilled airshipmen. For defense her designers had provided four machine-gun posts that were built into the outboard engine gondolas.

While heading in the direction of Ostend Warneford spotted something that was emitting the same blue-yellow flame as his Le Rhône engine. If that was Wilson or Mills, what were they doing up there toward Ostend? And what in heaven's name was that long black mass floating above them?

After continuing on for a few more minutes, Reggie suddenly saw he was coming upon a Zeppelin. He moved in fast to get a better look, and wondered how anything that large could be kept in the air. But there was no time for idle conjecture; the Zeppelin's machine guns suddenly opened up and slugs clattered through the wing of Morane Parasol Number 3252. Reggie wisely heeled over and cleared out of range.

He glanced around and saw that the ground mist below was clearing. The Ostend-Bruges Canal could be easily identified. He had decided the big airship was heading for Ghent, when she abruptly came roaring toward him. Two more streams of machine-gun fire snapped from the forward gondolas and converged only a few yards from the monoplane. Warneford gave his engine all it could gulp and tried to climb, but the crisscrossing tracers penciled in a definite warning, so he had to turn away and dive. As he studied the situation he wondered what he could do to attack this ungainly monster.

It is not certain what armament the Morane carried, but it is possible that Reggie fired off a few rounds from a short Belgian carbine carried by some of these pilots. If he did, his bullets had no effect, but the German gunners were generously peppering him. Commander Von der Haegen dumped some water ballast over Assebroek and left the young Englishman impotently potting away. The

Zeppelin then turned and headed toward Ghent, and Reggie knew he had better work to gain some more altitude.

Von der Haegen aboard *LZ.37* knew he had to maintain height to evade his attacker, but he also realized that he was not on an ordinary patrol. He had a number of important passengers aboard, and as it turned out, he worried more about them than he did about maintaining a safe tactical procedure.

By 2:25 A.M. Warneford was still stalking, and trying to get above the dirigible, when he was delighted to see the big airship nose down and head for a break in the 7000-foot cloud layer. The young pilot somehow forced his machine up to 11,000 feet, hoping to get into a position where he could use a number of incendiary bombs carried in a primitive rack. When Von der Haegen nosed down, Warneford for the first time was well above his target. He saw that the upper cover of the Zeppelin was painted what seemed to be a dark green, and it looked so big he felt he could have made a landing on her topside.

Von der Haegen had made a tragic mistake. He was in too much of a hurry to get his civilian passengers down safely, and ignored the possibility that the enemy airplane might be somewhere above him. Warneford made the most of his chance and nosed down at the 500-foot top panel of *LZ.37*. As he passed over the high elevator and rudder structure, he pulled the bomb release.

"One . . . Two . . . Three!" he counted as the little Morane jerked with the release of each bomb. He explained later that he had expected the dirigible to explode immediately after the first bomb had pierced the envelope, but nothing happened.

"Four . . . Five!" he continued to chant as he roared over the long envelope. Then, as he feared that all his bombs were duds, a blinding explosion ripped up through the upper covering baring the twisted tracery of the framework. Spellbound, Reggie continued his run-in until the airplane was swept up on a savage belch of flame and concussion. It was whipped over with great violence as Warneford gasped in astonishment. He rammed the stick forward and tried to force his machine into a dive. Chunks of burning framework hurtled past as he floundered out of the carnage. Over the next few minutes he was fighting for his life, getting back on an even keel, and frantically adjusting his air and gas mixture to dampen out a series of warning pops from the Le Rhône engine.

A few minutes later the doomed airship fell on the Convent of St. Elizabeth in the Mont-Saint-Amand suburb of Ghent. One nun was

40. The South African air hero few Britons ever knew. Captain A. W. Beauchamp-Proctor won practically every decoration the Empire could bestow. He was credited with fifty-seven enemy aircraft, a score he racked up in less than four months of front-line fighting. (*Arch Whitehouse photo*)

. Captain Roy Brown, Canadian pi-, has long been credited with ending e career of Baron von Richthofen, al-ough he himself never made such a aim. Today, evidence piles up to indi-te that the Red Knight was shot down Australian machine gunners. (*Imrial War Museum, London*)

42. Victor in sixty air combats, Raymond Collishaw failed to gain his deserved recognition during World War I. Nevertheless, he stayed on in the Royal Air Force and became an Air Vice Marshal. Today he lives in Vancouver, British Columbia. Here he is shown in a Sopwith Camel. (*Imperial War Museum, London*)

43. The man who foxed Anthony Fokker. Professor George Constantinesco, born a Roumanian, had become a naturalized British subject. His first contribution was the hydraulic-pressure interrupter gear for British aircraft. More than one hundred and five other inventions of great worth are credited to him. At the close of the war he was developing a motor patrol boat that would be capable of 200 mph—in a rough sea. (*Air-Britain Digest photo*)

44. The seldom-remembered Australian airman, Robert A. Little, was a master aboard the Sopwith Pup. A crack marksman and highly skilled pilot, he eventually downed forty-seven enemy aircraft. He was killed late in the war during a night flight to intercept an enemy bomber. (*Imperial War Museum, London*)

45. One of the most skilled and experienced airmen in the Royal Flying Corps, James B. McCudden rose from the ranks and became England's most popular fighting man. Son of a time-serving soldier, he won the Victoria Cross and commanded the famous No. 56 Squadron. He was killed in a tragic accident late in the war. (*Imperial War Museum, London*)

46. One of the few two-seater fighter aces, Andrew E. McKeever of No. 11 Squadron (Bristol Fighters), is credited with thirty victories while flying the famous Brisfit. He lived through the war, returned to Canada, and was killed in a Christmas holiday automobile accident. (*Imperial War Museum, London*)

47. Thousands of Canadian airmen know him as Black Mike, but his real name is Clifford Mackay McEwen. During World War I he destroyed twenty enemy aircraft and in the Second World War he commanded Canada's famous Sixth Bomber Group. (*Carlton-Yonge photo*)

48. Major Edward C. Mannock, son of a Scottish trooper, was born in the cavalry barracks at Aldershot. He turned out to be the fiercest Hun-hater of them all and gloried in watching his enemies go down in flames. Before he died in a flaming crash inside the German lines he had destroyed seventy-three enemy planes. (*Arch Whitehouse photo*)

49. Lieutenant W. V. Rhodes-Moorhouse was the first British airman to win the Victoria Cross. Flying an old B.E. 2c biplane he carried out a vital bombing mission over Courtrai until he was critically wounded. Instead of descending immediately, he flew on for thirty miles to British Headquarters in order to deliver a full report of the situation. He died two days later. (*Arch Whitehouse photo*)

50. The first Zeppelin shot down over Britain was destroyed by Lieutenant W. Leefe Robinson who was flying a B.E. 2c "Quirk" biplane. Later he commanded a Bristol Fighter flight and was shot down and taken prisoner. He died a short time after being repatriated following the Armistice. (*Arch Whitehouse photo*)

1. He downed twenty-two enemy aircraft, was himself shot down and taken prisoner, but the Huns couldn't hold Captain William Stephenson of Winnipeg, Canada. He escaped and returned to his Camel squadron, all ready to fly war patrols again. Today he is Sir Wiliam Stephenson, British-Canadian financier, living in Bermuda. (*Arch Whitehouse photo*)

52. On June 7, 1915, a youngster named Reginald Alexander John Warneford made his first night flight and came upon the Zeppelin *LZ.38* somewhere over Belgium. He attacked with a string of fire bombs and thus downed the first German dirigible to be destroyed in the war. Ten days later Warneford was killed in an air accident near Paris. (*Imperial War Museum, London*)

53. This quartet of Royal Naval Air Service pilots all took part in various air encounters in which Zeppelins were destroyed. From left to right: J. S. Mills, A. W. Bigsworth, J. P. Wilson and R. A. J. Warneford. (*Imperial War Museum, London*)

54. A pilot of No. 85 Squadron, flying S.E. 5s, chalks up their score over the past fourteen days. This was the squadron Major Billy Bishop organized and included several American pilots who were later transferred to the U. S. Air Service. (*Imperial War Museum, London*)

55. Major Edward McKelvie, commander of No. 22 Squadron, R.F.C., talks over flight plans with the squadron mascot. The black patch on Major McKelvie's jacket is still worn by a few British Fusilier regiments. It was originally used to protect their tunics from the grease of their wigs, so fashionable in the eighteenth century. *(Imperial War Museum, London)*

56. France's premier airman, Rene Fonck, with his Spad bearing the Storks insignia of Spa. 103. Other Escadrilles of the Storks group used variations of this classic stork design. In fact, there were six different insignia using the *Cigogne* motif. *(T. G. Miller photo)*

57. Captain Rene Fonck, the Allies ace of aces, is credited with seventy-five enemy planes. He was a remarkable marksman, a brilliant pilot and a redoubtable leader and one of the few to live through the war. After the Armistice he went into politics and served as Inspector of Fighter Aircraft for many years. He died in 1953. (*Arch White- house photo*)

58. This is the man who first fought with a gun that fired through the propeller. Roland Garros, concert pianist, devised a set of deflection plates which were bolted to the blades of his propeller, and which enabled him to down five enemy airmen in sixteen days, weeks before the Fokker fixed gun device was thought of. (*H. M. Mason, Jr., photo*)

killed and several seriously burned, but the helmsman of *LZ.37* had a miraculous escape. He was said to have jumped clear of the tumbling wreckage at about 200 feet, landed on the roof of the convent and crashed on through to land on an unoccupied bed. However, he suffered only minor injuries and was the only person aboard the dirigible to survive. (Possibly he was in a gondola that smashed through the roof.)

Warneford fully expected the parasol wing of his Morane to part company with the fuselage. Then the Le Rhône snorted and stopped cold. The gleaming propeller wigwagged to a halt just as Warneford figured he was at least thirty-five miles inside the German lines. There was nothing to do but accept the bad break and hope for a safe landing. So he put down his beat-up plane along a turfed stretch that was shielded on one side by a long strip of woods. There was a darkened farmhouse nearby but no one emerged to question his arrival, and his first impulse was to destroy the monoplane. A quick inspection disclosed that there was a reasonable amount of fuel in the tank, and Reggie then discovered that a fuel line had been broken. He worked hard to repair the damage, and legend has it that he used a piece of a cigarette holder; whatever it was he was able to join up the break and bind it with strips of his pocket handkerchief.

In a matter of minutes, the Le Rhône was running again, and Reggie made a successful take-off and roared away. As he approached the coast he encountered fog, so he dropped down at the first clear area which was at Cap Gris-Nez, about ten miles below Calais. He picked up more fuel and called his squadron headquarters.

Within hours the news was flashed over the Empire and Reggie Warneford's name was headlined in every newspaper. All that week his photograph was displayed on hundreds of theatre screens, to the delight of cheering audiences. On June 8 King George V awarded Warneford the Victoria Cross, and the French government added the Legion of Honor, but the young Englishman lived but ten more days. On June 17 he went to Paris to receive the French decoration, and after a short ceremony was ordered to pick up a new Farman biplane at the Buc field. The machine had been delivered minus much of its standard equipment, and there were no safety belts in either seat. An American newspaperman, Henry Needham, had asked to go along with Warneford to Furnes where he planned to write a complete story about Warneford's great victory. Reggie cheerfully agreed, and they climbed into the biplane and took off. Almost immediately, for some unknown reason, the Farman tossed and bucked. Rolling over out of control, it turned on its back, pitching out Warneford and Needham, both of whom were killed.

H. G. WATSON

Captain H. G. Watson, a New Zealander, often listed as an Australian, won the Distinguished Flying Cross, and accounted for ten enemy aircraft in a comparatively short career on the Western Front. He also gained a reputation as a fearless ground strafer, and was deadly when attacking enemy balloons.

A generous-sized, chunky man, Watson was born at Caversham, Dunedin, New Zealand. He enlisted first with the Australian Army Service Corps and spent considerable time packing supplies for the troops, but by 1917 put in for a transfer to the Royal Flying Corps. He received most of his training in England, and was finally assigned to the Australian Number 4 Squadron that was equipped with Camels.

Shortly after, the Germans opened up their March 1918 push and Watson soon realized that the high-in-the-sky air battles he had expected were postponed for the time being. He had to fly low-level missions, hoping to break the enemy's new ground offensive. For instance, on March 28 Watson was advised by an R.E.8 observer that there was considerable ground activity around Achiet-le-Grand, and within an hour Watson was attacking an enemy headquarters with Cooper bombs. When most of the buildings had been flattened, he turned his attention to a long column of troops, and for the next ten minutes created havoc with his machine guns, and left several motor trucks overturned. Then he went after a light field battery, and set fire to an ammunition dump.

While this low-level action was carried out, there was little opportunity for victories over enemy aircraft, and Watson did not down his first plane until May 11. At that time he was assigned to fly escort to a number of aircraft of Number 110 (Naval) Squadron that were to bomb a large ammunition dump at Armentières. The Navy boys did a splendid job until thirty-four Albatros scouts turned up.

Watson, one of ten Camel pilots assigned to this raid, went into the fray like an inspired fullback. He saw one Camel go down in flames, but Captain N. L. Petschler, the Australian flight leader, soon shot the wings off an Albatros. Watson found himself under the guns of two enemy planes, but he put a burst into a Mercedes radiator and one of the Albatros scouts darted into cloud cover. As Watson turned away he spotted a Pfalz which he attacked and sent down completely out of control. The melee ended soon after this.

Three days later Watson and Captain R. King attacked two L.V.G. two-seaters and sent both down, though neither could be confirmed as they disappeared through a low layer of mist and were not seen by the balloon observers.

Watson then went on a balloon-busting spree, often working with Captain A. H. Cobby. On one occasion, while returning from one of these attacks, they saw five Pfalz and an Albatros over Laventie. They immediately attacked, regardless of the odds, and Watson sent one Pfalz down in flames. Cobby tore one to pieces with a long burst, and then chased the Albatros until it piled up in a field. Watson plunged into the rest, killed the pilot of one, and then chased the others home.

All through July and August these two pilots played merry hell. On July 15, while attacking the enemy balloon line near Estaires, they were fired on by five Pfalz, so they darted into clouds to put them off. When they emerged again, they ran into a formation of eight Fokker triplanes. Ignoring these, they turned back and settled for the five Pfalz scouts. They each got one, and then went into a tail-chasing foray until Cobby shot the wings off the leader by which time the Fokker triplanes joined the fray. Over the next twenty minutes the two Camel pilots took pot shots at the enemy while darting in and out of available cloud cover. Only the greater structural strength of the Sopwiths enabled Watson and Cobby to reach their own lines safely.

On August 16 a large raid was staged against a German airdrome located at Lomme. Sixty-five British machines took part, including Watson's flight. His Camel pilots selected a group of officers' huts and some workshops on the edge of a wood, and Watson flew in so low he returned home with the greater part of a small bush entangled on the spreader bar of his undercarriage.

From that time on much of Watson's time was spent in tactical ground strafing, and he did not score his tenth official victory until September 16. On that day he and King were attacked by three Fokker D-VIIs northwest of Lille, and in the fight that followed both Camel pilots obtained single victories. Nothing more is available on Captain Watson after this. He may have gone to New Zealand on leave, and while there was swept up by the Armistice celebrations. We do know that he was never wounded, and lived to see the end of the war, but what happened after his tenth victory no one seems to recall.

HENRY W. WOOLLETT

Another unsung hero of the Sopwith Camel corps was Captain Henry W. Woollett, D.S.O., M.C., who is credited with thirty-five victories, and once bagged six Fokker fighters in one day. Yet he is only briefly mentioned in Britain's *Official History of the War in the Air*. In fact, there is no record as to when or where he joined the Royal Flying Corps, or where he came from.

We first encounter Henry Woollett in November 1916 when he was posted to Number 24 Squadron just one week after Major Lanoe G. Hawker was downed by Von Richthofen. Woollett took over a D.H.2 pusher fighter, soon gaining considerable experience, but no victories. It was not until the period of "Bloody April" in 1917 that his guns finally found their mark. He went to the rescue of three Fees and managed to shoot an Albatros scout down in flames. This seemed to trigger his ambitions, and the next day he downed an L.V.G. that was on a photographic mission over the Allied lines.

Woollett's bag did not mount rapidly, but he proved to be a dedicated airman and by July was promoted to Captain, and took over "A" Flight. Although burdened with leadership Woollett was soon scoring again. It should be added that the squadron had been outfitted with the little-known D.H.5, a back-staggered biplane that looked much like an astonished Sopwith Pup. It was powered with a 110-horsepower Le Rhône rotary, had a top speed of 102 miles per hour, and was armed with a fixed Vickers that fired through the propeller. It was a splendid machine in the air but difficult to land, possibly due to the back-stagger of the top plane that set up considerable loss of aerodynamic efficiency at low speeds, and was likely to go into a stall just as the pilot was leveling off for a touch down. Only five squadrons were equipped with this machine, and it eventually wound up as an operational training plane at the schools of aerial fighting.

Woollett scored another "double" on July 29, running up his score to six. He was sent on leave and then transferred to Number 43 Squadron that was then flying Camels. Aboard this plane Woollett began his best work and by the end of 1917 he had passed the even dozen mark. When the March Push opened up, Number 43, as were all Camel squadrons, was ordered to come down from 14,000 feet and carry out their long program of low-level attack shows.

But this in no way halted Woollett's fighting skill for as soon as he had dropped his quartet of Cooper bombs, he would range far and wide to seek enemy reconnaissance and contour-fighting ships. On one occasion he found two flights of Albatros scouts, and his team downed four in as many minutes. Captain J. L. Trollope was in this same flight, and on becoming detached from the general melee attacked six enemy planes and downed one of them. A few days later Trollope set a new fighting record by shooting down six German planes in one day.

Not to be outdone, Woollett, on his next patrol, shot the wings off a D.F.W. two-seater, and a few minutes later led his flight into an enemy formation. The Camels downed five of these, although the observers aboard other D.F.W. ships fought a great fight. Woollett's flying coat was slashed, but he finally killed a pilot who wore a black helmet. Following that he had to pull out and give some attention to columns of moving troops he had seen below.

On March 28, toward the close of the enemy's push, Captain Trollope was shot down while attacking eight enemy scouts, and Woollett took off that evening with the intent of evening the score. Over Estaires he caught a Pfalz that was shooting at an R.E.8, and with that in some small way made up for Trollope's loss.

During much of April 1918 the weather was not too good for wartime patrols, but Woollett went out to attack an enemy kite balloon that was still nestling in its ground bed. He risked a heavy barrage of "flaming onions" and managed to put enough bullets into the sitting balloon to deflate it completely. As he zoomed to clear, a Fokker triplane tried to get on his tail, but he completely outclassed it and shot it down in flames.

Woollett reached his peak on April 12 when he matched Trollope's six-in-one-day score.

Number 43 Squadron downed thirteen enemy aircraft on this day, and Woollett torched three during a morning patrol. After lunch he headed for Estaires and quickly shot down a Pfalz. He then spotted a two-seater and his first burst clipped its wings, and it fell in a wood. Before this patrol ended he had downed a Fokker—six enemy planes and eight airmen in the space of a few hours.

It must not be presumed from this that Woollett was the lone-wolf type of airman. On the contrary, most of his victories were won while leading his flight. He was a good pilot, a crack shot, but above all a devoted leader. He stayed on in the RAF after the war and when last heard of held the rank of Squadron Leader.

PART FOUR

French

FRENCH

France made a tremendous contribution to the Allied air arm in World War I, though she seldom has been given full credit for the part she played. What publicity was given to her aviation program usually was centered on the accomplishments of her fighting pilots whose scores generally were presented in a somewhat lighthearted vein—reports comparable to the routine announcements of golf or tennis tournaments—while the all-important tactical work of the two-seater squadrons was shamefully ignored. World interest, therefore, was centered more on France's efforts on the ground. On the other hand, Germany held the attention, first with her Zeppelin raids, then with her high-pressure propaganda based on the Boelcke-Von Richthofen Flying Circus claims, and later with her Gotha raids on British cities. Considering all this, it is clear why the neutral world assumed Great Britain fought her share of the war on the sea, France in the ground operations, and Germany with the bulk of the air action. This erroneous judgment is still retained in some quarters, and is perpetuated by many historians.

But records disclose that France was a military air power as early as 1870 when she manufactured and employed balloons to fly out important personages, to carry out reconnaissance, drop bombs, bear dispatches, and even airlift ammunition during the Prussian siege of Paris. Interestingly, in order to cope with these free balloons, the Krupp munitions factory designed the first true antiaircraft gun; the original high-angle weapon that became the basic gun for all antiaircraft defense.

France was the leading country for years, so far as heavier-than-air aviation was concerned, and was one of the few major powers to recognize the value of the Wright brothers' invention. French aeronauts and designers were quick to adopt the aeroplane, and most of the world's important aviation meets were held in France. Early in 1910 the Aero Club of France advised the War Cabinet that the heavier-than-air craft had great possibilities in warfare, and a few weeks later the French Air Service was formed. Again acting on the Aero Club's suggestion, the French Cabinet authorized their first aerial maneuvers in Picardy, and throughout 1911 flight exercises were carried out, and vital experiments were made to employ radio in artillery cooperation. By March 1913 a Naval Air Service was formed and about 160 aircraft of various types were available for France's airmen.

France also showed the way in the development of flying fields, and before the war had laid out Saint-Cyr, Villacoublay, Juvisy-sur-Orge, Issy-les-Moulineaux, Le Bourget, Buc, and a naval station at Juan-les-Pins. Each of these fields had a fleet of motor trucks, two breakdown cars, and a steam traction engine for service and transport. The personnel were trained to dismantle the sheds and hangars, and load them for moving within two hours.

But France also contributed a wealth of technical skills and aircraft design, and by the time the war broke out she had a wide selection of aircraft suitable for military and naval purposes. French designers had produced several first-class aero engines, such as Renault, Le Rhône, Canton-Unne, Monosoupape, and Gnome. Her aircraft factories were turning out the Astra C.M., several types of Blériot monoplanes, the Caudron two-seater, two types of Farmans, the Morane-Saulnier, and Voisins. In fact, French Aviation had 830 aircraft in flying condition, and 850 military pilots to fly them. The lighter-than-air arm had twenty-eight airships of various sizes and types, and full crews to man and maintain them.

France gave military aviation the first, fixed-gun, air fighter, a subject that has been debated for more than half a century, but unquestionably it was a French airman who first fired a burst of machine-gun bullets through the whirling blades of an aeroplane propeller, and downed an enemy plane. According to historical records Eugene Gilbert first conceived the idea of protecting the blades with deflection plates, and Roland Garros perfected the conception and flew such a machine in action, shooting down five German aircraft in the space of sixteen days.

Shortly after, Garros was forced to land in German territory where his Morane monoplane was captured and his "secret" fixed gun was discovered. From that point on legend and distorted claims took over. Anthony Fokker, the Dutch engineer, quickly produced his mechanical interrupter gear that was mounted on a number of his early Fokker monoplanes, and from then on, so the legend goes, Allied aircraft were shot down in wholesale lots, a statement that cannot be confirmed by a careful study of the fighting records. Actually, sage consideration has since agreed that the effect of the Fokker fixed gun was much overrated; that, like so many wonder weapons of the period, it was sadly misused, and that Allied pusher-type fighters that required no interrupter gear canceled out the impact of the Fokker gun gear. The record of Number 24 Squadron, R.F.C., that used the D.H.2 pusher-fighter puts the lie to the convenient alliteration "Fokker Fodder." Much of the credit that was showered on Anthony Fokker for years has been withdrawn in the face of the fact that sometime before the outbreak of the war a German engineer Franz Schneider patented a similar interrupter gear. Fokker is said to have borrowed the features of this device, and, according to French records, one of these had been found aboard an L.V.G. two-seater that had been shot down by Eugene Gilbert. It is also worth noting that Franz Schneider had once been associated with Edouard Nieuport (or Nieport), the designer of the French Nieuport aircraft.

Together with her first-class engines and aircraft, France must be credited with a splendid contribution of skilled airmen, both pilots and observers, many of whom must be included among the war's finest and most gallant air fighters.

MARIUS JEAN PAUL AMBROGI

This gallant gentleman with the impressive name is one of France's forgotten heroes, although he destroyed fourteen enemy aircraft in World War I and became a Deputy Group Commander in World War II, officially destroying a Junkers Ju 52/3m before his country was overrun by the Nazis. Yet who knows this remarkable man today?

Marc Ambrogi, as he prefers to be called, was born in 1896. He joined the French infantry at the start of World War I, and in February 1916 transferred to the aviation service, eventually becoming a Nieuport scout pilot with the rank of corporal. He put in considerable time flying escort to artillery spotters, and was next made a sergeant. Once he was permitted to roam on his own, he racked up victory after victory and on one occasion downed a German plane that fell inside the French lines. This feat brought him a commission as a *sous-lieutenant*. In due course he destroyed a kite balloon and another enemy aircraft for which his superiors awarded him the Legion of Honor.

Kite balloons attracted Ambrogi, and in the month of August 1917 he brought down three. During these successes, because he was down low, he usually finished his patrols by harassing enemy ground troops and road transport. A concentration of troops had been reported near a noted railroad station, and Ambrogi was sent out to attack. He used all his bombs and gun ammunition, so went back for another supply, and returned once more to complete the chaos.

Before the end of the war Marc had added four more balloons to his score, and was promoted to a full lieutenant. Today Marc Ambrogi retains his interest in aviation, and at one time was President of the Aero-Club de Province that guides the activities of France's light-plane flying clubs.

PAUL V. D'ARGUEEFF

World War I aviation is packed with careers of so-called mystery men, but Captain Paul d'Argueeff is possibly one of the more unusual of Allied pilots who ran up any kind of a victory record. A Russian by birth, he served with both the Russians and French. He was credited with fifteen victories, was decorated by the two countries under whose flags he served, and by all rights should have been invalided out of the service in 1915. Instead he took up flying, but how he passed the physical examination no one has explained.

Paul d'Argueeff was born at Yalta in the Crimea in March 1887, which made him twenty-seven years old when the war broke out. He was a lieutenant colonel in 1914, but for some unknown reason relinquished his Russian commission, and went to France where he enlisted in the 131st Regiment of Infantry. By early 1915 he had been wounded so severely he was invalided out of the service and sent home, but as soon as he could walk he applied for active duty with the Russian Army and was rejected. He continued his quest and was assigned to a staff post well behind the lines, and there he bided his time. There was an airfield nearby and he induced several pilots to give him free flights, and became so taken with flying he wangled a transfer to the Russian Air Service. He took a course of training at Sevastopol where he so shocked his instructors by spinning old Moranes, they got rid of him by ordering him to a scout squadron posted at Riga. Scout Squadron 4 was equipped with a heterogeneous inventory of Nieuports, Voisins, and Moranes that had been discarded by the French. One day an Albatros two-seater came over and dropped bombs on Riga, so D'Argueeff selected one of the Nieuports, took off, and calmly shot it down.

In March 1917 D'Argueeff was wounded by a shell splinter and was out of action for a week. Then, on April 1, while flying over Mitau (Yelgava) he was attacked by three Fokker D-IIIs, and although his Nieuport was badly shot up he managed to down one of the Fokkers for which he was awarded the Order of St. George with the Golden Sabre, and was also cited for the St. Vladimir Cross. He ran his score up to five or six—the records are not clear on this point— and with the upheaval of the Russian revolution D'Argueeff went back to France and volunteered to fly with his old companions.

He was first accepted to pilot ancient Bréguets, but after a wild display of aerobatics with one of these kites, he was quickly switched to a Spad escadrille, and by May 1918 was in the thick of the Allied general offensive aimed at ending the war. The German airmen were making a gallant stand, and both sides paid high prices for victory or defeat. During the action at Château-Thierry D'Argueeff was involved in low-level flying, mainly to protect French field batteries.

During one of these patrols, while a member of a mixed formation of Spads and Nieuports, he scored his first victory in a French uniform. The force had piled into a formation of Albatros and Pfalz scouts that were escorting a number of L.V.G. bombers. D'Argueeff saw a German observer torch a Spad, and then take time to watch the Frenchman go down in flames; the next thing he knew he was also going down in a burning plane. D'Argueeff had moved in fast to put in a burst in retaliation.

A few minutes later he suffered a long grazing burn in one arm, but it did not keep him out of the air. On May 31 he nailed a Rumpler that was carrying out a bombing mission, and his first burst caused it to explode in midair.

The next day Paul went on patrol with six other pilots to attack a German airdrome, but shortly after passing the enemy balloon line he was hit in the groin by a shell splinter and had to pull out and return to his own field. He had no sooner left his companions than he was intercepted by two Pfalz scouts and in the first brush he received two bullets through his left foot. He was fortunate to crash-land his Spad between the two front lines where he huddled in his wreckage for nearly three hours before a party of French infantrymen could drag him to safety.

When he was examined in a hospital it was decided that

D'Argueeff was again ready for discharge, but he refused the "ticket" and was back in the cockpit of a Spad by mid-August. Whether he was ready is a question, for on September 1 he engaged and shot down a Fokker D-VII, but the experience was such that he had to be lifted out of his cockpit by mechanics and armorers. He was then given two weeks' leave, after which he returned as chipper as ever, and finished out that month by downing a kite balloon. Then, while running from five Fokkers bent on shooting him down, he turned the tables and destroyed one that had dived too steeply and somehow worked itself out of control.

The next day, September 27, he found a two-seater flying just below a layer of cloud. It was a decoy ship, and when Paul moved in and fired a short burst, a formation of Pfalz and Fokkers came down out of the clouds and attacked him from all sides. Realizing he was in a tight spot, the Russian decided to take someone with him, and concentrated on the two-seater. His next shots caused it to break up in midair. He then expected to feel bursts of Spandau batter into him, but a formation of Nieuport 28s had dropped down on the Fokkers and Pfalz. One D-VII fell away from the foray and D'Argueeff tried to cut it off. He was very close and his first burst of fire folded the wings of the Fokker; the fuselage rolled over on its back and continued on with the engine roaring like a banshee. According to some statistics that was Paul's twelfth victory.

All through that October he was out every day that the weather permitted, and during one misty afternoon nearly rammed a Fokker, but recovered in time to take aim and press his firing lever; the Fokker crashed well inside the French lines. A short time later he downed an A.E.G. two-seater, for which he was awarded the Legion of Honor, and a ninth Palm to his Croix de Guerre. He ended the war with fifteen enemy aircraft. Paul d'Argueeff died in France in 1922.

JEAN-PIERRE LEON BOURJADE

One of the most unlikely candidates for glory in the air war was Jean-Pierre Léon Bourjade who was studying for the priesthood when World War I began. Although a militant man, he had no conception of the workings of the military machine. He joined an artillery regiment, and after surviving the First Battle of the Marne in 1914, he was made a quartermaster sergeant, a post he held until 1916.

In the long months of dreary footslogging this bearded aesthete noticed the activity in the skies, and after making several requests for a transfer, he was finally accepted. Given the routine training, he qualified as a pilot in late October 1917, and to his surprise was sent to the Vosges front to fly Nieuport scouts with N.152 Squadron.

Bourjade did not make much of an impression, but faithfully carried out his duties, escorting artillery-spotting machines or bomber formations. On March 27, 1918, he finally tasted the fruits of his long devotion to duty when he downed an enemy kite balloon. He pondered on this minor success and gradually turned his full attention to the Drachen. On July 17, 1918, he destroyed three of these bulbous bags—all three within five minutes! In the next eight days he downed six more, and before the war ended this priest-to-be ran his score to twenty-eight, twenty-four of which were kite balloons.

In his comparatively short spell on the front he became something of a legend. On his last show he risked following a balloon down to the level of 1000 feet where the ground fire was very heavy. He was severely wounded by machine-gun bullets and was still convalescent when the Armistice was signed.

After the war Bourjade gave up his military rank and decorations to resume his studies for the priesthood. He became a missionary in Waina, Oceania, in the Central Pacific, a mission that proved to be more dangerous than wartime flying. While ministering to a camp of lepers he contracted the dread disease and died on October 22, 1924.

MAURICE BOYAU

This renowned French ace began his career as an Army truck driver, although he had been a star cyclist, rugby and soccer player, and was especially remembered as a track man. At one time he captained the French International rugby team.

Maurice Boyau was born in Algeria in 1888, making him twenty-six years old when the war started, and somewhat older than the typical volunteer for flying, but by the middle of 1915 he had obtained a transfer to the French Aviation. Because of his natural skill and mature approach he was soon made an instructor at Buc, but Maurice wanted none of that, and began pulling strings that resulted in his being posted to N.77 Squadron (Nieuports) as a corporal pilot.

N.77 was just being formed at the time Boyau joined the squadron, so he had a chance to hone his flying skill and learn formation flying, and gunnery. One of his first missions produced one of those tit-for-tat encounters that are far from satisfactory. On March 16, 1917, along with several others, he was assigned to furnish escort for a Nieuport two-seater that was flying a photography patrol. Half way through the chore a battery of French antiaircraft guns began firing to point out a lone German plane. Some of the Nieuport pilots broke off to engage this threat, and in the diversion an Aviatik fighter slipped in, seemingly from nowhere, and dived on the camera plane. Boyau spotted it, but not in time, and the two-seater Nieuport was shot down. Boyau avenged the French crew by destroying the Aviatik, but such victories add up to poor arithmetic in air fighting.

Maurice Boyau could not stand inaction, and on one occasion when the enemy would provide no combats, he loaded his racks with incendiary bombs and flew deep into enemy territory to attack a German airfield at Marimbois. The timing was perfect, and he had an uninterrupted run in. By the time he had zoomed away three hangars were in flames, and not one enemy plane had had a chance to take off and intercept him.

Boyau also was interested in enemy kite balloons, and spent some time trying to solve the problem of torching the big bags. He made several lone attacks before he had success. On June 3, 1917, he attacked a balloon and made the observer take to his parachute before the bag actually caught fire. The next time he put his first burst into the basket, wounding, or killing, the observer, before turning his fire on the bag itself.

This sport so intrigued Boyau he made it a daily patrol, but on his next try he received a real fright when his Le Rhône cut out while he was maneuvering for the attack. He was far enough over the enemy lines to face being captured, and for a few minutes it looked as though he was headed for a Jerry prison camp. Then, just as his wheels touched down, the engine, for no accountable reason, picked up so he scrambled for altitude. Over the next few miles he had to dodge and dart through a storm of machine-gun and rifle fire until he dropped down just inside his own lines. Maurice Boyau was awarded the Médaille Militaire for that feat, and considering everything it would be of interest to know the actual wording of the official citation that accompanied the decoration.

✳

Later in that month of June, Boyau teamed up with a lieutenant and a sergeant pilot to attack a German balloon. This threesome drew a force of enemy single-seaters into their orbit, and five Fokkers went after the sergeant pilot. Maurice went to his aid, shot down one Fokker, and scattered the rest. He next trapped an enemy plane over Nancy, and on the way home made a low-level attack on a railroad station, and also destroyed several buildings occupied by enemy troops.

Boyau ran his score to seven, and was then awarded a commission, an honor that seemed to trigger a stretch of adverse luck. When he would find an enemy aircraft to attack, his guns would play him false. When the weapons crackled and sparkled, his targets would evade him. The weeks ran into months, and not until January 1, 1918, was success renewed. On that date, accompanied by Gilbert Sardier, he destroyed one balloon and shared another with Sardier. He also downed an Albatros D-V that he picked out of an eight-ship formation.

A short time later Boyau sighted two Albatros scouts that were attacking a Bréguet, but before he could get within firing range, the two-seater was shot down. Again, Maurice went in for revenge and downed one Albatros and engaged in a running fight with the other until that too went down. On the way back to his own lines he torched another kite balloon. Shortly after that his squadron turned in their Nieuports for new Spads.

Much of Maurice Boyau's record is puzzling, as the dates on which certain actions are quoted are at variance with those of the official records, and most historians have taken their data from the pilot's logbook. But there is no question that this man was an exceptional airman. When he had run his score to twenty-six he was given the Legion of Honor. On the day this award was announced Maurice celebrated by downing two balloons and an enemy aircraft. His thirtieth success was made on August 15 when flying with a Corporal Letz-Mitchell who, acting as bait, enticed an enemy two-seater to dive on him. Boyau went in like a dart and torched the *biplace*. Satisfied with this ruse and its victory, the two Spad pilots turned back for their own lines, when Letz-Mitchell's plane suddenly exploded at a height of 1000 feet and crashed.

Puzzled by this, Maurice turned sharply to investigate, and then realized that a second German two-seater had sneaked in to take revenge for Boyau's victory. Maurice knew that young Letz-Mitchell had been killed, and in a wild, savage reprisal he made a sharp climbing turn, fired a long burst, and then circled while the German two-seater spun down, completely out of control.

After a short leave in September, Boyau was soon back in action, and one evening he took on six enemy fighters, single-handed. This fight was a memorable thriller to the infantrymen below. Maurice damaged one of his opponents, but his own machine was shot to wreckage, and he had to make a forced landing near the front lines. What the German pilots had left intact of Maurice's Spad was quickly dismantled by a number of American infantrymen—for souvenirs.

With the war's end only a few weeks away, Maurice Boyau came to a tragic finish. While flying in company with a Corporal Walk, he went after another kite balloon that was aloft six miles inside the enemy lines. He made three dives on this bag before it burned, and by that time seven Rumplers had roared into the scene. Walk received an incendiary bullet in his back, and Maurice tried to escort him to safety. While the two were flying low over enemy territory, Boyau's Spad took a heavy burst of machine-gun fire. What happened to the pilot is not known, but Boyau's plane began to spin, and finally nosed in. The gallant Frenchman was killed. He was France's fifth ranking ace.

MICHAEL COIFFARD

A most interesting character in the French Air Service was a seldom-remembered native of Nantes, Michael Coiffard, who ended his flying career with thirty-four confirmed victories—twenty-eight of them enemy observation balloons. This was something of a record among the balloon busters, for the famous Willy Coppens of Belgium is credited with only twenty-six. Yet if a World War I enthusiast were asked who was the leading exponent in this field, it is unlikely he would know of this most personable man.

Born in 1892, Coiffard was called to the colors in 1910, and went to Africa as an artilleryman before the Great War was ever considered. He saw much fighting around Tunis between 1911 and 1914, and was wounded three times. For this early gallantry he was awarded the Croix de Guerre with two Palms.

Coiffard was convalescing in France when World War I broke out, and he immediately volunteered for active service. He was promoted to sergeant major for this gesture, and rushed to the front to join his battery. By September 10 he was again wounded, but he refused to go to the hospital, continuing in his madcap, reckless way. He was in the thick of the fighting all through that first winter and well into the following spring, and was awarded the Médaille Militaire.

But the artillery was too tame for Michael, so he applied for a transfer to the infantry. He was sent to the 13th Regiment, and this outfit took a terrific beating during the next twelve months. Coiffard was hit in the stomach by a machine-gun bullet and hauled to a hospital to die, but this iron-willed man soon recovered and then asked to be transferred to the Aviation Service.

By April 29, 1917, he had passed all his tests, and was posted to a Nieuport squadron. Nothing of great interest was recorded for about six months when he downed an Albatros photography plane. He was promoted to adjutant, and transferred to S.154 Squadron. While flying Spads he seems to have found himself once more. His luck was good, as he survived several combats in which he came off second best, and then early in 1918 he took on a trio of Pfalz scouts, and downed them all. He was awarded the Legion of Honor for this, but went to the hospital again with another bullet wound.

While he was convalescing he heard that a great deal of importance was being placed on downing enemy kite balloons. Also the exploits of Maurice Boyau were the talk of every airman on leave in Paris. Coiffard decided he too would try this sport and see if they were any tougher than Pfalz fighters. He did not get back to the line until early in May, and then, to his delight, found that balloon busting was far safer than engaging enemy airmen who could shoot back. In the next six weeks he downed eleven balloons and two airplanes, seven of this total falling in a period of four days.

A typical day was May 29 when he destroyed a balloon, and then followed it the very next day with a double "kill." He then ran into a dud spell, and it was late in June before his guns scored again. On

June 27 he downed an Albatros scout and a balloon, another balloon the next day, another on the next, and still another on June 30.

One day his plane was unserviceable, and he had to stay on the ground, but after lunch his commanding officer was called away for a staff conference, and the minute his back was turned, Coiffard ordered his leader's machine to be run out. He went up over Ploegsteert where he found three Drachens and, cutting his power, nosed down on the nearest, shooting it down in flames. Dodging the heavy ground fire, he darted in and out, and within eight minutes all three kites were piled up and burning. When he returned to his field, he was soundly tongue lashed by his CO, Captain August Lahoulle—a ten-Hun performer himself—but the denunciation turned into congratulations when it was learned that Michael Coiffard had destroyed nearly $10,-000 worth of valuable military equipment.

On July 10 Coiffard downed a Rumpler, and three days later added a balloon to his score. In August seven more balloons were burned, and on September 10 he destroyed his sixth and last airplane. This day Michael, and two companions, took on two Fokker D-VIIs and torched them both. Day after day, balloons fell in twos and threes until his score made him the ace of balloon busters.

Captain Lahoulle was wounded on October 12 and Michael was given his command, and while leading an escort formation for two Salmsons that were on a photography mission, they were attacked by twenty enemy scouts. Coiffard was hit during the ensuing melee. One bullet smashed his thigh and another ripped past his old stomach wound and tore out muscles in his back. Though in dreadful pain Michael managed to get back and make a good landing on his own field, but he died in the ambulance that rushed him to a field hospital. And thus ended the career of a man who had faced the enemy for more than seven consecutive years.

ALBERT DEULLIN

This scholarly gentleman, victor in twenty air combats, possibly was the most learned pilot in the French Aviation. A brilliant scholar during his early school days at Epernay in the Champagne region, he shone even more brightly at college, the Lycée de Pau. He also spent a year at a university in Germany before being called for military service in the 31st Dragoons. Fulfilling his national obligation, he next left for England where he continued his studies in the autumn of 1912. When war broke out two years later Deullin returned to France, rejoined his regiment, and took an active part in the early trench warfare, for there was little cavalry work for a Dragoon. During that period Albert Deullin saw all he wanted of footslogging warfare, and decided to apply for military flying.

He had made the transfer by April 1915, and by the middle of June had gained his brevet on Maurice Farmans. His first operational posting was with M.F.62 Squadron where he usually was assigned to photo or general reconnaissance. He was a workmanlike performer, and after nine months of this hazardous duty he was trained as a Nieuport pilot and sent to N.3 of the famous Storks group.

The association with such stars as Dorme, Heurteaux, and other aces of that period inspired Albert, and he soon scored his first "kill," downing an enemy plane near Verdun on March 31, 1916. He was hospitalized for a time with a bullet wound in one arm, but by mid-May was back with his squadron at Cachy and was delighted to find they had been equipped with the first Spads. Deullin took to the S.7 immediately, and quickly added to his score. By February 10, 1917, he had downed eleven enemy planes, won the Legion of Honor, and was assigned to the command of Spad 73, another Storks squadron. Three more enemy aircraft fell before his deliberate attacks.

The squadron was moved from one front to another to meet the various challenges made by the Flying Circus, but Deullin never failed in any of his assignments, and by February 1918 was given command of Number 19 Fighter Group that took a vital role in the battles of Saint-Mihiel and Château-Thierry. Before the war was over Deullin had registered his twentieth victory and had a rosette added to his Legion of Honor. He continued to fly after the war, and in 1921, accompanied by Lionel de Marmier, made a record long-distance flight from Paris to Istanbul. Deullin died at Petit Clamart, France, May 29, 1923.

RENE DORME

René Dorme who was an outstanding member of the Cigognes Group, downed twenty-three enemy aircraft and acquired the nickname Père (Papa), was only twenty-three years old when he died in 1917. His gentle, kind, paternal qualities marked his association with other airmen, but in the air he was a bitter, relentless foe, an unerring marksman, and above all a master of combat tactics. Georges Guynemer always claimed that Papa Dorme was the finest flier on the Western Front.

Dorme came from a modest home. His father was stationmaster at Aix Aubancourt near Verdun. For a time René toiled in a lawyer's office. In 1913 he was called up and joined the French Artillery. He was stationed in Bizerte, North Africa, and by the time the war broke out he was a quartermaster sergeant.

When he arrived back in France, René put in for a transfer to the French Aviation. He was accepted and went through the usual training, receiving his wings in April 1915. By June he reported to Escadrille C.49 that was carrying out patrols on Caudrons at Villacoublay. At one time Dorme suggested, along with a number of other pilots, that they try night flying, if only to prepare themselves for such work later on, and during one of these experiments René crashed one night and was hospitalized for several weeks.

In mid-March 1916 he was again flying Caudrons, and on one occasion encountered six German planes that seemed to be heading toward Paris. He attacked at once, driving one down and scattering the rest. For that action he was immediately assigned to the Cigognes and flew with Escadrille N.95. While flying the Nieuport he soon showed his mettle, shooting down a single plane. He was next assigned to Escadrille N.3.

From this point on Dorme's career was typical of all the leading aces. He scored regularly, had his share of "hair-raisers" and somehow managed to scramble home, engagement after engagement. His score increased as did his wealth of experience, but on December 20, 1916, he was struck by an incendiary bullet and was out of action until March 1917.

His end was tragic and legendary. On May 25, 1917, Dorme, along with Deullin, took off with the first light and crossed the line, dodging between piled banks of clouds. As they searched for action René saw a number of antiaircraft shell-bursts that warned him enemy planes might be in the area. The two pilots moved in cautiously and next spotted two enemy reconnaissance planes that obviously were engaged on a patrol of importance.

Dorme gave chase immediately when the reconnaissance planes headed for home. Deullin also found a scout that had been flying escort to the two-seaters, and was engaged with it for a time, finally shooting it down. He then looked for René, but he was nowhere to be found. Albert searched until his gas gauge warned him it was time to head back to his field where he was certain René would be waiting for him. As he crossed the lines he saw a French Spad burning on the ground below, so he went down for a closer look but the machine was completely consumed by that time, and he could not make any identification.

When Deullin returned to his field Dorme had not come back. It was presumed at first that he had been downed by a balky engine, or an empty gas tank, but as the hours rolled on no message was received from anywhere. Knowing the resourceful Dorme, his associates decided he had had to land in enemy territory, and perhaps was hiding out to await an opportunity to get into neutral or French territory. With that presumption no report was given out that the French ace was missing. His friends hoped that he would turn up again within a few days, explain what had happened, and relate his experiences. Papa Dorme would make a fine tale of it.

Nothing happened for two weeks, and then a German pilot flew over their field, and dropped a message that read, *"Pilot Dorme killed in combat."* But it was not believed as no date was included, and there were no particulars, no identifying item, and no explanation of where the body was buried. It must be a hoax, but if so, how did the Germans know Dorme was missing? That point had been kept a deep secret—or so everyone believed.

But Papa Dorme never came back, and it was obvious that, on May 25, 1917, he had made his last flight, fought his last fight, and in passing had left a great void in the ranks of the Cigognes.

RENE FONCK

René Fonck was the Allied Ace of Aces with a score of seventy-five, although some historians claim he could be credited with fifty-one more, that, for one reason or another, could not be made official. This is reminiscent of the claims for Captain Alfred Heurteaux who at one time was credited with 128 officially destroyed, and 132 others disabled. Actually, Heurteaux is generally credited with twenty-one victories. This shows how frantic were the claims and counterclaims to build up the records of scout pilots during World War I.

Whatever his score, René Fonck was undoubtedly one of the greatest duelists on the Western Front. Although he flew from mid-1915 to the end of the war he was never wounded, not even nicked. He took no unnecessary risks. He believed in conserving his ammunition, and spent hours considering the tactics of his opponents. He worked out in detail his plans for attack in all conceivable combinations of circumstances. He was a master of deflection shooting, and seldom expended more than five or six rounds on any victim.

Fonck was born at Saulcy-sur-Meurthe in the Vosges on March 27, 1894. Trained as an engineer, he took up flying as a sport, and had had his first lesson when war broke out. Thus, when he was called to the colors he was posted to Dijon for flight training, but after a month he was suddenly withdrawn and transferred to a regiment of engineers. For the next five months he was engaged in bridge-building, trench-digging, and road-repairing. But his persistence won out, and on February 15, 1915, he was sent to Saint-Cyr for aviation training, but not until April 1 when he was at Le Crotoy did he encounter an airplane.

On completion of his course he was posted to Escadrille C.47 that was flying Caudrons. In the following months he gained air experience on reconnaissance and light bombing patrols. He was cited for several first-class observation reports, and his observer was credited with fine camera work. It was not until July 1916 that he shot down his first enemy plane, which was accomplished aboard a Caudron that had been fitted with a forward-firing machine gun.

During his period on Caudrons, Fonck staged an astonishing show on August 6, 1916, when he attacked two enemy Rumplers. One immediately pulled out of the action, and with a number of bold, skillful maneuvers René forced the German pilot to surrender and land his plane inside the French lines. This is the simple outline of the feat, but it was learned later that René had accomplished this unusual exploit without firing a shot. His flying was so masterful he had the enemy crew at his mercy at all times, and the Rumpler gunner could not draw a bead on him. He also dominated the situation in such a manner the German pilot continued to lose height and finally had to land. The plane was a brand-new Rumpler C-III (6A.5), and was examined closely by Allied pilots and designers for new or valuable features.

Following this bloodless victory, Fonck was recommended for a transfer to a fighter squadron and finally joined Escadrille Spad 3 of the Cigognes. He began his Spad career on May 1, 1917, which would indicate he was given considerable training on single-seaters, but within twelve days after joining Spad 3 he had downed five planes and had become an ace. In August he shot down three more in three consecutive days. By autumn of that year his score had reached eighteen, and he was made a Chevalier of the Legion of Honor.

On September 14, 1917, René Fonck staged another thriller when he downed not only another enemy aircraft, but carried home the German's barograph as proof of his success. The barograph indicated that the pilot had reached the height of 20,000 feet, well above the clouds, and it was there that Fonck first spotted him. He attacked instantly, and both pilots fought savagely, but Fonck triumphed at last, and the enemy plane fell inside the French lines.

The story may be apocryphal, but it is worth relating. Apparently, Fonck landed nearby and retrieved the barograph, chiefly as an unusual souvenir. On examination it was noted that the instrument had recorded the complete range of the German's flight, and when the needle touched the 5000-foot mark it registered a sharp vertical stroke indicating that the pilot had been hit at that level, and instinctively yanked the stick back, putting the plane into a zoom. From there it stalled and spun down to crash, but fortunately the instrument was not badly damaged.

✳

Georges Guynemer, France's beloved airman and a member of Spad 3, was lost on September 11, 1917. No one knew what had happened to him, but eleven days later it was learned that Lieutenant Kurt Wisseman had been credited with shooting the French ace down. Wisseman, it was said, was a Rumpler pilot, but he had already been credited with five victories.

Commandant Felix Brocard and René Fonck were deeply distressed over Guynemer's death, and though nothing could be done about it, René was determined that some sort of retaliation should be made.

While cruising about the front line on September 30, Fonck spotted a two-seater moving back and forth at the 9000-foot level. He moved in carefully and noted that the enemy gunner had seen him and was alert to his moves. Nevertheless, Fonck nosed down and came up directly under the two-seater's tail in a position where the gunner could not fire at him. Two short bursts finished the two-seater, and it fell inside the French lines. Both the pilot and gunner were thrown out and when their personal possessions were examined it was discovered the pilot was Lieutenant Kurt Wisseman, the man who, according to the Germans, had killed Georges Guynemer. Officially, no trace was ever found of Guynemer or his plane, and according to other reports, his grave was obliterated by British shelling.

October of 1917 provided some inclement weather, and Fonck flew just over thirteen hours during that time. However, he was in ten engagements in which he claimed that many victories, but only four of these were confirmed officially. He continued to sharpen his skills, take plenty of exercise, and abstain from the use of alcohol. His score piled up week after week with relentless persistence while his friendly rivals either died, or were unable to keep up with Fonck's pace. On May 9, 1918, he destroyed six enemy planes, and from that date on his successes came in doubles and triples. By August 1 he had passed Guynemer's score, and his performances were becoming so standard that whenever it was announced that Fonck had been awarded another decoration, the interest was lukewarm. He was so completely in a class by himself, it is no wonder the war correspondents switched their interest to lesser lights who were concentrating on enemy kite balloons.

René Fonck continued to fly after the war ended, and for a time concentrated on aerobatic performances, but like so many others of the postwar period, he wanted to fly the Atlantic Ocean. With this idea in mind, he visited the United States and made the acquaintance of Igor Sikorsky who was developing his S.35, a three-engined transport. A deal was made, and Fonck flight-tested the machine for days, and was satisfied it was capable of making the long hop. On September 15, 1926, he made his first attempt, but a faulty fuel tank foiled him, so Fonck decided to try again on September 20. This time a defective undercarriage collapsed and the plane never left the ground, but piled up at the end of the runway and burned. Fonck and his co-pilot scrambled out but two other crew members were killed. Before another attempt could be made Charles A. Lindbergh had made the hop solo, and Fonck abandoned any further attempts. He died on June 18, 1953.

ROLAND GARROS

The man who gave the airplane a true talon, the man who first successfully fired a fixed machine gun through the whirling blades of an aircraft propeller, was Roland Garros—not Anthony Fokker.

This aristocratic Frenchman had started out to become a concert pianist not a military man, yet it was he who so completely revolutionized aerial warfare.

Born in 1888 at Saint-Denis on the island of Reunion in the Indian Ocean, he grew up in comparative luxury for his father was a noted lawyer who willingly provided a classical education for his artistic son. Roland was clever with his hands and could paint, draw and play several musical instruments. When it became apparent that he was exceptionally good on the piano, he was sent to Paris to develop his technique.

He arrived late in 1908 just in time to see the famous Alberto Santos-Dumont put on some of his early flying exhibitions. Instead of applying his available funds to piano instruction young Garros induced Santos-Dumont to teach him to fly. When the noted Brazilian coffee millionaire looked over the young Frenchman's hands he said: "You are lucky. With such hands you will make a splendid airman. I will teach you to fly, my friend."

Within a year the young music student had become one of the most skilled airmen in the world. In October 1910 Garros went to America with a French aviation team and competed in the memorable Statue of Liberty race which was won, after considerable controversy, by Count Jacques de Lesseps who flew a Blériot monoplane. Garros had selected a Paulhan biplane, but it was not maneuverable enough to make a tight turn around the harbor goddess and he had to be content with third place. In 1911 he won the $100,000 Paris-to-Rome race, was first in the Paris-to-Madrid feature, and led the field in the Grand Prix d'Anjou event that same year.

In the summer of 1914 Garros was in Germany giving exhibitions with an early Morane monoplane and held large audiences spellbound with his aerobatic displays. At nights he was usually honored at receptions and banquets where he frankly discoursed on the military value of the heavier-than-air machine.

He was most popular everywhere he went in Germany, and his

talks became regular newspaper features. Then one afternoon while returning to his hotel he learned that the Kaiser's troops had invaded his beloved France!

War had been declared!

For a few minutes Garros was in a state of panic. After all, he had been all over Germany, pointing out the value of the airplane in wartime, and had even showed how it could be used for reconnaissance and bombardment. Now, according to the rules of war, he could be interned—held as a prisoner—but even worse, the Germans might commandeer his machine and even fly it against his own people.

Garros hurried to his hotel, packed his bag and left by a rear exit. He scurried through the city and reached the exhibition grounds and crept into his hangar. Fortunately, most of the mechanics and guards had gathered in the nearest *Gasthaus* to toast the Kaiser and drink to Germany's success. Garros dragged his monoplane from its shed, checked the Le Rhône engine, stowed his bag in the nacelle and swung the propeller. Darkness had fallen by then but he got away safely.

At that time few men had risked night-flying, but Roland Garros made for the nearest border, and landed safely in Switzerland. Several days later he continued on to Paris where he immediately volunteered for military service, and, along with Armand Pinsard, went to Saint-Cyr, where he was put into uniform, and taught parade-ground drill. Then, both Garros and Pinsard were sent on simple cross-country flights to prove they were military fliers, after which they went to Paris for reassignment.

Morane-Saulnier Escadrille Number 25 was being formed at Buc, and Garros and Pinsard were ordered to report there and to their great delight were soon joined by several other exhibition pilots, including Adolphe Pégoud, Jules Védrines, Eugene Gilbert and Marc Pourpé. Over the next few weeks these former exhibition headliners were actively engaged in trying to stem Germany's dash for Paris, and were doing more than their share in turning the enemy's advance along the Meuse into a crushing defeat.

Over the following weeks Garros was thinking out an idea for arming the airplane, for he was convinced that what reconnaissance an airman could carry out in no way matched the observation work done by kite-balloon observers. Then his pal, Armand Pinsard, experienced engine trouble and had to land in enemy territory and was captured. Garros immediately conjured up an idea of flying in to rescue Pinsard, but realized that he would need an armed aircraft to make any such attempt. He knew he would have to fight his way through a number of German aircraft, and what would be needed was a plane that carried a useful weapon.

Another exhibition pilot, Eugene Gilbert, had been thinking along the same lines, and he decided that a gun mounted behind the propeller, firing along the line of flight was the ideal arrangement; but how could the rate of fire be controlled in order to avoid hitting the whirling blades?

Gilbert decided that only seven percent of the rounds fired would hit a prop blade, so he ignored any elaborate interrupter gear in favor of an armored collar bolted around the base of each prop blade. He tried out this idea, but in a test firing, two of his friends were killed by ricocheting bullets, and in remorse, Gilbert gave up the whole project.

Whether by coincidence or upon learning of Gilbert's experiment, has never been made clear, but Roland Garros began working on the same idea, using a Hotchkiss gun mounted on a Morane Bullet airplane. He devoted much attention to the design of the deflector plates, sacrificing some propeller efficiency, but he did devise a safe collar. Clip after clip of Hotchkiss ammunition was fired without one round causing any harm.

Then on April 1, 1915, Garros took off to try out his new device. He shot down a German two-seater with no trouble. Over the next fifteen days he accounted for four more enemy machines and was cited for the Legion of Honor. Parisian boulevardiers hailed him with the popular catchword of the day—ace! This appellation was applied to anyone who had performed anything unusual. The latest Grand Prix winner was an ace; the newest cycling hero was an ace; popular jockeys were included in this category and it was natural that it should be applied to Roland Garros.

The continued reference was noted by an American newspaperman who interpreted it to mean any pilot who had downed five enemy planes and, in his next dispatch to New York, he applied the reference to Garros without bothering to explain how the Frenchman had run up this score, or with what weapon. Thus, it became the journalistic standard by which a French fighter pilot was rated. The term "ace" and its requirements have lasted until this day. Only the British have ignored the designation.

✳

On the afternoon of April 19, 1915, Garros took off to bomb the railroad sidings at Courtrai. Why he was given such a mission has long been debated. He was by now the war's premier air fighter, but was still sent on routine bombing raids, for the importance of plane-to-plane combat was not yet fully appreciated.

He flew all the way to Courtrai without encountering enemy aircraft of any kind, but hoped he would be more fortunate on the way back. Once over his target area he cut his Le Rhône engine, went into the glide, swept over the freight yards, and dropped his bombs.

He had no idea what he hit, or whether he had missed the target completely; he was too concerned with getting the impact-fuse bombs overboard without blowing himself to bits. When he tried to switch on the rotary engine, the Le Rhône refused to pick up. Nothing happened! The propeller just windmilled in the slip stream. He knew immediately what had occurred and probably cursed his imbecility. In the long approach glide for the Courtrai freight yard he had allowed the spark plugs to oil up, and had forgotten to "burn" them off with intermittent blipping of the ignition switch. He had no alternative but to stretch his glide until he found a suitable spot to land.

Garros came down near Ingelmünster about forty miles from the Dutch frontier. His first concern was to destroy his plane and the details of the propeller's protective collar—the secret of the front-firing gun. He did his best to set fire to the Morane, even going to the effort of stuffing the cockpit with loose hay, but everything was damp and he was unable to create a flame. Had an enemy bullet flicked a spark off a metal fitting near a punctured gas tank, the whole machine would have gone up like a pan of gunpowder.

A squad of German soldiers soon arrived and Garros made one last desperate bid for freedom by running across the field and hiding in a swampy ditch. He stayed there until darkness fell, then crawled out and headed for the Dutch border, but as luck would have it he wandered straight into a group of soldiers who were out foraging for firewood. The game was up.

✳

The Germans were soon able to examine the captured aircraft and naturally wondered about the steel collars that were bolted around the propeller blades. Blued bullet marks next disclosed the purpose of the plates, and with that, the secret of the gun that could fire bullets through the whirling blades of the propeller was revealed.

From that point on the legend of how Tony Fokker invented the front-firing gun went into its first gear. It was said that Garros's Morane was flown to Schwerin where this young Dutch aviator was ordered to examine it. It was related that he took one look at the protective collars and immediately saw how the idea could be improved by some ingenious mechanical control. From that point it was easy to explain how Fokker had invented his E-I monoplane that became the scourge of the Western Front.

This fable was a long way from the truth. Fokker had no idea how to control the firing of a machine gun, but one of his assistants, Heinrich Luebbe, remembered that back in 1913, a German engineer named Franz Schneider, had received a patent for a gun-synchronizing mechanism; a device that had also been patented in France and Britain. Luebbe and another helper, Fritz Haber devised a like mechanism and showed it to Fokker, who immediately applied it to one of his latest monoplanes—and of course took full credit for the invention. Actually, the device was a Goldbergian gadget, which did not reach anything like perfection for five or six months.

But the gun-synchronization business is another story.

In the meantime Garros was placed in military confinement and was restrained there until he managed his escape in January of 1918. He of course requested reassignment and was given a refresher course on Spads. He returned to the front, but was shot down and killed on October 5, 1918, by a German pilot flying a Fokker D-VII.

GEORGES GUYNEMER

On September 11, 1917, Captain Georges Guynemer was lost over the enemy lines, leaving a history that over the years has become part legend, part assumption, part substantial truth. In the following decade he was a storybook hero and idol of every French schoolboy, yet during his military career he probably was one of the least admired airmen of his service. No one questioned his courage, tenacity, and faith in his cause, but to many of his acquaintances he was also unreliable, disorderly, self-willed, and quarrelsome. Nevertheless, he left an imperishable memory that to all French soldiers exalted the spirit of sacrifice.

Guynemer, whose complete name was Georges Marie Ludovic Jules, was the son of an ex-army officer. He was in delicate health for years and was spoiled and coddled by his mother and two sisters. He attended good schools but was never a first-class student, although in his early teens he had hopes of becoming a scientist.

Slight in stature and mousy in appearance Guynemer tried several times to enlist at the outbreak of war, but was turned down. His father's influence finally helped him to join the French Aviation as a mechanic trainee. He spent most of his time sweeping out dusty hangars and cleaning oily engine parts, but during this period he persuaded Captain Bernard Thierry to permit him to take pilot training. At the time Guynemer looked more like a candidate for a Boy Scout troop, and his uniform hung on him like a shapeless potato sack.

He started his training early in March 1915, and to the surprise of everyone who knew him became a reliable pilot and in the following fifteen months was credited with flying 350 hours over the line, and downing eleven enemy aircraft. Much of this front-line flying had been over the lush fields of the Valois country near his home, and at times he gave his family and village friends considerable concern with his wild aerobatics. One day his mother saw him loop over the family château, causing her to go into a deep faint, whereupon Georges gave up such schoolboy exhibitions.

How much of this is legend or messroom gossip is difficult to assess, as his several biographers have not been too concerned with facts or technical data. Most of them were so occupied with presenting the willful side of his nature, one cannot learn whether young Georges was handling a two-seater Morane or a single-seater Nieuport. In order to furnish pertinent conversation, some accounts have observers aboard either type of aircraft; in his air fights he runs out of ammunition belts when using a Lewis gun that was fed by a circular drum. In other situations he is supposed to have changed belts, which is quite a feat as Vickers belts of that time carried five hundred rounds of ammunition. And some historians record that Guynemer had an excessive amount of crashes, but his logbook mentions only one (when he wiped off an undercarriage after hitting a ditch).

However, Georges Guynemer must have been a persistent pilot for his close friends recall the many hours he spent sitting in his cockpit working the various switches and levers. He would also make take-offs and landings until he had everyone on the field frantic with the unending engine roar and undercarriage thumps. Despite his frail physical condition his rapidity of perception and immediate decisions were remarkable. He seemed to become an integral part of the machine the instant he tightened his safety belt. This young man was so perfect a pilot his instructors were convinced he had had flight training before he entered the service. Others said he wore himself out trying to become a centaur of the air.

It is generally agreed that Guynemer began his war career as a corporal pilot, flying Morane-Saulnier two-seaters, and carrying a gunner-observer. When in mid-July 1915 the first Nieuport scouts to be fitted with a forward-firing machine gun (one that fired over the tips of the propeller) were available, Guynemer was transferred to Escadrille N.3 that became the nucleus of the famous Storks Group. In fact, Guynemer is said to have been one of the first French pilots to be assigned to this particular aircraft.

Guynemer registered his first victory on July 19, 1915—but not with the Nieuport. For some reason he was aboard a two-seater with an observer named Guerder, and while searching for a German marauder that had been reported over Corcres they encountered a two-seater Aviatik. It must be presumed that the Morane-Saulnier had been equipped with a front-firing gun of some kind, as one report stated Guynemer shot the Aviatik down after using one complete belt. His observer was hit in the head by a single rifle bullet fired by the German observer as the enemy plane was going down in flames. Guynemer decided to land quickly to obtain medical assistance for Guerder, and in doing so came under heavy enemy shellfire. Georges piled into a haystack and broke his propeller. However, the episode was widely acclaimed, and both Guynemer and Guerder were awarded the Médaille Militaire.

Guynemer was a national hero for a few days, but nearly six months elapsed before he scored again. He was still frail and wan, and his CO was ordered to send him on leave as often as possible. Again, recorded events are confusing, for Guynemer is reported to have been flying two-seaters, either as a pilot or an observer, and in some instances it is related that he was engaged in delivering intelligence agents into the enemy lines, and returning a few days later to pick them up.

On November 6, 1915, Georges staged one of his wildest stunts. He was carrying a Captain Simon as his observer when he met an L.V.G. Guynemer maneuvered to give Captain Simon a good shot from below and behind, but when the observer's gun jammed, Guynemer turned to explain how to clear the stoppage and then found that his wing had interlocked with that of the L.V.G. He turned around and saw that the enemy gunner was aiming a Parabellum point-blank at him. Georges reacted so fast only one bullet of the burst went through the pads of his helmet, and with that both pilots decided they had had their thrills for that day, and both of them nosed down for home.

By December 8 Guynemer was back aboard a Nieuport single-seater when he intercepted another L.V.G. near Beauraignes. Moving in dangerously close he poured a sixty-round burst into it, sending it down in flames. For that feat he was made a sergeant, and a few days later he downed a two-seater Fokker, and then one of the single-seaters that was fitted with a fixed gun. When he went home for his Christmas leave he had reached his twenty-first year—but looked like sixteen—and was wearing the Legion of Honor for having shot down four enemy aircraft.

The year 1916 saw Guynemer move up into the front rank of fighting airmen, but with eight victories to his credit he was wounded on March 12, and almost taken prisoner. He had been assigned a new 120-horsepower Nieuport, and on meeting two enemy two-seaters had attacked from behind. The new mount's speed almost betrayed him for he was up to and zooming over the two-seaters before he had time to fire a burst. He was in a perfect spot for one of the enemy gunners and a burst riddled his engine's accessory grouping, and put two bullets through his left arm. Guynemer was lucky to get into his own lines, and only by the daring of French ground troops was he eventually carried to safety.

About this time the "ace" race went to ridiculous extremes in the French service. Dozens of first-class airmen were taking unreasonable risks to remain in the newspaper columns. The rivalry went to fantastic proportions, with single-seater fighter savagery continuing all through the summer of 1916. Guynemer scored his fifteenth, sixteenth, seventeenth, and eighteenth victories in September 1916, and it was clear that Charles Nungesser was in full cry with seventeen successes. The Storks Group was the pride and joy of the French boulevardiers.

✻

Late that October the much vaunted Spad fighter was available—this was the 150-horsepower version S.7 model that for a time enjoyed some rare renown, but it was not as good as early reports had it. The Spad was one of those attractive-looking machines that photographed well, and made inexperienced pilots drool, but it was not the ideal fighter. The later version, the S.13, was a great improvement, but neither ever reached the standards of the British S.E.5 or the Sopwith Camel.

Guynemer was one of the first to fly the new Spad, and it must be admitted his performance and victories were phenomenal. From November 9–27 he destroyed two L.V.G.s, two Albatros scouts, two Albatros two-seaters, and one Fokker. The Storks Group pilots won a second escadrille citation, and by the close of 1916 Guynemer led all the French "aces" with a score of twenty-five. Nungesser was second with twenty-one, Dorme had fifteen, Heurteaux fifteen, and Tarascon nine.

Guynemer scored one of his remarkable victories when he came upon a two-engined Gotha bomber, a type he had not seen before. He put on such a masterful exhibition the Gotha was forced down and landed almost intact. French and Allied designers had an excellent opportunity to inspect every feature of this new aircraft. Georges was again promoted, and Russia awarded him the Cross of St. George.

For all its new successes, the Spad was not widely accepted as yet for the Hispano-Suiza engine continued to give considerable trouble. The many "bugs" were gradually worked out, and the pilots displayed more confidence in the machine. Guynemer, who was still trying to obtain the ultimate in fighting aircraft, thought the Spad could be greatly improved by fitting a light 37-millimeter cannon as its armament. At the same time the Hisso engine was provided with a reduction gear box that allowed the designers to mount the gun behind the short hollow prop shaft. In this arrangement the one-pounder shell would travel through the center of the propeller boss.

Georges was selected to try out this new weapon, and on July 16 he came upon an Albatros D-III, and was fortunate enough to score a direct hit that blew the German aircraft to bits. But the recoil from the unwieldy gun was most unsatisfactory and the fumes from the expended shells almost asphyxiated Georges, so the Spad-cannon idea was abandoned for a time. Later on René Fonck adopted it and is said to have scored many victories with this unusual combination.

Guynemer's companions noticed a new surge of fanaticism in all his actions, and it was learned that he was suffering from tuberculosis. Never a rugged young man, the war was taking its toll. He should have taken his doctors' advice and retired, or at least have given the doctors a chance to prepare him for a recovery. But he was willful and obstinate. By August the "ace" race again was in full cry, and he was leading the pack with fifty kills to his credit. Twice he had fainted in the air, and somehow got down safely, but he would not listen to reason. The weather was uncertain, and his plane gave him considerable trouble, so he was denied his usual number of patrols and the opportunity to add to his score. He had forced landings all over the countryside, and he fumed and fretted about his ill fortune. His illness began to assert itself and his sallow complexion indicated how far the disease had progressed. His friends begged him to take a rest, and the squadron physician provided a private room in a nearby villa, but Georges stayed there for only a few days. Instead of resting he usually stripped off the jacket of his uniform and worked on planes; anything to keep the equipment flying and the guns firing.

His last day was one of those wartime epics. The morning opened with heavy fog and Guynemer decided to go over to the Buc aerodrome to find out why a new Spad was not available, but there was no train until that afternoon, which meant another delay. There was a report that Majors du Peuty and Brocard of the Office of the Ministry of Aeronautics were coming down by an early train, and someone suggested that a talk with them might expedite matters with reference to new equipment. Guynemer accepted that, but within half an hour the weather had cleared and he went off to the sheds where he found that *Vieux Charles,* his personal Spad, had been tuned, the guns checked, and a new water pump fitted. He decided to make the most of this chance.

Lieutenant Bozon-Verduraz and Captain Deullin were available and very willing to accompany Captain Guynemer, but someone suggested that it might be wise to await the arrival of Majors du Peuty and Brocard, but Guynemer waved the idea aside and climbed into his Spad. The majors from the Ministry of Aeronautics arrived five minutes after Guynemer, Deullin, and Bozon-Verduraz had taken off.

With Guynemer leading, the three Storks pilots flew southeast and picked up the Langemarck road and the shelled strip that had once been the railroad between Ypres and Thourout. They were next seen over the Saint-Julien-Poelcapelle road. There were no enemy formations in the area so Guynemer turned deeper into enemy territory and finally saw a two-seater and moved into a position below and behind the German's tail. Having had some back-seat gunnery, Georges had considerable respect for enemy gunners, and as he moved up, he flew a zigzag course.

His first burst was erratic but the German pilot nosed down and went into a spin, so Bozon-Verduraz took him on. He too missed, possibly because he was also watching a formation of Fokker D-V scouts approaching. Once the two-seater had cleared, Bozon-Verduraz continued on down to act as bait. Guynemer set himself in a position to move in and complete the trick. The enemy scouts made one half-hearted pass, but quickly broke up and scattered, probably sensing the decoy feint, so the "bait" pilot climbed back to join Guynemer but could not find him anywhere. Deullin also was nowhere to be seen.

Bozon-Verduraz flew back and forth, searching, but there was no trace of Guynemer. He stayed aloft as long as he could, and on arriving back at their field naturally inquired if the captain had returned. No one had heard anything from him.

At this point legend takes over. Some reports state that Deullin did not go on this tragic patrol, but others say he joined them on his own initiative, muttering he felt like getting a Boche. At any rate, if he went, he returned safely. Bozon-Verduraz said the scouts were D-V Fokkers, but this seems unlikely as that particular type was unpopular, and most of them had been relegated to the Italian front.

Anxious men got on the telephone, and the whole Poelcapelle area was checked out by observers in kite balloons, and by reconnaissance planes, but there was no sign of a downed Spad anywhere. At dinner that night deep depression fell on everyone as they feared Guynemer had been taken prisoner. They remembered that he had once said no Boche would ever take him alive.

Two days passed. Still no news, and it had to be announced that the great Guynemer was missing. Nothing was heard from the German side of the line, and none of the German newspapers claimed the French ace for either of the Von Richthofen brothers. In a few days a note was dropped on a British field, explaining that certain "English" fliers had been shot down in certain areas on such and such dates. Then, seemingly as an afterthought, there was an added notation concerning a Captain Guynemer that stated he had been shot down at 8:00 A.M. on September 10. The hour and day were wrong. Guynemer was alive and taking breakfast in his own mess at that particular hour; he did not leave the ground until 8:35 on the morning of September 11.

Bozon-Verduraz went over the details of the patrol, time after time, for no one could believe Guynemer was dead. Years later the French government created a commission to inquire into his fate and place of burial, but nothing came of that search. One poetic journalist in Paris offered an idyllic solution that to this day is told to French schoolchildren.

"Captain Guynemer flew so high he could not come down again!"

*

By October 4, 1917, the British had taken Poelcapelle, but the Germans counterattacked and regained the area. Five days later the British again took the village, and made a detailed search for Guynemer's grave but no trace of it was ever found. In fact, the Germans acknowledged officially that both the body of Guynemer and his Spad had disappeared completely.

There were some vague reports that he had been brought down from a height of 21,000 feet and had fallen near the Poelcapelle cemetery. It might be questioned that any Spad-13 was capable of 21,000 feet—certainly those used by Number 19 Squadron, R.F.C., could not reach such an altitude—and what was Guynemer doing up there when he was presumed to be going down to pick off the Fokkers that were taken in by Bozon-Verduraz's decoy maneuver? Three German soldiers swore later that they found the Spad with one wing shot off, and that the pilot had been wounded in the head and one shoulder. He also had one leg broken in the crash. A short time later the Germans published a list of French planes that had fallen inside their lines, but the numbers of Guynemer's *Vieux Charles* were not among them.

But the story could not fade away. There was a time when the Germans credited Lieutenant Kurt Wisseman, a two-seater pilot, with downing Georges Guynemer, and as explained before, Wisseman was shot down about two weeks later. We shall have to accept the possibility that Guynemer crashed somewhere in the Poelcapelle district, and that almost immediately after the heavy ground fire—preliminary to the British attack on the village—completely obliterated all traces of him and his machine. There had been no military funeral, so Guynemer had accepted nothing from his enemies—not even a wooden cross.

ALBERT HEURTEAUX

This famous French soldier, victor in twenty-one air duels, began his service as a sub-lieutenant of Hussars and at the outbreak of war was soon in action, and cited twice for exceptional bravery in the field. Then when the stalemate of trench warfare was an established pattern, Heurteaux transferred to the aviation service and began his flying career as an observer-gunner in a Morane-Saulnier squadron. Roland Garros, Eugene Gilbert, Armand Pinsard, and Marc Pourpe, Raoul Lufbery's former pilot, all came from this same Escadrille MS.23.

Heurteaux put in considerable time as an observer, and was a partner of Lieutenant De Druelle, the first French night-bombing pilot. In fact, on the night of February 11, 1915, these two men made a daring solo raid on the railroad station at Lutterbuck, and the ex-Hussar was again cited for his exceptional bravery.

But better still for him, he was selected to take pilot training and toward the end of 1915 had been passed out as a scout pilot. Almost immediately he was posted to the Storks Group where he learned the fine art of air fighting with the men who inspired this illustrious organization. However, Albert Heurteaux did not score his first kill until May 4, 1916. It was an L.V.G. two-seater that fell near Etain. On July 9 he had another victory, also a two-seater, but in the exchange of fire the V-strut of his Nieuport was hacked through, and when he landed the whole wing panel collapsed.

This experience in no way deterred him, for his score increased rapidly. Fokkers and Rumplers were in the air for the taking, and by August 17 Albert was an "ace."

René Dorme was also a member of Heurteaux's squadron, that became Spad 3, and in a short time these two fliers were friendly rivals. Dorme was a quiet, shy, small man who in two years of war flying received only two bullets in his plane, while Heurteaux, the typical devil-may-care type of officer, usually returned with his machine full of holes—a much-publicized airman of story and legend. Yet these two remained firm friends until Albert's luck ran out and he had to be withdrawn from the front to recover from his many wounds and crashes.

Though loyal companions and much concerned with each other's good or ill fortune, Albert and René seldom flew together. Albert was a typical lone wolf who ran up his score on the principle of dive, fire, and pull away—and if you miss, dive and fire again. A more conservative man, René played his role as a member of a patrol formation.

Heurteaux racked up his seventh Hun on September 18. This was a fast Roland scout, but he himself was hit in the right thigh. A week later he was back in action, and, with Dorme, ran into two Rumplers south of Barleux. The machine-like Dorme found a two-seater's blind spot and killed both the pilot and observer with his first burst. Heurteaux was having a more difficult time, and before he could score, two Rolands and a Fokker joined the action.

The Fokker pilot came head-on but the Frenchman refused to give ground and the German went down in flames. Then Dorme sent the second Rumpler to its end, or so he thought, but the pilot eventually regained control and made a safe forced landing. Together, Heurteaux and Dorme chased the two Rolands back to their field and then shot at the mechanics, pilots, and others who had dashed out to put planes into the air. In this foray Heurteaux silenced a machine-gun turret mounted on top of one of the hangars.

During the latter part of September 1916 bad weather set in and little war flying could be carried out. Then, in the middle of October, Heurteaux went aloft and found himself enveloped in fog where he almost collided with an Albatros, so he made the most of the contact and fired a short burst, setting the German machine on fire. The Nieuport was so close to the burning plane a gush of flame torched its wingtip, and Heurteaux had to put his machine into a slideslip to avoid burning up himself. He was fortunate to get back to his own field in safety. Three days later he met another two-seater, and sent that unlucky one down in flames.

Commander Felix Brocard, leader of the Storks, was due to retire, and Heurteaux was his obvious successor, and through the early winter of 1916–17 he had to concentrate on administrative work, so got in very little flying. After Brocard left in December 1916, Heurteaux ignored much of the paper work and celebrated his captaincy by downing three more enemy planes in two days. Some of his fights were thrillers, and most of them ended with his enemies going down in flames.

But 1917 was marked by increasing squadron responsibility and a change of fortune; he was wounded again, this time through the hand while he was thumbing his nose at a German attacker. When he could manage it he was back in action again, and raised his score to twenty-one. Then he ran into a number of patrols in which he was on the receiving end. In May 1917 he was so seriously wounded he was lucky to live long enough to get to a hospital. He was awarded the Legion of Honor, and was back with his squadron in September, again just in time to stop another burst of bullets while being shot down by five enemy scouts.

When he was eventually discharged from the hospital his legs were spliced with silver wire and his body was covered with scars from bullet wounds. He still tried to rejoin his squadron, but he was sent to the United States instead to give lectures on combat flying to American flight cadets. Later he was attached to the French Ministry of Aviation.

Between the two world wars he was Inspector of Aviation, and when France capitulated in 1940 Heurteaux joined the Resistance movement, but was soon arrested and imprisoned in Germany in the infamous Buchenwald camp. He lived through that experience and returned to France at the end of the war and was promoted to the rank of general. Today, he is France's highest-scoring living ace of World War I.

GEORGES MADON

This invincible Frenchman could be listed as the Miracle Man, for he not only downed forty-one enemy aircraft during his long career, but he survived a collision in combat, a fire in midair, a direct hit by an antiaircraft shell, and a court-martial for being shot down in neutral territory. Georges Madon did all the things often credited to the American type of swaggering hero so popular in magazines and motion pictures, whereas he was a mild, shy, self-effacing Frenchman whose only outstanding quality was his ingrained patriotism. To paraphrase the comedian George Gobel, "You can't hardly find them like that no more—anywhere."

Madon was born in Bizerte, Tunis, from where he was sent to Paris in 1911 to finish his schooling, but he joined L'Aviation Militaire instead and lived to see the war to its conclusion. He first learned to fly an old Blériot 39, and when the war started Corporal Pilot Madon was posted to Escadrille Blériot, then stationed at

Soissons. During those early days of trial and error while flying an observation mission his machine was hit by an artillery shell that lodged in his fuselage, but luckily it was a dud and Madon managed to make a landing just before the longerons buckled, collapsing the whole aircraft.

He was posted next to a Farman Shorthorn squadron, and while on a reconnaissance patrol became lost and cruised about looking for a familiar landmark. When his fuel supply gave out he had to land in neutral territory (Switzerland). Madon and his observer, a Sergeant Chattelain, were interned. The two Frenchmen made half a dozen attempts to escape, and on one occasion actually reached the Italian frontier where they were caught. Nine months later they were contacted by a French agent and new plans were made for freedom. Late one night their guard was chloroformed, and the agent led them to a waiting motorboat. They were rushed to France, and instead of a hero's welcome they were both court-martialed for violation of neutral territory and the loss of a French airplane. Madon was sentenced to sixty days of solitary confinement, and his observer received sixty days of ordinary imprisonment.

By May 1916 Madon was released and was back in the good graces of his superiors. He joined Escadrille M.S.218 and went on to fame and glory. On June 26 he shot down a Rumpler, and after several more weeks as a two-seater pilot he was transferred to S.38, one of the first Spad scout squadrons. By January 1917 he had downed an L.V.G., and had entered the glorious company of the aces.

Madon flew like a wild man all through that year, and while his score gradually mounted, his logbook read like an insane author's idea of melodrama. One time near Falvy he saw six Spads of his own squadron jousting with six Albatros scouts, so he went down to give a hand, and intent on lining his sights on one he completely missed another that was zooming from below. Madon's tail assembly cut the Albatros clean in two and the German went down in a heap, but Madon's Spad had a crumpled wing and the elevators apparently were torn away.

The damaged Spad started to spin and gyrate, and when Madon's squadron mates returned to their field they reported that Madon had been killed in action. None of them thought he could have recovered from that hopeless spin, but Madon sat calmly, using his engine power judiciously, and managed to put the hulk down, suffering nothing more serious than a broken finger.

One of Madon's wildest experiences was logged when he had roamed far over the line on an offensive sortie. His engine quit cold and he had to land in enemy territory. He waited around, expecting some German soldiers to come and take him prisoner, but whiled away his time cleaning the spark plugs. When no one came to apprehend him he tried starting the Hisso again. It ticked over like a brand-new engine, so he climbed back into the cockpit and took off. Two days later the same engine let him down once more and he again had to land in enemy territory. He tinkered with the Hisso, and again got it to run. In a short time he was back at his own field laying down the law to his mechanics.

Madon continued to have hair-raising experiences all through 1917, and his method of attacking enemy aircraft was considered by his companions to be suicidal, but he seemed to be guided by some special, lucky star. He always roared in dangerously close before firing his guns, and he continually risked collisions in the air. He had no respect for large formations, usually going in head first and circling in and out until his ammunition was expended. Under such circumstances he usually racked up doubles and triples that ran his score up at a tremendous rate. Once he torched a kite balloon, and then flew through great wads of burning fabric that set his Spad on fire, but he sideslipped and tangoed about the sky until he had put the fire out. Then he went home.

All through the early months of 1918 when the Germans were planning their March push, Madon flew patrol after patrol, and contributed to the defense by shooting down a number of enemy two-seater reconnaissance aircraft that were photographing the Allied lines.

Throughout that memorable offensive Madon's score increased, and then the Germans transferred Von Richthofen's Jagdgeschwader-I to the French Front where Madon was one of the first to be shot down by the charge of the Circus. This setback occurred on June 5, but he was back the next day, scoring his revenge by downing a black-and-yellow Fokker flown by Lieutenant Rudolf Otto, a five-plane ace who had just torched a French kite balloon. Otto was not killed, but he was badly wounded and his machine piled up a total wreck. Before the Circus returned to the British front, Madon had downed five more of its Fokkers, and then added an A.E.G. two-seater bringing his score to thirty-nine.

Madon's victories had run up to forty-one by the end of the war and he had received France's three chief military decorations. He continued to fly after the Armistice, and then on November 11, 1924, while putting on a display at the unveiling of a monument to Roland Garros, he crashed and died of his injuries.

JEAN NAVARRE

Another legendary Frenchman whose career has fascinated readers for years is Lieutenant Jean Navarre. A native of Jouy-en-Morin, he was born in 1895. Shortly before the start of World War I he became a pilot, and during the early days of the strife he flew with Escadrille M.S.12, and from all accounts ran up an impressive score flying Morane-Saulniers, armed only with military rifles. His observer was Lieutenant René Chambe who also performed so well he eventually became a scout pilot.

A number of Zeppelins were reported over Paris on the night of March 21, 1915, and Navarre was among a number of Morane pilots who went up to intercept. (It should be explained that Jean went aloft, carrying only a large kitchen knife, and spent most of the patrol chasing clouds that "looked like airships.") But in April of that year, with an observer, a Lieutenant Robert, Navarre intercepted an Aviatik and forced it down with ordinary rifle fire. Only three rounds were expended in this engagement, for which Lieutenant Robert was awarded the Legion of Honor and Corporal Navarre recommended for the Médaille Militaire.

Navarre progressed in his trade and found himself a member of Escadrille N.67 flying Nieuports over the Verdun battle area. At one time, while Georges Guynemer was in the hospital, Navarre was the leading ace in the French Aviation Service. By May 1916 he had eleven Huns to his credit.

Some historians have made much of the fact that Navarre was in the habit of wearing a woman's silk stocking in lieu of a helmet. Why this should be considered noteworthy is somewhat puzzling for many Allied airmen wore or displayed silk stockings to present an air of devastating cavaliers, or to proclaim their nocturnal conquests.

Actually, a silk stocking would have been of little practical use during the winter months.

On June 16 Navarre was shot down and seriously wounded, and with that the wheels of legend began to spin. One report had Navarre completely out of his mind, escaping from his hospital bed and making his way back to his field where he stole a plane and was never seen again. Another rumor stated that while deranged he was discharged from the hospital. He found an automobile, drove it like a madman and piled into a group of pedestrians. The story that perhaps comes closest to the truth is that Navarre's brother was killed in action, providing a shock that brought on Jean's temporary mental derangement. He was held in an asylum for nearly two years and then discharged as cured. At the time of Armistice he was taking a refresher course, hoping to get back into action.

Jean Navarre flew for a time after the war as a test pilot for the Morane-Saulnier Company, and on July 10, 1919, while practicing for a Victory Parade in which he was to fly through the Arc de Triomphe, he crashed and died of his injuries.

CHARLES EUGENE JULES MARIE NUNGESSER

Lieutenant Charles Nungesser who is credited with forty-three victories was wounded seventeen times. He was twice invalided out of the service, but he refused to retire and wound up third on the list of France's leading aces. It has been said that Nungesser spent more time in the hospital than he did on the front, but his courage was almost legendary, and it is recorded that he once escaped from a hospital with his leg in a plaster cast when someone told him that René Fonck had passed his score.

Is it any wonder the flying services were considered ragtime organizations when time after time certain members, when ordered to do this or that, generally took matters into their own hands and did what they pleased? They refused to go to a hospital after being wounded; they ignored orders to go on leave; some refused promotions and the accompanying responsibility. If they were grounded, they stole aircraft and went aloft to take on unjustified odds. Orders, discipline, or kindly suggestions were ignored, particularly in many French escadrilles.

In common with many airmen of that day, Nungesser began his war service as a cavalryman and within the first week had been awarded the Médaille Militaire for capturing a number of high-ranking staff officers who were heading for Paris in a motorcar. But the cavalry was soon dismounted, and by November 1914 Charles had transferred to the aviation service. He served some time in a so-called bomber squadron, but by early 1916 had managed his way into a Nieuport scout outfit, and the very next morning after joining the scouts he went over the line and downed a German kite balloon.

This success interested his superiors for it was unusual for a new-comer to find his way about the front so quickly. It then turned out that he had taken a month's leave to convalesce after a wound he received while flying bombers, and in that time had spent about a week flying with the American Lafayette Escadrille. In fact, he downed one enemy plane while on this unofficial duty.

But he soon proved that his balloon kill was no fluke. He started a string of victories that made his name well-known all along the French front. Still, he seemed to get creased or nicked almost every time he engaged an enemy aircraft, but by mid-June 1916 his score stood at ten. On June 22 he downed an L.V.G. over Forges, and less than a week later he was wounded in a shoulder. Most of his injuries seemed to have been the result of his pet maneuver known as the "whip-stall" in which the pilot noses down hard and then whips up in a terrific zoom to get under the belly of an enemy plane. If the burst went home, all well and good, but if the pilot missed he found himself stalling at the top of the zoom with little flying speed left. There was nothing to do but to stall off, giving the enemy a sitting target.

By the end of 1916 Nungesser had downed twenty enemy planes, and his twenty-first provided an unusual situation. He had had trouble with his engine, and after a complete overhaul he took off on the morning of December 19 for a test flight. He spotted an L.V.G. two-seater over Chaulnes Wood and immediately dived for its tail. The observer was alert and quickly sprayed Charles' Nieuport, so he went into one of his whip-stalls, and to his consternation saw there was no Lewis gun on the top-wing mounting. He had taken off, forgetting that the weapon had been removed during the engine overhaul.

This was a desperate situation and Charles had to fly as though he intended to ram the two-seater. He worked these maneuvers so well the German quit, nosed down, landed in a clearing inside the French lines, and set fire to his machine the minute it stopped rumbling across the turf.

A few days later Nungesser was wounded again, and offered an honorable discharge, but by April 1917 he was back once more in a new role, a free-lance pilot with a roving commission. In other words, he could fly whenever he wished, on any patrol he cared to devise, or join any squadron formation. Needless to state, this amazing man was always found where the fighting was thickest. He hobbled about the aerodrome supported by two walking sticks, and his sense of humor prevailed all through this period. He created an insignia that he had painted on his plane. It was a cracked skull, representing his own cracked head, and two crossed thigh bones, duplicating his own broken legs.

From May 7 to August 3 he ran his "kills" to thirty-nine, but was wounded three times more in that period, and René Fonck passed his score. Flying a Hanriot scout that was fitted with a "lanser" fireproof fuel tank, he managed to get safely down after a flight of Fokkers torched him. He had only a scorched foot and a slightly burned hand.

On August 14 Nungesser took off to attack a number of enemy kite balloons, and two went down within a few minutes. The ground fire then became too stiff so he drew away and went down to fifty feet. He attacked a third balloon, shooting it down in flames. He saw the observer jump, but not in time for the burning envelope fell on the descending parachute. Less than a week later five Fokkers trapped Nungesser, inflicting his seventeenth wound. It was a serious puncture, but this invincible Frenchman refused to die. However, the war was over before he could crawl out of bed and stagger toward another warplane.

After the war he gave lectures, made films, and in 1927, in company with Captain François Coli, attempted to fly the Atlantic from France to the United States in a Levasseur P.L.8. This time the Grim Reaper had his way for no trace of the machine or the two men was ever found.

ARMAND PINSARD

Armand Pinsard was twenty-five years old when he joined the new Aviation Militaire, France's aviation arm, in 1912. He had been a cavalry officer as early as 1905 and had served with distinction in the Moroccan War, but apparently saw a future in the air and was one of the first of twelve officers to enter the new service.

Pinsard gained his ticket on an early Morane and was awarded the Médaille Militaire for a number of daring performances during Army maneuvers held in Picardy in 1913.

Shortly after the outbreak of war Armand was assigned to Escadrille M.S.25, and immediately started a career of astounding experiences that were rewarded with eight citations for courage and devotion to duty. On one occasion he brought his plane home over a distance of forty miles though one wing had been shattered by shellfire. Late in that October he was forced to land with oiled-up plugs, but as so often happened in those early days of the war, he had time to remove each plug, clean it, and attempt to fly off before he was noticed. But just as he was taxiing for his take-off a troop of Uhlans galloped across the field. Completely undaunted, Pinsard ruddered his machine directly at the charging horsemen and opened up a space wide enough for his getaway.

Late in February 1915, however, Lady Luck beamed her smiles in other directions. While on a long-distance reconnaissance flight Pinsard's plane was struck by rifle fire and he had to crash-land in German-held territory. He broke two ribs and suffered a slight concussion that put him in a German hospital for five weeks. On his recovery he was held in a nearby prisoner-of-war camp where he made two attempts in three weeks to escape, but was recaptured both times.

Although Armand was put in solitary confinement for his audacity, he made twelve more attempts to get away, and one time he had reached within two miles of the Dutch frontier where he was betrayed by a group of farmers. He was then put in the "escape-proof" Prinz Karl Fortress at Ingolstadt where three months elapsed before he was missed again. With a Captain Meynard, Armand Pinsard had dug his way through a wall twelve feet thick and had a six-hour head start before an alarm was sounded.

Pinsard and Meynard endured a rigorous journey in the next three weeks, but finally crossed the Swiss border and presented themselves to a French consulate—and asked to be assigned to active service.

*

On his return to Paris, Pinsard soon realized that military aviation had made amazing strides since his days on a Morane-Saulnier. It was now May 1916. Aircraft had improved, engines were more powerful, and all planes were provided with machine guns. It was obvious he would have to start all over again, but within a month Armand had mastered the new Nieuport scout, and because of his new skill was sent to Spad 3 of the Storks Group. In a short while, under the guidance of Captain Heurteaux, he downed his first victim, a Rumpler that fell in flames near Verdun.

But this air fighting took a long time to learn. Pinsard did not become an ace until March 6, 1917. However, once he was in his stride he became a worthy Storks pilot. Like many of the others, he had a spell of balloon-busting, and went through all the trials and problems of ground fire and counterattacks by Fokker packs that were guarding the enemy Drachens. Pinsard believed that attack was the best defense, and when he went for a balloon he usually added at least one cover plane.

He was a most reliable pilot, experienced on long-distance patrols, and because of these qualities was often asked to carry out certain special missions. These flights usually were concerned with the planting or recovery of intelligence agents, but one mission in particular makes interesting reading.

To recapitulate, it should be explained that Roland Garros, who devised the first fixed-gun arrangement for fighter aircraft, was still a prisoner in Germany as was *Sous-lieutenant* Pierre Marèchal who had once made a flight over Berlin to drop propaganda leaflets. The French were concerned about the plight of these two air heroes and undercover plans were made to get them out.

Garros and Marèchal were confined in a Cologne prison, but certain instructions were gotten to them, and arrangements completed for their escape. They were to "break out" on January 23, 1918, and the following day a multi-seat plane would pick them up at a prearranged spot. All they had to do was to get there. Meanwhile Lieutenant Pierre Quette was to fly in with a three-seater Farman, and Pinsard was to cover it with his Spad. All went well. Garros and Maréchal somehow slipped out of prison, and by 12:15 A.M. the next day Quette picked them up, and, still covered by Pinsard, flew them to a sequestered spot near the Swiss border. How all this was planned and accomplished has long been one of the secrets of the French Bureau Militaire, but the two rescued men followed instructions and both were returned to France by way of England.

Like Pinsard, Garros wished to return to active-service flying, but he could not pick up the new trade as quickly. He took a refresher course, but it was not enough and Roland Garros was shot down and killed near Vouziers on October 5, 1918.

Pinsard continued his routine combat patrols, and flew all through the March Push and the succeeding Allied counterattack. His last victory, his twenty-seventh, was scored against an A.E.G. armored ground-strafer that was harassing French infantry. Armand had only a few rounds left in his belts, whereas the German machine was armed with two machine guns and plenty of ammunition, but Pinsard worried the attacker so as to make the rear gunner expend all his ammunition. Parabellum slugs spattered around the darting Spad as the Frenchman took incredible risks. Then, when he felt there was a reasonable chance, Armand went down to close quarters and killed both the gunner and pilot with his last few rounds.

His amazing career would have been enough for most airmen, but Pinsard decided to remain in the service after the Armistice, and for a time he was a colonel in charge of the 7th Escadrille based at Dijon. He died at Bourg on May 10, 1953.

MARC POURPE

Marc Pourpe, who has been known for many years only through the reflected glory of Raoul Lufbery, made great contributions to French aviation. He started flying some time before the war, and appears to have made his living giving exhibitions. He had once flown the English Channel in an early Blériot, and then made exhibition flights in India, Indochina, and Cambodia. While he was giving demonstrations in Calcutta Lufbery wandered into his parking area and was taken on as a mechanical assistant. Marc Pourpe taught Lufbery all the tricks of his trade, and they became fast friends.

Their wanderings took them to Egypt in 1913 where General Horatio H. Kitchener had become interested in aerial reconnaissance. To prove a number of points Pourpe decided to attempt to fly from Cairo, Egypt, to Khartoum in the Sudan, and return, a flight of about 2700 miles. This was one of the epic aerial conquests of that day, and Pourpe's name was placed high on the list of international pilots.

Hoping to make the most of this well-earned publicity, Marc hurried back to Paris to purchase another airplane and begin a new schedule of exhibitions. He took Lufbery with him, and they planned to buy a new Morane Parasol monoplane and take it to the Far East, but before all the details of the purchase could be completed World War I had broken out. Pourpe offered his services and was accepted immediately by the French Aviation.

Marc bid Lufbery goodby and left to join M.S.23 while Lufbery, now an American citizen, was disconsolate and uncertain of his future. As related earlier, Lufbery joined the Foreign Legion as an infantryman, but by the end of August 1914 had transferred to Pourpe's squadron as an aviation mechanic. Marc was killed in action the following December, and little has been recorded of his wartime experiences.

XAVIER DE SEVIN

This almost unknown French hero is credited with twelve confirmed victories, and probably learned more of military aviation than any man in the French service. He began his career as a cadet at the military academy at Saint-Cyr, from where he was commissioned a *sous-lieutenant* in an infantry regiment. After being wounded in the Argonne in April 1915 he transferred to the French Aviation.

He was posted first to Escadrille N.12 which was equipped with the Baby Nieuport 11s. He served with this squadron until early in 1917. His first victory came on July 12, 1916, when he forced a German aircraft to land in French territory. The following December his name appeared in the citation list again after he had made an important reconnaissance flight during very inclement weather conditions. He completed this mission by scattering a force of enemy reserves with a daring low-level attack by machine gun.

De Sévin accounted for his second victory on March 4, 1917, and was transferred to command Escadrille Spad 26 of the G.C.12 Storks. He marked this promotion by scoring his third kill, and from that time on downed an average of one enemy a month until he had run his score up to twelve.

After the Armistice De Sévin took further staff training at Saint-Cyr and in 1921 became Commandant of the First Group of the First Air Regiment. He was later appointed Professor of Air Fighting, and finally was head of the Bombardment Command at Le Bourget. When World War II began De Sévin was a high-ranking officer and was made Commandant of the Air School at Salon. He was captured in 1943 and imprisoned by the Germans, but managed to escape and serve with the Free French in Italy. By his retirement in 1945 he was a general, and for many years after the war lived in Casablanca where he headed an organization of pioneer pilots.

HENRI JOSEPH DE SLADE

Another high-scoring French ace who survived the war and became a noted racing pilot was Henri Joseph de Slade. He was born in 1895, attended the Saint-Cyr military school and served with cavalry units until late in 1916. After he joined the French Aviation he spent weary months carrying out the important, but unpublicized, reconnaissance, ground-support, and artillery-spotting work of two-seater squadrons. When he was posted later to Spad 159, a scout squadron, he scored his first victory when he downed a D.F.W. from 15,000 feet.

After the Somme-Aisne campaign De Slade was made a captain, after which he seems to have devoted his time to enemy kite balloons and two-seater aircraft. He became an ace on December 5, 1917, when he attacked a Rumpler at 18,000 feet. Three months later he destroyed another Rumpler over Noyon, and on May 18, 1918, he attacked a German two-seater that was escorted by eight Fokkers. Despite the fury of the opposition De Slade destroyed five enemy machines in as many days, bringing his final score to nineteen which included two observation balloons.

MARQUIS A. O. DE TURENNE

This gallant airman who is credited with fifteen enemy aircraft was a direct descendant of the famous French family of De Beaufort that had always made memorable contributions to the country's history and valor. The Marquis de Turenne was born in 1891, the son of a distinguished infantry officer. At the outbreak of the war he was a *sous-lieutenant* in the 2nd Dragoons, and after nearly a year of active service as a cavalryman he transferred to the French Aviation, flying Farmans on reconnaissance and bomber missions. While returning from one of these forays he was shot down and landed in no man's land but crawled to safety under a barrage of machine-gun fire to bring in valuable information, for which he received the Croix de Guerre.

In February 1917 De Turenne was posted to a Nieuport squadron, and a month later scored his first aerial victory when he encountered a German two-seater that was spotting for Jerry artillery. He made the most of the situation and downed the enemy plane inside the Allied lines. He did not concentrate on simple air fighting, but whenever possible used the reconnaissance tricks he had learned with the Farmans, often bringing in valuable information.

While patrolling with a companion on July 6, 1917, he sighted seven German scouts of a new type. They were Pfalz-IIIs, and De Turenne's companion was soon spinning down out of control and the Marquis was left to face the seven enemy pilots. While moving to make his dive for home he noticed that these machines were painfully slow in climbing, so he enticed three to nose down at him. When he zoomed to clear all three were left at the top of an obvious stall, and De Turenne caught one with a direct burst. It rolled over on its back, and the pilot was seen to fall out of the cockpit.

The remaining six Pfalz went into line abreast and tried to get him with deflection shots. One of them, apparently unfamiliar with the aircraft, overcontrolled and floundered in front of the Frenchman's guns. A snap burst exploded the German's gas tank, and the resulting flareup dispersed the rest of the enemy. De Turenne was able to escape and reach his own lines with nothing more than a grazed cheek.

*

During that year only one more victory came his way when he downed a Rumpler that was on a photographic mission. It fell near Fismes. After that French officials decided that De Turenne's leadership was most valuable, and he was placed in command of Spad 12. One of his first problems was to select a patrol to attack an enemy balloon that was spotting the Chemin des Dames. Instead of calling for volunteers De Turenne tackled the job himself. Loading up with belts of incendiary ammunition he sallied forth. He met no opposition, and the balloon was falling in flames within a short time. The Germans then responded with a heavy barrage of artillery fire and De Turenne received a piece of shell casing on his head that staggered him. He was half blinded by the flow of blood, but managed to regain control of his spinning Spad just as two Albatros scouts skimmed into the picture. Luckily, a formation of Nieuports came to his rescue and escorted him back to his field.

De Turenne was in the hospital for nearly six weeks, but returned to the front on March 23. Two days later he was back over the Chemin des Dames and shot down an Albatros for his seventh victory. Administration work curtailed his flying, but he continued to score regularly. Then, during a foray over Soissons on June 13, he lost two of his pilots and saw another going down with a shattered propeller, as he himself was harried by two Albatros scouts. He finally nailed one, sending it down in flames, but four more nosed in to cut him off, and he was lucky to get down inside his own lines with a shot-up engine, a splintered propeller, and a punctured fuel tank. He emerged from the wreckage with only a few bruises.

De Turenne was in the thick of the fighting throughout the rest of 1918 for his escadrille had been assigned to escort packs of French bombers that were now assuming the problems of strategic aviation. These missions usually drew dozens of Fokkers and Albatros scouts, and on one of these escort flights De Turenne did his best to down every enemy plane in sight, but the opposition was too much and he was once more seriously wounded and had to feign "dead" to ease out of one heavy melee. When a Fokker pilot saw he had been tricked he tried again to get the Frenchman, but De Turenne had just enough strength left to put up his last fight and send the German down out of control.

De Turenne's Spad came to rest in a shell hole inside the French lines, and the Marquis was rushed to a hospital. He was still there when the Armistice was celebrated. When he had recovered he returned to L'Aviation Militaire and for many years commanded one of France's fighter escadrilles. He had been awarded the Legion of Honor, the Croix de Guerre with eight Palms, and the Italian Medal for Valor.

PART FIVE

German

GERMAN

Shortly after the Wright brothers made their historic flights in 1903, a few German officers were among the first military men to appreciate the airplane as a potential war machine. To encourage German scientists, a fantastic sum, approximating $20,000,000, was offered as prize money and for financing the development of aircraft and aeronautical engines. Little came of this since most Germans were more interested in lighter-than-air craft. Count Zeppelin's dirigibles were establishing new air-transport records all over Europe. There was money to be made in Zeppelins; the heavier-than-air machines seemed to have no financial potential of any kind.

In 1911 an Austrian engineer, Igo Etrich, produced a Taube, or dove-design airplane that was highly satisfactory. He tried to sell his first models to his own government but the easygoing Austrian monarchy of the days of the Emperor Franz Josef had no interest in any military organization that did not seem to promise something new in gaudy uniforms. Finally, a German secret-service agent contacted Etrich with the result that his Taube design was purchased outright by the Rumpler factory at Berlin-Lichtenberg, and German military officials ordered Rumplers to turn out twenty Tauben at once.

In a very short time twenty factories were producing several versions of the Taube type, powered either by the Argus or Mercedes engines, but the Rumpler models surpassed all others. On July 9, 1913, Herr Linnekogel, chief pilot of the Rumpler factory, took one of their machines up to 20,000 feet, and as a result, the German government decided to concentrate on this type for photography and reconnaissance—missions in which height and a rapid rate of climb were more important than over-all speed.

In the spring of 1913 the German High Command was placing orders for large numbers of aircraft, half of which were to be biplanes, half monoplanes. The latter were practically all Taube types, while the biplanes were manufactured by the Rumpler, A.E.G., Euler, L.V.G., A.O.G., and D.F.W. companies. Twelve months later when Germany was preparing for an undeclared war an army bill was passed granting $2,000,000, and what was left of the original prize money of $20,000,000, to the Imperial Air Service. More aircraft were ordered, and all early types replaced. A rider in the contracts stated that all new machines were to have seats for a pilot and a passenger; they had to be entirely of German manufacture, and were to bear bomb racks, and fittings for an aerial camera; no engines of less than 100-horsepower would be accepted, and a minimum speed of sixty-five miles per hour, and a flight duration of at least four hours were mandatory.

When the bugles sounded for the invasion of Belgium, Germany's air force was far superior to that of any other belligerent nation. They had thirty-eight dirigibles and more than eighty airship pilots. In the heavier-than-air hangars they had several hundred airplanes, 250 of which were fully equipped for military operations. In addition, they had acquired 36 seaplanes. About 2600 skilled mechanics were on the rolls.

There were no aircraft for specified work, and the pilots flew any mission they were assigned, aboard any machine available. At the outset the pilots were considered mere chauffeurs and were graded as NCOs. The passengers, or observers, were commissioned officers, but with the course of the war the NCO pilots were gradually promoted from the ranks. Also many cavalry officers applied for transfer to the Aviation Service, and in time the NCO airman became a rarity.

The German Air Force struck its first offensive blow on August 13, 1914, when Lieutenant Franz von Hiddeson flew to within a mile of the outskirts of Paris, dropped two 4-pound bombs, and scurried home. Two weeks later Von Hiddeson was shot down by a battery of antiaircraft guns near the Bois de Vincennes, and thus was the first raiding airman to fall in the war. But Von Hiddeson was not the first German airman to die. On August 24 a Sergeant Kausen was shot down by the British near Quesnoy while he was carrying out a scouting flight aboard an Aviatik. Another German airman, unnamed, was forced down in a 90-horsepower Mercedes Rumpler-Taube by Lieutenant H. D. Harvey-Kelly and his gunner, a Sergeant Major Street. The machine was captured, but the German crew escaped.

The German Air Force, like its opposing organizations across the line, seemed to attract the most intriguing characters. The crack German cavalry regiments, tossed into the discard by trench warfare, contributed hundreds of heroic fliers to their cause. All prejudices and personalities aside, it must be admitted that many German airmen were as high-minded, noble, patriotic, and valorous as could be found in any military organization. Those of us who encountered these gentlemen daily never considered them in the same class as the detested Prussian militarists. Nor did we count them among the savage, unbridled exponents of barbarism that were to be found in the German land or sea services. They fought boldly and died valiantly. They usually treated their captives with sympathetic courtesy, and it was not until Allied airmen were turned over to German Army officials that cruelty and inhumane treatment were suffered. Most German airmen lived up to the great tradition, fighting to the end. They were the last to surrender when famine, disorganization, and revolution had ended all ground and sea resistance.

Although a certain degree of knightly gallantry may have been observed between airmen in combat, it should be noted that only in air action could such behavior occur. There could be no Galahadian gestures during a bayonet charge, or at the height of a trench-bombing raid. Gentlemen could not exchange salutes during naval salvos of 16-inch guns. It would be impossible for the crew of a destroyer to requite courtesies with U-boat crews after they had dropped their racks of depth charges. Such knight-errantry was limited to the duels in the sky—and to the imagination of the writers of fictional combat.

Action between airmen mounted in single-seater aircraft comes reasonably close to the combat of the tournaments recorded in *Ivanhoe* or *The Idylls of the King,* but while individual instances of gentlemanly courtesy may have been experienced, it should not be inferred that such behavior was the rule. It most certainly was not. Those infrequent gestures more often were the act of adjusting goggles or helmets, not traditional salutes, but they were newsworthy at the time, and later were grossly exaggerated by hack writers and motion picture scenarists. In fact, most of the screen "epics" of the postwar years were nothing more than phony sentimentality—totally unrealistic.

But there were courtesies of a kind. Enemy airmen who fell in Allied territory were always buried with the honors due them, but these were routine gestures—not to pay homage to a particular foe. Whether these rites or ceremonies were carried out inside the German lines, we do not know. There are few, if any records of such gestures.

In the case of Baron von Richthofen a wreath and a photograph of his grave were dropped by British airmen. In some instances lists of downed airmen and their conditions were exchanged, but these were not daily occurrences. When British airmen, who were prisoners of war, learned of Oswald Boelcke's death, they drew up a sincere message of regret and asked that it be forwarded to his family, but British prisoners of war expressed no such sympathy when they heard that Von Richthofen had fallen.

It should be pointed out that for every gentlemanly gesture credited to wartime airmen there were dozens of instances—on both sides —when just the opposite behavior was encountered. There were reports of observers, who had jumped from burning balloons, being fired on by the gentlemen who had torched the inflated bags. Also both sides were reported to have put up balloons "loaded" with high explosive rather than observers, and when enemy airmen dived on them the explosive was ignited, usually blowing the airmen to bits. Was that gentlemanly conduct?

Spokesmen for both sides have long argued that while it was important to destroy the balloon, it certainly was more important to "eliminate" every trained observer, whether still in the basket or trailing down in his parachute. The methods of protecting the balloons could take any form—ground gun fire or booby-trap deception.

Many fighting airmen were unashamedly sickened after downing an enemy plane in flames, whereas others displayed glee in announcing a like victory.

With reference to kite balloons and such inflated aircraft, the Germans always felt that the British had resorted to "frightfulness" when they developed and used various types of incendiary ammunition, and there was a period when any Allied airman who was captured while carrying such ammunition was given an immediate court-martial and sentenced to solitary confinement or hard labor.

It is of interest to reflect that the German Cavalry Staff that had originally put up many hindrances to the full development of the air arm should in time furnish so many of its fighting stars. This was noticeable on both sides of the line. Hundreds of ex-cavalrymen became aerial aces, and whether this phenomenon can be credited to the fact that men who had managed horses with the skill of their hands and the sensitivity of their seats were better suited to the "feel" of the joystick and rudder so necessary in the aircraft of that day, or that cavalrymen could be spared more easily than skilled infantry, engineers, and artillerymen, the fact remains that a large percentage of German airmen had previously been members of crack mounted regiments.

Owing to the remarkable score credited to Baron Manfred von Richthofen it is widely accepted that the Germans were premier in the air-fighting lists. This will always be debated, of course, and no study of the relative scores will ever settle the question. It was never a matter of whether Germany had the finest aircraft or the most skilled airmen. The basis of all consideration must be that the great bulk of air fighting took place over German territory, and many of the Allied planes that had suffered only engine trouble, lack of fuel, or were unable to cope with adverse winds, were unequivocally lost, and in many instances credited to some German airman who had only followed the victim down. The Allies had to carry the air war to the enemy, and under such conditions it was natural that their losses were always greater than those of their enemy. Whenever a German pilot shot down an Allied airman the aircraft and pilot fell within the German lines, and the victor had no trouble in gaining a complete confirmation. On the other hand an Allied pilot might engage a German for several minutes, and never know whether he had killed his adversary or wounded him. He might fire a number of bursts at some individual aircraft, and if the German seemingly escaped, there was no manner in which the Allied airman could learn if he had scored. Thus, he could not claim a kill, although his adversary might have floundered home to wind up in a hospital, or to die within a few hours. In consideration of all this, it is easy to see how the Germans had an advantage in compiling their lists of victories.

As another example, during World War II when the Luftwaffe was carrying out its part during the Battle of Britain they suffered dreadful losses in the air, and most of their downed aircraft could be found scattered all over southeast England or in the English Channel. Later in the war when British and American airmen carried the bombardment to Germany, Göring's pilots racked up lengthy scores with proof of their claims. In many instances these Allied losses were not the immediate result of air combat, but could be traced to ground fire, engine trouble, lack of fuel, or adverse weather conditions. Yet night after night the Germans could report so many aircraft downed—and have the battered hulks to prove it.

＊

For many years I have been concerned about the disparity in claims and credits of the aces of all nations. Some writers of popular histories, and of aviation features usually contrive to add to the scores of their favorites. Either that, or they resort to the old plaint that their hero should have been credited with many more, but unfortunately most of his fights took place so far over the enemy line it was impossible to obtain the required information.

In the light of my own experience I still wonder how these records could have been compiled with any degree of accuracy. I saw all kinds of air action involving most types of machines on both sides of the line, and in most cases I would hesitate to declare who shot down whom. How can one tell how many planes he shoots down during a dogfight? There isn't time to make certain that a victim catches fire, or is seen to crash. There isn't time for members of your formation to look on your handiwork and confirm your claims. At best, it must be some kind of gentleman's agreement in which any reputable member of the flight has his claims fully substantiated by those who were in the air at the time. And again, what about the pilot who is hit during this dogfight and wisely sneaks out and goes home. He is certainly out of action for some time—or he may eventually die. Who is to be given credit for his elimination?

As pointed out by many historians, many victories were never confirmed, and many "confirmed" victories were erroneous. Unquestionably many pilots on both sides of the line could have been listed as aces, but their names have never appeared in any official lists. The most successful fighter, regardless of his score, was one who carried out his flight obligations to the full, day after day. If he scored often, yet lost his own pilots and machines, his worth was negligible. The headstrong and unpredictable were whirlwind copy for the war news, but they hardly can be credited with carrying their weight or earning their pay. Generally speaking, the lone eagle had a fairly cushy time. He could attack or ignore the opposition, depending on how bloodthirsty he felt that day. There was no one to question his mood or degree of courage. But if a scout pilot was a member of a flight or element that was detailed to do a specific task, there was no backing out. He stayed in formation, played his part in the team, and distributed his allotment of fragmentation bombs and machine-gun ammunition.

It is well to consider all these points and observations when perusing the history and experiences of a representative list of German aces.

KARL ALLMENROEDER

This renowned German ace is credited with thirty victories, and was awarded the famous Pour le Mérite, a decoration that was romanticized recently as the Blue Max. It was instituted by Frederick the Great who rarely spoke German because he felt the language lacked officer-like qualities.

Allmenroeder died before the black Sopwith of Ray Collishaw, but aside from these few salient facts little had been related of this World War I airman.

Karl Allmenroeder was born in Wald, a small town in the Rhineland, in 1895. He was the son of a German minister, and after a routine schooling, took up medicine. His family had high hopes of his becoming a doctor, but the Prussian war machine began to roll before he could complete his studies. He first joined the field artillery, and by early 1915, after various postings, he served some active-service time in Poland, gained a commission and was awarded the Iron Cross First Class. His brother Willi, with whom he shared a warm affection, talked of the benefits and advantages of the flying service, and together they applied for a transfer.

The wheels of progress ground slowly, and the red tape seemed unlimited. It was March 1916 before they were finally sent to a flying school at Halberstadt. On completing their courses they were assigned to a service squadron. Karl showed unusual skill and was able to arrange a transfer to Boelcke's Jasta 11, and reported to Douai in November 1916. Boelcke had been killed about a month before.

There seems to have been an immediate rapport between Von Richthofen and Allmenroeder, for they often went hunting together after their regular circus forays, but the man from Wald did not score until February 16, 1917. However, by May 26 his victories had reached twenty. In the meantime his brother Willi had a memorable experience. He had downed a British pilot in German territory, and hoping to make sure of his man, had landed to take him prisoner personally. But the Englishman, after setting fire to his plane, turned on Willi and drilled him with a pistol bullet, putting this Allmenroeder out of action for the rest of the war. The records, however, do not disclose what happened to the English pilot. Did he escape? Was he eventually credited with a victory? After all he had eliminated another German airman.

But fortune smiled on Karl, and he was awarded the Pour le Mérite in June, and by the twenty-fifth of that month had raised his score to thirty when he brought down Gerald Nash of Collishaw's famous Black Triplane Flight. Nash was the only pilot of this renowned team to be lost during its long period of service, and there is an interesting sequel to the incident.

On June 27 Nash was still a prisoner in the forward area and when he heard the bells of a nearby church tolling mournfully, he asked his jailer what it meant. He was told that it was for the funeral cortege of Karl Allmenroeder, one of the stars of Jasta 11. His body was being taken back to Wald for formal burial. Later, Nash learned that Allmenroeder had been shot down by a member of the Black Triplane Flight.

At the time Allmenroeder was leading a flight of Albatros scouts and Collishaw, from a level somewhat higher, had tried a long-range burst at the leader of the German ships below. He saw the Albatros leader go out of control momentarily, but he could not follow through as he and the two Triplane pilots with him were suddenly attacked from above. However, Allmenroeder dived to his death, and from all accounts Collishaw did not know whom he had attacked until after the war when Gerald Nash reported what he had learned while being held prisoner. Some accounts state that Collishaw knew whom he was engaging, and that he had gone out to seek revenge for the loss of Nash. Today Ray explains, "There was nothing of the kind. It was nothing spectacular in any way."

PAUL BAUMER

Born in Duisburg in 1896, Paul Baumer is one of the more interesting persons in the long list of German aces. His first association with aircraft was when he cycled all the way to Friedrichshafen to see a Zeppelin rise into the sky. After his formal schooling, Paul was a dental assistant and in his work met an unnamed pilot who encouraged Paul to spend his pocket money on a short course in flying. He was not what is known as a born airman, but when the war started he had progressed to the point where he was making short solo flights.

He immediately tried to join the German Naval Air Service, but was turned down. Disgusted with the Navy he enlisted with an infantry regiment and was soon in action in the Saint-Quentin area. Later his regiment was hurried to the Russian front where he was wounded in his left arm and hospitalized. While convalescing he made another attempt to enter one of the air services, but again was unsuccessful. When he learned that "technicians" were being recruited for the Army Air Service, he made still another application on the assumption that a dental assistant might be considered a technician, and to his surprise was immediately accepted and sent to Döberitz where Von Richthofen and Heinrich Gontermann were taking their first flying lessons. Although Baumer had been flying before the war he was first employed in mounting guard or in pioneer work around the airfield.

Frustration and desperation taunted Paul into demanding an interview with his CO who, when he learned that Paul had taken flying lessons, had him transferred to a student group where he showed better than average ability to learn. By September 1916 he was flying two-seaters, carrying out routine reconnaissance missions. By May 1917 he had been posted to Jasta 5 where he flew Albatros scouts. He immediately went on a balloon-busting spree, downing three in four days.

After Baumer had run his score up to thirteen he was shot down in flames by the gunner of a Bristol Fighter, but by this time a few German airmen had been furnished with Paulus parachutes, and Paul managed to get down to earth safely. This may have been the first such escape made by any front-line German airman, for Paul Baumer seems to be the first mentioned.

He was such a proficient workman, he soon ran his score into the forties, after which he was commissioned a lieutenant. He closed his war career with a score of forty-three, and after the war formed his own aircraft company, and did much test flying. While checking out a new Rohrbach cantilever monoplane on July 15, 1927, he was killed when the aircraft seemingly stalled and crashed in Öre Sound near Copenhagen.

RUDOLF BERTHOLD

All the air services had their most fabulous character, a man who combined personal magnetism, fanatic patriotism, flying skill, and unbelievable heroism. To the ordinary individual some of these men are incomprehensible, and some patently were the result of public adulation, publicity, the product of the writer's imagination.

Rudolf Berthold is Germany's contribution to this gallery of incredible airmen. The details of his life have been taken from several sources, and as far as possible, arranged to make some kind of believable picture. Like so many aces in the German Air Service he was given a flamboyant nickname—the Iron Knight—a cognomen probably intended to advertise his determination to continue flying although seriously wounded—which he was on a number of occasions.

Rudolf, whose father was a forester, was born in the little town of Ditterswind in southern Germany. His first military service was with the 20th Infantry Regiment, but late in 1913 he transferred to the Aviation Service. He served first as a pilot-observer with Section 23, but nothing unusual came his way until September 1915 when the L.V.G. in which he was flying was attacked and shot down by a British airman. In this case, however, Berthold managed to glide the machine down to a safe landing and crawl away from the general wreckage. He then spent some uneventful time aboard A.E.G. two-seaters until January 1916 when he began to fly one of the new Fokker E-IIIs. This was a midwing monoplane, powered with the 100-horsepower Oberursel rotary, and fitted with the M.14 type of interrupter gear that increased the rate of fire from 400 rounds per minute to 450–600.

With this new machine, and the freedom of the scout pilot, Berthold made his first kill over Péronne, and in a short time had five victories, but soon ran into trouble himself when he was shot down and seriously wounded, suffering several broken bones. At this juncture the old routine of the junior officer not obeying orders to remain under medical care comes up. Rudolf refused to be taken from the field hospital, or even sent to a back-area convalescent ward where he could recuperate. "No power on earth will get me home," he raged. "I'll keep on flying, if I have to be carried out to my plane."

By October 9, 1916, he was aloft again, which proves that he rested somewhere for many months, but on that date he was honored with the Pour le Mérite. In another year of war flying he had increased his score to twenty-eight. At that point he was again wounded by a machine-gun burst that damaged his right arm so severely the muscles withered and became useless. Once again, after treatment he made his way to the front by early March 1918 where he flew a Siemens-Schuckert D-III that was specially rigged for him to fly despite his latest disability.

Now bearing the title the "Iron Knight," Berthold continued to fly even as his old wounds oozed pus and blood. Flying under such conditions must have been torture, but he insisted on continuing in action, raising his score to forty-four. Then one day he crashed into a house and had to go back to the hospital. By the time he could leave his bed again, Germany had signed the Armistice.

Still aflame with patriotism Berthold could not believe what was happening to his country, and he organized a civilian-military unit to fight the Communists, but his small force was fated for tragedy. Overwhelmed, they were forced to lay down their arms, and Berthold was picked out, battered with rifle butts, and finally throttled with the ribbon of his Pour le Mérite that was around his neck. He is buried in East Berlin near Von Richthofen and Ernst Udet.

OSWALD BOELCKE

Oswald Boelcke, who contributed the most to Germany's power in the air, who conceived the Flying Circus, and devised the most successful combat tactics used by the aces of the Iron Cross, is today a shadowy, dim figure. The name Boelcke "rings a bell" with most enthusiasts of aviation, but strangely enough, he is seldom included in lists of such greats as Von Richthofen, Immelmann, or Göring. Yet his story is one of the more engrossing war biographies. His modest personality, his orderly mind, and his sincere patriotism deserve consideration. Although he contributed much to the art of air fighting, he did not run up a staggering score and so never won his rightful place in the international hall of honor. Military aviation was a new art, and if it completely eluded the General Staff, it certainly baffled the men who were assigned to write its early history.

Oswald Boelcke was born in 1891, the third son of a German schoolteacher who had spent some years in Argentina where he taught at the German Protestant School in Buenos Aires. On returning home he accepted the post of assistant master at the high school in Halle, and later became a professor at the Antoinette School in Dessau. Oswald's brothers, Wilhelm and Friedrich, were born in Argentina, but he first saw the light of day in Giebichstein near Halle. It was decided early that Oswald would be a teacher, whereas his older brothers would choose more masculine occupations. As a youth Oswald was croupy, studious, and retiring. He seemed to show little promise, and was never considered for any team sport.

Left much to himself, Oswald decided to become a good swimmer, and while improving his stroke and kick he also improved his stature and gained vitality. A voracious reader, he was a first-class scholar, particularly proficient in mathematics and physics. Although Professor Boelcke still considered his son as schoolteacher material, the martial music of the times, the uniforms, and the bombastic talk about Germany's place in the sun, generated a quiet, but consuming desire in Oswald to be a soldier.

Although his brothers also aspired to military glory, Oswald did something about it. He bypassed all the regular channels and wrote directly to Kaiser Wilhelm. He pointed out that his father was only a schoolteacher and could not afford to send him to a military academy, but he presumed there was some magic method of a palace appointment—at the time he was but thirteen years old.

He had not confided with the rest of his family, and one day when an impressive envelope was slipped under the door, the family was aghast to learn that little Oswald had actually written to the Kaiser. Evidently touched by the boy's sincerity his Emperor had enclosed an appointment to a nearby cadet school, and had warned in a friendly tone: *"But you will, of course, complete your grammar school subjects. After that you will report to Leutnant General von Schwartzkoppen at Coblenz."*

Wilhelm and Friedrich were outraged and envious, and their father astonished that this youngster would have the effrontery to contact the Kaiser personally, but there was no ignoring a cadet appointment awarded by their Emperor. So Oswald, who finished grammar school and grew to some stature, first saw military service as a color guard in a cadet telegraphic battalion. Later he was moved to Darmstadt where he first came in contact with the aviation branch of the military service. He had devoted much time to being a skilled telegrapher, and realized he might be selected for aerial observation, but because of his enthusiasm and scientific background was given the opportunity to become a pilot. He received his initial training at Halberstadt where he required less than seven weeks to qualify as an NCO pilot.

In the meantime Wilhelm had enlisted in the aviation service, but because he did not have Oswald's training, he could qualify only as an NCO observer. Shortly after the war began both of them were sent down to the Champagne front and found themselves in the same squadron. This created an unusual situation for Wilhelm immediately assumed the role of the older brother, bossing and bullying Oswald to let him fly as his observer. This did little to raise Oswald's standing in the squadron as the other pilots had little respect for a man who allowed himself to be ordered about by a brother who was "merely an observer."

Throughout early September 1914 the Boelcke brothers carried out many routine patrols together, and when inclement weather set in they were grounded for considerable periods of time. One day an observer lieutenant requested Oswald to fly him out to perform a special mission. As Oswald was only an NCO he could not refuse, but when they returned Wilhelm was on the Tarmac fuming because Oswald had taken an officer for his observer, and a marked coolness developed between them. On October 12 Oswald was awarded the Iron Cross for his determination and devotion to duty while flying many routine observation patrols. A week or so later Wilhelm was awarded a higher decoration, the Iron Cross, First Class, for having flown more miles on observation than any German observer at the front.

There followed a dreary period of observation patrols, reorganization, and the mud and slush of that dreadful first winter. Early in 1915 Oswald's bronchial troubles returned, and he was withdrawn from the line to convalesce. When he had recovered he was posted to the Inspectorate Division where he served for about two weeks. He was then forwarded to Döberitz where Section 62 was being formed, and it was here that Oswald Boelcke first encountered Tony Fokker's M-VIII two-seater monoplane, an artillery spotter powered by a rotary engine. This was listed later as the Fok.A., and was under general test for front-line service. He also met Max Immelmann, a boisterous man who up to this time had accomplished very little, except to break up service aircraft. However, these two men became bosom friends.

It was at Döbertiz that Tony Fokker demonstrated his first E-I monoplane that had been fitted with the much publicized interrupter gear, and Boelcke and Immelmann were ordered to take a one-hour course in the handling of this machine and its mechanism. Early the next morning Section 62 was aroused by the roar of engines and the crash of exploding bombs. Ten British B.E.2cs were attacking the airfield, but by the time the German pilots reached their hangars to retaliate the British aircraft were on their way home.

Both Boelcke and Immelmann took to the air with their new Fokkers. Near Vitry, Immelmann overtook the rearmost B.E.2c, and triggered about five hundred rounds from the new Parabellum weapon. (This gun was replaced later by the more suitable Spandau-Maxim.) The British pilot went into a spin, pulled out, and made a hurried landing in German territory. When taken into custody it was discovered that he had been wounded in one arm and about forty rounds had passed through the observer's cockpit which was unoccupied. And so Immelmann received credit for the first victory with a Fokker fixed gun. Some historians claim that it was Boelcke who downed this Britisher, but his official logbook discloses that he did not destroy an Allied plane until July 6, 1915, when he downed a French Morane over Vouziers. In fact, Boelcke's logbook shows that he downed only five enemy planes between the time of the first Fokker delivery and the opening of the new year. He was, however, giving considerable thought to a more efficient handling of the fixed weapon, and was to become the guiding light of the German Air Force.

Actually, few German airmen liked the Fokker E-I, despite its superior armament. Most of them preferred the new Halberstadt D-I, which was ready for front-line action by February 1916, or the Albatros D-I that came along shortly after. In fact, Boelcke, who later formed the famed Jasta 2, openly preferred the Halberstadt, and Tony Fokker's prestige began to decline.

Noting the gradual improvement in Allied fighter offensive, particularly in the employment of the Nieuport scout that carried a

59. The famous and legendary Georges Guynemer is shown here aboard his first Nieuport Scout. The primitive gun-mounting is interesting in that it bears an infantry-type Lewis gun with the standard stock. The weapon was mounted to fire over the tips of the whirling propeller. *(Arch Whitehouse photo)*

. Jean Navarre, one of France's tragic roes. Among the first of the fighting airmen to achieve fame, he suffered a mental eakdown after being wounded in 1916. was killed after the war while practic-; for a Victory Parade air display. *(T. G. ller photo)*

61. Displaying some gallows humor in his personal insignia, Charles Nungesser, France's third-ranking airman, was credited with forty-five victories. In an Atlantic attempt after the war, he was lost along with Captain François Coli aboard the Levasseur P.L. 8 named *Oiseau Blanc* (The White Bird), on May 8, 1917. *(Paul A. Rockwell photo)*

62. Germany's ace of aces, Baron Manfred von Richthofen, is credited with eighty victories. Always a powerful figure in the Imperial Air Service, his exploits played a great part in the buildup and morale of his country's aviation service. *(German Archives photo)*

63. On July 6, 1917, Baron von Richthofen was bested and shot down by an aerial gunner aboard an F.E. 2b pusher. His name was Second Lieutenant Albert E. Woodbridge, a young Englishman who had joined up at the age of eighteen. Here the Baron is seen with his nurse, who, legend has it, was his secret sweetheart. *(Imperial War Museum, London)*

64. One of the more interesting characters of the German Air Force, Paul Baumer of Duisburg paid for his own training, served with the infantry and then wangled his way into the aviation service. He accounted for forty-three Allied planes and was then killed after the war while acting as a test pilot. *(Egon Krueger photo)*

65. The true creator of the Flying Circus, Oswald Boelcke trained to become a school teacher, instead became the mastermind of the German Air Service. Here he is seen before a Fokker E IV. He was credited with forty victories. *(Egon Krueger photo)*

66. Stemming from a long line of professional soldiers, Hermann Göring had none of the discipline of the old school. He bullied his way into the aviation service and amazingly enough became a first-class fighter pilot, and was credited with twenty-two Allied aircraft. The rest of his history is bespoiled in the tragedy of World War II. *(Egon Krueger photo)*

67. A group of German air aces who had been awarded the Pour le Mérite. From left to right: K. Degelow, J. Veltjens, J. Jacobs, O. von Boenig, E. von Schleich, Ernst Udet, Bruno Loerzer, Paul Baumer, Hermann Göring and H. Bongartz. *(Egon Krueger photo)*

68. The man known as the Eagle of Lille, Max Immelmann, is shown settling himself in the cockpit of one of the first Fokker E. 1 monoplanes equipped with a synchronized gun. Never a great pilot, he won the affection of Oswald Boelcke and was fortunate enough to be assigned to one of the first Fokker fixed-gun fighters. *(Egon Krueger photo)*

69. Beginning his career as an NCO flier, Max Müller turned out to be a natural pilot and rose to command Jasta 22. Later he took over the famed Jasta Boelcke. Müller was credited with thirty-six Allied aircraft before he died after leaping from his burning Albatros. *(Egon Krueger photo)*

70. This handsome German airman has been called the Second Eagle of Lille, possibly because he was taken over as Max Immelmann's protege. Max von Mulzer downed ten Allied planes before he was killed when his Albatros broke up in midair. *(Imperial War Museum, London)*

71. Baron von Richthofen, seated in his all-red Albatros, is posing with members of his special flight. Seated on the ground in front is Lothar von Richthofen, Manfred's brother, who was to down forty Allied aircraft before the war ended. (*Imperial War Museum, London*)

72. Von Richthofen was shot down near Bertangles on April 21, 1917. Flying officers of No. 3 Squadron, Royal Australian Air Force, provided full military rites and a firing party, and copies of this photograph were dropped in the German lines a day or so later. The body was eventually moved to Berlin. (*Imperial War Museum, London*)

73. Credited with thirty-five victories, Eduard von Schleich, sometimes known as The Black Knight, became something of a colorful figure before the war ended. He was particularly fascinated with decorating his planes in gaudy colors and symbolic emblems. Before World War II he helped in the creation of the German Luftwaffe. *(Egon Krueger photo)*

74. One of the most popular of the German aces, Ernst Udet, who scored sixty-two victories and who later made friendship tours throughout the Allied countries, could only rid himself of the Hitler regime by committing suicide. *(Egon Krueger photo)*

75. Two of Germany's most respected airmen, Ernst Udet (left) and Bruno Loerzer. It was Loerzer who was most instrumental in getting Hermann Göring into the flying service. Bruno was credited with downing fifty-five Allied aircraft. *(Imperial War Museum, London)*

76. Fregattenkapitän Peter Strasser, Leader of Airships of the German Naval Airship Division, was awarded the Pour le Mérite for his outstanding efforts to defeat Britain by bombing London with his fleet of Zeppelins. *(Luftschiffbau Zeppelin photo)*

77. Germany's boldest airman. Werner Voss was one of the few who dared combat over the Allied lines. After scoring forty-eight victories, he was finally brought down by pilots of Jimmy McCudden's No 56 Squadron. Voss still retains the respect and affection of all British World War airmen. *(Imperial War Museum, London*

front-firing gun on its top wing, and the British D.H.2 pusher, Boelcke decided to put air fighting on a more efficient basis. He insisted on tight formations, accurate gunnery, and fighting well inside the German lines in order to gain all the advantages that came with the selection of the battlefield. As mentioned before he destroyed only five enemy planes in 1915, but started well in 1916 by destroying four British machines in January. One of these was a Vickers Gunbus, a two-seater pusher powered with a rotary engine. This encounter gave Oswald an unforgettable scare. He had never met one before and probably expected to make short work of it, but the British plane flipped around so nimbly and the gunner was so skilled and alert Boelcke had to move fast to get out of range. He went back in hoping to outmaneuver the Vickers, but the pusher machine outmaneuvered him, and for twenty-five minutes they had a thrilling duel. Gradually, both ships lost altitude until they were practically down over Boelcke's Douai airdrome. At this point the British pilot became alarmed and made a foolish move. Boelcke took advantage and fired a short burst; the pilot was killed and the machine piled up on the edge of the Douai field.

Oswald Boelcke was awarded the Pour le Mérite for this feat, and the medal was personally presented by Kaiser Wilhelm. A few days later Oswald rescued a young French boy from a canal, and the local residents were so appreciative of this and the fact that Oswald had carried out the resuscitation, the mayor recommended that he receive the French Life Saving Medal. To Boelcke's amazement this civilian award was conveyed to him five months later. He was the only airman of the war to receive a decoration at the request of his enemies.

＊

Boelcke did not score another victory throughout the month of February, but his Jasta was transferred to the French front to take part in a proposed offensive against Verdun. Germany was determined to overrun the old fortress area, firstly for the morale effect, and secondly to clear a new path to Paris. No sacrifice was to be too great, and the cream of the land and air services were moved into the area. Every available airman was expected to take part in an over-all program of aerial reconnaissance and low-level bombing. Air fighting, as such, was to be avoided.

Boelcke had little appreciation for this plan, but he was not important enough to make any contrary suggestions. He believed each squadron should do the job it had been trained for, and his Section was presumed to be a fighting unit. However, he had to send his men and machines out on individual missions, and on March 13 while flying alone he spotted a French Voisin formation returning from a raid over German territory. He noticed a laggard that seemed to be having engine trouble, and he moved in like a shrike. The Voisin fluttered, tried to zoom, fell off after a stall and began to spin. Oswald thought this could be a trick, so he followed the big biplane down until both machines had slithered into a layer of cloud. When Boelcke came out in the clear he saw the Voisin floundering in a wide circuit with the French gunner clambering along the lower wing trying to provide leverage that would right the aircraft. He was so close he could see the Frenchman's face with his fear-stricken eyes flashing like jet ornaments in a chalk skull.

A touch of humanity restrained Boelcke's hand until several anti-aircraft bursts snapped him back to reality, and he knew it would be folly to act humanely when he himself might be shot down in hostile territory. But he never fired another shot. While he had been considering the quality of mercy, fate took a hand. The left wing of the Voisin dropped to earth, and the plane fluttered like a great bird in the torment of agony. There was a quick flash-scene of a helpless man being hurled from his frail platform and tumbled into the dreadful nothingness of the sky. With an ache in his heart, Boelcke turned back toward his own lines.

In successive days this German flier shot down three Farmans, and now had thirteen planes to his credit. He became the idol of his Fatherland, and only Max Immelmann came anywhere near him in the victory lists. Immelmann was a more spectacular showman and possessed that personal magnetism that attracts the masses, but Boelcke was entertained more often by German nobility.

At the beginning of September 1916 Boelcke was given a command of his own that was known as Jasta 2, and with this honor came the usual reams of paper work and time-consuming administrative duties. He was also asked to make an inspection of the complete German Air Service, following which, on his return to Douai, he saw that his air fighters were no longer having things their own way. The British, in particular, with their two-seater pushers and the D.H.2 were giving the Fokker and Albatros fixed-gun fighters several new lessons in air combat.

Boelcke also realized that the Aviation Staff was handling their two-seaters with little understanding of their full capabilities. They had been practically useless during the siege of Verdun; their observation planes had been sent into the air with little, or no, fighter protection. There was no real cockpit cooperation between the pilots and observers, and as a fighting element they were not worth the fuel they were consuming. But as Boelcke was temperamentally a fighter pilot, he could not devise or suggest an acceptable two-seater strategy. The fixed gun had set up a mental block as far as two-seater fighting was concerned. On the other hand British aerial gunners were more than earning their flight pay and rations.

When Immelmann was shot down by an aerial gunner aboard a British F.E.2b Boelcke realized that war in the air was no longer a one-sided sport. Now it was a deadly game in which many factors played vital roles. This new administrative concern needled him into making childish denunciations and braggart threats against the hated English. Making the most of these tirades the German High Command encouraged him to direct his wrath to devising new tactics and to assuming a more disciplined leadership—to use against the British.

Within a short time his new fighting maneuvers were quite productive, and the Boelcke Staffel became outstanding for initiative, dash, and boastful confidence. All this was grist to the German press, and as the focal figure Boelcke was in an unenviable position; unless he shot down a Britisher every day he was looked upon as something of a slacker.

It must be said to his credit that he put on a great effort. During that month of September while showing his fledglings how it should be done he destroyed eleven British machines. Between patrols or during bad weather he made hurried visits to Berlin to push his fighter-squadron ideas and theories, hoping to inject some of this up-to-date viewpoint into the minds of the General Staff which still thought in terms of kite balloons and long-range artillery to fight the stalemated war.

While on one of these visits he became acquainted with a little-known pilot, Baron Manfred von Richthofen, who was a member of an Albatros two-seater squadron but wished to become a single-seater fighter pilot. Boelcke needed ambitious young men of this type, and within three days Von Richthofen was heading for Jasta 2.

By this time the Jasta had been fully equipped with the new Albatros D-I, a tough, sleek-bodied biplane that carried *two* fixed guns. Flying this trustworthy machine, Boelcke set out to stem the new

British offensive, and, beginning on September 17, Jasta 2 was flown as a circus formation, meaning every available plane and pilot went into the air in a tight formation sweep with Boelcke leading. Anything in small numbers was doomed, and as the days slipped by Oswald raised his score to forty. What the rest of the German Air Force was accomplishing was something else, but the Boelcke Circus was holding its sector of the line above the Somme.

Boelcke always led the first morning patrol when the rising sun was in its favor, and as long as a tight formation was maintained, it enjoyed snug protection and security. Any Allied aircraft trapped in their three-dimensional charge was downed by someone, and the new pilot, Von Richthofen, was credited with fifteen victories during the last four months of 1916.

Boelcke no longer cared about his own military fortunes, or his score; his schoolteacher destiny had caught up with him. He spent hours drilling his newcomers, lecturing his flight leaders, devising new fighting tactics for the men who were flocking to his banner. He wrote out his views, attached tactical drawings, and toured the whole area, giving talks and spreading his doctrines. He set up skeletal formations that were to become other Jagdstaffeln, and to make certain his pupils would recognize him in the air he had his machine painted all black, a feature his understudy Von Richthofen was to adopt and take credit for.

Another airman of wide experience was Erwin Boehme who was doing particularly well. As a matter of fact Oswald Boelcke considered Erwin to be superior as a pilot to Manfred von Richthofen, and had not a tragic event occurred that affected Boehme's spirit, Boelcke's preference might have been justified.

On October 28, 1916, Boelcke led a six-ship element on a formation drill. Von Richthofen and Boehme flew close behind on his right and left. They were there to observe the master's technique. Near Pozières inside the German lines two D.H.2s of Number 24 (Hawker's) Squadron, flown by Lieutenants A. G. Knight and A. E. McKay, were out on an offensive patrol.

The Staffel leader raised his hand, folded his fingers down, and signaled the attack. Moving in from behind, he led his formation up and under the blind spots of the D.H.2s. In trying to maintain his protective position Boehme somehow slipped into Boelcke's Albatros. To the pilots in the rear it looked as if the two planes scarcely touched, but the machine in which Boelcke had so much confidence was stricken immediately. Boehme's upper wingtip had sliced through the two interplane struts, collapsing the wing of the famous black plane. As the wing slowly folded back, the leader's Albatros turned with the drag of the fractured airfoil. The stick went dead in Boelcke's hand, and there was little height in which to attempt a recovery. The ponderous 160-horsepower Mercedes took the crippled Albatros to its doom, plowing into the blood-drenched territory of the Somme that had gathered in so many of Boelcke's victims.

It is said that they had a difficult time with Erwin Boehme. He was heartbroken, and when he landed begged for a minute alone with a service Luger. Wiser heads talked him out of self-destruction, and eventually he commanded the Boelcke Jagdstaffel. His fate, too, was explicit. Erwin Boehme was killed on November 29, 1917, just before he was to be decorated with the Pour le Mérite.

Oswald Boelcke was buried from the cathedral in Cambrai with the staff of Germany's Imperial Forces and the ruling princes of the Empire in attendance. Among the floral offerings was one that might have meant much to Boelcke could he have known. It bore a card that read:

> *To a much admired and honorable enemy.*
> FROM: *British officers who are prisoners*
> *of war at Osnabrück.*

CARL BOLLE

This German airman, credited with thirty-six victories, spent considerable time in England before the war. He had been a popular student at Oxford where he made many friends, but when war broke out he returned to Germany and after some colorful service with a crack cavalry regiment, he transferred to the Air Service. It is highly probable that in the ensuing months he engaged many of his former college mates who had selected the Royal Flying Corps.

Carl Bolle was soon awarded the Iron Cross for gallantry in action against French patrols in Belgium, and in 1915 was sent to the Eastern Front where his regiment stagnated as the result of the establishment of the trench system, so he and several other brother officers requested transfers to the Aviation Service. Their CO refused at first to forward their applications, but Bolle persisted and managed to make the transfer late in 1915.

By May of the following year Bolle was flying an Albatros C-III two-seater on the French front. He soon claimed to have downed a Nieuport Baby scout and a two-seater Farman. Then in October while on an observation patrol he was attacked by four Nieuport scouts. He shot one down in flames, and his observer accounted for another. But the other two Nieuports refused to be driven off, and Bolle's Albatros was finally riddled. He managed to land his machine and crawl out with four bullets in one leg, another through his left arm, and his flying suit in ribbons.

Carl Bolle spent many months in a hospital and was discharged as unfit for further service. One leg was painfully crippled and he was warned by the doctors not to fly again, but Carl was made of sterner stuff. He devised a program of exercises that though most painful resulted in his being accepted again for active-service flying. And to prove his point Bolle took a type of machine he had not seen before, and staged a wild display of stunting that left his superiors with no reason for refusing him an acceptable medical report.

On March 17, 1918, Bolle was assigned to the Boelcke Staffel just when the great German offensive was reaching its peak. The sky was cluttered with all types of machines, and considerable action was being staged down low where British Camel squadrons were carrying out their hour-by-hour bombing of moving troops. Bolle who was still somewhat convalescent managed to down a Sopwith 1½-Strutter that was making a low-level reconnaissance. He did little more until April 30 when he downed a second Sopwith.

As the summer approached the air war was increased and on May 8 he was mixed up in what was sometimes called a dogfight when his portion of the Circus tangled with a number of Sop Camels and S.E.5s. Bolle picked off a Camel, and then found an S.E.5 pilot who was concentrating on an Albatros. Bolle's guns spat and the Britisher went down, crashing only a few yards from the Camel. About two weeks later he was victor over a Bristol Fighter, and following that his Staffel was transferred to the French front.

The opposition was less concentrated here, and he discovered that the vaunted Spads gave little trouble. He downed three in a short time. On one occasion, while engaging a small formation of French machines, Bolle's guns jammed and he found himself harried by one determined Frenchman. While he worked to clear the stoppage, he carried out a fake fight, and when the Spad appeared in his sights momentarily, his guns, for no apparent reason, fired ten rounds each, and the Frenchman went down in flames.

On June 9, 1918, he scored a double, the third time in his career, and by the end of that month he had raised his score to eighteen. On July 5 he attacked three French Nieuports, quickly downing one. The other two acted uncertainly, so Bolle chased them all the way back to their airdrome but was unable to put in a telling burst. He scored his twentieth victory on July 15 when he downed a Sopwith Camel, for which he was awarded the Pour le Mérite. Over the next two days, to celebrate his decoration, Bolle downed three more Allied planes, and after that the Staffel returned to the British front.

Back in action against their traditional enemies, Captain Otto Hartmann, who had been credited with seven victories, was shot down, and Carl Bolle was appointed to the command. Unfortunately, he took over his new post with the opening of Germany's "Black August" when the British Army started its final move, and the new Royal Air Force had reached the peak of its strength. The greats of the Boelcke Circus began to go down one by one, but Bolle continued to add to his score, and seemed to bear a charmed life. During one wild melee on August 9 he torched a D.H.4, destroyed an S.E.5, and on his way back to his field downed an R.E.8 that was spotting for the British artillery. The R.E.8's gunner gave him a bad time while he lasted. Fourteen holes were found at vital spots near his cockpit, and one bullet had clipped off the buckle of his safety belt.

All through that dreadful month of August 1918 when Germans fought Britishers in what proved to be the climactic period of the war, Bolle continued to fly and keep what was left of his formation together. On August 26 he downed a Sopwith Camel, his thirty-first victory, and hoped he was on his way to break the half century mark, but the German Air Staff decided his squadron should be withdrawn from the front for rest and refit. They rested for six welcome weeks, and eased jangled nerves while refreshed mechanics put their aircraft and armament into first-class condition.

After six weeks, rest or no rest, the handwriting was on the wall, plain for all to see. Bolle and his comrades went back into the maelstrom for one last fling at the enemy. They must have known their cause was lost, but one and all they were determined to finish in a blaze of glory. In the next ten days Bolle and his crew slammed into dogfights and combats, but little glory came to their pennons, and not until November 1 did their leader score again. An S.E.5 went down, but it was a mere pittance in the disaster that was engulfing the whole Imperial German Air Force.

On November 4 the entire Staffel took off in the general retreat and as they climbed into that gray and bitter sky they were blocked off by great formations of British planes—the Flying Circus stunt was being played in reverse. This classic engagement took place over Englefontaine. Every German pilot, realizing this would be his last chance to strike a blow for the Fatherland, flew like a madman. The sky blazed with colorful machines and burning aircraft. Tracer fire weaved a taut web across the battle scene as Fokkers, Snipes, Albatroses, and Camels charged with reckless abandon. Bolle had one close shave when a blazing Snipe roared at him head-on. He just managed to sideslip out of the way, and the maneuver placed him directly on the tail of an S.E.5. He fired instinctively, and the snap burst instantly killed the pilot. Then the fuel tank exploded and the S.E.5 went down like a winged torch. Before this memorable melee dissipated Bolle downed another S.E.5, and led what he had left for a clearing.

Fifteen minutes later his battered squadron fought a ten minute battle with a formation of Sopwith Snipes over Villerau. Two of his men were lost, but Bolle put one Snipe down in flames, and drove three more down apparently out of control.

By this time fuel was running low, and Bolle sought out his reserve field, but before they could move into their landing pattern another flight of Snipes came into the picture. Abandoning all restraint, Bolle went in, shot the wings off one, and drove three others out of the action, and with that the squadron finally landed, only to learn that what they feared had become a reality. Germany was to sue for an armistice and all aircraft were ordered to move away from the front.

An ironical touch came up at this point. Because of his knowledge of English and his British university background, Carl Bolle was appointed to be one of the officers to carry out the formal surrender of all German fighter aircraft to the Allies. One Fokker, bearing the colors of the Boelcke Staffel bore an additional citation:

Rittmemeister Carl Bolle—36

Following the strictures of the Peace Terms, there was no commercial aviation for German pilots to fall back on, but as the years rolled by Carl Bolle, who had once been warned that he would never fly again, became actively connected with the Deutsche Lufthansa and other commercial transport companies. When last heard of he was still associated with German aviation.

WALTER von BÜLOW

In some aviation histories Walter von Bülow is listed as a prince, and certainly he was a scion of that famous family and a worthy member of the Boelcke Staffel. He was credited with twenty-eight victories and led a charmed life on two fronts until at last he disappeared on January 6, 1918. Who downed him and where he was buried have long been subjects of controversy.

Von Bülow was born in 1894, and educated at the University of Heidelberg where he gained high scholastic honors and was head of the Cadet Corps. At the outbreak of war he was commissioned in the Seventeenth Hussars and distinguished himself during the early German advance. In January 1915 he was awarded the Iron Cross, Second Class, for gallantry on the Lorraine front, and two months later was made a full lieutenant for his services in the field. He applied for and quickly received an appointment to the Imperial Air Service, taking his training at the Hanover Flying School.

His first assignment was with a two-seater squadron operating on the Champagne front, and on October 10, 1915, while flying over Metz, he encountered a French Voisin. Before the observer could fire a shot Von Bülow had put in a telling burst and the Voisin plunged to the ground in flames. A second victory was gained the following afternoon, but the circumstances were somewhat reversed. This time Von Bülow was attacked by a Farman and two Voisins and he had to take cover in a cloud. His plane had received many bullets, and his engine was running roughly, but he nursed it along and stalked the French machines, biding his time for more than thirty minutes. He then noticed that the Farman was lagging behind the two Voisins so he moved in fast and sent it down out of control before the Voisins could get back into the action.

A third French machine fell before his guns in December, and in February 1916 he was transferred to the newly formed Abteilung 300 (two-seater general purpose flight) that was sent to Palestine where Germany was contesting the British right of way to the Suez Canal. The unit was stationed at El Arish and given the duty of patrolling the vital waterway. Only two antiquated two-seaters were available and Von Bülow was in little action until six Rumplers and two Pfalz E-III scouts (machines that looked suspiciously like the French Morane Parasol, and armed with a single Spandau gun) were assigned to the squadron.

Von Bülow put in a stint of general reconnaissance and light-bombing patrols, while the aircraft of the R.N.A.S. in the Near East continually plastered the El Arish field. Walter decided to retaliate, and flying one of the Rumplers with a Lieutenant von Hesler as his observer, he intercepted a Short seaplane and two Sopwith "Baby" seaplanes as they approached the field. The Sopwiths opened fire but the Rumpler cleared, outmaneuvering them. Von Bülow finally sent one down in flames, the other continued to fight but Von Hesler at the Parabellum drove it down, causing it to crash-land on the Mediterranean Sea. Heading for the Short, Von Bülow fired at long range and apparently put a burst into the Sunbeam engine's radiator for the seaplane dived away, trailing a plume of steam. It then alighted beside its mother ship, the *Ben My Chree*.

A short time later, in September, Von Bülow was flying one of the Pfalz scouts, powered with a 100-horsepower Oberursel rotary, and found himself under fire from four B.E.2cs, so he joined in the action, shooting one of them down. Then he received a burst in one shoulder that caused him to crash inside the Turkish reserve lines. He spent about a month in a Jerusalem hospital, and did not return to his squadron until late in November.

We next hear of him back on the Western Front where he was posted to an Albatros squadron in the Champagne area where they encountered squadrons of French Spads and Nieuports. Von Bülow soon added two of the latter to his score. He seems to have had a successful tour of duty on the Champagne front for he scored regularly. Then the Albatros Staffel was moved up to Arras where they found several British squadrons equipped with the new Bristol Fighter. In two weeks three of his squadron's planes were shot down by gunners in Bristols, and he himself had a very narrow escape. While engaging a couple of Brisfits, it was seen that these aerial gunners were smart and well-trained, and before either could be shot down a flight of Camels streamed into the scene and an Albatros piloted by a man named Gortach was sent down in flames by a Bristol gunner and three Camels immediately boxed in Von Bülow. He was rescued just in time by a formation of Fokker triplanes, but did receive a flesh wound in his thigh.

Von Bülow was back in action by July and soon disposed of an R.E.8 and a Camel, and by the end of that month his score reached fifteen.

The Bristol Fighters scored again in August and Von Bülow went down once more but escaped serious injury. He had been attacking a Brisfit when his guns jammed, and the pilot of the two-seater shot his engine to pieces, and he crashed in a plowed field near his own airdrome. He gained some satisfaction that evening when he borrowed a machine and went up over Saint-Julien and downed a Spad of Number 19 Squadron, R.F.C. Half an hour later he attacked a British two-seater and wounded the observer, but the pilot managed to land the machine under full control, so Von Bülow could not claim a complete victory.

All through the heavy air fighting of late 1917 Walter had his ups and downs, but was awarded the Pour le Mérite, and had scored twenty-eight victories. His last two successes came on December 3, 1917. He had left the ground early in the morning and encountered several large formations of French and British machines, and although he led his pack full tilt into the opposition he did not have any success. Two of his pilots had to return with engine trouble, and at that point four Bristol Fighters appeared nearby.

Von Bülow had a force of seven Albatros scouts, and he signaled for an attack, but before either side could start firing three S.E.5s and a small formation of French Spads slipped out of nearby clouds. A Spad and an Albatros collided in midair and another Albatros was driven out of the play with a shattered propeller. In the melee a Spad flew into Von Bülow's sights and he put a snap burst dead into the cockpit sending the Frenchman down. A Bristol Fighter then banked into the scene and his next burst shot its controls away, and the Brisfit went down in a tight spin. These were the last two planes to fall before his guns.

On December 17 Von Bülow was transferred from Staffel 36 to take command of Jasta Boelcke, but he did not enjoy this command for long. He fell on January 6, 1918, during a dogfight over Saint-Julien. German records state he was shot down by a British two-seater, but French records credit Walter von Bülow's fall to Pierre Marinovitch, the youngest of the French aces. Von Bülow's family tried for years to solve the mystery, claiming that it was another Von Bülow who had been downed by the young French pilot. In looking through the records we note that no less than five Von Bülows were killed in air action from 1914–18, which perhaps accounts for the confusion and sets up another mystery of the Great War.

FRIEDRICH CHRISTIANSEN

Nicknamed "The Fighter of Zeebrugge" Friedrich Christiansen was an outstanding character in the German Air Service. At the peak of his career he was thirty-seven years old. He never flew a single-seater in action, yet is credited with twenty-one victories by some historians. These successes were gained over airplanes, flying boats, and submarines.

Born to the sea in the town of Wyk on Föhr Island, December 12, 1879, Christiansen served some time as a conventional sailor, but in 1914 switched to aviation and learned to fly a Gotha-Hansa Taube machine. Early in 1915 he was proficient enough to be posted to a seaplane squadron based at Zeebrugge, presumably to furnish air protection for the German naval base there, but not until early 1917 had German naval aircraft been built with suitable offensive power to justify combat with enemy machines. One of these was a plane, the idea for which had been suggested to the Brandenburg designers by Christiansen. This was probably the W-29, a low-wing mono-plane seaplane powered by a 150-horsepower Benz engine. Armament varied; some were equipped with one fixed gun and a radio set, while others dispensed with the wireless and carried two Spandau weapons. It was seaplanes of this type that harried British coastal motorboats that were out the day Stuart Culley downed the Zeppelin *LZ.53,* after he had taken off in a Sopwith Camel from a towed lighter.

Friedrich Christiansen was given charge of a large force of these W-29 machines, and two days after the historic attack on the Zee-brugge Mole, he was leading a flight of seven W-29s when he at-tacked two F.2a flying boats from Felixstowe. One was shot down in flames, the other suffered a broken fuel pipe and landed on the beach in Holland where the British pilot set it afire before he was interned.

Christiansen also took credit for destroying a British submarine listed as *C-25,* although there is no record of any such undersea craft being lost during World War I. On December 11, 1917, he did attack and destroy the British airship *C-27* off the East Anglian coast for which he was honored with the Pour le Mérite.

Friedrich Christiansen had a dappled career after the war. He commanded a Hamburg-American Line steamer for a time, and then returned to flying, and skippered the famous Dornier Do.X on its flight around the world. He became Adolf Hitler's first commander of the Nazi Air Service, and did much to renew German interest in flying. During World War II he had a besmirched record when he was military governor of the Netherlands. He was arrested by the Allies after the war and convicted of many cruelties. He was given a long sentence, but was pardoned later, and is said to live in West Germany.

RUDOLF von ESCHWEGE

This German ace who is credited with twenty victories was known for a time as "The Eagle of the Aegean." His career was staged mostly in Macedonia, a front that is almost completely unknown to American readers. Nevertheless, considerable action occurred in that far-flung area, and some interesting air history inscribed.

Rudolf von Eschwege was born February 25, 1895. On his eighteenth birthday he enlisted in an Austrian cavalry regiment and saw twelve months' service as a trooper. In February 1915 he was sent home to train for aviation, and by July was a pilot in a two-seater reconnaissance squadron. Nothing but ill luck seemed to dog him over the next six months, and weird accidents happened almost daily. Once he landed on top of another plane that was about to take off, and his CO threatened to return him to the cavalry.

The threat worked, and in a short while Rudolf became a skilled pilot, and by May 1916 was recommended for single-seater training, but instead of being posted to a Fokker squadron on the Western Front, he was posted to Drama in Macedonia. Three days later he scored his first kill when he downed a Farman biplane, but as it fell deep inside the Allied lines he did not receive credit for it. A few days later he downed a British B.E.2c directly over his own airdrome, and there was no question of that victory. On January 6, 1917, another Farman appeared over an advanced field near Drama and the pilot who was evidently confused, started to come in for a landing.

Enemy gunfire roused him, and he sheered off. Eschwege who was nearby took off and quickly forced the pilot, a Serbian sergeant, to land. It was learned that the Farman pilot had mistaken the German field for his own.

On February 12 Rudolf shot down a B.E.12 of Number 17 Squadron, R.F.C. Two Sopwith 1½-Strutters were shot down in March, and after running his score up to seven, he received his first wound. While attacking two B.E.s over Angista his main fuel tank went dry and the Fokker fell off into a spin. After switching over to the reserve tank, Eschwege returned to the fight and put a burst through one B.E.'s engine, and while watching it glide down, the pilot of the other B.E. slammed a long burst into the Fokker, holing both tanks, and putting two bullets through Rudolf's right arm. He was lucky to make a dead-stick landing on the Drama airdrome.

On returning to his squadron he became doubly interested in his engine, guns, and general maintenance of his aircraft, and as a result his uniform was usually more soiled than those of his mechanics.

Eschwege learned one day that eight enemy planes were covering a naval cruiser that was shelling Kavalla, so he took off and within thirty minutes had made contact with the enemy machines. Using a cloud for cover he sought out the Farman that seemed to be spotting for the cruiser's guns. Moving in fast to avoid the others, he fired a heavy burst that caused the Farman to break up in midair. Eschwege then raced away and avoided further contact with the Allied planes.

Although harried with malaria Eschwege continued to add to his score through the spring and summer of 1917, but his fourteenth victory gave him a hearty scare. He was attacking four Sopwith two-seaters that were returning from a raid on Xanthe, and after picking out the leader and sending him down in flames, he was startled to hear a terrifying explosion that shook his own machine and enveloped him in a thick cloud of oily smoke. He waited for the end, but evidently the other Britishers assumed he was going down out of control and continued on their way. He did not know what had caused the explosion, but in a short while he was able to restart his engine and return to his base.

On October 3 Rudolf shot down a Sopwith Pup, his sixteenth success, and then he decided to become a balloon buster. He found a British bag over Orjlak. It took three bursts of incendiaries before it went down, but this seemed like sport, so two days later he tried it again. His first burst made the observer jump, and he saw the unfortunate man go to his death when the parachute failed to open.

Turning back to the balloon Rudolf triggered his guns—but nothing happened! Both were hopelessly jammed, and by that time the anti-aircraft ground guns were making things miserable, so he hedge-hopped back to his field.

On November 15 another balloon was up at Orjlak, and although there was a distinct drizzle, Eschwege was determined to try out his new Halberstadt scout. Two Allied machines were flying protection over the balloon, so he made a couple of fake passes at them, and then suddenly nosed down and set fire to the kite.

Evidently someone then decided that this flier, called *Bjelomors-sko Orel,* The Eagle of the Aegean, was becoming too offensive, and a trap was set for him. On November 19 another balloon was put up, and Rudolf set out to get it. This time the British had two B.E.12s and a Sopwith 1½-Strutter to intercept him soon after he crossed the lines. He immediately attacked one of the B.E. aircraft and shot it down. In the engagement a bullet clipped the heel of Eschwege's flying boot, but that was as far as the opposition went at that point. The new Halberstadt was too much for the ancient craft the British were flying.

At dusk that same day he again sought out the British balloon, but the ground crew was too fast for him and the bag was hauled down quickly. So he poured several bursts at the winch and then turned on four B.E. biplanes and chased them back to their field at Thasos. Ensuing rain put off flying for a few days, but early in the morning of November 21 Eschwege was anxious to get into the air again and continue bursting balloons. At the same time on the opposite side of the line two officers of the Royal Engineers were busy loading the basket of a decoy balloon with a dummy observer and a load of high explosive. Thus, to all intents and purposes, a British balloon was in the air with an observer leaning over the edge of the basket. Eschwege made certain there were no enemy aircraft in the area and then went down full tilt with both guns blazing. Watchers below saw flame spurt from the perforated bag, and then, as the German flier nosed in close to zoom in triumph an engineer on the ground pressed a plunger and the aerial mine exploded blowing Eschwege's Halberstadt to smithereens. The Germans claimed later that it was not a gallant way to fight an air war, but they soon used the same device on the Western Front.

The R.F.C. buried Eschwege with full military honors and dropped photographs of his grave on the Drama airdrome. Later, the Bulgarians erected a monument to his memory.

HERMANN GÖRING

This notorious man who did as much to besmirch the reputation of the German people as did Adolf Hitler was a typical Prussian of the old school. Although he was born in 1893 in Rosenheim, Bavaria, the most unwarlike of the German states, he came from a long line of professional soldiers. His father served in the struggle against Austria in 1866 and in the Franco-Prussian War of 1870–71, and later was the first Governor of German West Africa.

For a time young Hermann was placed in the care of wealthy friends while his parents were at their overseas post, and during that interval he grew up and turned into a reckless, self-willed young man. His parents had not planned on his continuing the military line, but they finally placed him in a cadet school from which he graduated in 1912 with the rank of second lieutenant, and was assigned to the 112th Infantry Regiment.

He was still an undisciplined young man, and during the annual maneuvers he thought nothing of deriding his commanding officer for his field tactics. Had it not been for his father's influence in Berlin he probably would have been cashiered out of the service.

Fortunately for him, the Great War broke out and there were many opportunities for him to relieve his recklessness. His regiment was sent to Alsace where he immediately formed a cyclist corps with the intention of harassing French outposts. On one occasion he was sent out to reconnoiter the advancing enemy with strict orders to avoid actual contact. With seven other men he cycled into a village that sheltered about one hundred French troops, and with a surprise move put most of them to flight; the rest were killed. Had it not been for the fact that one of his men, as undisciplined as he, opened fire from a hayloft before Hermann could place the rest of his men into position, he might have captured the whole French force. He was awarded the Iron Cross, Second Class, for this action—and then suitably dressed down before his own troops for disobeying orders.

But the swashbuckling Göring was not a physical marvel, and by 1915 he was placed in a hospital with a severe attack of rheumatism. While convalescing he was visited by his friend Bruno Loerzer who had recently transferred to the Aviation Service. Bruno spent the whole afternoon extolling the thrills of flying, and the fun of engaging the enemy in the air. Hermann decided, then and there, that he too would become an airman, but when he brought up the subject later on with his CO it was vetoed immediately. But he would not be put off with mere words, and he arranged for Bruno Loerzer to land his two-seater Albatros near his camp. Without permission Hermann climbed in and flew off and landed at Loerzer's field.

For the next few days Göring flew as Loerzer's observer, and since no one did anything about it, he stayed on and never went back to his infantry regiment. So much for the vaunted discipline of the German Army.

In the next two months both Loerzer and Göring were awarded the Iron Cross, First Class, for a number of daring reconnaissance missions carried out over the French lines. During this period in early 1916 the French sent a formation of Farmans to bombard the German Crown Prince's headquarters at Stenay, and Loerzer and Göring "just happened" to be in the area while the Frenchmen were unloading their bombs. Loerzer nosed down and went right through the Farman formation, his front gun being used in the manner of a garden hose. Göring in the rear sprayed the formation with his Parabellum. None of the raiders was shot down, but the interception must have interfered with the bomb-aiming.

A short time later these two fliers were attacked by a French Nieuport, but Hermann drove the Frenchman off by simply brandishing and firing his pistol. At least that is how Hermann explained the action. At any rate it proved that he was being wasted as an observer, and in the spring of 1916 he, with thirty others, went to Courtrai to become pilots. Göring was soon in trouble again, for he ignored the routine dual-control instruction, arguing that Loerzer had shown him how to fly during all their weeks in the Albatros. To prove this he "borrowed" a Rumpler and headed back to the front.

✻

German military discipline having been shown up, the powers-that-were decided to let Hermann Göring discipline—or kill—himself, and within a month he had managed his way into a front-line flying section before Verdun. The rest of the story can be foretold with little difficulty. After flying two-seaters for a short time, he was transferred to scouts, and joined Loerzer who by now was flying Fokkers with Staffel 5.

Before the end of 1916 Göring had accounted for three French machines and unquestionably had saved Loerzer's life. One day in December their squadron was engaged with a flight of Nieuports and Bruno was forced out of the action with machine-gun trouble. A pair of Nieuports made the most of this and Loerzer's plane had several control cables severed. At this point Göring went to his rescue and drove one Nieuport off. The other tried to spin away, but Göring finally put in a heavy burst which caused the French machine to break up in midair.

The inclement weather in early 1917 gave everyone a respite, but in mid-February Hermann took off with two other Fokker pilots. A low mist broke up this formation and Hermann found himself alone and looking down on a twin-engined biplane that was crossing into German territory. He attacked it at once and his first burst put one engine out of action. As the bomber turned to fly toward home, Hermann decided to look over his shoulder. It was well he did, for two flights of Spads came out of the mist above, and the pilots took turns pouring gunfire into the Fokker.

Göring staged a grim but losing battle for fully fifteen minutes, and only through amazing luck did he stay airborne. His machine was riddled and he received a bullet through his thigh. With that he went neck-or-nothing for his own back area and managed to land a short distance from an emergency hospital where immediate treatment saved his life, but he had an eight-inch scar to remember the event for as long as he lived.

He returned to the front by May and on one of his early flights his friend Bruno Loerzer was able to repay Hermann for saving his life several months before. Engaging a flight of Spads, Hermann had his propeller shot away, and Bruno came to his rescue, enabling him to land safely at an advance airdrome.

By the end of that May, Hermann Göring had scored seven victories, and late in June was given command of Jasta 27 that was made up of fledgling pilots straight from flying school. He led this new element into action at once, and two of his pilots scored victories, but Hermann had to wait for three days before he added to his score. On this occasion he led his ten-plane flight toward Arras where he encountered a small formation of British Nieuports. Putting up a signal, Göring went down with one of his birds behind him. The others stayed aloft to watch. Göring was soon in trouble with a Nieuport that was shooting him to pieces, but he managed finally to turn the tables and with a lucky burst disable the Englishman's engine and force him to spiral down into the German lines. The vanquished foe was Lieutenant F. D. Slee of Number 1 Squadron, R.F.C.

A week later Göring's score reached ten. He encountered a formation of Fees and Camels over Cambrai well inside his own lines. He downed one of the two-seaters, at which point five Sopwiths attacked him and his seven Albatri. A burst of incendiary bullets torched one Albatros and Göring retaliated by downing a Camel. When another element of Camels surged in Göring took his flight home.

By the end of that year, 1917, Hermann Göring had been credited with sixteen kills, but 1918 started ominously. On January 1 he took on an F.E.2b near Moorslede, but the British gunner made a colander of Hermann's gas tank, and then followed him down as he spun earthward. Only the timely arrival of two other Albatri from his own squadron saved him. The F.E. was shot down in flames.

While leading a flight of five machines, early in February, Göring was attacked by two Sop Camels, and one of his pilots was shot down before he knew what was going on. One of the attackers then selected him, and Göring stated later, "Never in all my years of experience had I met such an adversary!" His Albatros was riddled from prop to rudder and he agreed that it was more by luck than skill that he finally put a burst into the Camel's cockpit. The Sopwith dived to earth near the German second line, and when the pilot was extricated from the wreckage it was found that he had received seven bullets in his head and chest. The victim was Lieutenant W. B. Craig who had been credited with five victories.

During May two more enemy machines fell before Göring's guns, and on June 24 he scored a double to bring his score to twenty-one and with it the award of the Pour le Mérite. On July 8, 1918, Göring was appointed commanding officer of the Von Richthofen Squadron, a promotion that enraged many Circus aces who had double the number of Hermann's victories. The new commander took no notice of the dissension and was soon ruling with an iron hand. All signs of jealousy and unrest disappeared as if by magic. Ten days after his appointment Göring led his Circus against a formation of Spads and downed one for his twenty-second and last victory.

❊

After the Armistice Göring went to Sweden and became a pilot with an air transport company. Later he returned to Germany where he met Adolf Hitler. The rest of his story is tragic, bloody history.

HEINRICH GONTERMANN

Probably one of the greatest pilots developed by the Imperial Air Service, and unquestionably the finest marksman among the list of German aces, was Heinrich Gontermann, a young Westphalian farm youth whose victory score of thirty-nine Allied aircraft included eighteen balloons. How far he might have gone had he not been killed while testing a new Fokker triplane is interesting to consider.

The son of a farmer, Gontermann was born in Siegen in 1896. He had a limited schooling, and joined the German Army at age fifteen. When the war broke out he was a trooper with the 6th Uhlan Regiment. He soon applied for admittance to the air service, but did not receive a transfer until late 1915. He went through the usual routine of learning to fly both Albatros and Roland two-seaters.

While serving at the front he showed rare skill and courage, willingly taking on Allied scouts in any number, and usually escaping scot-free by his amazing ability in stunting. One time he took on four Sopwith Pups, and after tangoing all over the sky in his lumbering two-seater he finally put a burst of five bullets into one and shot it down.

During inclement weather Gontermann spent his time studying enemy planes and working out their blind spots. As a result he could maneuver to within point-blank range where one burst generally was enough to finish the opposition. Using this trick and his skill at stunting, Heinrich Gontermann scored five kills within three weeks. Pups, F.E.2bs, and Sopwith two-seaters were his special dish, but on March 24, 1916, he was outstunted by a British Spad and had to land his Albatros behind the German lines. Why he wasn't killed in that one-sided combat was a mystery.

The next day Gontermann was up over Cambrai where two Sop Strutters took him on. He made but one snap-burst, but it was enough. One of the two-seaters went down in flames. His burst had caught the fuel tank, setting a tremendous explosion.

During "Bloody April" of 1917 Gontermann scored his eighteenth victory, for he had been retrained to fly single-seaters. On the strength of his stunting ability he was moved along to Jasta 5, and the following August saw him blazing his mark across the skies of the Western Front when he was credited with thirteen kills, most of them kite balloons. But from the point of view of true air combat his display in April had been his most outstanding.

His balloon-bursting actually began when he downed two in the Armentières sector. The next day he scored again, and was given command of Max Reinhold's Jasta 15, Reinhold having been killed by a French Spad pilot. While capable and satisfactory in his period of command, Gontermann did not possess the ability to make friends. He was officious, overbearing, and distrustful of any opinion other than his own.

He continued to score, however, and with his twentieth victim was awarded the Pour le Mérite, which by that time seemed to come up with the rations any time a German pilot reached the magical "twenty." Gontermann was sent on a brief tour of recruiting for the Imperial Air Service, but had to return hurriedly when it was learned that most of his Staffel had been wiped out. Picking out one of the few available planes left, Heinrich went aloft and shot down a French Spad.

In the next three weeks four more balloons fell before his guns, but by this time his Staffel was so badly cut up it had to be withdrawn from the front for a rest and a refit. They were not back in action until August 12. A few days before, however, Gontermann was flying on his own and shot down a balloon near Verdun. On heading for a second one he discovered that the observer had been supplied with a machine gun, for bullets buzzed all round him. He darted about and finally put a snap-burst into the basket, killing the French observer. Another burst torched the bag.

Three days later Gontermann returned to this same area and on this occasion he learned that his enemies had prepared a special welcome for him. He found one bag and his first burst made it smoke and cause the observer to dive overboard. Then suddenly three Spads nosed down for his tail and Heinrich had a fierce fight on his hands. But again his skill as a stunt pilot served him well. One of the Spads was shot down and the others gave up the quest.

On August 18 the same French balloon line furnished two more targets, and both went down, bringing Gontermann's score to thirty. Two days later he staged his greatest show, booking four victories during one lone patrol. This time he tackled the British balloon line near Soissons, and so flashy was his opening attack two observers in the first basket were killed and going down under their flaming bags without having seen this avenging Albatros. Continuing on, Gontermann downed two more with little trouble. Then a French pilot, noting the smoke and flame of the burning balloons, moved in to intercept. Gontermann waited calmly, did two quick turns, and then put twelve bullets into the body of the Frenchman.

When his score had reached thirty-six it was evident that the strain was beginning to tell. He was tired, irritable, and in no shape to command his Staffel, so he was sent home for a month's rest. He returned to the front on September 24, but his leave apparently had had little effect for he was still irritable, unfriendly, and sleeping badly. On his first flight after his return he damaged his Albatros with a bad landing. On September 29 a British Camel pilot out-stunted Germany's aerobatic star and sent him home with twenty-seven bullets in his aircraft. On October 1, however, some of his old skill and verve returned, and during a melee involving seven Albatros scouts and five Sopwith Camels he shot the tail off one Camel and sent another down in flames. Two days later he destroyed his thirty-ninth and last victim.

Heinrich Gontermann went to Berlin on leave and during that time put in a bid for one of the new Fokker triplanes, a mount Tony Fokker had copied from the Sopwith triple-winger. One of these planes, Dr.I Number 115/17, was delivered to his field. Gontermann, of course, insisted on making the first trial flight aboard it. The fateful day was October 29, 1917.

The new Fokker was drawn out of the hangar early in the morning and Gontermann took it aloft, knowing everyone expected him to stage a show of stunting. At about 1500 feet he began a series of test maneuvers, including a couple of loops, when those below saw the triplane suddenly whip into a steep dive. Parts began to break away, and then the whole top wing buckled. The new Fokker crashed less than five yards from where it had taken off.

Gontermann was still alive when removed from the wreckage but the best available medical attention was not enough. He died within twenty-four hours. It was reported later that he had suffered severe head injuries from contact with the breeches of the machine guns. But for this he might have survived. It was admitted that this particular model did have a weak wing structure that had to be strengthened before it could be used on the front. The Fokker triplane was not used widely or respected outside of the Richthofen Circus, and only 320 were built.

MAX IMMELMANN

The self-styled Eagle of Lille was Germany's bad boy of the war skies. Arrogant and self-assured, Max Immelmann became the subject of more phony credits than any airman on the Western Front. For instance, he was credited with dropping the first bomb on Paris in September 1914, a time when he was not a member of the German Air Service. Later, a simple reverse maneuver was credited to him, and in some quarters is still known as the Immelmann turn. This "stunt" was known to European aeronauts and was seen in the early air shows before World War I broke out.

Max Immelmann was born in Dresden in 1890. On his fourteenth birthday he entered the Dresden Cadet Corps where he rose to the rank of ensign in an engineer regiment. He was a brilliant mathematician and a first-class mechanic, but was in the same category as Hermann Göring in regard to deportment and military discipline. He was so dissatisfied with the Army he resigned his commission in 1912, feeling the service had no technical future for him. From all accounts the Army was glad to be rid of him.

But with the outbreak of the war Max was mobilized at once and ordered to report to his old regiment, but before leaving home he put in for a transfer to the Aviation Service. He had no intention of becoming a pilot. It was the mechanical features of aircraft that appealed to him. His transfer papers came through in November 1914 and he was told to report to the Aldershof Flying School. He was surprised to learn he had been selected for flight training, rather than aviation engineering.

Immelmann survived more than the usual number of training-school crashes, and with some limited experience was sent to Section 10, located at Vitry. Shortly after his arrival he crashed a brand-new L.V.G., and two days later, after picking up another one from an aircraft park he brought it in and scattered it all over the airdrome.

His published history is confusing, for some historians say he was a natural pilot and marked by unusual coordination, but others claim he was a ham-fisted performer who couldn't be trusted with a wheelbarrow. Apparently he had some service influence behind him, for he was retained and by May 1915 when his squadron was moved up to Douai he had corrected most of his piloting faults.

At Douai, this abstemious vegetarian, who roistered more wildly than an inebriated seaman, attracted the attention of Oswald Boelcke. Immelmann ignored all the concepts of teamwork, formation flying—and the niceties of social behavior. He was more of a liability than an asset to his squadron for a considerable time. While carrying out a photography patrol on June 3 he and his observer were downed by the gunner aboard an old Henri Farman. The ignition system of his engine had been shot away and he had to land in a nearby field, but, to the astonishment of his comrades, Max was awarded the Iron Cross, Second Class, "for bringing his aircraft down safely." The citation also made a reference to his coolness under fire.

Shortly after this incident Tony Fokker arrived at the Douai airfield with two new Eindekkers that carried his synchronized gun. Boelcke and Immelmann were given a one-hour course in handling the machine and its mechanism. As explained before, Max scored the first victory credited to this winged weapon, and received the Iron Cross, First Class, for his display. He did not score again until September, which confounds the general impression that both Boelcke and Immelmann went on a killing spree from the day Fokker delivered his first two Eindekkers. Immelmann scored on September 9 and 21, but on September 23 was caught napping again by the gunner of a Farman two-seater. In this instance the Frenchman shot away Max's undercarriage, riddled the engine, and put nine slugs through the fuel tank. How Immelmann survived this hail of lead is one of the puzzles of the air war, but he was a doughty type and was soon back in action, downing a B.E.2c near Lille. While flying over Arras he suddenly encountered a British biplane as he swept out of a thin cloud bank. The R.F.C. machine went down before the observer could fire a shot. On November 7 Max downed another B.E.2c, and on December 5 torched a Morane, bringing his score up to seven in about six months.

It can be seen that the "secret" of the front-firing gun was woefully exploited. Its surprise factor was utterly wasted when the machine was placed in the hands of a few ambitious pilots of the Boelcke Staffel, just as the surprise factor was dissipated in the careless introduction of poison gas, the armored tank, the flame-thrower, and the mine galleries bored under the enemy trenches. Had the Germans first organized a complete wing or group of these early Fokkers and trained a special corps of destroyer pilots in the use of the weapon, the effect might have been devastating. As it was, the synchronized gun was wasted, and the Allies knew of it within a few days after Boelcke first flew the new machine. Most certainly no German airman employed the front-firing gun as efficiently as had Roland Garros who destroyed five enemy planes in seventeen days.

Actually, only a few German airmen trusted the Fokker E-I, despite its superior armament, and most of them switched their preference to the new Halberstadt D-I that appeared in February 1916, or to the Albatros D-I that came along a short while later. Few historians explain that the Fokker E-I was quickly matched by the Nieuport with its fixed top-wing gun, and the D.H.2 that needed no interrupter gear of any kind.

Immelmann enjoyed considerable popularity when he went on leave, and Tony Fokker cultivated him and saw to it that he was the first to get one of his new two-gun models, and later produced for Max's special use a three-gun machine, sometimes known as the Eindekker-IV, a mount that looked remarkably like the French Morane-Saulnier monoplane.

There were many "unofficial" complaints about these multi-gun models, most of them valid, though some of the objections were initiated by other German aircraft manufacturers. In particular they argued that the Oberursel rotary engine was not worthy of a military plane, being nothing more than an uninspired copy of the French Le Rhône. In fact, the Germans never produced a rotary comparable to the Le Rhône, Clerget, or Bentley engines. Fokker's gun gear was also criticized, with some justification. It was pointed out that many propellers *were* being pierced by bullets, even when the Eindekker carried but one Spandau weapon, and it was predicted publicly there would be dire results if these scouts ever carried two or three guns.

Starry-eyed with the adulation that was showered on him, Max made the most of his popularity, and when Fokker suggested that three fixed guns might increase his score, Max jumped at the idea.

On April 16, 1916, he took the latest Eindekker aloft and tried out its three guns. The mechanical interrupter gear was not selective enough to control three weapons, and Immelmann's prop disappeared in a pattern of splinters. The engine ran wild and almost tore itself out of the bearers.

And so the Eagle of Lille, as he was being headlined, had to be content with a two-gun mount, but even with this precaution he was destined for mishaps. On May 31 he "shot himself down" while attacking a British bomber formation when his guns ran amok and ripped his propeller to shreds. One chunk flew back and tore a gash in his flying helmet.

The month of June saw the opening of the Battle of Verdun, and the German High Command sent a special squadron of these fixed-gun fighters down to that front. Boelcke must have had something to do with this decision, but instead of leading this new fighter command, he was sent on an inspection of German airdromes, and Immelmann was selected to take his place. From all accounts, the general plan was not completed immediately, so Immelmann went off hunting whenever he could find the time.

On June 18 he took off with a Sergeant Prehn, and two brothers named Heinemann. They met four Fees of Number 25 Squadron R.F.C., and one manned by Lieutenants Robinson and Savage went down under the concentrated fire of the three Fokkers, but Corporal J. H. Waller, aerial gunner for Lieutenant G. R. McCubbin proved to be Immelmann's nemesis. Just out of the trenches, and a skilled machine gunner, Corporal Waller had little respect for these Fokkers. His first burst killed Immelmann immediately, and the Fokker went down like a dart, and then broke up under the strain. All these facts, the time brackets, and details have been confirmed by the R.F.C., and antiaircraft gunners in that area.

The Germans immediately put out a different version, for they did not like to admit that an aerial gunner aboard a pusher Fee could so easily destroy one of their two-gun Fokkers. It was announced officially that Max Immelmann had again shot off his propeller, that the engine ran wild and tore itself free of its bearers, and with that the Fokker air-frame began to disintegrate.

Today, Max Immelmann lies buried beneath a great statue in Dresden. His remains were taken there in 1928, and the inscription on the statue reads, *Immelmann, der Adler von Lille*. No one explains the reference to Lille, although Max was born in Dresden and did most of his war flying out of Douai.

BRUNO LOERZER

A long-time companion of Hermann Göring, Bruno Loerzer was never as popular, or so widely publicized. He was never included among the Prussian elite when special events were being arranged. He was simply an ex-farmer turned airman who admittedly hoped the Aviation Service would add prestige to his colorless existence. As early as 1913 he joined an engineer regiment, and his being selected for pilot training reads like a comedy of errors. He had made his first flight on a dare, and later when volunteers were sought for aviation training he put his name down, thinking he was volunteering for a card tournament to be held at a nearby officers' mess. We have told how he progressed through the two-seater squadrons, always trailed by Göring, but after several months on the Lorraine front as a two-seater leader, Bruno was relieved, and told to form a fighter Staffel of his own.

He began this task in January 1917, and the first man he selected was Göring, his brother Fritz Loerzer, known as the Flying Pastor, was second, and Walter Blume, another veteran, was third. This squadron was eventually built up to strength with Albatros fighters and became known as Jagdstaffel 26. They fought so well under Loerzer's leadership that Manfred von Richthofen is said to have urged Bruno to adopt some special squadron marking. This seemed to be the thing to do in the German service; to be identified as a unit upon which all other German fliers could depend.

Not too enthusiastic about the idea, Loerzer finally put it up to his pilots. Walter Blume, a chess player, reminded Bruno that he had trained his men to fight with their heads and always to fly one thought ahead of their opponents. Why not select a chessboard for an insignia? This seemed to satisfy everyone. The design had a certain dignity, and could be recognized at a good distance, so it was painted on the sleek sides of their Albatros machines. In fact, Jagdstaffel 26 became known as the Chessboards. Loerzer further capitalized on the idea by devising moves on chess strategy. His pilots were taught to be far-sighted, daring, and quick to open fire at the right time—and retreat when victory had been attained. He stressed above all that victories alone were not real evidence of success, but could be justified only against the right proportion of losses. This was a point Von

Richthofen missed during his whole career. The Baron was extremely upset when losses piled up, but he never developed a defensive policy.

❊

The area around Arras provided a hundred combat situations. One time a British D.H.2 patrol was flying above a cloud layer unaware of the Chessboards. They were watching the upper sky, and were completely off guard when Loerzer's Jagdstaffel 26 zoomed through a rift in the layer to riddle the de Havillands from below. The leader went down with a shattered propeller; another curled out of the formation with his engine smoking badly; three others dived for the security of the cloud below to evade this unorthodox attack. From that day on a signal went out along the British lines, "Watch out for those Huns flying Chessboard-design Albatroses!"

Loerzer downed his fourth victim in that skirmish, and added four more over the next two weeks. In quick succession he received the Iron Cross and the new Order of the House of Hohenzollern, and by midsummer had twelve planes to his credit.

All through 1917 bitter air fighting was the lot of those who were with active-service squadrons. The ground forces were locked in deadly combat, struggling for Passchendaele, and the Third Battle of Ypres was to open on July 31. A new air offensive was released in which the British lost but 217 aircraft while downing nearly 500 black-crossed planes. The new Sop Camel, the S.E.5, and the Bristol Fighter had more than taken the initiative.

The Chessboards flew all through that offensive, and before the year was ended Loerzer had brought down twenty planes. Early in 1918 he was awarded the Pour le Mérite and given command of a complete flying Circus. Promoted to first lieutenant, he finished the war with Jagdgeschwader 3, having run his victories up to forty-five. His organization was among the last to disintegrate under the final thrust of September 1918. When it was all over Loerzer and his arrogant companion Hermann Göring were left to wonder about their doubtful future.

Bruno Loerzer took a job in a German aircraft factory, and retained his interest in flying. When Hermann Göring became Minister of Aviation Bruno was given the rank of colonel, and is said to have developed the cooperation technique between aircraft and armored vehicles, so well displayed in World War II. He was made president of the Air-Sport League which was only a ruse to train military pilots. By 1938 Loerzer was a general, and eventually took command of one of the air fleets that led the initial attack on Poland. Later he was involved in the Battle of Britain and became Göring's Chief of Staff.

When Germany was defeated Loerzer was among the Nazi leaders interrogated by Allied officials, but he was cleared of any war atrocities, and he finally went into business. He died on August 22, 1960.

ERICH LOEWENHARDT

One of Germany's most interesting aviation personalities, ignored for years by historians, was Erich Loewenhardt who downed fifty-four Allied planes before meeting a fate as tragic as that which engulfed Oswald Boelcke.

Loewenhardt was born in 1897 in Breslau. At the outbreak of war he was enrolled in the Lichtfelder Cadet School, and was immediately posted to Groudez with the 141st Infantry on the Eastern Front. Before the conflict was a month old he had received his first wound, but he remained with his battalion all through the Battle of Tannenberg, and in reward for his gallantry was promoted to lieutenant.

In October he was given command of a company of ski troops that were to fight valiantly in the Carpathians, and in January 1915 he was awarded the Iron Cross, First Class, and transferred later to the Austro-German Alpine Corps for service in the Dolomites. He took part later in the advance through Serbia. During this latter campaign, Loewenhardt contracted a fever and was sent home, unfit for active service. He was nineteen years old at the time, and after five months of convalescence he applied for and received a transfer to the Aviation Service. He passed through the training schools in record time, proving to be so skilled a pilot he was posted in July 1917 to Jagdstaffel 10 of the newly formed J.G.1, the Richthofen Geschwader.

Very little is known of his early flying days, but it would seem he first scored against an Allied kite balloon. On August 14 he selected an R.E.8 and sent it down near Zillebeke. On September 5 he was among a formation that attacked a flight of Sop Camels. Loewenhardt destroyed one, and four days later downed another balloon that was up over Wevelgem.

On September 20 a lone Camel made an attack on a nearby air-drome inflicting casualties on several men and machines. A flock of Circus planes took off and ran into a large formation of Camels over Roulers. Loewenhardt was boxed in by five Britishers and received a slight wound in one shoulder, but he was aloft again the next morning and on this occasion downed another balloon.

Early in November, Erich Loewenhardt had a very close shave when he was flying over Saint-Eloi and was under heavy attack from two mobile antiaircraft guns. One shell which failed to explode tore off a large section of his left wingtip and his plane fell in an uncontrolled spin. He was less than fifty feet from the ground when he at last gained control, but he did hit hard, turned over twice and finished in a hedge. He was badly shaken but miraculously unhurt.

By the beginning of 1918 Loewenhardt had run his score up to eight, and early in that January triumphed over a Bristol Fighter, and downed still another balloon. After Baron von Richthofen had passed out of the picture, Erich began to cut loose and show his true ability as a fighter pilot. He took on everything and anything. In June 1918 his squadron was transferred to the French front where it had a field day. Between June 1 and June 8 no less than forty French machines fell before the guns of Geschwader 1, and Loewenhardt became the top man of Germany's surviving aces.

August 1918 saw the beginning of the end for the German Air Service. The Allies were breaking through at all points of the line. Fuel and ammunition stocks were very low, and British scout fighters were everywhere. The Bristol Fighters were mopping up German airdromes every hour on the hour of daylight. Still, Loewenhardt continued to score, and Berlin began to wonder if this youngster would pass the renowned Von Richthofen before the end came.

Shortly before midday of August 10, Staffel 10 joined with Staffel 4 to take on a swarm of S.E.5s that were orbiting over the town of Chaulnes. Erich gave the signal to attack just as several more planes from Staffel 11 joined the fray. One of these pilots, a Lieutenant Wentz, nosed down on an S.E.5 just as Erich had made his move. The left wheel of Wentz's Fokker D-VII tore through Erich's upper wing, and the two planes were locked together for a few seconds. Then, the upper plane's wheel tore loose, and both machines started to fall. Both pilots took to their new Heineke parachutes that had been available since the middle of 1917. These were packed in a bag that was fastened to the pilot's shoulders. A release cord ran from the parachute and was attached to a snaffel inside the cockpit. All a pilot had to do was breathe a prayer—and jump.

By a strange freak of luck Wentz landed safely, but Loewenhardt plummeted to earth, his unopened parachute trailing behind him.

WILHELM REINHARD

This German ace who is credited with twenty victories scored on many fronts, is probably best known as the man who succeeded Von Richthofen to command the Richthofen Circus, after the Red Knight had been downed inside the British lines. Apart from that, he was like so many others of that famous group, always eclipsed by the high-pressure publicity of his leader.

Reinhard was born in 1892. He was a commissioned officer in a Prussian Artillery Regiment when war broke out. He was slightly wounded in Belgium, and by July 1915 was transferred to the Air Service. He first put in time on the Verdun front as an observer for Section 205. He spent more than a year on important reconnaissance missions, and then by August 1916 was sent to Darmstadt to be trained as a pilot.

From this time on Reinhard's war career reads like a chapter from *Baedeker's Handbook for Travelers*. In October 1916 he was flying L.V.G. two-seaters over the swamps of Salonika. From there he went to Russia, after which he joined an Albatros C-III squadron stationed in northern Italy about March 1917. Two months later he was back on the Western Front with Flying Section 28, but before he had time to learn where to put his personal belongings, he was sent to Germany to a flying school and made an instructor. He performed so well there with the almost obsolete equipment, he was returned once more to the Western Front to join the newly formed Richthofen Jagdgeschwader 1, which at the time was flying Albatros D-Vs.

Reinhard's first victory was scored when he downed a Sopwith 1½-Strutter that had to land with a shattered propeller. Willy, as he was known to his comrades, had trouble confirming this kill since two other pilots claimed to have fired the telling burst. The decision was made by Baron von Richthofen who was positive Reinhard was most deserving of the victory.

There was an amusing sequel to this incident. The pilot and observer of the Sopwith were captured, and when they were interviewed by Reinhard the pilot claimed to have destroyed seventeen German planes, and the gunner added that he had downed no less than fourteen. Willy put all this down in his report of the fight, but in his excitement at having vanquished such doughty opponents, forgot to include their names. It would be interesting to know who had been "pulling Reinhard's leg," for no Sopwith 1½-Strutter crew ever ran up such a score.

A workmanlike airman, Willy's score increased day by day. On August 13 he "shot the wings" off a Camel, and within twenty-four hours had added two more Allied ships to his record. One was another Sopwith 1½-Strutter, and the second a Spad that had been in the escort party. His next victim was an R.E.8 that broke up over Bixschoote, and then he downed another Camel on September 1.

This September was a most unlucky one for Staffel 11, for the British killed Kurt Wolff—a very promising airman—and Bocklemann, G. W. Gross, and Reinhard were wounded. While engaged with nine Camels over Houthulst Forest, Willy suffered a serious thigh wound and just managed to land his machine before fainting.

Reinhard was not back in action until late November when he was appointed to command Staffel 6, but did not add to his score until the new year, 1918. On January 4 he tangled with a Bristol Fighter, and after a long, hard fight sent it down in flames. In February two more Brisfits fell before his guns, and on March 27 he overcame an R.E.8 near Mourcourt to register his tenth victory.

When Manfred von Richthofen was killed on April 21 an examination of his papers revealed that he left an order for Willy Reinhard to take command of the Richthofen Geschwader. Thus, even after death the Baron's word was law; the Imperial Air Service confirmed the appointment. All of which makes one wonder what would have happened in the British or American air services had a wing commander drawn up a will designating the successor to his command. But the Baron could do no wrong, and as they had idealized him as the leading figure in their service, they had to go along with this policy.

As it turned out, Reinhard was not a good leader. He could instill no discipline and was no judge of men. He allowed all kinds of would-be heroes to join the Circus, for he was not particular about who moved in to replace experienced pilots, and casualties were alarmingly high in the next two weeks. H. Weiss and E. Scholz of Staffel 11 went down, a Lieutenant Just was seriously wounded, and two others were reported missing.

The Circus moved south to the French front where things became easier, and through the month of June no less than seventy victories were claimed. Reinhard himself destroyed seven machines in thirteen days. Although he had downed the same number on the British front, those victories had taken him seven months. Over this period in June he lost two of his best pilots, one of them a Lieutenant Rautter (?) who had been credited with fifteen victories.

Early in June Reinhard's outfit encountered a large formation of Spad single- and two-seaters. The two-seaters, known as the XI-A2, were inferior types and they had little trouble in downing four of them. Willy was credited with one, but before the kill was completed the gunner put a burst into his Fokker triplane, cutting a fuel line and perforating the instrument panel. Loewenhardt moved in and made certain his leader would have protection on the way back, and Willy managed to guide his damaged Fokker toward home, reaching safety just as his engine quit cold. When he touched down the undercarriage buckled, and it was found that the Frenchman had severed the spreader bar.

Later that day Reinhard took his flight back into French territory and found another formation of Spads that were backed up by some Breguets. Willy downed another Spad two-seater and later claimed a second, after a long chase. In the first two weeks of June Willy's score climbed to twenty, and then on June 18, after the last German offensive had fizzled out, he and Hans Kirchstein were ordered to attend an aircraft-testing session at Aldershof, Berlin. These two airmen spent a pleasant week helping select new planes, and then on July 3 Willy expressed a desire to fly a Friedrichshafen D-2A quadruplane that had been in the course of development for many months. This machine was expected to outclass the Fokker D-VII, but when Reinhard tested it the top wing broke away, the fuselage buckled, and he was thrown out. He was equipped with a parachute, but again the device refused to open, and Reinhard died, leaving the Richthofen Circus in the hands of—of all people—Hermann Göring.

MANFRED von RICHTHOFEN

During the early weeks of the war in 1914 a young lieutenant of the 1st Uhlan Regiment was riding at the head of his troop six miles from the German-Russian front. On the morning of August 3 they entered a Russian village near Kielce, and Lieutenant Richthofen went to the front door of a low wooden building and banged imperiously on the portal with the butt of his riding crop. A tall man in black robes responded to his knock. The young officer clicked his heels and said, "Father, I inform you that war has been declared between Germany and your country. Your village is now occupied and surrounded by my men. At the first sign of hostility from your villagers you will be executed, and I shall take such measures as are necessary for the protection of the men under my command, and the proper pacification of the inhabitants."

Five days later this officious young man's force was trapped and ambushed by a patrol of Cossacks. Von Richthofen was asleep in bed when his orderly roused him, and on looking out the window Richthofen saw at least thirty Russian cavalrymen, so he scurried out a rear door and raced to a nearby field where two of his men had horses waiting. Two days later his tattered party crept into a German garrison town and erased their names from a list of German soldiers "wiped out by the Cossacks." His squadron was mentioned in the next official communiqué, withdrawn from the Russian front and sent to France.

Manfred von Richthofen was born in 1892, and his brother Lothar who also became a noted German ace was born two years later. After his experience on the Russian front Manfred lost all interest in the cavalry and especially in horses. He made several attempts to transfer to the Air Service. He did not seem to have immediate pilot potential, so he was trained first as an observer, and by May 1915 was serving with Section 7 near Cologne, and later joined a like unit on the Eastern Front. By August of the same year he was with a two-engined bomber squadron based at Ostend, but this work did not interest him, and he next managed a transfer to a two-seater squadron where he is supposed to have downed a French Farman, but the victory was never confirmed.

Later that year Manfred met the incomparable Oswald Boelcke, and after friendly discussion with him, was determined to fly as a pilot. From all accounts he was not too good, for he required more than twenty dual-control, instruction flights before he went aloft solo. He gradually gained some skill and during the Battle of Verdun was permitted to pilot a two-seater reconnaissance plane. During this period he mounted a machine gun on the top wing of his Albatros, *à la* French Nieuport style, and soon claimed to have shot down a Nieuport, but again, this was never confirmed.

Up to this point Richthofen's career was spotty and undistinguished. He was given a few flights on a Fokker single-seater, but apparently impressed no one, for he was soon back on the Russian front flying two-seaters on bombing raids. It was during this tour of duty that Boelcke again met the young Prussian nobleman, and on this occasion decided to "invite" him to join his Staffel. Whether Von Richthofen's skill as an airman, or his Prussian background had impressed Boelcke has not been clearly defined. At any rate it was soon evident that the Baron was one of the elect and destined for better things.

So much has been written to delineate Von Richthofen's long victory list, further elaboration would be repetitious. He was credited with eighty kills during his eighteen months with the Flying Circus. This score is accepted generally, although, as has been pointed out time and time again, twenty-one of his successes have never been confirmed, although all records impounded at the German Archives have been carefully examined. Sixty of the machines claimed are fully confirmed because the names of the pilots or observers were produced. Twenty others were not clearly identified, and as practically all of Von Richthofen's victims were shot down in his own area, there should have been some way to identify the machine or the crew.

Baron von Richthofen's career has always attracted two distinct groups of interested readers. One accepts everything that has been credited to him, never questioning his score; the other refuses to believe anything in his favor, arguing he was a manufactured hero and that many machines that make up his score should have been credited to his companions. This group also claims that if there was any question about who had shot down any aircraft in battle the credit was always given to the Baron. Some British airmen hated his name and argued that he was a Prussian phony; the French ignored him completely. Some Royal Flying Corps pilots have written ecstatic pages lauding his skill, courage, and noble character and behavior. Some were joyful when it was reported that he had been shot down —particularly Mickey Mannock. Others solemnly penned sincere regrets and dropped wreaths on German airdromes to show their respect. It must be remembered, of course, that by late April 1918 it was obvious that Germany had lost the war, and that the sporting spirit of the British was bubbling to the surface. They were more than willing to show their true feelings under these circumstances, but it must also be remembered that no such response was made by the

Germans when on July 9, 1918, Major James Byford McCudden, RAF, was killed on the Western Front.

It is agreed generally that Von Richthofen was an arrogant disciplinarian who rode roughshod over all his inferiors. He had no compassion, no sense of humor, but lived and died the overbearing Prussian of song and story. Nevertheless, he has remained a legendary figure, an accepted hero, and the idol of the widespread group of American hobbyists who collect memorabilia of World War I.

✻

By comparison Lothar von Richthofen, the Baron's younger brother, was an attractive young man. He was credited with forty victories, and from all accounts was a far more skillful pilot than his illustrious brother. He transferred from the cavalry in May 1916, and by November of that year had taken part in thirty-eight bombing raids. Later, when he had asked for single-seater training, he amazed the Baron who was on hand to see him fly his first solo flight, for he put on a finished performance, whereas the Baron in his first solo flight aboard a Fokker crashed it in a most ungainly display.

Lothar was always overshadowed by his titled brother, and strangely enough his logbook is most puzzling in spots. It shows that on March 13, 1917, he downed an R.E.8 and an F.E.2b, yet in a letter to their mother, dated March 25, the Baron stated that Lothar was doing well but had yet to register his first victory. We can also look back in an earlier chapter to his claim of having downed Albert Ball. Flat on his back in a hospital Lothar was asked to write out a report of the fight, and Ball was officially listed as his twenty-second victim, despite the fact that he had identified Ball's S.E.5 as a Sopwith triplane and incorrectly stated the date on which the fight was supposed to have taken place.

After being shot down by a Sopwith Camel Lothar was again in a hospital when the Armistice was signed. By 1922 Germany was beginning to emerge as an air-transport power, and Lothar was selected to be a pilot aboard one of their Junkers airliners. On July 4, 1922, he was piloting a plane chartered by an American film actress and her manager on a trip from Hamburg to Berlin. The machine was a converted bomber, and when halfway to its destination the engine failed, and the aircraft tangled with an electric cable. Lothar was killed, but his two passengers were pulled out, though seriously injured.

EDUARD von SCHLEICH

In 1932 Hauptmann von Schleich, another German baron credited with thirty-five victories, accepted an invitation from a representative group of British fliers to visit England and meet some of his old adversaries. The author was in London at the time and saved a number of newspaper items that related this unusual occasion.

In his speech before these ex-R.F.C. airmen Baron von Schleich stated: "At last my dreams have been realized, and I have met your 'knights of the air' on terra firma. I have met the pilots in the flesh and blood who dived and spun and flirted with death in those well-remembered machines, each of which seemed to reflect the individual characteristics of the brain that guided it. Within twenty-four hours we have become fast friends. I pledge myself to do my utmost to continue this band of peace for as long as I live."

Seven years later Von Schleich was a Nazi commander, heading Jagdgeschwader 132, and working with Hitler and Göring in their plans to enslave Europe and the rest of the free world. He had become one of the earliest members of the Nazi party and a determined worker in the infamous S.S. (Blackshirts).

Von Schleich was termed "The Black Knight" in the First World War by the authorities who dispensed such appellations in the German Air Service. He was born near Munich on August 8, 1888. He was soon swept into the military machine, and at age twenty was a member of the 11th Bavarian Infantry Brigade. He had been commissioned in 1908, but saw little action in the early days of the war. Late in August 1914 he was wounded in a shoulder and had to spend several months in a hospital during which time he came to appreciate the social and service advantages of the German flying men. He applied for a transfer, and received training both as a pilot and an observer. By December 1915 he was serving with a two-seater squadron. On one patrol Von Schleich was wounded in an arm by a chunk of ack-ack shell, but he had his observer, Hans Adam, bind up the gash, and he continued on his mission, for which both he and Adam were awarded the Iron Cross, First Class.

Von Schleich put in many months piloting various types of two-seaters, and carried out a wide program of missions.

He apparently was fascinated with highly decorated aircraft and on any pretext would paint one up, and enjoy himself tangoing about the sky in his newest plaything. Once he took a captured Spad, daubed it with an Iron Cross insignia and flew it into a formation of French machines. None of the Spad pilots noticed anything unusual for several minutes, but finally one of them spotted the black crosses and took immediate action. Von Schleich managed to escape, but on flying over one of his own antiaircraft batteries came under heavy fire. He considered himself lucky to reach his own airdrome unscathed.

At another time he did much the same thing with a captured Nieuport, but the German High Command took a dim view of these pointless tricks, and sent him to a special fighter-pilot school, and eventually he joined Jasta 21. While he was there one of his particular friends, Erich Limpert, was shot down by a pack of French Spads. This inspired a new gesture. Von Schleich had his own Albatros painted inky black to mark his friend's loss. According to legend his outfit was for a time known as the Dead Man Squadron, but the black Albatros may account for the nickname of Black Knight that marks him to this day.

The loss of Limpert and Von Schleich's gesture seemed to have sent the Jasta on a victory surge. During September 1917 they downed forty-one Allied aircraft with the Baron accounting for seventeen. A bout of dysentery put Von Schleich in bed for a few days, but, living up to German military tradition, he soon ignored his doctor's orders, got out of bed and headed for the front line. He went on patrol and encountered a flight of Spads, and suffered severe abdominal pain. He shot one down for his twenty-fifth victory, and was fortunate to escape the rest and fly back to his field. On landing he was placed under arrest, confined to his quarters, and forced to submit to proper medical attention.

Once he was fit again the testy Baron was ordered to take a six-week furlough. When he returned he was surprised to learn he had been relieved of his command. Jasta 21 had been given over to a Prussian. It was pointed out that the Baron was only a Bavarian, and thus ineligible to command an All-Prussian Jasta. Later he was given command of Jasta 32, an all-Bavarian outfit, and awarded the Pour le Mérite. Then his stomach trouble returned and he was given light duty—running an instruction school in Schleissheim, and was not at the front again until April 1918.

Von Schleich rose to command Jagdgruppe 8 which was composed of three Jastas, and his score mounted until thirty-five Allied planes had fallen to his guns. Late in October of that fateful year

Von Schleich, like so many others of his skill, was ordered to Berlin to fly new machines in the fighter-plane competition, and by the time he got back to the front the war was over.

Von Schleich escaped being murdered by the Communists by only a hair's breadth. Later, he was attracted to the growing Hitler regime, becoming one of the first members of the party. He organized youth flying movements, and with the creation of the Luftwaffe he once more took up military aviation. On December 11, 1938, he became the first commander of the group that produced Adolf Galland, one of the leading aces of World War II. When last heard of Baron von Schleich was a retired major general of the Luftwaffe. When he was in London in 1932 he said:

I would not call myself a pacifist. That word has a doubtful flavor. I would call myself a *fighter* for peace. To my mind, the nations seem to have spent the best part of the hundred years between Waterloo and Mons in preparing for wars of revenge. Isn't it time they tried to struggle to get reconciled?

ERNST UDET

Another tragic figure in the history of the German Air Service was Ernst Udet who as Chief of the Technical Office of the Luftwaffe ended his life with a pistol on November 17, 1941, thus ridding himself of the taint of Nazism and of the Hitler regime. During World War I when he shot down sixty-two Allied planes he had been a happy-go-lucky character, quite different from most German Air Force types. In his service with the Jagdgeschwader, he provided a continual series of dramatic or amusing episodes that make his career more interesting than that of any other top-flight German airman. The youngest ace in the German service, and the runner-up to the great Von Richthofen, Udet was still considered a playboy by his dour companions.

As did Jimmy McCudden, Ernst Udet fought through every year of the war, but in contrast to the ill-fated Englishman, Udet was more fortunate in that his service provided him with a parachute during the last phase of the war. He was shot down twice, and on both occasions was saved from certain death by this aerial life preserver.

The son of wealthy parents, Ernst Udet was born at Frankfurt am Main on April 26, 1896. A sensitive, artistic boy he developed an interest in flying and built model aircraft before he entered high school. There is one report that he once built a boy-carrying glider, but it is certain that he owned a motorcycle in his early teens and with the outbreak of the war offered himself and his mount for despatch riding. He was so frail he was repeatedly rejected, but eventually the motorcycle won out, and he was attached to a reserve Württemberg division. He was not a skilled rider, and early in the war took a toss and wound up in a hospital with a broken shoulder. His superiors willingly permitted him to transfer to the Aviation Service, hoping to be rid of him.

The Aviation Service also had little use for Ernst, and he was buried in some unimportant job miles behind the line. In his spare time, thanks to his wealthy parents, he took a private flying course and proved to be far better than average as a pilot. As soon as he had soloed he was picked up and sent to Darmstadt where he completed the required training, and he thought he was ready for honor and glory, but there were hundreds of rookie pilots, but few machines to be flown. Udet wound up as a private in a flight battalion where he endured the indignity of manual toil and parade-ground drill. But finally his name sifted to the top of the list and he was sent on a cross-country test of about 200 miles. He invited a friend, a Lieutenant Gerlich, to check his route. He took off across the Rhine and landed at Bonn with no trouble. The two men went into town to register their arrival, but of course they had to strengthen the inner man with beer and baloney. The refreshment session was long and satisfying and when they returned to the field they discovered that one tire of their plane was flat. Neither man was in any condition to make a suitable repair, so Ernst took off both tires and flew the rest of the circuit on the steel rims.

To mark that masterly effort Udet was confirmed a service pilot and sent down to a fairly quiet sector in southern Alsace. During his first flight in the area, he made a showy take-off and completely wrecked the airplane. He was rushed to a hospital, placed under arrest and told that on his recovery he would be cashiered out of the service. Ernst soon talked himself out of that sentence and returned to his squadron.

His second patrol was more encouraging. He had drawn a Lieutenant Justinus as his observer, and over the enemy lines they came upon a French Farman, but Justinus ignored it, knowing the opposition was no more offensive than they were. After almost an hour of observation they turned for home.

Udet's next approach to the enemy lines was almost his last. All the Aviatiks in the area had been ordered to bomb the town of Belfort. Each plane was to carry eight missiles and two Mauser automatic rifles. Shortly after take-off the weather turned bad, and heavy clouds were encountered at 15,000 feet. As their aircraft could fly no higher, the formation was forced to break up. Udet, up front as the leader, gave the order and then as he started his turn something fouled his controls and it was impossible for him to work the machine back to an even keel. It fell off in jerky sideslips, but after some anxious moments, the Aviatik returned to a fairly level position. Udet then noticed a broken control cable that threatened to leave the elevator in a depressed position. He tried to yank it loose, but this only increased the speed of the dive.

At this point, Lieutenant Justinus, who was again acting as his observer, suggested that they try to get down in Switzerland to avoid being taken prisoners by the French. When Udet hesitated the observer left his seat and crawled out on the wing, trying to shift the weight to level the machine. But nothing happened, so Justinus kicked out some fuselage panels, found another elevator cable and pulled and tugged until the nose of the plane came up slightly. By easing back on the throttle Udet was able to maintain a fair amount of control, and they finally landed the Aviatik inside the German lines. Justinus was awarded the Iron Cross, First Class, and Udet the Iron Cross, Second Class.

But greater honors were to come to the youthful Ernst. He was transferred to a new Aviatik squadron, but given a new Fokker fixed-gun fighter with which he was expected to provide air protection for the observation planes. A short time later he had his first real air fight when he came upon a Voisin biplane and opened fire from a range of about 600 yards. The Voisin gunner replied in kind, both men continuing to fire away at this ridiculous distance until they had expended their ammunition. A second encounter had a different ending when Udet met a Caudron and this time moved in closer before opening fire, but his gun jammed and as he attempted to clear the stoppage the Frenchman peppered him generously. He was forced to dive and run for home.

However, victory was over the horizon. He was aloft one day over Colmar when he saw twenty specks heading for Mülhausen. He climbed to escape their notice, and sat it out. Finally, he decided they were a mixed pack of Caudrons and Farmans. When the formation was directly below him he nosed down and fired from about fifty feet. A Farman burst into flames, a spectacle that so fascinated him he forgot about the others until he found himself in the midst of a frantic melee with gunfire streaking in from all directions. This continued until at last a large formation of German planes came to his aid. Thus ensued one of the first dogfights on the French front, and Udet was given the Iron Cross, First Class, for this performance.

Some time after, while returning from the lines, his engine stopped and he made the mistake of selecting a cornfield for his forced landing. The Fokker turned turtle and Ernst was trapped for fifteen minutes. He finally freed himself just before the hulk went up in flames.

Udet took part in the German defense of the Oberndorf munitions works, a target the French and British had been watching for a long while. The first big attack came on March 18, 1916, and when the raiders appeared every German fighter plane in the area took to the air to head them off. Udet, who had become separated from his flight, spotted seven Allied aircraft heading toward the Rhine with two Nieuport scouts flying above them. Then the seven two-seaters below suddenly became twenty-three and Udet hesitated, wondering if a lone Fokker should risk so many guns. Below were well-known towns, houses, hotels, gardens, cafés, and the geometrical pattern of streets. There were a thousand round discs that represented upturned faces. Udet realized he was alone and had every right to await the arrival of his comrades. Years later he wrote that he had been torn between two great emotions, one based on the law of self-preservation, and the other on honor.

"I somehow realized that if I failed to open battle immediately I should never have the courage to do so afterward. In that case I would land, go to my room, and then in the morning my roommate would have the task of writing my father, telling him that there had been a fatal accident while I was cleaning my revolver."

He took the plunge, and opened the most decisive battle of his flying career. He went down on a big Farman nestling in the center of the Allied formation. As he opened his throttle and dived with the engine full on, the bomber spread its wings, seeming to grow in size. For a few seconds he could distinguish every detail, as if examining the machine under a microscope. The observer turned around and Udet could see his leather helmet which became the bull's-eye for his machine gun. He opened fire from a distance of about ninety feet, and the Farman faltered almost immediately. A glaring blue flash stabbed from the exhaust, followed by a plume of white smoke, and Udet knew he had punctured the fuel tank. A second or so later a spatter of enemy machine gun bullets drew his attention away from his victim. Turning sharply, he saw he was under the fire of two Caudron gunners.

He accepted this ordeal with no concern. He was perfectly calm, carrying out the rest of his maneuvers with the poise of a student of advanced aerobatics. Diving once more he caught up with the Farman that by now was roaring across the sky like a giant torch hurled in anger. A figure with outstretched arms and legs was catapulted from the wreckage.

"I never considered that either of the men was a human being. That never occurred to me. I was only conscious of one sensation —victory . . . triumph! The iron band about my chest snapped, and the blood coursed freely through my body. The tension was over. I had been blooded in action," he related afterward.

What happened then was typical of all general engagements. Other German aircraft joined the battle, and other Allied planes were shot down and some German aircraft lost. Ernst Udet did not get another, although he saw and caught up with a laggard Caudron. His gun jammed after he fired a burst into one of its engines. He saw the propeller wigwag to a halt, but the Caudron eventually limped home.

Udet continued to add to his score in Alsace, and by December 1917 was credited with twenty-one victories, and was then transferred to the Aisne sector where he was posted to Jasta 15, commanded by Heinrich Gontermann. He flew the Albatros D-III, and did so well against the stiffer opposition in this sector, he was given command of Jasta 37. On one occasion he was badly mauled by a Bristol Fighter gunner, but just as everything seemed hopeless, the Brisfit exploded in midair, probably from a chunk of antiaircraft shell.

Udet was switched from Jasta to Jasta, mainly to spark their pilots with his wild daring and skill. He was awarded the Pour le Mérite, and invited to fly tail guard to Baron von Richthofen.

During the last few months of the war Udet put in many hours, flying many patrols. In the March Push of 1918 he had a close call after attacking a British B.E.2c. He disposed of the rear gunner and then became careless. The pilot put in a burst that dismembered the Fokker triplane, and Udet, carrying a parachute, went over the side. Apparently the device opened too soon and a portion of the canopy fouled on the plane's rudder and fin. For a minute or so the Fokker whirled in helpless circuits and Udet was slung about on the ends of his shroud lines and harness. The canopy was only partly open, and it looked for a time as though Udet would go down with the whirling wreckage, but fortunately the gunner in the Quirk had so damaged the rudder assembly that the weight of Udet swinging about eventually tore it apart. The parachute floated free and the German ace landed safely.

In August 1918, Ernst, who seemed destined for scrapes and near disasters, was flying a low-level patrol with several other German pilots when a lone Camel came down from above with both guns chattering. Ernst did a tight bank, went into a reverse turn and finally worked his way to the tail of the Britisher. The Camel went into a dive and Ernst followed.

At about a thousand feet the RAF pilot zoomed suddenly and twisted into a tight turn. Udet stuck to his original course, expecting his foe to swerve aside, but determined not to give the German a clean shot the Britisher made a new move and the Fokker and Sopwith collided. There was a terrible crash as Udet's undercarriage crashed into the Camel's wing. For an instant both planes clutched each other, then fell apart gradually with the Camel starting into a tight spin. The Fokker held together and, with rare good luck, Udet put her down in a nearby field. The British pilot finally pulled his damaged plane out of its spin and pancaked the hulk on plowed land.

This was Udet's forty-seventh victory, a very questionable credit and one in which the fortunes of war played the most important role. Had the encounter taken place over the British area, and Udet been forced to land in British territory, the credit would have been reversed.

Weeks later Udet's sixty-second, and final victory, was scored over a British D.H.9 bomber that was heading for Metz. Udet had dispatched another of the same type a few minutes before. This ended the war career of the ranking living German ace, probably one of the most picturesque figures to wear the uniform of the German Air Service. It was tragic that a few years later a man named Adolf Hitler was to emerge from the debacle and sully the glory of so many gallant gentlemen.

WERNER VOSS

It is perhaps appropriate to close this chapter of representative German aces with a profile on Werner Voss, sometimes known as the Hussar of Krefeld, who by all British fliers was considered the bravest man in the German Air Service. He won their complete admiration when he died in a grim, one-sided battle, fighting a full flight of S.E.5 aces of Number 56 Squadron while another flight of Bristol Fighters of Number 22 Squadron circled nearby to make sure he did not escape. This was a typical Voss engagement. He was one of the few German airmen who boldly crossed the British lines and tackled the opposition over its own grounds.

Werner Voss was born on April 13, 1897, and according to some records released before World War II, his parents were Jewish. Later on it seemed expedient to claim that he was sent to the Evangelic Lutheran Church. His father certainly was a German but his mother may have been of the Hebrew religion. Werner's father was a dyer and there was no money to send his son to an expensive military school, so Werner spent some time before the war with a local militia Hussar squadron. When the war broke out his regiment was rushed to the Eastern Front, and by May 1915 he had become a corporal, and awarded the Iron Cross, Second Class.

In September of that year Werner managed a transfer to the Air Service, and showed rare skill as a rookie pilot, so much so in fact, he was retained for a time as an instructor. According to some historians there was some inexplicable stigma attached to being an instructor, completely ignoring the fact that someone had to teach others how to fly. However, hewing to the general line, Voss soon relieved himself of this stain on his logbook and made his way to the front with a two-seater squadron. He arrived on the Somme in time for the great engagement where "slow two-seaters were 'cold meat' for the swift Allied fighters of the period." He managed to live through this, however, and by September 1916 had gained a commission, and was to be groomed as a fighter pilot with Boelcke's Staffel 2. Early in November he downed two Allied planes, beginning his long score of forty-eight enemy aircraft to become the fourth ranking ace in the German Air Service.

Through the early months of 1917 Werner Voss often threatened Manfred von Richthofen's lead in the ace sweepstakes, but whenever he caught up with the Baron's score he was withdrawn from the front or given administrative duties that occupied much of his attention and certainly lessened his keen aggressive skill. This point has always been argued by those who are most ardent admirers of Von Richthofen, but the fact remains that not only Voss was so treated; Karl Allmenroeder and Karl Schaefer were switched about in a like manner.

Werner Voss was a dedicated airman, one of the few who, after carrying out routine patrols with definite missions, would take off again on lone wolf forays in which he usually ranged far and wide over the British lines. He also spent much time in murky overalls working on his plane and its guns alongside his mechanics. He flew in old noncommissioned uniforms and civilian sweaters, but when on the ground, or on leave, he was possibly the best-dressed airman of them all. He wore smart uniforms, all his decorations, and kept his field boots highly polished. Unlike the Von Richthofens, Werner always had an eye for a pretty girl.

His skill in the air was legendary, and his score was made in an amazingly short time. He was master of the flat-spin maneuver, and when the Fokker triplane was made available he took to the new aircraft and made a fetish of his affection for it.

There has long been heated discussion as to what personal design or insignia Voss selected for his various mounts. In some photographs we find he favored an Albatros D-III on which was daubed a candy-box heart, a wreath of flowers, a swastika—which at the time was as acceptable as a primitive ornament or symbol—as well as the official Maltese cross of the service. He also had a Pfalz scout that bore nothing more than the Iron Cross insignia. There has always been an argument as to what personal design Voss selected for his triplane. The least vociferous advocates claim it was painted an oyster white and bore a checkerboard design. Others insist that it was painted a light sky blue and provided with a scarlet nose that was further daubed to give it some tribal god effect. These are matters of high import to hobbyists who are intrigued with such decorative factors of aerial warfare. The author was an aerial gunner aboard a Bristol Fighter the day Voss was brought down, but for the life of him cannot remember what design or color the young German preferred.

On September 23, 1917, Werner's two brothers Otto and Max, also members of the German forces, met on Voss's field and were photographed looking over his equipment. Later that afternoon Werner took off alone aboard his personal triplane and they never saw him alive again.

From all accounts he climbed to 18,000 feet and headed for Ypres. Below he could see six Bristol Fighters that appeared to be escorted by a flight of S.E.5s. Actually, these were two elements, each out on an offensive patrol. Voss nosed down to select one of the S.E.5s, but before his guns could open up he sensed that he was being attacked from above. Six more S.E.5s were on his tail. This was the formation headed by Jimmy McCudden, and Voss foolishly tried to stay and mix with this particular flight. In the element were Mayberry, Hoidge, Rhys-Davids, Bowman, and possibly Cecil Lewis, although the latter makes no mention of the Voss battle in his book, *Sagittarius Rising*. At any rate, Voss had taken on more than he could handle and he never had a chance.

Once, a flight of gaudy Albatros scouts hove into sight, but after making one uninspired pass they all raced away, leaving Voss to his fate. There were several instants when he might have fought his way out, instead he resolved to see it through to its finish. Every pilot in the McCudden flight took long bursts at the German youth who had just passed his twentieth birthday. Finally Rhys-Davids, who also had not yet reached his majority, went below Voss, tilted his top-wing Lewis gun upward and fired a short burst. Werner's plane rolled over on one wingtip and began to sideslip down. Rhys-Davids followed him and saw the triplane finally crash in British territory.

His body was recovered, and was buried with full military honors a day later. Major McCudden stated: "As long as I live I shall never forget my admiration of Werner Voss, who singlehanded, fought seven of us for ten minutes, and also put some bullets through all of our machines."

And so, at the age of twenty, passed a storybook hero who lived up to the great tradition of the heroes of the sunlit sky.

CONCLUSION

The Armistice brought an end to the war and peace again came to the world. The bells in the churches pealed their thanks, the triumphant bugles shrilled to fill the silence left by the dead engines and unloaded guns. The lights went on again to gladden the darkened streets with life and hope.

The war was over and many men who had flown for months never went into a hangar again. Most who had gloried in their skill in the sky lanes never flew again. Only a few ever talked of those epic days or remembered the details of their conquests. Only a handful still desired to fly. One or two remembered enough to put their history down on paper for their sons to read and digest. Some were satisfied with the war's conclusion, a few resented the unfinished business, for keen instinct warned them that it would all erupt again a quarter of a century later. They were solemnly aware that history repeats itself.

Thus ended the Great War in the air. It was the first such conflict —and most certainly the last of its kind. Nothing has approached it for drama, heroism, devotion to duty, or the high dignity of its patriotism. It was the last great war in which man, not the weapons, played the major role. The same dauntless spirit moved one and all —on both sides of the line.

Today, half a century after the conflict had reached its zenith, there are few of these men left: men who can still remember "what it was like" and what part they played. Alas, so many have gone on to their destiny, bowing to the toll of time. More disturbing is the number who died at the peak of their careers, not in the glory of battle, but under circumstances that seem cruel and unfair.

Here is how some of our air-war heroes ended their gallant careers.

Hamilton Coolidge—Killed when his Spad took a million-to-one shot direct hit by an antiaircraft shell.

Edmond C. C. Genêt—Fainted in the air during a patrol after refusing to rest after an illness.

Bert Hall—Killed in an automobile accident after the war.

Field E. Kindley—Killed in a flying accident shortly after the Armistice.

Raoul Lufbery—Died after jumping from a burning airplane after attacking an enemy Albatros reconnaissance plane.

Frank Luke—Killed while resisting arrest by a German platoon, after being forced down in enemy territory.

James R. McConnell—Lost during a patrol he had been forbidden to join. Probably fainted in midair.

Paul Pavelka—Died of injuries suffered while attempting to master a fractious horse.

Norman Prince—Died from injuries suffered when his plane struck a high-tension cable.

Charles Trinkard—Killed while stunting to amuse a gathering of infantrymen.

Edmond Thieffry—Killed while making a survey flight for a commercial air line.

Albert Ball—Shot down by a German machine-gunner hiding in a church tower.

William G. Barker—Killed while testing a service aircraft in Canada.

A. W. Beauchamp-Proctor—Killed shortly after the war while practicing for an RAF air show.

Albert D. Carter—Killed while stunting a Fokker D-VII shortly after the Armistice.

J. Ira T. Jones—Died from injuries caused by a fall from a ladder.

Robert A. Little—Killed after being blinded by a searchlight beam.

James B. McCudden—Killed when his engine stalled on take-off while flying back to France to take command of Number 60 Squadron.

Andrew E. McKeever—Injured in an automobile crash in September 1919, he died on Christmas Day.

Alan McLeod—Died of influenza five days before the Armistice.

Francis G. Quigley—Died of influenza on October 20, 1918.

William Leefe Robinson—Died of influenza after long confinement in German prison camp.

R. A. J. Warneford—Killed with a newspaper correspondent when his plane became unmanageable. There were no seat belts and both were thrown out.

Jean-Pierre Léon Bourjade—Died shortly after the war while ministering to a camp of lepers.

Georges Madon—Died of injuries suffered after a crash while putting on a display at the opening of the Roland Garros Stadium in Paris.

Jean Navarre—Killed July 10, 1919, while practicing for a Victory Parade in which he was to fly through the Arc de Triomphe.

Charles Nungesser—Lost while attempting a trans-Atlantic flight in 1927.

Paul Baumer—Killed after the war while testing a Rohrbach cantilever monoplane.

Oswald Boelcke—Killed in a midair collision during a formation flight exercise.

Rudolf von Eschwege—Killed while attacking a British kite balloon sent aloft with basket loaded with high explosive.

Hermann Göring—Committed suicide while awaiting sentence of death for his role in World War II.

Heinrich Gontermann—Died of injuries suffered in a crash while testing new Fokker triplane.

Erich Loewenhardt—Killed when his parachute failed to open after midair collision with a squadron mate.

Wilhelm Reinhard—Killed while testing a new Friedrichshafen D.2A quadruplane.

Lothar von Richthofen—Killed while flying postwar Junkers transport.

Ernst Udet—Committed suicide during World War II.

EXPLANATION OF GERMAN AIR FORCE ORGANIZATION

Deutschen Luftstreitkraft—German Air Force.
Kampfeinsitzerkommando—Single-seater fighter unit.
Schutzstaffeln—Protection flights.
Schlachtstaffeln—Battle flights.
Fliegerübungsabtielung—Training section.
Jasta—Fighter squadron.
Jagdstaffeln—Group of fighter squadrons.
Jasta Boelcke—Oswald Boelcke's squadron.
Jasta 11—Von Richthofen's squadron.
Jagdgeschwader—A fighter wing.
Jagdstaffelschulen—Jagdstaffel schools.
Jagdgruppen—Fighter groups.
Geschwader—A generic term for Flying Circus.

Kampfeinsitzerstaffeln—Home defense squadrons.

Kampfstaffel—Bomber battle squadron.

Brieftauben Abtielung—Multi-gun battleplane unit.

Kampfgeswader—Twin-engined bomber group.

Bombengeschwadern—Bomber wings.

Marine Luftschiff-Abtielung—German Naval Aviation.

Befehshaber der Marine-Flieger—Naval Aviation Administration.

Marine-Landflieger—Landplanes of Marine Corps.

Armeeflugparks—Aircraft parks or supply depots.

Reihenbildzüge—Serio-photographic unit (Mosaic).

INITIALS USED IN GERMAN AIRCRAFT

A.E.G.—Allgemeine Elektrizitäts Gesellschaft.

A.G.O.—Aerowerke Gustav Otto.

D.F.W.—Deutsche Flug-Werke.

L.V.G.—Luft-Verkehrs Gesellschaft.

INITIALS USED IN BRITISH AIRCRAFT

B.E.—British Experimental (Royal Aircraft Factory).

F.E.—Fighter Experimental (Royal Aircraft Factory).

S.E.—Scouting Experimental (Royal Aircraft Factory).

R.E.—Reconnaissance Experimental (Royal Aircraft Factory).

Ack-W.—Armstrong-Whitworth Company.

D.H.—De Havilland Company.

BIBLIOGRAPHY

Archibald, Norman, *Heaven High, Hell Deep,* Albert and Charles Boni Inc., 1935.

Ashmore, E. H., *Air Defence,* Longmans, Green and Co., 1929.

Biddle, Charles J., *The Way of the Eagle,* Charles Scribner's Sons, 1919.

Bishop, William A., *Winged Warfare,* George H. Doran Company, 1918.

Bordeaux, Henry, *Georges Guynemer, Knight of the Air,* Yale University Press, 1918.

Bowman, Gerald, *War in the Air,* Evans Brothers, Ltd., 1956.

Boyle, Hugh, *Trenchard, Man of Vision,* W. W. Norton & Company, 1962.

Brett, R. Dallas, *The History of British Aviation,* John Hamilton, Ltd., 1933.

Coppens, Willy, *Days on the Wing,* John Hamilton, Ltd., 1929.

Cosgrove, Edmund, *Canada's Fighting Pilots,* Clark, Unwin & Company, Ltd., 1965.

Cutlack, F. M., *Australian Flying Corps,* Angus and Robertson, Ltd., 1953.

Duke and Lanchbery, *The Saga of Flight,* John Day Company, Inc., 1961.

Ellis, Frank H., *Canada's Flying Heritage,* University of Toronto Press, 1954.

Funderburk, Thomas R., *The Fighters,* Grosset & Dunlap, 1965.

Genêt, Edmund, *War Letters,* Charles Scribner's Sons, 1918.

Gibbons, Floyd, *The Red Knight of Germany,* Garden City Publishing Co., 1927.

Golding, Harry, *Wonder Book of Aircraft,* Ward, Lock & Co. Ltd., 1929.

Gray and Thetford, *German Aircraft of the First World War,* Putnam, 1962.

Gurney, Gene, *Five Down and Glory,* Putnam, 1958.

Hall, Bert, *One Man's War,* John Hamilton, Ltd., 1928.

Hall, James Norman, *High Adventure,* Houghton Mifflin Company, 1918.

Hall and Nordoff, *The Lafayette Flying Corps,* Houghton Mifflin Company, 1920.

Harris, John N., *Knights of the Air,* The Macmillan Company, Toronto, 1960.

Herlin, Hans, *Udet—A Man's Life,* Macdonald & Company, 1960.

Heydemarck, Haupt, *War Flying in Macedonia,* John Hamilton, Ltd., 1930.

Hyde, H. Montgomery, *Room 3603,* Farrar, Straus and Company, 1962.

Immelmann, Franz, *Max Immelmann, Eagle of Lille,* John Hamilton, Ltd., 1933.

Jackson, A. J., *De Havilland Aircraft,* Putnam, 1962.

Jane, Fred T., *All the World's Aircraft,* Sampson Low, Marston & Co., 1919.

Johns, W. E., *Thrilling Flights,* John Hamilton, Ltd., 1934.

—— *The Air V.C.'s,* John Hamilton, Ltd., 1932.

—— *Fighting Planes and Aces,* John Hamilton, Ltd., 1929.

Jones, Ira, *Tiger Squadron,* W. N. Allen & Company, 1954.

Jones and Raleigh, *War in the Air,* (6 volumes) Oxford University Press, 1931.

Joubert de la Ferte, Philip, *Birds and Fishes,* Hutchinson, 1960.

Kahnert, M. W., *Jagdstaffel 356,* John Hamilton, Ltd., 1934.

Kemp, P. K., *Fleet Air Arm,* Herbert Jenkins, 1954.

Kerr and Granville, *The R.N.V.R.,* George G. Harrup & Company, 1957.

Kiernan, R. H., *Captain Albert Ball,* John Hamilton, Ltd., 1933.

Kingsford, A. R., *Night Raiders of the Air,* John Hamilton, Ltd., 1932.

Leigh, Howard, *Planes of the Great War,* John Hamilton, Ltd., 1929.

Lewis, Cecil, *Sagittarius Rising,* Harcourt, Brace and Company, 1936.

Lewis, Peter, *British Aircraft, 1809–1914,* Putnam, 1962.

Loosbrock & Skinner, *The Wild Blue,* Putnam, 1961.

Loraine, Winifred, *Head Wind,* William Morrow Company, 1938.

McConnell, James R., *Flying for France,* Doubleday, Page and Company, 1916.

McCudden, James T. B., *Flying Fury,* John Hamilton, Ltd., 1929.

Marben, Rolf, *Zeppelin Adventures,* John Hamilton, Ltd., 1927.

Mason, Herbert Molloy, *The Lafayette Escadrille,* Random House, 1964.

—— *High Flew the Falcons,* J. B. Lippincott Company, 1965.

Masters, David, *So Few,* Eyre & Spottiswood, 1942.

Monk & Winter, *Great Exploits in the Air,* Blackie & Sons, Ltd., 1932.

Moore, Samuel Taylor, *U. S. Air Power,* Greenberg, 1958.

Musciano, Walter A., *Eagles of the Black Cross,* Ivan Obolensky, Inc., 1965.

—— *Lieutenant Werner Voss,* Hobby Helpers Publications, 1962.

Nielson, Thor, *The Zeppelin,* Allan Wingate, 1955.

Norris, Geoffrey, *The Royal Flying Corps,* Frederick Muller, Ltd., 1965.

Parsons, Edwin A., *The Great Adventure,* Doubleday, Doran & Company, 1937.

Payne, L. G. S., *Air Dates,* Heinemann, 1957.

Poolman, Kenneth, *Zeppelins Against London,* John Day Company, Inc., 1960.

Pudney, John, *The Camel Fighter,* Hamish Hamilton, 1964.

Rickenbacker, Edward V., *Fighting the Flying Circus,* Doubleday & Company, 1965.

Roberts, Leslie, *There Shall Be Wings,* Clarke, Irwin & Company, 1959.

Robertson, Bruce, *Air Aces of the 1914–1918 War,* Harleyford Publications, Ltd., 1959.

Robinson, Douglas, *The Zeppelin in Combat,* Foulis & Company, 1962.

Rockwell, Paul A., *American Fighters in the Foreign Legion,* Houghton Mifflin Company, 1930.

Saunders, Hilary St. George, *Per Ardua,* Oxford University Press, 1945.

Sims, Edward H., *American Aces,* Harper & Brothers, 1958.

Slessor, Sir John, *The Central Blue,* Cassell and Company, Ltd., 1956.

Stark, Rudolf, *Wings of War,* John Hamilton, Ltd., 1930.

Strange, Louis, *Recollections of an Airman,* John Hamilton, Ltd., 1932.

Sunderman, James F., *Early Air Pioneers,* Franklin Watts Company, 1961.

Sutton, H. T., *Raiders Approach,* Gale and Polden, Ltd., 1956.

Swanborough, F. G., *United States Military Aircraft Since 1909,* Putnam, 1963.

Taylor, J. W. R., *Warplanes of the World,* Ian Allan, 1966.

—— *Central Flying School,* Putnam, 1958.

Thetford, Owen, *British Naval Aircraft Since 1912,* Putnam, 1962.

Ticknor, Caroline, *New England Aviators* (2 volumes), Houghton Mifflin Company, 1919.

Toliver and Constable, *Fighter Aces,* The Macmillan Company, 1965.

Turner, John Frayn, *V.C.'s of the Air,* George G. Harrup & Company, 1960.

Ulanoff, Stanley, *Fighter Pilot,* Doubleday & Company, Inc., 1962.

Vaeth, J. Gordon, *Graf Zeppelin,* Harper & Brothers, 1958.

"Vigilant," *German War Birds,* John Hamilton, Ltd., 1931.

—— *Richthofen—Red Knight of the Air,* John Hamilton, Ltd., 1930.

Walbank, F. A., *Wings of War,* B. T. Batsford, Ltd., 1942.

Wellman, W. A., *Go, Get 'Em!,* The Page Company, 1918.

Werner, Professor J., *Knight of Germany—Oswald Boelcke,* John Hamilton, Ltd., 1929.

Weyl, A. R., *Fokker, The Creative Years,* Putnam, 1965.

Whitehouse, Arch, *Fighters in the Sky,* Duell, Sloan & Pearce, 1959.

—— *Hell in the Heavens,* W. & R. Chambers, 1938.

—— *Billy Mitchell,* Putnam, 1962.

—— *Squadrons of the Sea,* Doubleday & Company, Inc., 1962.

—— *The Years of the Sky Kings,* Doubleday & Company, Inc., 1959.

—— *The Fledgling,* Duell, Sloan & Pearce, 1964.

—— *Heroes and Legends of World War I,* Doubleday & Company, Inc., 1964.

—— *Decisive Air Battles of World War I,* Duell, Sloan & Pearce, 1963.

—— *Legion of the Lafayette,* Doubleday & Company, Inc., 1962.

—— *Zeppelin Fighters,* Doubleday & Company, Inc., 1967.

Wortley, R. Stuart, *Letters from a Flying Officer,* Oxford University Press, 1928.

GLOSSARY

Ace—Term used to designate any fighter pilot who had downed five or more enemy aircraft. Adopted by the U. S. Air Service but not by the British.

Ack-Ack—Front-line expression for antiaircraft. The letter *a* was pronounced "ack" by signalers to avoid mistakes in transmission. Thus *a-a* was pronounced ack-ack.

Aerodrome—The original name for any field used for flying. The term was used by the French and British throughout World War I.

Archie—A derisive term for antiaircraft fire originated by the British.

Art-Obs—Vernacular for artillery observation.

Aviate—A professional expression for flying. "Let's aviate."

Balloon—An inflated gasbag used for military observation. As a kite, it was tethered by a steel cable to any desired height. It carried a basket below in which two observers stood and watched the enemy areas. A barrage balloon was one of a system used around London to hinder attacking aircraft.

Barrel—Rolling the aircraft over and over in the air.

Besseneau hangar—A canvas-covered shelter large enough to accommodate a flight of six aircraft. It could be taken down or assembled in about three hours.

Biplace—A two-seater aircraft.

Biplane—An aircraft with two sets of wings, one above the other. A triplane had three. A quadruplane four. (There were such planes.)

Blériot—A generic term applied to all early monoplanes after Louis Blériot, who first flew the English Channel in 1909.

Breeze up—One has a breeze up when he is frightened. A gust up means one is practically scared to death.

Brevet—Originally referred to a commissioned rank in which an officer is given a higher grade than that for which he receives pay. Later it was taken to mean that a student had received his wings and commission at the same time. Thus "brevet" was often understood to mean a man had won his wings.

Brisfit—A term of affection for the Bristol Fighter.

Brolly—A British phrase meaning umbrella. During the war it was applied to the parachute by balloon observers. "I went over the side and took to my brolly!"

Bung off!—Trench parlance meaning to get going, clear out, mooch, vamoose, or get-the-hell-out-of-here!

Cashiered—To be dismissed from any government service in disgrace and disqualified from further government employment.

Ceiling—The limit of an aircraft's altitude. When it won't climb any higher it has reached its ceiling.

Center section—A small airfoil set above the fuselage to which the outer wing panels are bolted.

Chandelle—To go into a corkscrew climb. Often talked about but seldom performed.

Chasse—French for "chaser." All scouts were supposed to be designed to chase the enemy. Americans later changed this to "pursuit."

Contour fighting—Engaging enemy troops and defenses low down. The pilot follows the contour of the terrain and makes the most of the cover afforded.

Coupez—To "cut" or switch off the ignition after landing.

Dogfight—A wild aerial melee in which dozens of aircraft participate and fight at very close quarters. As a result more planes were lost in midair crashes than by the exchange of gunfire.

Dud—Anything that doesn't work. A shell that doesn't explode is a dud. A pilot who can't stay in formation is a dud. A plane that doesn't fly correctly is a dud.

Dump—Any area used for storing military supplies.

Drachen—The German word for kite balloons.

Empennage—The complete tail assembly of an aircraft. It includes the fin, rudder, tail-plane, and elevators.

Epaulet—The shoulder strap of a military jacket, tunic, or blouse on which a man's rank or regimental insignia is affixed.

Essence—French term for gasoline. To the British, gasoline is petrol —a petroleum product. Americans called it "gas," "juice," or "sauce."

Fee—Familiar term for British F.E.2b pusher biplane.

Feldwebel—In the German service, a warrant officer.

Flechettes—Small steel darts dropped from an aircraft on massed troops.

Flight—Usually a unit of six planes.

Flight Sergeant—Chief NCO of a flight, responsible for all the mechanics and aircraft maintenance.

Fourragère—A braided cord decoration worn by members of a regiment or squadron after the organization has been awarded that honor. Sometimes called an *aiguillette*.

Free lance—A pilot who elects to fly lone patrols after his regular missions have been carried out.

Funk hole—Any handy shelter used to avoid enemy fire—or any unpleasant duty.

Gazette—The official journal of the British government.

Gravel crushers—A disdainful expression applied to the PBI (Poor Bloody Infantry).

Ground strips—Colored cloths laid out on the ground by the infantry for signaling purposes.

GS—General service (British). There were GS jackets and GS wagons. It is the British variant of GI—general issue.

Hauptmann—German rank, equivalent to a captain.

Haversack—A bag of heavy web or canvas, used by British soldiers for personal gear and rations. Comparable to the French musette bag.

Hoik—To pull up sharply from level flight. To zoom.

Incidence—The angle at which the wings are set to the line of flight. The angle of incidence determines the aircraft's ability to climb or produce much of its lift.

Joy rags—Your best uniform, reserved for furlough or special occasions.

Joystick—Slang for control column. A stick device invented by an Englishman named Joyce. Thus, the phrase may have originated as Joyce-stick.

Kanone—German term for a fighter pilot who has destroyed ten enemy aircraft.

Keel surface—All aircraft surface seen when viewing the plane from either side.

King post—The short lever above or below a movable surface to which the control cable is attached.

Kiwi—Royal Flying Corps vernacular for any nonflying officer. It alludes to the flightless bird of New Zealand, called a kiwi.

Landing wires—All wire cables supporting the wings when the plane lands or stands on the ground. Flying wires take over the support of the plane when it is in the air.

Longerons—The main structural members running the length of the body or fuselage.

Main spar—Chief structural member of a wing to which all ribs and bracings are attached.

Monocoque—A type of fuselage or airplane body in which the main loads in the structure are taken by the skin covering.

Nacelle—The body that encloses the crew or an engine.

Oleo—The shock-absorbing portion of an undercarriage leg.

Pancaking—Landing the airplane slowly so that it drops hard and flat—like a pancake.

Pitot tube—An air-inlet tube set outside the cockpit and connected to the air-speed indicator, the pressure from which actuates a diaphragm and indicator needle.

Pocket—There is no such thing as an air pocket. Nature abhors a vacuum. Aircraft in flight may experience violent upward or downward lurches, but these are caused by turbulent air, rising or falling. There are no holes or vacuum spaces in the atmosphere.

Quirk—This has two meanings. It can mean a very new and very unskilled student, or it may refer to the British B.E.2c biplane.

Radial engine—An aviation engine with its cylinders arranged radially around a master crankshaft. The cylinders are stationary and the crankshaft revolves.

Rigger—One employed in assembling or servicing the complete airframe. A fitter took care of the engine.

Rotary engine—An aviation engine in which the cylinders are also set radially around its crankshaft, but in this case all cylinders and the engine shell revolve around the crankshaft.

Scarff ring—A movable machine-gun mounting used on most Allied two-seaters. It was invented by Warrant Officer Scarff of the Royal Naval Air Service.

Tarmac—Permanent artificial paving made of tar, macadam and iron slag. A registered trade-mark for the paving usually laid down in front of British overseas hangars.

Tractor airplane—A plane in which the propeller or propellers are mounted in front of the main planes. A pusher mounts the engine or engines behind the main planes.

INDEX